LETTERS FROM HOME
A Guide To Symbols –
Awake or Dreaming

STONE PEOPLE PUBLISHING COMPANY
Apache Junction, Arizona

LETTERS FROM HOME
A Guide To Symbols –
Awake or Dreaming

By Patricia Troyer

Published by:

Stone People Publishing Company
P.O. Box 4650
Apache Junction, Arizona 85278-4650 USA

This book is a reference book based upon research by the author and those listed in the bibliography.

Requests for permission to reprint, reproduce, etc., to:

Patricia Troyer
250 S. Tomahawk No. 30
Apache Junction, AZ 85219-5469 USA

Other books by Stone People Publishing:

Crystal Personalities, A Quick Reference to Special Forms of Quartz
by Patricia Troyer, $17.95 Soft Cover US

Includes Glossary and Bibliography

Cover Design: B.J. Graphics
Typesetting and Book Design: *AV Communications*
Printed and Bound: Griffin Printing

Library of Congress: LC-96-067360
ISBN 1-885975-02-3 $19.95 Soft Cover US Dollars

DEDICATION

This book is dedicated to all of you who have contributed to its creation and birth, not the least of whom were the participants in our workshops over the last several years who so openly and unself-consciously shared your dreams and personal symbol meanings.

It takes a genuine desire to know yourself to have the courage to keep working with your dreams, and to keep searching for the real You. Thank you, and keep on keeping on.

And a very special thank you to Steve Ellman for believing in us and helping us make our dreams come true.

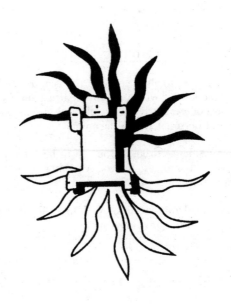

TABLE OF CONTENTS

Meeting Yourself 1

Universal Symbols 3

Question Everything 4

The Stuff Dreams Are Made Of 5

"Beyond This Point There Be Dragons" 7

Catching Your Dreams 9

Building Your Dream Journal 13

Cleaning The Windows Of Your Subconscious 14

This All Sounds Like A Lot Of Work To Me! 18

Will The Real Expert Please Stand Up? 19

Spotting Your Waking Symbols 20

Glossary 389

Stages of Sleep 392

Questions to Question Your Questions 393

Bibliography 401

Additional Reading 402

Order Forms

❖❖❖❖❖❖❖❖❖❖❖❖❖❖❖❖❖❖❖❖❖❖❖❖❖❖❖❖❖❖❖❖❖

This Table of Contents was especially created to be used as both an index and table of contents. We have arranged everything alphabetically within each category. So, if you are looking for DOG, go first to ANIMAL and then alphabetically to Dog, and so on. If you can't find your particular symbol, just go to the one closest to it and see what pops up for you.

A

ACCIDENT 23
ADULTERY 23
AIRPLANE (see Vehicle)

ALARM 24
ALCOHOL 25
   FERMENTATION
   WINE
ALIEN (see Foreign)
ALLEY 26
ALLIGATOR (see Animal/Crocodile)
ALPHABET 26
AMBER (see Color)
AMPUTATION 26
ANGEL 27
ANGER (see Emotion)
ANIMAL 28
   ANTLERS (see Horns)
   BAT 28
   BEAR 29
   BOBCAT 30
   BUFFALO 30
   BULL.. 31
      Bull-Man
      Calf
      Drawing a chariot
      Head of
      Riding a
      Slaying of
      Thigh of
   CAGED 31
   CAMEL 32
   CAT 32
   COUGAR 33
   COW 33
   CROCODILE... 33
      Being swallowed by
      With mouth open
   DANGEROUS... 35
   DEER 35
   DOG.. 36
   DOMESTICATED 37
   DRAGON 38
      Azure
      Biting each other's tail
      Common
      Fire of
      Imperial

   Killing
   Rescuing princess from
   Struggling with
   Two fighting
   Undulating
   Winged
   With pearl or crystal ball
   With Phoenix Bird
   With tiger
ELEPHANT 40
   Skin
   White
ELK 40
FANGS (see Teeth)
FROG 41
   In a well
HELPFUL 41
HORNS 42
HORSE 43
   Black
   And carriage or chariot
   Red
   And rider
   White
   Winged
   Pegasus
LAMB 45
   With lion
LEOPARD 45
LION 46
   Back-to-back
   With crescent
   And dragon
   And lamb
   Pair of
   With solar disk
   And unicorn
   Winged
LIZARD 47
LYNX 47
MENACING 47
MOOSE.. 48
MOUNTAIN LION (see Cougar)
MOUSE.. 48

PANTHER 48
RABBIT 49
SEAL 49
SCORPION (see Insect)
SHEEP 49
SNAKE 50

    Celestial or Rainbow Serpent
    Child playing with
    Coiled
    Coiled around egg
    Coiled around tree
    Coiled around woman
    With eagle or stag
    Eggs of
    Fiery Serpent
    Fights of
    Holding herb or fruit
    Horned serpent
    Kundalini
    White cobra as
    Lidless eyes of
    On a pole
    Ouroboros
    Passing through circle
    With a pig
    Plumed
    Poisonous
    Ram-Headed
    With a rooster
    With a rooster and pig
    And Tree of Knowledge
    And Tree of Life
    Two around tree
    Two biting each other's tails
    Two together
    Two with upward & downward movement
    Two wound around each other
    Undulating
    White cobra
    Winged
    With a pig
    With a rooster
    With both rooster & pig

TIGER 57
    Black
    Blue
    Fighting dragon or serpent
    Red
    Riding the
    White
    Yellow
TORTOISE 59
TOTEM ANIMAL 58
TURTLE 59
TUSK 60
    WILD (see Dangerous)
WOLF 60
ANKH (see Geometric Shape/Cross)
ANKLE (see Body)
ANT (see Insect)
ANTLERS (see Horns)
APPLE (see Food)
APRICOT (see Food)
AQUAMARINE (see Color)
ARGUMENT 61
ARM (see Body)
ARROW (see Weapon)
ARTWORK 61
ATTACK 61
ATTIC (see Building)
AUDIENCE (see Stage)
AUTHORITY FIGURE (see Leader)

B
BABY 63
BALD (see Body/Hair)
BAND (see Orchestra)
BANK (see Building)
BAR (see Building)
BASEMENT (see Building)
BAT (see Animal)
BATH (see Water)
BATHROOM (see Building)
BEAR (see Animal)
BEARD (see Hair)
BEDROOM (see Building)

BEE (see Insect)
BEIGE (see Color)
BELL 64
BIG 64
BIRD 65
   BLUE JAY 65
   CARDINAL 66
   CHICKEN 66
   CRANE 66
   CROW 67
      Black
      Gold
      Red
      With white heron
   DOVE 67
      Black on oak tree
      Pair of
      Turtle dove
      White
      With olive branch
      With palm branch
   DUCK 69
   EAGLE 69
      In Aquarian symbol
      Carrying victim
      Conflict with bull
      Conflict with serpent
      Devouring a lion
      Double-headed
      Perched on a pillar
      Soaring
      With human arms
   FALCON 71
   FEATHER 71
      Cloak of
      Crown of
      Eagle
      Feathered stick
      Ostrich
      Peacock
      Three
      Two
      To wear
      White

GOOSE 72
    Flying
HAWK 73
HERON 73
    Gray
    White
HUMMINGBIRD 74
MAGPIE 74
OSTRICH 75
    Egg
    Feather (see Feather above)
OWL 75
PEACOCK 76
PELICAN 76
PHEASANT 76
PIGEON (see Dove)
RAVEN 76
    Red
ROBIN 77
SPARROW 77
SPARROW HAWK 78
STORK 78
SWAN 78
TURKEY 79
VULTURE 79
WINGS 79
    On Caduceus
    On cap
    On horse
    Pegasus
    On sandals
WOODPECKER 80
WREN 80
BLACK (see Color)
BLEEDING (see Blood)
BLOOD 80
    BLEEDING
    BRIGHT RED
    INTERNAL
    DARK RED
BLUE (see Color)
BOAT (see Vehicle)
BODY 82

ANKLE 82
ARM 83
   Bent
   Both raised
   Extended
   Left
   Multiple
   None
   One raised
   Right
EARS 84
   Big
   Broad
   Elongated lobes
   Pointed
   Right
ELBOW 84
EYE 85
   Both closed
   Both open
   Eye of the Heart
   Eye of Horus
   Eye and eyebrow of Horus
   Left
   One
   One or more
   Peacock feathers as
   Right
   Third Eye
   Triangle with eye in center
   Two winged
EYEBROW 85
FACE 87
   Faceless
   Multiple
   Someone you know
   Your own
FINGER 88
   By side of nose
   Index
   Index raised
   Index and ring
   Index, middle, and ring
   Little

Middle
Pointing
Raised in benediction
Raised to lips
Ring finger
Thumb
Two raised
FOOT 89
Absence of
Bare
Deities with object under
Footprints
Going in both directions
Kissing
Other forms taking place of
Sole of
Stamping
Washing
Winged
HAIR.. 91
Bald
Braids
Beard
Black, Dull
Black, Shiny
Blond
Body Hair
Combing
Curly
Cut in geometric patterns
Cutting
Dirty
Golden
Gray
Long
Losing (see Bald)
Red
Red, Golden
White
HAND 95
Closed
Covered or hidden
Extended
With its five fingers

With fingers spread
Folded
Handshake
Injured
Left
Open
Placing in hands of teacher
Raised
Right
With three fingers raised
HEAD 99
Animal
Bowing
Decapitated
On fountain
Four heads of Brahma
Of Horus
Male & female joined
Nodding
On a pillar
With ring in mouth
Of Set
Two-headed beings
Triple-headed beings
Skull
Skull and cross-bones (see Thigh)
Veiled
Winged
HEART 101
Trouble with
JAW 101
Crushing
Locked
KNEE 102
Kneeling
Someone seated on
LEG 103
One-legged being
MOUTH 103
Closed
Opened
Speaking
NECK 104
With necklace

NOSE 104
    Using to smell
SKELETON 105
STOMACH 105
TEETH 106
    Baring of
    Braces on
    Crooked
    Decayed
    Fangs
    Gnashing of
    Loose
    Loss of
    Oral surgery
THIGH 108
    Skull & crossed bones of
THROAT 109
    Chakra
    Choked or strangled
    Laryngitis
    Sore
    Wounded in
TONGUE... 110
    Fleshy or fat
    Long
    Of an Angel
    Protruding from animal
    Sticking out your
WRIST 111
BOGEYMAN (see Monster)
BOOK 111
BOW AND ARROW (see Weapon)
BOWL (see Container)
BOX (see Container)
BOY 111
BRAKES (see Vehicle)
BREAD (see Food)
BRIDE... 112
BRIDEGROOM (see Bride)
BRIDGE... 112
    OF HEAVEN
    HIGHER SELF AS
BROTHER (see Family)
BROWN (see Color)

BUFFALO (see Animal)
BULL (see Animal)
BUG (see Insect)
BUILDING 113
    APARTMENT 113
    ATTIC 114
    BANK 114
    BAR 114
    BARN 115
    BATHROOM 115
    BASEMENT 116
    BEDROOM 116
    CATHEDRAL (see Church)
    CEILING 116
    CHURCH 117
    CLOSET 117
    DINING ROOM 118
    DOOR 118
    ELEVATOR 119
    FAUCET 119
        Leaky
    FLOOR 120
        Falling apart
        Ground
        Main
        Unfinished
    FOUNDATION 121
    GARAGE 121
    GATE 121
    GROUND FLOOR (see Floor)
    HALLWAY 121
    HOTEL 121
    HOUSE 122
    INSIDE 122
    KITCHEN 122
    LIBRARY 123
    LIVING ROOM 123
    MAIN FLOOR (see Floor)
    MANSION 123
    OUTSIDE 124
    PATIO 124
    PLUMBING 124
    PORCH 124
    PUBLIC BUILDING 125
    RESTAURANT 125
        Angry at waiter
        Waiter

Waitress
Waiter behind schedule
Waiter rushed
ROOF 126
ROOM 126
Closed or sealed
SCHOOL 127
Back in
Taking test
SHOPPING CENTER 128
STAIRS 128
Leading underground
Individual steps of
Spiral
Stairwell and landing
SUPERMARKET 130
TENT 130
TOILET 130
Excrement
TOWER 131
Ivory
Princess or virgin in
WINDOW 131
YARD 132
Back
Front
BULL (see Animal)
BUTTERFLY (see Insect)

C

CADUCEUS (see Animal/Snake)
CAMEL (see Animal)
CAMELLIA (see Flower)
CANDLE 133
BOTH SIDES OF ALTAR or CROSS
CANDELABRA
MENORAH
ONE
THREE
CANDLESTICK (see Candle)
CANYON 134
CAPE (see Clothes)
CAPTIVE (see Victim)

CAR (see Vehicle)
CARP (see Fish)
CAT (see Animal)
CATHEDRAL (see Building)
CAVE (see Container)
CEILING (see Building)
CEREMONY 134
    AWARD
    BAPTISM
    BIRTH
    CHRISTENING
    FUNERAL
    GRADUATION
    INITIATION
    NAMING
    SACRIFICIAL
    WEDDING
        Marrying former love
CHAIR (see Furniture)
CHAKRA 137
    1ST
    2ND
    3RD
    4TH
    5TH
    6TH
    7TH
    8TH
    9TH
    10TH
    11TH
    12TH
CHARIOT (see Vehicle)
CHASE 152
CHEW (see Eat)
CHILD (see Family)
CHILDREN (see Family/Child)
CHURCH (see Building)
CIRCLE (see Geometric Shape)
CITY 153
CLIMB 154
    DOWN
    UP

CLOTHES 154
    CAPE
        Flowing out like wings
    CHANGING
    DIFFERENT FROM YOURS
    FROM ANOTHER TIME PERIOD
    GLOVES
        Dirty
    HAT
        Changing
    SHOE
        Missing
        Removing before entering sacred space
        Shopping for
    UNIFORM
    WHITE SHINING
CLOUDS (see Weather)
COBWEB (see Insect/Spider)
COLD (see Weather)
COLOR 158
    AMBER
    AQUAMARINE
    BEIGE
    BLACK
    BLUE
    BLUE-GRAY
    BLUE-WHITE
    BROWN
    CANARY-YELLOW
    CHARTREUSE
    CRIMSON
    EMERALD GREEN
    GOLD
    GOLD-WHITE
    GRAY
    GRAY, DARK
    GREEN
    GREEN, DARK
    GREEN, LIGHT
    INDIGO BLUE
    LAVENDER
    MAGENTA
    MAUVE
    MUDDY COLOR

NAVY BLUE
ORANGE
ORANGE, DEEP
ORANGE, GOLDEN
ORANGE-PINK (see Peach)
PASTEL COLOR
PEACH
PINK
PURPLE
RED
ROSE
ROSE-RED
ROYAL BLUE
RUBY RED
SCARLET
SILVER
SKY BLUE
TURQUOISE BLUE
VERMILION
VIOLET
VIOLET-PINK
VIOLET-WHITE
WHITE
YELLOW
YELLOW, CLEAR
YELLOW-GOLD
YELLOW-GRAY
COMET (see Planet)
CONTAINER 167
BOWL
BOX
CAVE
CUP
Drinking from
On top of a pillar
Overturned
PITCHER (see Vase)
VASE
Fluid flowing from
Full
Of wine
COOK 169
COSMETICS 169
COW (see Animal)

CRAB (see Fish)
CRANE (see Bird)
CRESCENT (see Geometric Shape)
CROCODILE (see Animal)
CROSS (see Geometric Shape)
CROSSROAD (see Road)
CROW (see Bird)
CROWD 170
CRY (see Emotion)
CUBE (see Geometric Shape)
CUP (see Container)
CURTAINS (see Furniture)

D

DAISY (see Flower)
DANCE 171
    AROUND OBJECT
    CHAIN DANCE
    DANCE OF SHIVA
    RING DANCE
DANGER (see Emotion)
DARK (see Day)
DAY 172
    DARK
    DAWN
    LIGHT
    MIDDAY
    MIDNIGHT
    NOON (see Midday)
    NIGHT
    TWILIGHT
DEATH 175
DECAPITATION (see Body/Head)
DEER (see Animal)
DEEP (see Direction)
DESERT 176
DESTRUCTION 176
DIAMOND (see Wealth/Jewel)
DINING ROOM (see Building/House)
DIRECTION 177
    DEEP
    DOWN
    EAST

HIGH
   On the edge of cliff
NORTH
SOUTH
UP
WEST
DISASTER (see Destruction)
DISH (see Container)
DITCH 179
   DRIVING OR WALKING NEAR
   WATER RUNNING IN
DIVORCE 180
DOG (see Animal)
DOLPHIN (see Fish)
DOOR (see Building)
DOT (see Geometric Shape)
DOVE (see Bird)
DOWN (see Direction)
DRAGONFLY (see Insect)
DRAPES (see Furniture)
DRAW 180
DREAM 181
DRINK 181
DRIVE 181
DRIVER (see Vehicle)
DROWN (see Water)
DRUM (see Circle)
DUCK (see Birds)
DUSK (see Day/Twilight)

E

EARTH (see Planet)
EAGLE (see Bird)
EAST (see Directions)
EAR (see Body)
EAT 183
   CHEW
EGG (see Food, Geometric Shape/Oval)
ELEPHANT (see Animal)
ELEVATOR (see Building)
ELF (see Fairy)
ELK (see Animal)
ELLIPSE (see Geometric Shape)

EMOTION 184
   ANGER
   CRY
      Tears
   DANGER
   FEAR
   GRIEF
ENEMY 187
ERUPTION (see Explosion)
EROTIC (see Sex)
ESCAPE 187
   IN SLOW MOTION
EYE (see Body)
EYEBROW (see Body)
EXCREMENT (see Building/Toilet)
EXPLOSION 188

F

FACE (see Body)
FAIRY 189
   ELF
FALCON (see Bird)
FALL (see Seasons)
FALL 190
FAMILY 190
   BROTHER
   DAUGHTER
      Daughter of Man
   FATHER
   GRANDMOTHER
   GRANDFATHER
   HUSBAND
      Ex-husband
   INCEST
   MOTHER
      Earth Mother
      The Great Mother
      The Terrible Mother
   RELATIVE
   SISTER
   SON
   WIDOW
   WIDOWER

WIFE
  Ex-wife
FAMOUS 196
FANGS (see Teeth)
FARM 197
FAST 198
  TO BE ON A
FAT (see Big)
FATHER (see Family)
FAUCET (see Building)
FEAR (see Emotion)
FEAST (see Party)
FEATHER (see Bird)
FEED (see Eat)
FEET (see Body/Foot)
FEMALE 198
FENCES 198
FIGHT (see Struggle)
FINGER (see Body)
FIRE 199
FIREFLY (see Insect)
FISH 200
  CARP
  CAUGHT IN NET
  COSMIC FISH
  CRAB
  DOLPHIN
    Deities riding on
  SCALES OF
  STRANDED
  OCTOPUS
  OYSTER
  SALMON
  SEA URCHIN
  SERVED WITH BREAD & WINE
  SHARK
  STARFISH
  STRANDED
  SWIMMING DOWNWARD
  SWIMMING UPWARD
  SWORDFISH
  THREE INTERTWINED
  THREE WITH ONE HEAD
  TROUT

TWO
TWO TOUCHING NOSE-TO-NOSE
WHALE
    In belly of
FLAME 204
FLOAT 205
FLOOD (see Water)
FLOOR (see Building)
FLOWER.. 206
    AZALEA
    BASKET
    BLUE
    BUD
    CAMELIA
    CARNATION
        Pink
        Red
        White
        Yellow
    CHILD RISING FROM
    CHRYSANTHEMUM
    DAISY
    FIVE-PETALLED
    GARDEN
    GARLAND
    GOLDEN
    GOLDENROD
    GROWING or UNFOLDING
    IRIS
    LILAC
    LILY
    LOTUS
    MARIGOLD
    ORANGE
    PEONY
    RED
    RED & WHITE
    ROSE
        Blue
        Five-petalled
        Four-petalled
        Garden
        Garland
        Golden

     Red
     Red & white
     Rose-Cross
     Rosette
     Rose of Sharon
     Six-petalled
     Thorns of
   SCENTED
   SIX-PETALLED
   TULIP
   VIOLET
     White
   YELLOW
   WHITE
FLY (see Insect)
FLY, TO 211
FOG (see Weather)
FOOD 212
   APPLE
   APRICOT
   BREAD
     Breaking of
     Served with fish and wine
     And wine
   EGG
   FRUIT
   ICE CREAM
   MILK
   PEACH
   STRAWBERRY
FOOT (see Body)
FOOTPRINTS (see Body/Foot)
FOREIGN 215
FOREST (see Tree)
FOUNDATION (see Building)
FOUNTAIN (see Water)
FRIEND 215
FROG (see Animal)
FROST (see Weather/Snow)
FRUIT (see Food)
FUNERAL (see Ceremony)
FURNITURE 215
   BED
     Pillow

CHAIR
CURTAINS
    Closed
    Open
    Parted
    Thrown over something
TABLE

G

GANG (see People) 219
GARAGE (see Building)
GARDEN 219
GATE (see Building)
GEMS (see Wealth/Jewel)
GEOMETRIC SHAPE 220
    CIRCLE
        Circumference of
        Concentric
        Drum as a
        Large
        Overlapping or divided
        Three interlocked
        Small
        White
        With cross in center
        With double cross
        Within a square
    CRESCENT
        With a star
    CROSS
        Ankh
        Double-barred
        In a circle
        Within a square
        With wheel in center
        With equal arms
        Of St. Andrew
        Tau cross
        Rose cross
        Six-rayed
        As a swastika
    CUBE
    DOT
        In a circle

HEXAGRAM
LINE
    Horizontal
    Straight
    Undulating
    Vertical
    Wavy (see Undulating)
MANDALA
OCTAGON
OCTAHEDRON
PARALLELOGRAM
    Leaning to left
    Leaning to right
PENTACLE
    Reversed
    Shield of David
PENTAGRAM (see Pentacle)
RECTANGLE
    Horizontal
    Vertical
SPHERE
SPIRAL
    Double
SQUARE
    Celtic triple
    Surrounding a circle
    Within a circle
TRIANGLE
    Downward pointing
    Equilateral
    In a circle
    Double
    Horizontal and touching at apex
    Three interwoven
    As triad
    Upward pointing
GHOST (see Monster)
GIFT 231
GIRL 231
GLOVES (see Clothes)
GOLD (see Color)
GRANDFATHER (see Family)
GRANDMOTHER (see Family)
GRAVE 231

GRAY (see Color)
GREEN (see Color)
GROTESQUES (see Monster)
GUARD 232
    PRISON
    SECURITY
GUEST 233
GUN (see Weapon)

H

HAIR (see Body)
HALLWAY (see Building)
HAND (see Body)
HANDICAP 234
HANG 234
    CLOTHES
    THE HANGED MAN
    NOOSE
    SWINGING WHILE
HAT (see Clothes)
HAWK (see Bird)
HEAD (see Body)
HEART (see Body)
HEAT (see Fire)
HEAVY 236
HEIGHT (see Direction)
HERON (see Bird)
HIDE, TO 236
HIGHER MIND (see Will, Human)
HILL 236
HOMOSEXUAL 237
HONEY (see Insect/Bee)
HORNS (see Animal)
HORSE (see Animal)
HOT 237
HOTEL (see Building)
HOUSE (see Building)
HUMMINGBIRD (see Birds)
HUNGER 237
HUNT 238
    AN ANIMAL
    BEING HUNTED
HURT (see Pain)

HURRICANE (see Weather)
HUSBAND (see Family)

I

ICE (see Weather/Snow)
ICE CREAM (see Food)
INCEST (see Family)
INJURY (see Pain)
INSECT 239
   ANT
   BEE
      Honey
   BUTTERFLY
      On chrysanthemum
      Pair of
      With a plum
      White
   DRAGONFLY
   FIREFLY
   FLY
   SCORPION
   SPIDER
      Cobweb
      Spiderweb
ITCH (see Rash)
INVASION 243
ISLAND 244

J

JADE (see Wealth/Jewel)
JAIL 245
JAW (see Body)
JEWEL (see Wealth)
JOURNEY (see Trip)
JUDGE (see Law)
JUMP 245
JUNK 246
JUPITER (see Planet)
JURY (see Law)

K

KEY 247
   ANKH AS

    FINDING
    GOLD
    GIVING
    RECEIVING
    SILVER
    THREE
KIDNAP 249
KILL 249
    BEING KILLED
    CHILD
    PARENT
    SUICIDE
KISS 250
KITCHEN (see Building/House)
KNEE (see Body)
KNEELING (see Body/Knee)
KNIFE (see Weapon)
KNOCK 251
KNOT 252
    CUTTING
    ENDLESS
    KNOTTED CORD
    LEMNISCATE
    SLIP-KNOT
    UNTYING
KUNDALINI (see Animal/Snake)

L

LADDER 254
    CLIMBING DOWN
    CLIMBING UP
    RUNGS OF
    TWO SIDES OF
LAKE (see Water)
LAMB (see Animal)
LAMP 255
    FLAME OF
    OIL OF
    WICK OF
LANDSCAPE 256
LATE 256
LAUNDRY 257
LAVENDER (see Color)

LAW 257
LAWYER (see Law)
LEADER 257
LEAVES (see Tree)
LECTURE.. 258
LEFT 258
LEG (see Body)
LEOPARD (see Animal)
LETTER (see Mail)
LIBRARY (see Building)
LICENSE 259
LIGHT (see Day)
LIGHTNING (see Weather)
LIMB (see Tree)
LION (see Animal)
LIQUID (see Water)
LIVING ROOM (see Building/House)
LIZARD (see Animal)
LOST 260
LOVER 260
LOWER MIND (see Will, Human)
LYNX (see Animal)

M

MACHINE 261
MAIL.. 261
    LETTER
    NOTE
    PACKAGE
        Receive
        Send
MALL (see Building/Shopping Center)
MALE 262
MANSION (see Building)
MARRIAGE 263
MARS (see Planet)
MARTYR (see Victim)
MAZE 264
MERCURY (see Planet)
METEOR (see Planet/Comet)
MIRROR.. 264
    HAND

MISSING 266
  CONNECTION
  OBJECT
MISTLETOE (see Plant)
MONEY (see Wealth)
MONSTER.. 266
  BOGEYMAN
  DEFEATING A
  DESTROYING A
  FIGHTING A
  GHOST
  GOLEM
  GROTESQUES
  LAND
  VAMPIRE
  WATER
  WEREWOLF
MOON (see Planet)
MOOSE (see Animal
MOTHER (see Family)
MOUNTAIN 270
  CLIMBING DOWN
  GOING AWAY FROM
  CLIMBING UP
  GOING TOWARD
  TOPS OF
  SEEN IN DISTANCE
  VOLCANO
    Dormant
MOUNTAIN LION (see Animal/Cougar)
MOUTH (see Body)
MOVIE 272
MUD 272
MUTILATION (see Amputation)
MUSIC 273
  HEARING
  SACRED
  MUSICIAN

N
NAIL 275
NAKED 275
  UNDRESSING

NATIVE AMERICAN 276
NECK (see Body)
NECKLACE (see Body/Neck)
NEPTUNE (see Planet)
NET 277
NIGHT (see Day)
NORTH (see Direction)
NOSE (see Body)
NOOSE (see Hang)
NUMBER... 277
    ZERO
        String of zero's
        Zero's next to another number
    ONE
    TWO
    THREE
    FOUR
    FIVE
    SIX
    SEVEN
    EIGHT
    NINE
    TEN
    ELEVEN
    TWELVE
    THIRTEEN
    FOURTEEN
    FIFTEEN
    TWENTY
    TWENTY-ONE
    TWENTY-TWO
    TWENTY-FOUR
    TWENTY-SIX
    THIRTY-THREE
    THIRTY-SIX
    FORTY
    FIFTY
    SIXTY
    SEVENTY
    ONE HUNDRED
    666
    888
    1001
NUDE (see Naked)

O

OAK (see Tree)
OAR (see Boat)
OCEAN (see Water)
OCTAGON (see Geometric Shape)
OCTAHEDRON (see Geometric Shape)
OCTOPUS (see Fish)
OPERATION 290
ORANGE (see Color)
ORCHESTRA (see Band)
ORGY 290
OSTRICH (see Bird)
OUROBOROS (see Animal/Snake)
OVAL (see Geometric Shape)
OWL (see Bird)
OYSTER (see Fish)

P

PACKAGE (see Mail)
PAIN 292
    EMOTIONAL
    PHYSICAL
    PSYCHOLOGICAL
PANTHER (see Animal)
PARALLELOGRAM (see Geometric Shape)
PARTY 293
PASSENGER (see Vehicle)
PASSPORT (see License)
PATH (see Road)
PATIO (see Building/House)
PEACH (see Food and Color)
PEACOCK (see Bird)
PEARL (see Wealth/Jewels)
PENTACLE (see Geometric Shape)
PENTAGRAM (see Geometric Shape)
PEOPLE 294
PHEASANT (see Bird)
PHOTOGRAPH 295
PIGEON (see Bird/Dove)
PILLOW (see Furniture/Bed)
PILOT 295
    AIRPLANE

SHIP
PINE (see Tree)
PITCHER (see Container/Vase)
PLANT 296
    GREEN
    MISTLETOE
    WEED
PLANET 297
    COMET
    EARTH
    INNER
    JUPITER
    MARS
    MERCURY
    MOON
        Crescent
        Dark phase
        Full
        Half
        Waning
        Waxing
    MORE THAN ONE
        NEPTUNE
    OUTER
    PLUTO
    SATURN
    SEEN AS WHOLE
    STAR
        Falling
        Five-pointed
        Pointed down
        Pointed up
        Six-pointed
        To be a
    SUN
        Light of
        Straight lines of
        wavy lines of
    URANUS
    VENUS
PLUMBING (see Building)
PLUTO (see Planet)
POCKET 305
POLICE 305

POSTMAN/WOMAN (see Mail)
POVERTY 305
PREGNANT 306
PRISON (see Jail)
PURPLE (see Color)
PURSE 306
    LOST
    STOLEN
PYRAMID 307
    APEX
    CAPSTONE (see Apex)
    WITH CIRCLE ON TOP
    WITH DECORATIONS and LIGHTS
    ENTRANCE
    LOWER PASSAGES
    OF STONE
    PASSAGES TO KING/QUEEN'S CHAMBER
    STEPS
    STONES OF

Q
QUARTZ CRYSTAL 309
    BALL
    POINT OF
    SIX SIDES OF

R
RABBIT (see Animal)
RACE, HUMAN 311
RACE, TO (see Run)
RAIN (see Weather)
RAINBOW (see Weather)
RAPE 311
RASH 312
    ITCH
RAVEN (see Bird)
RECTANGLE (see Geometric Shape)
RED (see Color)
REDWOOD (see Tree)
RELATIVE (see Family)
RESTAURANT (see Building)
RIGHT 312

RING 313
    FINDING
    LOSING
    AS NECKLACE
RIVER (see Water)
ROAD 314
    BEND IN
    CROSSROAD
    STRETCH OF
ROAR 315
ROCK 315
    CLASHING
    DUAL
        THE LIVING
    WATER GUSHING FROM
ROOF (see Building)
ROOM (see Building)
ROPE 315
    CLIMBING
        AS NOOSE
    PASSING THROUGH WINGED DOOR
    TIED BY
ROSE (see Flower)
RUBY (see Wealth/Jewel)
RUN 317
    AWAY
    IN SLOW MOTION
    RACE
    TOWARD

S

SALMON (see Fish)
SATURN (see Planet)
SCAR 318
SCHOOL (see Building)
SCORPION (see Insect)
SEASONS 318
    FALL
    SPRING
    SUMMER
    SUMMER SOLSTICE
    WINTER
    WINTER SOLSTICE

SECRET 320
SECRETARY 320
SERPENT (see Animal/Snake)
SEX 320
SHADE (see Tree)
SHADOW... 321
SHARK (see Animal/Fish)
SHELL 322
    CONCH
    MOLLUSK
    SCALLOP
SHEEP (see Animal)
SHIP (see Vehicle/Boat)
SHOE (see Clothes)
SHOT 323
SHOOT (see Shot)
SHOPPING CENTER (see Building)
SHOULDER (see Body)
SHOWER (see Water/Bath)
SICK... 323
SILVER (see Color)
SISTER (see Family)
SKELETON (see Body)
SKI 324
    TRACKS AHEAD
    TRACKS BEHIND
SKULL (see Body/Head)
SKULL AND CROSS-BONES (see Body/Thigh)
SKY 324
    BLACK
    BLUE
    GRAY
SLEEP 325
SMOKE 326
SNAKE (see Animal)
SNOW (see Weather)
SON (see Family)
SOUL 326
SOUTH (see Directions)
SPARROW (see Bird)
SPARROWHAWK (see Bird)
SPHERE (see Geometric Shape)
SPIDER (see Insect)
SPIRAL (see Geometric Shape)

SPORTS 327
SPRING (see Seasons)
SQUARE (see Geometric Shape)
STAG (see Animal/Deer)
STAGE 327
    AUDIENCE
      Applause
      Bored
STAIRS (see Building)
STAR (see Planets)
STARFISH (see Fish)
STATION (see Building)
STEER (see Animal/Bull)
STEER, TO (see Vehicle)
STOMACH (see Body)
STONE 328
    BEING THROWN
    BUILDING
    CARVED
    CORNER
    CUBIC
    COVERING ENTRANCE
    KA'ABA
    TALL UPRIGHT
    UNCARVED
STORE (see Building)
STORK (see Bird)
STORM (see Weather)
STRANGER 329
STRUGGLE 330
    FIGHT
STUMP (see Tree)
SUICIDE (see Kill)
SUITCASE 331
SUMMER (see Seasons)
SUMMER SOLSTICE (see Seasons)
SUN (see Planet)
SWAN (see Bird)
SWASTIKA (see Geometric Shape)
SWIM 331
SWORD (see Weapon)
SWORDFISH (see Fish)

T

TABLE (see Furniture)
TEACHER 332
TEARS (see Emotions)
TEETH (see Body)
TELEPHONE 332
    FAX
    INTERNET
TELEVISION (see Movie)
TEMPLE (see Building/Church)
TEST 333
THIGH (see Body)
THIRD EAR (see Chakra/5th)
THIRD EYE (see Chakra/6th & 7th)
THORN (see Flower/Rose)
THROAT (see Body)
THUNDER (see Weather)
TIGER (see Animal)
TIRES (see Vehicle)
TOILET (see Building)
TONGUE (see Body)
TOOL 333
TORNADO (see Weather)
TOWER (see Building)
TOY 334
TRAP 334
TREASURE (see Wealth)
TRIP (see Journey)
TREE 335
    ALMOND
       Nut
    ASH
    BIRCH
    BRANCH
    BONSAI (see Tree/Twisted)
    CEDAR
    CHERRY
       Blossom
    CHRISTMAS
    CLIMBING A
    COSMIC TREE

CYPRESS
DICIDUOUS
ELM
EVERGREEN
FIG
FOREST
    Lost in a
INVERTED
LEAFLESS
LEAVES
    Autumn
    Dead
    Green
    On the ground
LIMBS
MAPLE
MULBERRY
OAK
    Acorn
    Leaves
    Wreath
OLIVE
ORANGE
PEACH
PEAR
PINE
    Pine cone
    White pine cone
SHADE
SNOW-COVERED
STUMP
    Pulled out
TREE OF LIGHT
TREE OF LIFE
TREE OF KNOWLEDGE
TWISTED
    Bonsai Tree
WILLOW
    Wand of
WOOD
WORLD TREE (see Cosmic Tree)
YEW
YULE LOG
TRIANGLE (see Geometric Shape)

TRIP 347
TROUT (see Fish)
TRUCK (see Vehicle)
TULIP (see Flower)
TUNNEL 348
TURKEY (see Bird)
TURQUOISE (see Wealth/Jewel)
TURTLE (see Animal)
TUSKS (see Animal/Horns)
TWILIGHT (see Day)

U

UMBRELLA 349
UNDERGROUND 349
UNDRESSING (see Naked)
UNEMPLOYED 350
UNIFORM (see Clothes)
UNIVERSITY (see Building)
URANUS (see Planet)
UP (see Direction)

V

VALLEY 351
VAMPIRE (see Monster)
VEIL (see Head)
VEHICLE 351
    AIRPLANE
    BOAT
    BRAKES
    CAR ....
    CHARIOT
    DRIVE
    PASSENGER
    STEER
    TIRES
        Flat
        Missing
    TRUCK
    WHEEL
VENUS (see Planet)
VICTIM 357
    CAPTIVE
    MARTYR

VIOLET (see Color or Flowers)
VOLCANO (see Mountain)
VULTURE (see Bird)

W

WAITER (see Building/Restaurant)
WAITRESS (see Building/Restaurant)
WALLET (see Purse)
WAR 359
WATER 360
   AGITATED
   AND CLAY
   AND FIRE
   AND WINE
   BATH
   CALM
   CLEAR
   CROSSING OVER
   DEEP
   DIRTY
   DIVING INTO
   DROWN
   FLOOD
   FOUNTAIN
      In center of anything
      Of Life
      Of Light
      Sealed
   THE HIGHER WATERS
   IN UNFORMED STATE
   LAKE
   THE LOWER WATERS
   MUDDY
   OCEAN
   OVERFLOWING
   POND (see Lake)
   RIVER
      Crossing
      Flowing
      Four Rivers of Paradise
      Mouth of
      Of Death
      Of Life
   RAIN (see Weather)

RUNNING WATER
SHOWER (see Bath)
SURROUNDING
WALKING ON
WATERFALL
WAVES
WELL
    Closed
    Drawing water from
    Falling down a
    Fed by stream
    Sacred
WATERFALL (see Water)
WAVES (see Water)
WEALTH 371
    JEWEL
        Diamond
        Emerald
        Glowing
        Jade
        Pearl
        Ruby
        Turquoise
    MONEY
        Bills
        Coins
    TREASURE
WEAPON 373
    ARROW
        Feathered
        Flight of
        Heart pierced by
        Shot from bow
    BOW AND ARROW
    DAGGER (see Knife)
    GUN
    KNIFE
        In sheath
    SWORD
WEATHER 376
    CLOUD
        Angel standing on
        Hand emerging from
        Dissolving in sky

COLD
CYCLONE (see Hurricane)
FOG
HURRICANE
LIGHTNING
RAIN
 Causing flood
 Torrential (see Flood)
RAINBOW
 Colors of
SNOW
 Frost
 Ice
 Trapped in or by
STORM
 Wind storm (see Hurricane)
THUNDER
TORNADO (see Hurricane)
WHIRLWIND
WIND
WEDDING (see Ceremony)
WEED (see Plant)
WELL (see Water)
WEREWOLF (see Monster)
WHALE (see Fish)
WHEEL (see Vehicle)
WHIRLWIND (see Weather)
WHISPER 384
WHISTLE 384
WHITE (see Color)
WIDOW (see Family)
WIDOWER (see Family)
WIFE (see Family)
WILL, LAST 384
WILL, HUMAN 385
 HIGHER MIND
 LOWER MIND
WIND (see Weather)
WINDOW (see Building)
WINGS (see Bird)
WINTER (see Seasons)
WINTER SOLSTICE (see Seasons)
WOLF (see Animal)

WOOD (see Tree)
WOODPECKER (see Bird)
WORM 385
WORSHIP (see Ceremony)
WRECK (see Accident)
WREN (see Bird)

X
X 386
X-RAY 386

Y
YARD (see Building)

Z
ZODIAC 387
ZOO 388

❖❖❖❖❖❖❖❖❖❖❖❖❖❖❖❖❖❖❖❖❖❖❖❖❖❖❖❖❖❖❖❖❖❖❖❖

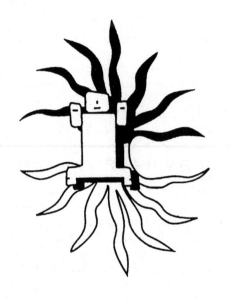

Meeting Yourself

Your symbols are *your* symbols, whether you are awake, asleep, day dreaming, dozing in the sun, or meditating. In fact, if your symbols did not already mean something to you, your subconscious wouldn't bother using them in your dreams, or anywhere else.

While *Letters From Home* is slanted slightly toward your dream world, it is just as true that the situations and events in your waking world have the same significance, and use the same symbolism. We guarantee that if you begin looking at your world symbolically, the events in your life will immediately become more interesting, helpful — and infinitely more creative and fun.

Letters From Home is not meant to be used in place of analyzing your own symbols. It was created to help you when you get stuck and to give you some different ways of looking at the symbols surrounding you at any given minute. *Letters* is also aimed at helping you dive deeper and deeper into your private symbolic world. And it is geared toward helping us here in the Western part of the planet understand how much we have lost by losing the incredible perception of meaning of some of our most common symbols. We have also attempted to put back some of the older archaic words and meanings, hoping that this will spur you to do your own research into your unique use of these ancient universal symbols.

Please don't let the size of this book deter you from browsing through it. As you work with your dreams and symbols, you will be surprised at how little this guide book actually does cover, and will more than likely be frustrated at not finding every symbol you want.

There will always be symbols of yours not included here precisely because they are so uniquely yours. No one has lived your life or had your experiences, and no one will use your symbols in precisely the same way.

Letters From Home is meant to be very personal to you, and you are encouraged to add interpretations of personal recurring symbols as you experience them by either beginning your own symbol dictionary, or by writing in the margins of this book. It is your book, after all.

Universal Symbols

Researchers estimate that most of us still dream from three to four universal symbols every night of our lives, and as we each have an average of 1,000 or more dreams a year, that adds up to a lot of universal symbols. The definitions in this guide book represent a compilation of the most common symbols dreamed in some form by almost everyone on our planet. For instance, an animal dreamed by a Kalahari Bushman would be different from one dreamed by you, but ANIMAL itself would have the same underlying, or "universal" symbolic meaning.

The symbols included in *Letters* were collected from many different kinds of sources after extensive research into material both ancient and modern, including interpretations found to be the most common among the people attending our workshops over the past several years. We have tried to give you as many possible interpretations for any one symbol all in one place as we can, always remembering that in the final analysis only *you* know what your symbols mean, even your universal ones.

And since your symbols are *your* symbols, even when you are awake, you can use *Letters From Home* to lead you through the maze of your own consciousness, to find and understand the many, many sign posts you place around yourself each moment of your existence. There is really no difference between the interpretations of your personal symbols — waking, meditating, day dreaming, or sleeping — or even out-of-body for that matter.

Question Everything

But *Letters From Home* doesn't stop at giving you alternate ways of looking at your symbols; it equips you with questions to ask about and of them. Each of the many possible interpretations of the symbols include questions to ask yourself when analyzing your use of that symbol.

The key to unraveling your symbols is really in asking the right questions at the right time — and in keeping at it. Be merciless. You are an investigative reporter, and you insist on knowing who, why, where, when, and how, and you won't stop until you get the information you want.

But again, your symbols are *your* symbols, no matter where you bump into them— dreaming, meditating, day dreaming, drowsing, or wide awake. If something was not already a recognizable symbol to your conscious mind, your subconscious wouldn't bother to use it in your dreams, or anywhere else. It really is trying to communicate with you in the best ways it knows how. It's a little as if your conscious mind spoke English and your subconscious only Swahili, so in order to communicate at all, they have to use sign language — in other words, symbols.

The Stuff Dreams Are Made Of

Your dreams are all yours. No one else has had exactly the same collection of experiences you have, in the same sequence, and no one else will use your dream symbols exactly the same way. Your dreams are your own private movies, plays, short stories and novels — as individual, distinctive, and unique to you as your DNA.

Every single dream is unveiling your deep subconscious feelings about the subject of your dream. Your dreams can help you understand what you feel, both consciously and subconsciously, and accept yourself for who you really are — and who you are in the process of becoming at the time.

Most experts recommend that you work with your dreams for at least six months to get the hang of it before you either drop dream work altogether or cut back in the amount of time you spend working on them. You don't have to make dream analysis your life's passion, but it does require some time, effort, and commitment.

You cannot over-analyze any dream or symbolic event. Continue to unravel it until it bores you blue — and then go look up blue under COLOR. Each and every interpretation you feel is right for you, is right for you. There is no fast, simple way to understand your symbols and dreams. There are no slick easy answers, and to not instantly understand the meaning of a dream is the norm. Most of us have the same problem, and that's why books like this one get written.

Symbols can and do have more than one meaning for you. **And everything in your dream has meaning. Nothing, absolutely nothing, is in your dream by accident.**

There is never just one interpretation to any symbolic event, waking or dreaming. You are a multi-layered, multi-dimensional entity, and your life happens on many levels at one time. So any meaning and insight you get from working with your symbols only brings you closer to the real you. In other words, you can't lose, no matter what, if your willingness to understand and your honesty with your self stays in good working order.

Although each dream isn't a pearl of wisdom, divine or otherwise, it is always you communicating directly to you, all about you, and always about something beneficial or useful to you at the time you dream or experience it. Dreams show you things you have consciously missed or ignored, for instance, and feelings of which you are not consciously aware, or aware of enough, at the time.

Dreams themselves are first and foremost always, always about your feelings at the time, and at a deeper level than you are aware of when awake. If you were totally and completely aware of the depth of these feelings, you would not need to dream them. This one is hard to believe until you start working with your symbols, so for now take it on trust. We guarantee you will find it is so.

So never take any dream or symbolic event at face value. Learning to interpret your personal symbols helps you keep the bridge between your conscious and subconscious mind strong and in good repair. Once this bridge or channel is relatively cleared of the dust and underbrush, it is much easier for your superconscious to get through. How's that for an exciting challenge?

"Beyond this Point There be Dragons"

This phrase was found written on very old maps, maps made when human beings believed that you could literally sail right off the end of the earth, and that beyond a certain point "there be dragons" and other unsavory experiences. Which makes this phrase a very good analogy for what many people believe about dreams.

But the truth is, there is no such thing as a "bad" dream. There are dreams that frighten you, of course, or make you uncomfortable, but after working with your dreams and personal symbols for even a short time, you will find that any nightmares or negative feelings are your very best friends — and kind of fun at that. They certainly get your attention, don't they? Which is exactly what they were designed by some part of you to do.

Remember, everything in your dream is a symbol. Monsters are symbols, fear is a symbol, running is a symbol, blood is a symbol — well, you get the idea. Step out of the nightmare, and into its real message; see MONSTER, etc. We absolutely unconditionally guarantee you that the Count is not hiding under the basement stairs, waiting to catch your ankles as you step down.

Your dreams and symbols are safety valves, early warning systems, allowing you a protective way to experience and release stress and tension before they get out of hand and cause damage in the physical world. They can help you make changes in your life, try out alternatives, and get comfortable with any shift or change before you or some part of you takes conscious action on any of them. Many dreams even warn you of potential health problems, and always in plenty of time to fix it before it breaks.

Remember that no matter how mundane or simple your symbol, it almost always has deeper levels of communication for you to explore. Your dreaming self is multi-layered, just like your waking self. Keep digging. And remember that you, and only you, have the final answer. Don't give up until it feels right to you, no matter how it feels to anyone else.

And watch your dreams and symbols change as you change. They will tell you things about yourself and your beliefs long before you are consciously aware of them. This is especially true of any healing taking place, at any level. And laugh and have fun with yourself while you grow. That's really what this is all about, isn't it?

Catching Your Dreams

Most of us do not remember our dreams during our work week or if we have to leap out of bed the minute our eyes open. Holidays, vacations, nap time, and weekends are usually the best time to remember your dreams — anytime you can wake up on your own schedule, within your own natural sleep cycle. And when you are traveling, pay particular attention to how your dreams change with your environment, not to mention the altitude.

Tracking your dreams by keeping either a written or spoken record of them allows you an easy step-by-step view of your personal inner growth. Dreams you have now can give you unique insights into how you got from A to B, or how you *can* get from A to B, and then move on to C, D, and E.

They also can show you quite clearly that you may not really want to go from A to B after all, and then quietly go about pointing out some of your many alternate routes. And collecting information about your dreams is absolutely mandatory if you want to learn to use lucid dreaming to its fullest potential (see Glossary/ Lucid Dream).

So, to catch a dream:

- Keep a pen and paper or journal by your bed, even if you choose to use a voice-activated tape recorder to record your dreams rather than writing them down. This reinforces to both your conscious and subconscious mind that you are serious about remembering your dreams.
- Write the date at the top of the page. Include a few words about anything during the day which had an emotional impact, something that's on your mind most of the time. Or choose a problem that is bothering you that you would like to explore. Or maybe you want to make a decision about something you are ambivalent about when you are

awake, or want an alternate suggestion on how to cope with a difficult situation. Including this type of information on the page will help you unravel the information communicated by your subconscious during your dream; see Glossary/Incubating.

- Recording the time of day or night, the season, the phase of the moon, and the weather can be a good way to begin to track your personal cycles, if you know that you are sensitive to any of these things. If you know you are particularly sensitive to astrological influences, you might want to include that information as well. Couldn't hurt.

- If you are incubating a dream, write your dream intent or question into your journal. Keep it short and sweet — the simpler the better, and only one question per night, please. Dream questions can be anything from "Why do I eat so many potato chips?" to "How do I really feel about getting out of this job or relationship?" You will always get an answer, but since it is always in symbols, you will want to be sure you write them all down to examine at length later, even months later.

- Suggest to yourself several times during your waking day and just as you are falling asleep that "Tonight I remember a dream." Keep your instructions to yourself in the present tense — don't put them in the future; in other words, never use phrases like, "I am going to remember my dreams" or "I want to remember my dreams". Your subconscious mind literally does not comprehend the future; it accesses past memories, not future ones. Your conscious mind, however, loves the "I'll think about it tomorrow" way of doing things, so make sure it understands that you mean NOW, and that you are not going to give up, so it may as well get on with it.

- Some people who have a difficult time catching a dream set their alarm (a soft one, not piercing or annoying) to go off approximately two hours after they go to bed. Since most of us dream in 90 to 100 minute sleep cycles, you are more likely to catch the first dream of your sleep cycle this way. This method won't guarantee that you will catch yourself in a REM period, but at the very least it reinforces to your

10

brain that you are really serious about catching a dream. Sleep labs wake people during REM, giving them an edge most of us don't have, although there are now excellent electronic devices geared to signal the brain when it is dreaming.

- When you wake, without moving more than necessary, reach for your pen and paper or your tape recorder. The more physical and mental you get when you first wake up, the faster your dream will dissolve. Run the dream backwards, starting with the last scene you remember or felt. Don't worry about where the dream started, and never assume that because you have replayed it in your mind that you will remember the dream later. Record it, record it, record it. Dreams are elusive little critters, especially the ones in your first 90-minute sleep cycle. So immediately record any feelings, sounds, colors, and/or smells you remember.

- If you can't remember your dream, record how you felt when you first woke up; be as specific as you can. And don't try to find the beginning. Start from the last thing you remember, and run it backwards. Let the dream flow naturally. Don't edit, analyze, judge, or try to make it logical, just get it down. Dreams are seldom "logical", and you can analyze it to your intellect's content later.

- Record the dream exactly as you remember it. Never add or subtract anything, and especially don't create an end that did not actually happen. For instance, if you see yourself falling, don't assume that you went splat! if you didn't actually experience the impact. (And, no, you don't die if you do go splat!). And don't put dream scenes in logical sequence if they didn't really happen that way in your dream. There is no linear time when you're in dreamland, and this alone can be a symbol. Why did X come *before* K, for instance? What does that remind you of that's going on in your life at the time?

- It is not necessary to work on a dream the minute you record it. In fact, some authorities recommend that you not even attempt to really dig into your dream for at least 24 hours. You have plenty of time to work on it once it's been recorded. And the operative word here is "work." Don't take anything for granted or at face value. *Everything* in your dream has meaning. Believe this. Your sleeping self went to a lot of trouble to create these movies and the least you can do is show this part of yourself that you appreciate its considerable efforts and creativity.

- Keep your dreams and any interpretations in chronological order. Refer to them again and again. They are excellent reminders of how far you've already come, something we all have a tendency to downplay and forget.
- Highlight or circle any recurring dream symbols. Check and recheck periodically for any recurring themes or patterns. Remember that everything in your dream is a symbol, even action and non-action. There is a very good reason why you are walking instead of driving a car, for instance, or why you are in an office building rather than a hospital. You could have put yourself anywhere, so why did you choose the scene you did? (See LANDSCAPE).

And save plenty of room after each dream to add things you remember later, because you will.

Building Your Dream Journal

Your journal can be anything with which you personally feel comfortable. It doesn't have to be expensive or fancy, and in fact having a beautifully bound book to start with can even keep you from writing down your real thoughts and feelings. We were, after all, trained in school not to make mistakes, and to write perfect compositions. There can be no mistakes in your dreams (or anywhere else in your life for that matter, but that's a whole 'nother book).

If you have difficulty recalling your dreams, don't worry about it. No matter how good you get at this, some of your dreams will always melt away the minute you open your eyes. You don't remember everything you think or experience every day, so why should you remember everything you dream? If you remember even one dream a week, you have plenty of material to work with, probably more than you want. And if you only remember one a month, you're still doing great. Keep in mind that on average, you will have 1,000 or more dreams every year, so don't worry about it. Just catch the ones you can.

Cleaning the Windows
of Your Subconscious

One of the best ways to download your day-to-day emotions and experiences so they don't need to take up valuable dream time is to run your day backwards in your mind while getting ready for bed. Start from where you are, then keep moving back, scene by scene until you replay waking up that morning. This helps to clear the decks of your more mundane emotions so that your subconscious can get right down to the good stuff.

The key to unlocking your dream and your symbols is as simple as asking the right questions, or the right sequence of questions, and keeping at it until you are satisfied with your answers. Cross examine your symbols. Be merciless. You are an investigative reporter and you mean to get all the facts.

Here are some basic questions to get you started, but we have included plenty of sample questions with each symbol in this book, and please add your own as they come up for you.

- Where is your dream taking place? Describe the setting in detail. Nothing in your dream landscape is there by accident. Each piece has something specific to tell you about yourself and your life. Dreams are primarily about feelings, and dream scenery and landscapes almost always shows you the *primary* emotional background for the whole dream. Every time a dream scene changes it usually is telling you about a change in your emotions. What kind of people would normally like your dream setting? Why? What kind of people would normally avoid it? Why? (See LAND-SCAPE).

- In or around which type of building do the majority of your dreams take place? Are you usually inside or outside? (Women tend to dream themselves in enclosures of some kind, while men prefer the wide open spaces; but this is not a given, just the "average"). What kind of people would like

14

your most common dream buildings? Why? Who would avoid them like the plague? Why? How are those two types of people different from one another? (See BUILDING).

- What role do you play most often in your dreams? For instance, are you usually the leader, or the follower; the aggressor, the victim, or the rescuer; the seeker, or the teacher; the driver, or the passenger? How does it feel to play that role? How would your dream be different if you changed roles? Watch for your roles to change in any way at all. They are important clues to your inner subconscious feelings and growth. (See STAGE).

- Are you usually alone in your dream, or with other people? Are they most often people you know, or "faceless," nameless people? It is common to dream these known-but-unknown strangers, a dead giveaway that these are unfamiliar or unrecognized characteristics or tendencies of your own personality. (See STRANGER).

- What kinds of people are you with most often in your dreams? Why? What part of you does each one of these people represent? What would they say to you if they wrote their own dialogue? What kind of people are they? Where would these people work? What would they do for fun? What would they be afraid of? What do you think these people are like as people? How are they different from, or the same as, the people in your life when you are awake? What personality qualities do they have that you might like to have? What qualities do they have that you might like to get rid of? How would you like to hang out with these people when you are awake? Why, or why not? Where would you have to go or how would you have to change your life in order to meet people like this? How do you feel about that? (See PEOPLE).

- What type of clothes do you wear most often in your dreams? Why? How are they the same as, or different from, the ones you usually wear? What does this tell you? (Clothes often show you the role you are taking in your dream, or ones you would like to play in waking life; see CLOTHES).

- Which sex are you most often in your dreams? Do you ever change from one gender to another in your dream? Why, or why not? What does that tell you about yourself? How does it make you feel? Why? (See FEMALE, MALE).

- Which emotions do you most commonly feel in your dreams? What are the emotions most often felt by the other people in your dreams? What does this tell you about your deep subconscious feelings at the time of your dream? How are these feelings the same as, or different from, the feelings you are aware of when you are awake? What does this tell you about something going on in your life at the time of your dream? (See EMOTION).

- How do you most often deal with any conflicts, danger, or struggles in your dreams? How is that the same as, or different from, the way you would handle the same situation when you are awake? Most of us tend to be a little less assertive in our dreams than we might be when awake; we are, after all, trying to work things out in our dreams; see EMOTION, STRUGGLE.

- What is the main action taking place in your dream? If it changes, at what point in your dream did it change? Why did it change? How did the change in action change the dream? (See CHASE, FIGHT, RUN).

- Which objects are in your dreams the most often? For many of us, these are familiar everyday objects like cars, houses, office buildings, etc. How are your recurring dream objects the same as, or different from, the same object in your waking life? What kind of a person would own your dream objects? Your recurring objects will always be some of your key symbols. Nothing is in your dream by accident; each object was chosen by your subconscious in its efforts to communicate with you. (See BUILDING, VEHICLE).

- What type of situations are you most often involved in? *Are* you involved, or are you most often a passive observer, the passenger in the vehicle, a bystander? How do you feel about that? What does this remind you of that is going on in your life at the time of the dream?

- What plot or story line do you act out the most often in your dreams? Why? What kind of publisher or movie producer would want to buy it? Why? (See MOVIE).

- Try to give your dream a title. You can get some terrific insight just by the titles you choose. If your dream were a movie or a story, what would it be titled? Why?
- If your dreams over the past few months were chapters in a novel, what would that tell you about your recent past, and about which direction you are headed right now? Would you like to change the main plot of the novel? Why, or why not?

As we said, become a dedicated investigative reporter. You are determined to find out who, what, why, where, when, how. Be absolutely merciless with yourself in your questioning. After all, you can't get too nosey about yourself. This time it really *is* your business — and no one else's.

This All Sounds Like
A Lot of Work to Me!

One of the biggest reasons to record your dreams is that you will now be able to find your recurring themes, symbols, and situations over long periods of time. While your dreams can each be interpreted individually (and should be), they can also be interpreted as acts in a play or chapters in a novel. So answer questions often, especially when you get good enough at unraveling your dreams to be sure you have all the answers. Because this is precisely the point where you get serious about cleaning away the debris on the way to your superself, so don't sell yourself short. Question especially any and all natural resistance to recognizing your symbols.

And never settle for just one interpretation of any dream. Your dreams are occurring on several levels at once, just like your waking life. They are like Chinese boxes or stories in *The Arabian Nights*, they are stories within stories, layers upon layers. Keep at it until you are either bored silly or have more than one possible interpretation.

And look for the paradoxes. A dream will frequently have two interpretations which seem to be the opposite of one another. But both interpretations can be equally true at the same time. You do live in a world full of duality, remember? And, as we said earlier, there is seldom just one interpretation to any one dream or experience anyway. Anything that feels right to you, is probably a valid answer. At the very least, you have just learned something else about yourself that you probably weren't consciously aware of, so how can you lose?

Will the Real Expert Please Stand Up?

No one, absolutely no one, can approve the final interpretation of your dream or your symbols but you. Don't let anyone talk you out of any interpretation that feels right to you, no matter how intellectual or spiritual the other person's interpretation sounds. You will always know when you've hit the mark, and don't be satisfied until you get to that **Aha!** feeling. Accept that you will not necessarily get a satisfactory interpretation to every dream or symbolic happening right when you want it. And some you may never ever completely understand at the conscious level.

Professionals can, of course, help you see angles and perspectives that you may be too involved with at the time to see. Dream and symbol dictionaries work the same way, giving you deeper, broader, and many, many more facets of an interpretation than you might have recognized by yourself. Dream groups or dream buddies are good at this, too.

The bottom line is that you just cannot over analyze your dreams, and it is *your* interpretation that counts.

Spotting Your Waking Symbols

Symbols are symbols, no matter where they show up. Once you begin to recognize your own highly unique use of symbols in your dreams and meditations, it's easy to make the jump to seeing them in your day-to-day living. And life gets a lot more interesting, instructive, and just plain fun.

In fact, if you have trouble remembering your dreams, begin with your waking life. If the situation or event were a dream, what would it mean? What does it tell you about what you want, where you are going, who you really are or would like to be?

For example, if on your way to work every intersection light you approach is yellow — beyond the obvious Caution! message — you might be getting a message to slow down a little, take it easy, look around you, take your time, get centered in what's really important. Does two seconds really make that much difference? Or your yellow light symbol might be telling you to be a little more aware of your own human nature, and to treat yourself and others with a little more respect during your day; see COLOR/Yellow, or anything at all that yellow means to you at the time.

If you are working on your prosperity beliefs and you see a lot of Rolls Royce automobiles during your day, you just may be getting a message to aim for the best, reminding you that there are no limitations on how well you can do. How do you feel about a Rolls Royce? What kind of people own them? Why?

What kind of food do you eat during your day? Why? What is it telling you about yourself and your deep subconscious feelings? Be especially aware of any food cravings. There's a reason why you want what you do, when you do (see FOOD).

Do you lose things a lot? Why? And it's not because you're "just that way," or careless, or dumb. What things do you lose most often? Why those things and not others? How do you feel when you lose something? Why? What does this remind you of? (See LOST, MISSING).

What kind of clothes do you wear most often? How do you feel about that? Why do you pick the color and texture you do? How would you rather dress? How is that the same as, or different from, the way you dress in most of your dreams? (See CLOTHES).

You've just hurt your right foot? How does that affect the way you move through your day? What does that remind you of going on in your life at the time? What do you gain, or lose, by limping? What kind of people normally limp? Why your right foot and not your left? Which foot do you lead out with when you begin to walk? Why? What does this tell you about yourself? (See BODY/Foot).

What kind of bird do you notice most often? What kind of tree, flower, plant? What do these things represent to you personally? (See BIRD, FLOWER, PLANT, TREE).

What kind of weather do you like best? Why? (See WEATHER). And on and on. Begin to take nothing for granted, and believing that there are no accidents. If you can manage this without becoming obsessed with yourself, you are well on your way back home.

Unravel your waking life exactly the way you would a dream. All of the symbolism applies, just as if you were tucked in your bed REMing like crazy. Using either the dreaming or waking approach to your symbols will get you to the same destination. As one sage said, "All roads lead home."

So stop taking your environment and life for granted. It doesn't just happen to you, and some part of you is trying very hard to let you know what you need to know every single step you take. And, yes, this is where the trust part comes in. But it gets a lot more fun from this point on — we promise.

Good hunting!

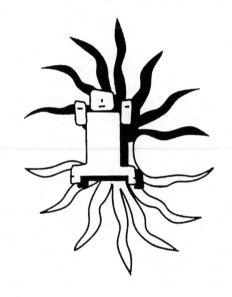

ACCIDENT

Accidents are most often trying to tell you that some part of you feels you are not paying enough attention to what is represented by the accident, usually some personality trait or habit.

An accident may also be warning you that you are trying to go much too fast in the area of your life represented by the dream, meditation, or experience, that you are probably not thinking through the consequences of your actions and the way you are handling things.

In waking life, if you find yourself suddenly accident prone, it is probably a clear message that you have allowed your energy to get way, way too low. Slow down, get your priorities back in order, and pay closer attention to what's going on around you. For instance, are you maintaining your equipment (your body and emotions) properly on a regular basis?

Accidents also make great puns. What is it you may be in danger of wrecking? What have you done lately that was accidental, not done intentionally at the conscious level? Who got hurt or damaged as a result of this action, or non-action?

What kind of an accident is it? Who was at fault? How did it happen? Who or what was involved? What was the damage and injury? What part(s) of the body were damaged? What objects were damaged or destroyed? What does this remind you of that is going on in your life at the time?

How did you feel about the accident in your dream or meditation? What actions would you have to take to have the same type of accident in your waking life? What does this remind you of?

See also BLOOD if present, BODY if involved, PAIN if pain is felt, VEHICLE, and any other objects involved in the accident.

ADULTERY

Dreaming that you or the love of your life commits adultery almost always symbolizes that you are giving too much attention or importance to something that is preventing your growth, and that as a result you are literally "cheating" on yourself.

But dream adultery can also represent a strong need to merge your inherent Yin-Yang (female-male) qualities with the qualities of the dream partner with whom you or your significant other is committing the adultery.

How is this third party different from you? What is he or she giving your partner in the dream that you may not be doing yourself when you're awake? What is this trying to tell you about your relationship as it is at the time?

What is your mate like as a person? Be very, very detailed and specific in your description. Keep in mind that this is not about criticizing yourself or others; it's about understanding how your subconscious is using these people as a symbol.

If you are the partner who is committing the adultery, it can symbolize that the quality you are attracted to in your dream lover is missing in your mate, or in yourself in some way, or in the relationship as a whole.

Adultery can also symbolize that some part of you feels a need to break free from conventional cultural limitations, a need to break the rules imposed by your society, and not just sexually. Does this remind you of anything going on in your life?

To dream of your lover committing adultery, of course, can also symbolize a fear of losing that person or what that person represents

to you, usually a strong message to look closely at self-esteem and relationship issues. After all, why would anyone in their right mind want to cheat on you?

As an archetype, adultery symbolizes the human ego's turning away from a higher existence in favor of a lower, more worldly physical one. It is a strong symbol of choosing union with physical and emotional sensations over Divine Wisdom and Truth.

Conversely, this symbol can also point out a strong inner desire to integrate Spirit with Matter, the Divine with the physical. How you feel about the adultery at the time will lead you to your best interpretation.

Who is committing the adultery? Why? What do they really get out of it? How do you feel about it in your dream or meditation? Why?

How do you feel about adultery in general? What kind of person commits adultery? How will your life change if either you or your partner commits adultery? Why? See MARRIAGE; FAMILY/Husband, Wife; SEX.

ALARM

An alarm of any kind frequently tells you that some part of the Self is waking up, becoming much more aware — or that it is time to let it do so.

An alarm can also be a clear message that you need to wake up in your day-to-day life and pay attention, get moving, open your eyes, stop being a couch potato.

It can also be telling you to snap to attention when working with the situation represented by your dream or meditation. The bell has rung, and what are you doing still asleep?

What type of alarm is it? What sound does it make? Who would normally react to this alarm? Why? How is that different from, or the same as, the type of person who would react to it in the waking world? Is the alarm automatic, or does someone or something have to activate it and turn it off? What triggered the alarm?

How does the alarm make you feel in your dream or meditation? What actions do you take because of the alarm? How would your dream be different if the alarm did not sound? See also BELL, YELL.

ALCOHOL

Dreaming of any alcoholic beverage often symbolizes a strong desire to relax, meditate, or otherwise change your usual state of consciousness. Alcohol has the physical effect of soothing the rational mind while at the same time inhibiting many cultural restrictions you have accepted as a result of your personal belief systems.

Alcohol is a temporary and artificial means of breaking free from your everyday restrictions and limitations, a way of not being responsible for all of your thoughts, words, and behavior. What does this remind you of going on in your life at the time?

Drinking any alcoholic substance can also symbolize ingestion and absorption of Divine life and power, a desire to literally be intoxicated by Spirit. How you feel in your dream will give you your clue as to how your subconscious is using this symbol.

As an archetype, alcohol is an ancient symbol for the power of combining the elements Fire and Water, the two elements necessary to create the human soul.

The fermentation process itself is symbolic of the ability of the human soul to go beyond its ordinary limitations, to free its intuitive powers to produce penetrating and profound dreams and visions.

Alcohol automatically and with little or no personal effort helps to produce an altered state of consciousness and for this reason is often a symbol for transformation, especially when the alcohol is wine.

Wine is, and has been for thousand of years, a universal symbol for spiritual growth and intoxication with the Divine or the Beloved.

Traditionally, wine is a symbol of Wisdom, Truth, and the spiritual life which intoxicates or paralyses the lower (physical) instinctual characteristics of human nature, but which brings fulfillment and joy to the higher (spiritual) nature.

What kind of alcohol is being consumed? Who is drinking it? Who offers or sells it? How do you feel about alcoholic drinks in general? Why? What will happen once all of the alcohol is gone? See also CONTAINER/Cup or any other object holding the alcohol, and BUILDING/Bar.

ALLEY

An alley often symbolizes a shortcut or an unexpected change in direction, a redirection or alternative path for your current plans or direction.

An alley is also narrow, limiting, and often a route you would not normally take for one reason or another. Alleys can be dangerous.

And, like hallways, alleys can be purely sexual symbols.

Alleys can, of course, be great puns. Is something "right up your alley"?

What are the objects in the alley? Are there people or animals in it? Is it littered with trash?

Is your alley (your Way) light or dark? How do you feel about being there? Why are you there? Who would habitually use this alley? Who would avoid it? Why? What does this remind you of? See also BUILDING/Hallway.

ALPHABET

In general, the letters of the Arabic alphabet (or any alphabet for that matter) are symbolic of the communication of ideas and beliefs and the ability to record their meaning for all future generations. This universal symbolism is intensified by what the letter means to you personally.

For example, the letter A has been used to label adulterers in many cultures, X marks the place of buried treasures, and letters are

often used to tell us how well we do on tests.

And the individual letters can also be interpreted numerically:

1	2	3	4	5
A	B	C	D	E
J	K	L	M	N
S	T	U	V	W

6	7	8	9
F	G	H	I
O	P	Q	R
X	Y	Z	

To the ancient Greeks, the vowels *a, e, i, o, u* symbolized the Spirit and the Seven Heavenly Spheres (the Greeks had two letters for *e* and *o*). The consonants symbolized Matter.

So the Greek alphabet was functional on several levels, reminding them of the relationship between Spirit and Matter, and how this could be accomplished through "correct composition," the combining of Spirit with Matter. This multi-level use of language and the alphabet in general is common to many cultures, and, unfortunately, the English language is not particularly well suited to conveying many spiritual concepts. See also NUMBER represented by the specific letter.

AMPUTATION

Loss of any part of your body, or a serious mutilation or injury, often symbolizes a deep subconscious feeling of loss of energy or personal power, or a fear of the imminent loss of either or both of these.

The part of the body amputated or mutilated will give you your clue where this may be happening, or in danger of happening.

Conversely, amputation can symbolize cutting away or cutting back no longer necessary or diseased parts of yourself, and in this context represents a healing of some kind. The general overall content of your dream or meditation will tell you which of these interpretations fits. Remember that growth is about integration, not denial or suppression (amputation).

Decapitation was performed as a sacred ritual in several early human cultures because it was believed that the head contained the spirit or soul. Mastheads, busts, and sculptures of heads share much of the same symbolic meaning; see HEAD/Decapitated.

What was the action leading up to or causing the amputation? Are you in danger of cutting something off or out of your life?

Which side of the body is affected? Which part of the body? Was there any blood or pain? How do you feel about the amputation in your dream or meditation? What does the amputation or mutilation instantly make you think of? Why?

See also BODY part amputated and the instrument used in the amputation or mutilation, BLOOD and PAIN if either was present, and SURGERY.

ANGEL

Angels are literally beings made of Light and almost always symbolize a Messenger of God.

Angels represent spiritual freedom through your ability to attain the capacity for complete unconditional love, to love as the angels love.

Angels also symbolize "God's Ideas" or "Gods Thoughts in action," ideas or thoughts which have separated from God for the sole purpose of accomplishing very specific assignments. What was this angel sent to do?

And Angels often bring warnings, symbolizing that you are not only forewarned but well protected in the situation symbolized by your dream, meditation, or experience.

In some systems of belief, angels are divine influences created specifically to aid the human soul in its evolution. Within these systems of belief, human beings are considered capable of rising higher than the angels, and are in fact served by them at all times.

Any dreams or meditations with angels or other spiritual beings are always of special significance. These are generally direct messages from your Higher Self to your personality self.

Angels usually show up in your dreams or meditations to give you a message to help you act from your higher nature, rather than your lower reactive physical nature, in the situation represented by the dream or meditation.

What does your angel look like? What is its name? Is it male, female, or androgynous? Why? Where did it come from? Where will it go?

What is it wearing? Does it fly? What part of you is your dream angel? How do you feel about that?

If your dream angel could sit down and chat with you, what would be the first thing it would say?

See also BIRD/Wings and DAY/Light.

ANIMAL

The general interpretation of animals in dreams is that they are a symbol of some part of your human emotional and instinctual nature, the "earthy" part of you.

There are different interpretations for each animal (see individual animal by name). Use your intuition and common sense to tell you which interpretation applies to your dream, meditative, or waking event.

If you are in the process of searching for your true emotional nature, animals can be very effective guides and allies, and direct symbols for which part of your nature your subconscious wants you to pay particular attention to at the time of the experience.

Even to Carl Jung, animals represented very specific archetypes.

Animals also represent your own natural survival instincts. They correspond to the 1st, 2nd, and 3rd Chakras combined, or any one of the three alone, but can also represent any of the Chakras,

including those above the 7th. How you feel about the animal will give you your clue as to which Chakra this might be; see also CHAKRA.

And dream, meditation and animals actually experienced can, and often do, represent your personal totem or guardian animals. Shamans often refer to certain altered states of body and mind as "becoming the animal," a state of consciousness reached by integrating and identifying with the qualities of the animal.

How is this particular animal different from the same animal as you think of it? How do you feel about animals in general? What is the natural behavior of this animal? What is its natural habitat? And what does this remind you of?

What is the animal's overall physical condition and health? How do you feel about the animal in your dream or meditation? Why? What does it remind you of? Why?

See also COLOR of animal and individual animal below.

COMMON ANIMAL SYMBOLS:

BAT

The bat as a symbol has a long history of ambivalent interpretations.

In the Far East, it is a symbol of good fortune and represents immortality and the gateway to the heights. In Africa, the bat was a symbol of intelligence, and to the ancient Alchemists the bat symbolized all ambivalent phenomena in

Nature since it was both bird-like and a mammal.

But the bat is also a symbol of death, dark depression, of dark sexual desires and passions, an enemy of the light, and an enemy of the natural order of things since it sleeps upside down.

This one is also a great pun. Who is batty? Is something about to get tangled up in your hair? Would you like to bat someone? For whom or what would you like to go to bat? Is someone at your throat?

How do you feel about bats in general? Why? What do they make you think of?

BEAR

Bears almost always symbolize enormous power and strength. Dream or meditation bears will usually be either cuddly or dangerous, depending upon how you feel about your personal power or strength at the time.

Bear also represents a desire or a need to dream more, a need for silence, a need or deep desire to meditate or contemplate something going on in your life, to hibernate with it for a time.

And bear was used as a symbol of a mediator between Heaven and Earth, and believed by many ancient cultures to be an ancestor of human beings.

Bear is considered to represent the West (the direction of maturity or ripening for harvest) and the intuitive right side of the brain.

Bear also symbolizes illusions or passions that hug the mind and stifle or crush your intellect and ability to reason (breathe).

Bear can also symbolize truth that is heard but not clearly understood, warning you that as a result you may be coming to a wrong or even potentially dangerous conclusion, opinion, belief, or action.

Bears are nearsighted and don't like surprises. And bear is often much too quick to anger, instantly becoming angry enough to hurt, maul, and kill things, including humans. Does this remind you of anything?

And bears take their power and strength for granted and take on any opponent, even when they should be more cautious.

In some Native American traditions, bear symbolizes introspection or a time to hibernate and digest the experiences of the previous Spring, Summer, and Fall to prepare for new growth; see also SEASONS. Rest is as important to your growth as expansion — a hard one for most of us to accept.

Bear is a good pun. Are you telling yourself to "bear" something? Have you substituted bear for "bare"? What or to whom would you like to give a big bear hug? Are you touchy as a bear lately?

What is this bear doing? What color is it? What species of bear? Why? How is this species different from the others?

Is it male or female? Adult or cub? How do you feel about this particular bear? Can it talk to you? Is it friendly, or dangerous? Why?

Where would your dream bear normally live? If it could talk, what would it tell you? How do you feel about bears in general? Why?

BOBCAT

Bobcats frequently symbolize strong independence. They are rarely seen by human beings since they hunt at night. And this cat has no problem jumping into water, especially when single-mindedly tracking its prey, which it does very well.

Bobcats don't recognize boundaries of any kind, including fences. So if you have dreamed of a bobcat you might be telling yourself it's time to ignore any old boundaries and beliefs which have kept you from exploring new territories or hunting grounds. The only real boundaries you have are the ones you set for yourself.

Or have you just overstepped the boundaries and ignored the "keep out" signs concerning the subject of your dream or meditation? Are you trying to move into areas you aren't really ready to tackle yet?

And, of course, this one is prime for a pun — do you know a cat named Bob?

What is this particular bobcat hunting? Will it be successful? Why, or why not?

BUFFALO

The buffalo or bison symbolizes enormous supernatural and mystic power in most cultures where it is found. For example, the Buddhists often portray Yama, the god of the dead, with the head of a buffalo.

Riding on a buffalo symbolizes your mastery over your basic physical animal nature. For instance, Lao Tzu was often shown riding a buffalo, and was said to have been riding a green one when he disappeared into the West. How's that for good symbolism?

In some Native American traditions, the buffalo is a symbol of strength and the power to endure, and the whirlwind (see also WEATHER/Whirlwind). Many, many stories and legends center around the buffalo.

Buffalo is often the bringer of healing medicines. Both the male and female buffalo have horns, and buffalo horns themselves were powerful healing tools; see also Horns below. And buffalo symbolizes abundance and one who supplies all physical survival needs.

But buffalo, by keeping to its old strategies when faced with a new enemy ensured it would be easy to hunt, nearly to extinction. So could your buffalo be trying to warn you that you have become an easy target for something or someone by refusing to see that things have changed?

What is this buffalo doing? How is that the same as, or different from, what a buffalo normally does? What does this buffalo remind you of going on in your life at the time?

BULL

The bull is an ambivalent symbol, sometimes depicted as solar and sometimes lunar. It is often used as a symbol of the first Chakra; see CHAKRA/1st.

The bull itself as a sky and weather deity is found in the earliest human cultures, its consort often one of many goddesses. For instance, the bull as a symbol is a common thread among all Sumerian and early Semitic cultures.

Bulls symbolize the procreative powers and energies, including the fertilizing powers of the sun, rain, storms, lightning, and thunder.

To the Buddhist, bulls symbolize the moral self and the ego. The ancient Celts used the bull as a symbol of divine power and strength, while the early Christians used it as a symbol for unthinking brute force.

To the ancient Egyptian, the bull Apis was an incarnation of Osiris, a servant of the Great God Ptah, and sacred to Ra and Neb.

In ancient Greece the bull was sacred to Poseidon, Dionysos, Zeus, and Aphrodite.

In Persia, it was the Soul of the World, and the first created animal from whose soul came all later creations.

And of course the Minoans saw the bull as The Great God. A bull was a common sacrifice to the earth and all earthquake deities, while in Crete it also symbolized the reproductive forces of Nature.

Or your bull may just be a good pun. Are you giving someone a lot of bull? Are you wading through the bull to get to something? And don't forget the astrological sign of Taurus. Is there a Taurean in your life?

A BULL-MAN FIGURE is often shown guarding a center (usually some kind of maze), and doorways, gateways, and treasures.

A BULL CALF or a bull is often used to symbolize the 1st Chakra or physical energy center; see CHAKRA/1st.

BULLS DRAWING A CHARIOT or RIDING ON A BULL is a common solar god-warrior symbol, associated with sky, storm, and solar deities. So to ride a bull or have it pull your wagon shows mastery and control over the symbolism of the bull.

A BULL'S HEAD is an ancient symbol for a sacrifice of some kind; see also AMPUTATION.

SACRIFICING A BULL AT THE NEW YEAR symbolizes the death of Winter and the continuing rebirth of the creative life force.

THIGH OF THE BULL: To the ancient Egyptians, the thigh of the bull represented the phallic leg of Set as a symbol of strength and fertility.

CAGED
A caged animal almost always represents your imprisoned strong feelings and emotions.

But a caged animal can also represent the free, natural parts of you that feel caged or hampered by something in your life.

What is this cage made of? Why that and not some other material? How is the animal reacting to being caged? What kind of an animal would normally be placed in this cage? Why? What does this remind you of going on in your life at the time? See also JAIL, ZOO.

CAMEL
Camels symbolize royalty, dignity, great stamina under harsh conditions, obedience, and temperance.

Camels can travel great distances under extremely hostile desert conditions because of their ability to so efficiently store water.

But they are respected by those who know them well for their tempers and their penchant for spitting on people they don't want too close to them.

To the ancient Persians, the camel was a symbol of the dragon-serpent; see Dragon and Snake below.

And there's always the old saying, "A camel is a horse created by committee." Does this remind you of anything going on in your life?

CAT
Cats have been sacred to many cultures throughout human history and invariably carry dual symbolism wherever they are found.

For instance, the ancient Egyptians believed cats were the protectors of the home, mothers, and small children.

And they were associated with the moon and sacred to the goddesses Isis and Bast (the guardian of marriage). But cats were also sacred to Set in his representation of darkness.

Cats often symbolize your female (Yin) quiet, independent qualities and characteristics, whether you are male or female. Cats can see in the dark and have infinite patience when hunting.

Cats are also uncooperative (by purely human standards, not cat ones of course), setting their own priorities and following their own agendas.

Cats are always self-possessed, often loners and totally unconcerned with the opinions of anything or anyone around them, and, of course, sensual.

Cats are often cruel to smaller animals, especially ones they like to play with before killing.

To the early Buddhists, cats were closely associated with the symbolism of the serpent, while the Japanese used cats to symbolize the power of transformation and peaceful rest and sleep.

In general, it was not until the Middle Ages in Europe that cats were labeled as bad luck and accused of consorting with and being familiars of witches, and a sure sign of the devil and "evil forces".

A cat is also a great pun. Are you being catty? Are your claws out? Are you playing a cat-and-mouse game? Who's a fat cat?

What color is this cat? Why? Do you like cats? Why, or why not?

What kind of a person would like this cat? Who would avoid it or be allergic to it? Why? How would it feel to be this cat? Why? How are cats different from dogs and other pets?

COUGAR (Mountain Lion)

In some Native American cultures, the cougar frequently symbolizes leadership and the lessons that come with being a leader.

Mountain lions don't roar, they scream or purr, depending upon their message.

Cougars teach their young for approximately one year, training them to hunt by bringing them live prey to kill.

Cougars are generally nocturnal and elusive, not easily seen by the ordinary person.

So is your cougar telling you that you have been staying in the background too much? Or that you might want to melt into the shadows for awhile? Do you have a tendency to hang back until conflict is unavoidable? Or maybe that now is the time to do just that?

Are you quietly staking out your territory? What might be waiting on the ledge above, ready to pounce? See also Lion below.

COW

Cows are ancient symbols of The Great Mother. Virtually all moon goddesses were associated with the cow, and symboled her nourishing, life-giving qualities.

Cows also symbolize the productive power of the Earth, procreation, material plenty, and the maternal instincts.

To the ancient Celts, the Celestial Cow was red with white ears, and represented the Yin (female) principal and the Earth, while the horse symbolized the Yang (male) principle and the heavens.

To the ancient Scandinavians, it was a cow, the Nourisher, who licked the ice and produced the first human.

And the cow is still a sacred animal to the Hindu, representing fertility, plenty, the Earth, Prithivi, and Nandini, the wish-fulfilling cow.

Hathor was The Great Mother of ancient Egypt, and when portrayed with two heads represented Upper and Lower Egypt. The legs of the Celestial Cow, Nut, the Lady of Heaven, represented the four quarters of the Earth (Nut is usually shown with stars on her underbody). And Isis was also sometimes symbolized by a cow, or just by the cow's horns, representing the crescent moon — symbols within symbols.

What color is this cow? What is it doing? How contented is it? What do you think cows are like as animals? How is this cow different from other cows? Why? How would your dream or experience be different if another animal were substituted for this cow? Why? What does this remind you of going on in your life at the time?

CROCODILE

Crocodiles are strong symbols of The Great Devourer, a reminder of the necessity or process of passing through death to reach new life.

And since they can live quite comfortably in water and on land, crocodiles symbolize the dual nature of humanity, with all of its inherent potential.

In many cultures, crocodiles are strongly associated with the fertility of the waters, and are often guardians of doorways, ways to other dimensions of reality.

Crocodiles and alligators are ancient survivors, and can symbolize your strong will and power to survive the subject of your dream. They can eat almost anything and have been here much, much longer than we have.

So your dream crocodile or alligator may be telling you to take care of your own survival needs first. How's your diet? Are you living in your optimum environment?

Are you working in a job or associating with people who will ultimately be a danger to you, eat you alive? It is, after all, human beings who are the only natural enemy of crocodile and alligator.

Both crocodiles and alligators are excellent mothers, and their young are born fully-formed and ready to go. So these reptiles are also strong symbols of fertility and instantaneous power.

And they can survive in two elements, land and water. They constantly patrol shorelines, symbolic of the ceaseless search for knowledge and the meaning of life and death.

The crocodile was sacred to Apep, Serapis, and often shown sitting at the feet of the Great God Ptah. It is one of the emblems of the ancient Egyptian god Set, and Sebek is also often crocodile-headed, in this instance symbolizing vicious passions, treachery, deceit, and hypocrisy.

It was an ancient belief in many cultures that the crocodile was tongueless, and therefore silent, and that it routinely swallowed the moon, for which deed it constantly wept, giving us the still current phrase "crying crocodile tears".

So any way you look at it, crocodiles and alligators are strong primal symbols, bound to get your immediate attention.

What is this particular crocodile or alligator doing? How do you feel about it? Is it a danger to you or anything else around you? How are you reacting to its actions?

What color is it? Who would like it and want to protect it? Why? Do you like crocodiles? Why, or why not?

BEING SWALLOWED BY A CROCODILE is an ancient symbol of the descent into the Underworld, of going deep into the Inner Self.

CROCODILE WITH ITS MOUTH OPEN may be telling you that you are heading into danger, going against the current, that you are somewhere you don't belong.

But in a purely spiritual or moral sense this may be telling you that you are also headed in exactly the right direction, just not the easiest one. You are about to descend into the Underworld, the Inner Self.

DANGEROUS

A dangerous animal can symbolize that you have, or feel you have, wild uncontrollable emotions and feelings, the emotions specifically represented by the animal.

Dangerous animals can also represent suppressed or unacceptable (to you) anger and frustration.

A dangerous animal can, of course, also represent an actual physical danger your subconscious has picked up from your waking environment, again, symbolized by the particular animal.

Who or what does this dangerous animal remind you of? How does the animal itself feel in your dream or meditation? If it could write its own dialogue, what would it say?

How would you feel about meeting this animal face to face? Why? What would it take to domesticate this animal? How would things change if this happened?

DEER

The deer and the stag are both ancient symbols of swift movement, long life, wealth, success in public office, and meditation.

But while the deer and the stag share much of the same symbolism, the deer was associated with the moon and the stag was a solar animal, representing fire, creation, the dawn, renewal, and usually the animal associated with the Tree of Life; see TREE/Tree of Life.

And deer often symbolize your more peaceful, gentle, undemanding qualities and actions, or needs. Deer also symbolizes meditation, meekness, and gentleness.

Deer were associated with the fairy world by many cultures and believed to be supernatural creatures and messengers of the gods.

And a deer portrayed on either side of the Wheel or Circle of Life symbolizes the Buddha's teaching in the deer park at Sarnath, a teaching which set the Wheel of Life in motion again.

Conversely, deer was one of the three senseless creatures of the Buddhists, symbolizing love-sickness. (Tiger represents anger and the monkey greed and covetousness).

To the ancient Celts, deer represented supernatural beings of the fairy world and were "fairy cattle" and always divine messengers. It is for this reason as much as any other that deer skin and antlers were ritual garments.

To the ancient Chinese, deer symbolized longevity, high rank, official success, and wealth.

In some Native American traditions, deer or a fawn often symbolizes your ability to use your gentleness or passive resistance to open the hearts of others.

The Japanese saw deer as a dual symbol, representing longevity but also melancholy and solitariness, especially when associated with a maple leaf or tree; see TREE/ Maple.

Deer was sacred to the goddess Isis in ancient Egypt, and to

Artemis, Athene, Aphrodite, Diana, and Apollo in Graeco-Roman cultures.

All deer are vegetarians and exceptionally sensitive to their environments. Their awareness is heightened at the slightest disturbance or change. But being too sensitive can also ultimately be detrimental, especially in today's environments. Does any of this remind you of something taking place in your life at the time?

Dreaming of a deer can of course be a good pun, a play on words substituting deer for "dear".

What color is your dream deer? Is it a fawn, a doe, or a stag? Why? What actions is it carrying out?

If it could speak, what would it say to you? Why does it belong in your dream or meditation? How would your dream be different without the deer? What does it remind you of that is going on in your life?

DOG

Dog has a long history of symbolizing the Will of the Higher Self (see WILL, Human). Dogs also often represent the male (Yang) qualities and characteristics, whether you are male or female.

Dogs symbolize strong loyal friends, patience, fidelity and unswerving devotion, a forgiving nature, loving completely and unconditionally, nobility in action, watchfulness, protection, and the conservative, philosophical principle of life.

And dog is a common popular culture and mythical hero, and when associated with fire also takes on sexual symbolism. The belief that dog brought fire to human beings is historically a common one, and dog was often considered a master of fire.

In some Native American traditions, dog often represents service to others and is often interchanged with Coyote as the fire-inventor and rain-bringer.

It was a white dog which was sacrificed by the Iroquois at the New Year to take their prayers to the next world. And to shamans even today, dog is often the messenger of forest spirits.

To the ancients, dog was also believed to be the keeper of the boundaries between this world and the next, a guardian of the passage to and of the Underworld, even an attendant of the dead (a Psychopomp).

When used as a lunar symbol, dog is the intermediary between various moon deities; when used as a solar symbol, dog was Yang in the day, but became Yin at night.

But dog was solar to the ancient Sumerians and Egyptians and associated with all messenger gods and goddesses, including gods of destruction.

To the Egyptians, dog was a guide of the hawk-headed solar god, keeping the sun on its correct path. Dogs were sacred to Anubis and later to the Greek Hermes.

A dog accompanied all hunter goddesses and the Good Shepherd, symbolizing the compassion of healers. Dog is associated with Aesculapius, the Great Healer. It

A   *Letters From Home*

healed by rebirth into a new life, its faithfulness surviving even physical death.

And the Mother Goddess was often shown as a dog giving birth, and called "the Great Bitch".

Dog is also a wind symbol and can chase away drought and the boar and bear of winter, depending upon which culture you are in at the time.

To the ancient Chinese, the arrival of a dog was a symbol of future prosperity. The Red Celestial Dog was Yang and drove off evil spirits. But as a guardian of the night, dog becomes Yin and symbolizes destruction, catastrophe, and is connected with meteors and eclipses, when the dog goes mad and bites the moon or sun.

To the early Christians, the dog symbolized fidelity, watchfulness, and faithfulness in marriage. To the Greek poet Homer, the dog was shameless, but was also a Psychopomp (guide of the dead) and an attribute of Mercury in his aspect of both messenger and mind. Mercury was often accompanied by his dog Sirius, representing the "all-seeing vigilance." And it is the dog Sirius which also accompanies the hunter Orion.

And the three-headed dog Cerebus guards the entrance to the ancient Greek Underworld, while it is the goddess Hecate who controls the dogs of war. The dogs of Hades symbolized the gloomy periods of pre-dawn and pre-dusk which were believed to be inhabited by dangerous demonic beings.

To the ancient Semitic peoples, the dog represented evil and demons, but to the Phoenicians dog was symbolic of the sun and a representation of Astarte, and of Gala, the Great Physician, an aspect of the Mother Goddess.

And as if all of this weren't enough, the dog is considered a "clean" animal by some cultures and "unclean" by others. For instance, a dog was considered a clean animal by the Zoroastrians and to kill one was a sin.

Dog is also a good pun. Is something "dogging" you? Are you being "treated like a dog?" Or are you in danger of treating someone or something that way? Should you let sleeping dogs lie?

How is this dog different from the same dog in your waking life? What breed of dog is it? Why? How is that breed different from other breeds?

What color is the dog? What physical condition is it in? How old is it? How do you feel about dogs in general? What kind of a person would own this dog? Who would not want it around? Why? Would you like to have a dog like it? Why, or why not? What does this dog make you think of first?

DOMESTICATED
Any type of domesticated animal most often represents the taming of your wilder and potentially dangerous natural animal behavior and instincts. The kind of animal it is will tell you which of these behaviors has been trained to behave in polite society.

What kinds of animals are easy to domesticate? What were they like before they were trained? Who is responsible for their care? What happens if they are released back into nature? What does this remind you of going on in your life at the time? And how do you feel about all of that?

DRAGON

Dragons are winged serpents and have always been powerful and highly complex symbols. Dragons have symbolized the mystical and magical, the highest spiritual power, and even the origins of life throughout human history.

In general, dragons have the same symbolism as that of snake or serpent — just bigger and more of it.

The symbol of a dragon was often used by the ancients as a symbol for the Higher Self. Dragons can also represent a personal mythic image, or a personal dream pun, as in "slaying your dragon."

In the beginning, dragons were considered to be a completely positive symbol and represented the merger of the serpent (Matter) and bird (Spirit), and as such symbolized the physical manifestation of Spirit.

They also symbolized the combined powers of the life-giving water (the serpent) with the breath of life (the bird).

Dragons were associated with all sky deities and were their ambassadors on Earth, especially when associated with royalty.

In the Orient, the dragon is still viewed as a celestial power, and it is only in the Western world that it has been relegated to the darker powers.

In the East, the dragon symbolizes ancient wisdom, strength, hidden knowledge, the Son of Heaven, and supernatural and celestial powers, while in the West it is still generally associated with evil, chaos, and our untamed natures. The exception to this is the association of the dragon with the Logos, itself a symbol of the Higher Self manifesting on the Upper Mental Planes of Existence as a Divine outpouring of life and form, the outpouring of creative energy, or the Word.

As monsters, dragons are "masters of the ground," masters against which human beings must fight for their own mastery of the land. They are also fierce and deadly guardians of treasures, and the gates to esoteric knowledge and wisdom.

In early Greek tales, it is a dragon that draws the chariot of the goddess Ceres.

Dragons are also great puns. What are you draggin' around? Who has dragon breath? Is there a dragon lady in your life? Which dragon do you want to slay?

What color is this dragon? Why? What is it doing? How are you interacting with it? What brought it into your dream or meditation landscape? Where does it normally live?

How does it feel about being called into your dream? Does this tell you anything about something that is going on in your life at the time?

THE AZURE DRAGON is symbolic of Vital Spirit, the very highest level of Power.

THE COMMON DRAGON has four claws, and symbolizes worldly or earthly power and authority.

DRAGON WITH A FLAMING PEARL or CRYSTAL BALL is an ancient symbol of the "Pearl which grants all desires," the Pearl of Perfection containing Wisdom, Enlightenment, and the Spiritual Essence of the Universe. It also symbolizes instant illumination and enlightenment.

DRAGON WITH THE PHOENIX BIRD symbolizes the union of Heaven and Earth, the Emperor and Empress, the Divine potential contained within all opposites, the interaction of the Microcosm and the Macrocosm, birth and death.

DRAGON WITH A TIGER most often symbolizes strong sexual passions and anger.

THE FIRE OF THE DRAGON symbolizes the purifying power of Spirit.

IMPERIAL DRAGON has only three claws (see Common Dragon above), its head is to the South and its tail to the North. It often symbolizes the East and the life-giving, fertilizing rain.

The three-clawed dragon was not used in Chinese artwork after the Red Revolution.

KILLING A DRAGON symbolizes the conflict between light and dark, humanity overcoming its own darker nature and attaining self-mastery, especially over our passions. A dragon is often the opponent of a hero or deity in myths and legends.

RESCUING A PRINCESS FROM A DRAGON symbolizes the release of pure forces and energies after killing the darker powers, our more physical instincts and passions.

It is for this reason that the dragon is often the opponent of a dying god or hero in many myths.

STRUGGLING WITH A DRAGON TO GAIN A TREASURE symbolizes the habits or traits of your personality which must be overcome and mastered before you can gain the treasure of inner wisdom.

TWO DRAGONS BITING EACH OTHER'S TAIL is an ancient symbol that the forces and things within the world of duality actually have their origin from the same source and principle, even though they give the appearance of being in direct opposition to one another.

TWO FIGHTING DRAGONS symbolize the dualism of Yin and Yang, all opposites and complements, Celestial and Terrestrial powers, and Eternity. They are often shown with either the sun or the moon behind them or in their claws.

UNDULATING DRAGONS are ancient symbols for the cosmic rhythms and power of the waters.

WINGED DRAGONS are ancient solar symbols and represent the union of Spirit with Matter and the union of all opposites

ELEPHANT
The elephant symbolizes tremendous strength, power, fidelity, a good and long memory, wisdom, peace, marital happiness, and faithfulness and protection of a pregnant mate.

In Asia, elephants are the "steed of the ruler," a supporting structure for one in absolute control and authority.

Elephants also sometimes symbolize the 4th or Heart Chakra; see CHAKRA/4th.

Under normal conditions, elephants are dangerous only when severely provoked. And elephants have allowed themselves to be made beasts of burden by human beings, even though they have the strength and intelligence to resist and change this situation whenever they want. Does this remind you of anything?

Who or what is as big as an elephant? Do you have big ears too often? How's your memory?

How is this elephant different from other elephants? How large is it? What age is it? Why? What is it doing? What color is it? What do you think elephants are like? What natural characteristics do they have? Does this remind you of anything going on in your life at the time? See also COLOR of elephant.

THE ELEPHANT'S SKIN often symbolizes ignorance, thickness or toughness, and conversely your invulnerability to the stings of small things.

THE WHITE ELEPHANT is a common symbol in Buddhism and always solar in its qualities; see PLANET/Sun.

It is a white elephant who appears to Queen Maya to announce the birth of a new world ruler and symbolizes compassion, kindness, love, and the Jewel of the Law.

The white elephant also often symbolizes the 1st Chakra (as do the horse and bear).

And it is, of course, a wonderful pun. Are you still lugging that old white elephant around?

ELK
Both the elk and moose symbolize supernatural power and the power of the whirlwind; see WEATHER/Whirlwind. The feeling of being caught in a whirlwind is also

described by many people who experience out-of-body dreams, so your elk may be your signal to be aware of this.

Elk also symbolizes elegance and majesty in bearing. So your elk may be telling you to remember to carry yourself proudly, even regally, to hold your head up high.

Elk reminds you to be aware of and value your natural talents and gifts. Elk may also be warning you to be more careful who you show these talents to, since too much antler-waving just calls attention to the fact that you have something worth stealing.

Elk never graze at night. When attacked, the herd scatters in every direction to confuse its hunter, and elk can run for a very long time. Sound like you?

But unlike deer, elk won't usually run from a good fight, and have even been known to take on bears. Does this remind you of anything going on in your life?

FROG

Frog is another of the ambivalent symbols, representing both good and evil in many cultures.

Frog is the rain-bringer and symbolizes fertility and one who is able to bring strength out of weakness. And frog is also a cleanser of the emotions and a symbol of life and resurrection.

The frog was an emblem of Isis and one of the attributes of Hekt as the protector of mothers and the newly born. Frog later became an emblem of Aphrodite and Venus and was believed to bring harmony between lovers.

Frog is usually considered a lunar Yin (feminine) symbol, and sometimes called the Great Frog who carries the Universe on its back, the basis of all created matter.

But A FROG IN A WELL symbolizes a person of limited perception and understanding; see WATER/Well.

And some frogs secrete special poisons to make them unpalatable to predators. So this frog can be telling you that you are not only jumping to conclusions, but are protecting yourself in ways out of all proportion to the actual situation. Remember that defenses in place for too long can become prisons rather than defenses. On the other hand, maybe froggy is telling you to make yourself a less desirable target.

Frogs also make great puns. What part of you is feeling like a big frog in a small pond? "It's not easy being green" you know. And don't forget the obvious pun "You have to kiss a lot of frogs...".

How are frogs different from toads? What is this frog doing? What color is it? How do you feel about frogs? Why?

HELPFUL

Any helpful animal usually symbolizes a particular ability or trait of yours that is surfacing into conscious awareness at the time of the dream or experience. For example, a helpful animal often represents inner growth of some kind which incorporates or somehow relates to the qualities you attribute to the animal.

Helpful animals can symbolize deep hidden unrecognized emotions and feelings which are trying to reassure you that it's okay to let them out, that they are not really dangerous after all.

And a helpful animal can represent your present relationship with nature and our planet, and a good relationship between you and your natural human physical instincts.

Any helpful animal can also, of course, symbolizes your totem animal at the time of your dream or experience; see Totem Animal below.

HORNS

All animal horns are ancient symbols of power, especially spiritual and magical or mystical power. They symbolize the powers of Truth and victory over the lower (physical) qualities of mind and spiritual ignorance.

Traditionally, horns also represent human aspirations which are now growing toward the ideals of Divine Love and Wisdom.

There are several passages in the Judeo-Christian Bible describing horned altars, and when Yahweh angrily breaks off the horns in the Temple and throws them to the ground (Amos 3:14), it is a symbol of Divine anger and reproach.

In many ancient cultures, one of the most distinctive features of any divine being was a horned head. Crowns and masks of deities were often depicted as horned animals.

Conversely, horns can symbolize excessive pride and ambition, great vanity, all sexual excesses, and arrogance and conceit.

Horns are an animal's defense weapons and therefore can symbolize aggressiveness, power, and the ability to protect yourself through your own natural attributes.

And horns are associated with one of the oldest Tantric beliefs concerning male virility — that by the suppression of ejaculation, mystic or spiritual energy flows up the spine and from the head, greatly amplifying wisdom and mystical power. The horns themselves thus represent this discipline physically visible and can now be of practical use.

Horns were also strong symbols of the penetration of intuition, able by its very nature to transcend and go beyond the ordinary performance of the human mind.

Horns also show us that the powers of the head are so strong that they have become protuberances — horns. See also BODY/Head.

Horns were used by many ancient cultures as containers for sacrificial beverages, or were painted with the blood of sacrificial victims. They were also used as instruments for the call to prayer, to war, to a meeting, to the hunt, and used to sound a warning.

Primitive sacred art in virtually every human culture shows human beings wearing the horns of bulls, goats, deer, and other animals, usually representing a shaman, priest, sacred leader, or sacred sacrificial victim.

Horned animals or beings were often associated with The Great Mother, and with a consort of The Great Mother. It was not until the European Middle Ages that horns became a strong symbol for lustful passions and the devil here in the western part of the world.

Horns can be a good pun. What is horny? Has someone given you horns? Do you need to blow your own horn?

Why do animals have horns? How is an animal with horns different from one without them? How do you feel about horns? Why?

HORSE

Horses often symbolize your great driving energy and power, very often sexual energy and power. They represent intense desires and instincts but now powered by the strong energy of the horse.

Traditionally, a horse symbolizes the cosmic forces which literally surge forth from Cosmic Chaos, the Origin.

Horse also symbolizes the intellect, wisdom, reason, the mind, nobility, swiftness of thought, the wind, and the waves of the sea. Horses are the energies capable of carrying the directing spirit of humanity.

Horse represents both the sun and the moon, and is therefore historically associated with both solar and lunar deities. Horses often pull the chariots of sun, moon, and oceanic deities.

The horse is also one of the ancient universal symbols for the Will of the Higher Self, and horse represents the powerful driving force behind this type of determination. It is only when your "horses" are under your control that your Spirit or Soul can move forward.

Horse can also represent consciously controlled body movements during ordinary actions, especially a horse and rider or horse and chariot or carriage.

In many ancient tales and myths, horses are often clairvoyant and have the ability to speak to humans.

And in true symbolic fashion, the horse itself can be symbolized by fire, light, the wind, and sea foam — symbols within symbols.

In the *Upanishad*, the horse is a symbol of the Cosmos itself. Horse is the seventh sign of the Chinese zodiac and corresponds to the astrological sign of Libra.

In many cultures in the Far East and Europe, horse had the ability to find water and to free springs of water from the ground with its hooves; see WATER/Gushing From Rock. Horse was also believed to be a Psychopomp, a guide of the Soul after death, and for this reason was often buried with its owner.

In some Native American traditions, horse often symbolized both physical earthly powers and extraordinary non-earthly powers. Horse is believed by some to have been the first medicine animal of humankind.

No less an authority than Carl Jung believed that the horse symbolized the magical side of mankind, the "mother within us," our intuitive understanding.

Another potential pun, are you hungry enough to eat a horse? For what? Is this a horse of a different color?

What color is this horse? Why? How would the scene change if the horse were a different color?

How many horses are there? How do you feel about this particular horse? Why? What actions is it carrying out? What does this remind you of?

Do you like horses? Do you ride? Is this horse easy to handle, or is it giving you trouble? Why? What does this remind you of?

COMMON HORSE SYMBOLS:

BLACK HORSE: A black horse symbolizes the Unknown, the Great Mystery, the subconscious. A black horse can also symbolize a death, that some part of you is dying; see DEATH.

It may also be telling you that you need to balance some of the qualities of the Will of your Higher Consciousness, especially when the horse is not all black.

And a black horse can represent a mistake or incorrect knowledge and information. How do you feel about the black horse? See also COLOR/Black.

HORSE and CARRIAGE or CHARIOT: A horse and chariot or horse and carriage symbolizes the innate potential and ability of humanity to control its instinctual physical (lower) nature by harnessing, directing, and controlling its power in the directions chosen by the higher mind, not just by instinct alone. How well is the horse being handled by the driver?

HORSE and RIDER: A horse and rider symbolizes that you feel in control of your own will power, your emotions and feelings, and/or your own sexuality, depending upon how successfully the rider is controlling the horse.

It can also be telling you that a message is on its way. Why would the message come by horse and rider rather than E-Mail?

RED HORSE: A red horse represents your intense powerful energy and persistence. And it often symbolizes Mind energized by Spirit. A red horse can also be a message to Stop! Has your will power gotten out of control? See also COLOR/Red.

WHITE HORSE: A white horse represents your creative and spiritual energies. A white horse is a solar heavenly animal, the "steed of the gods." It is a strong symbol of the force of the will subdued by reason, and of the pure and per-

A

fect Higher Mind with its aspirations and ideals. See also COLOR/White.

WINGED HORSE: A winged horse is a symbol of the aspiring Higher Mind, the wish to literally soar to new levels of being by miraculous and non-ordinary or magical means.

A winged horse has all four hooves on the ground (Matter), but has the ability to fly in the air (Spirit). A winged horse is a solar symbol, the Cosmic Horse, and is ridden exclusively by various heroes or heroines who have earned that right.

Winged horses combine the strength of the horse with the freedom of the birds from the bondage and limitations of the ground or Matter.

Winged horses, especially legendary Pegasus, are common symbols of poetic inspiration. Pegasus was also a symbol of the intellect through which wisdom (by proper training and discipline) could be attained. Some mythologists see Pegasus as symbolic of the higher aspects of the symbolism of the horse, while the Centaur represents the darker aspects. See also BIRD/Wings.

LAMB
A lamb has almost always symbolized gentleness, quiet, peace, youthful naiveté and innocence, exceptional vulnerability, purity, simplicity, and tolerance.

Lambs were favorite sacrificial animals of many ancient cultures, since to many of them a lamb was a symbol of the newborn initiate and his or her mystic rebirth through transformation.

A lamb can also be a good pun. Are you a lamb being led to the slaughter? Are you meek as a lamb, mother's little lamb?

How is this lamb different from all other lambs? What color is it? Why? What is it doing? What kind of a person would own this lamb? For what reason or purpose?

How does the lamb feel in your dream or meditation? If it could talk, what would it say to you?

A LAMB WITH A LION is an ancient symbol of Paradise attainable through the reconciliation of these opposite natures; see also Lion below.

LEOPARD
Leopards are another ambivalent symbol and represent bravery, swiftness, and ferocity, but also impetuous behavior, aggression, and cruelty.

Leopards are the Great Watcher in some cultures, possibly because the spots on a leopard resemble eyes.

To the ancient Chinese, the leopard symbolized bravery, especially in connection with battle.

And leopard was one of the emblems of the ancient Egyptian god Osiris, and to the ancient Greeks, leopard represented Dionysos as both creator and destroyer.

LION

Lions have almost always been symbols of absolute power and authority through their individuality, courage, tremendous strength, and ability to rule absolutely.

The lion is most often a sun symbol and connected to all solar deities. But in ancient symbolism, the lion was often both solar and lunar since it was believed to never shut its eyes, and therefore was "ever watchful."

As a solar symbol, lion represents courage, justice, the law, military strength, the king, strength, and the fiery Yang principle, but also symbolizes cruelty, war, subhuman instincts, and ferocity.

As a lunar symbol, the lion or lioness symbolized all virgin war goddesses, especially if they either accompanied The Great Mother or were shown drawing her chariot (which represented her maternal instinct and the Earth); see also VEHICLE/Chariot.

To the Buddhists, a lion is the Defender of the Law, the Wisdom of Buddha, an Enlightened One.

To the Ancient Egyptians, the lion was a protector and guardian.

A lion can also be a symbol of your need to face your fears by "taming the lion." And your lion can, of course, also be a symbol for the astrological sign of Leo and the qualities you normally associate with that sign.

Dreaming of a lion can be a good pun. Who has the lion's share of something? Are you "lyin'" and to whom or what part of you? Is there a regal Leo in your life?

What are lions like as animals? How do you feel about them? What color is this one? Why? Is it male or female, adult or a cub, alone or in a pride? Is it docile or dangerous? What actions is it performing in your dream or meditation? Why? How is it different from other lions?

COMMON LION SYMBOLS:

TWO LIONS BACK-TO-BACK: This is a very old symbol of the past and the present, yesterday and tomorrow.

A LION WITH A CRESCENT: The lion with a crescent symbolizes the ancient Egyptian deities Isis and Osiris, and all that they symbolize.

THE LION AND DRAGON DEVOURING ONE ANOTHER: This is an ancient symbol of union, union which results in a loss of identity.

THE SOLAR HERO or DEITY SLAYING THE LION: Any deity slaying a lion symbolizes the sun god taming or lessening the "heat of the noonday sun," acting as a mediator between humanity and our Original Source.

THE LION AND THE LAMB: The lion and the lamb together is an ancient symbol of Paradise, attainable by the reconciliation of these two opposing natures.

PAIRS OF LIONS: Pairs of lions symbolize a master of double strength and double the power and energy of lion symbolism. It was for this reason that pairs of lions were made guardians of gates, doorways, treasures, and even the Tree of Life.

LION WITH A SOLAR DISK: This is an ancient Egyptian symbol and one of the many emblems of Ra, the Supreme Sun God.

LION THRONE: A lion seated on a throne or a throne shaped like a lion symbolizes a ruler's subjugation and mastery of cosmic forces, and therefore his or her divine right to rule.

THE LION AND UNICORN: The lion and the unicorn together symbolizes the dualities of the Yin-Yang (female-male) forces and qualities.

WINGED LION: A winged lion symbolizes the completed and successful union of two natures, the true androgyne.

LIZARD

Lizard frequently symbolizes divine wisdom, good fortune, and silence, and was a characteristic of the Greek Serapis and Hermes.

To the ancient Romans, lizard symbolized death and resurrection, since they believed it slept through the winter.

To both the Zoroastrians and early Christians, lizard was a symbol of evil and the devil, but to the Australian Aborigines, lizard is still a hero figure even today.

Lizard is able to save itself from predators by leaving part of itself behind, its tail. The tail can be regrown by the lizard, but only once. So is it time to give some part of yourself up, a part you can replace if you decide to?

And lizards eat insects, so your lizard may be telling you its okay to pay attention to the small things that bug you, but it's all just nutrition in the end.

How do you feel about lizards in general? Why?

LYNX

The lynx symbolizes watchfulness and secrets, especially magical mystic secrets.

Lynx also symbolizes clear perception and clairvoyant abilities, and some cultures even believed it had the ability to see through walls. How's that for a symbol?

MENACING ANIMAL

A menacing or threatening animal often represents your deep subconscious feelings threatening to overwhelm you, a feeling of being vulnerable, unprotected, or unsafe in your environment.

The species of animal menacing you will show you which part of you is feeling this threat, in which of your environments, and often exactly why.

Threatening animals can also represent suppressed and unrecognized frustration and anger, symbolized by the natural behavior of the animal.

A menacing animal can also be telling you about a real threat somewhere in your life, a menace picked up by your subconscious when you are awake.

And it can symbolize subconscious emotions generated by a part of you feeling threatened at the time of the experience.

What type of animal is menacing? What does this tell you about yourself? Would you normally feel threatened by this animal? Why, or why not?

In what way is it threatening you? How do you react? What does this remind you of going on in your life at the time?

MOOSE

Both moose and elk often symbolize supernatural power and the whirlwind. The whirlwind symbolizes the dynamic evolution of the Universe; whirlwinds also symbolize vortices, energy points, and rapid change helped by this energy force. And the feeling of being caught in a whirlwind is described by many people who experience out-of-body dream. See also WEATHER/Whirlwind.

Moose also symbolizes unpredictability and total spontaneity. There's just no way we can predict what a moose will do or when it will do it.

And nothing, absolutely nothing, gets between a male moose and the female who has answered his call.

MOUSE

Mouse symbolizes illusion and the ability to go just about anywhere, even into or through places where it looks like there is no way in or out.

Mice are evasive, usually exceptionally quiet. And one of the most interesting things about the symbol of mouse is that at the same time mice are considered destructive and disease-carriers, they have managed to get themselves thought of as cute, playful, funny little cartoon characters.

So this mouse may be telling you to see things the way they really are, not how you would like them to be. How do you feel about the mouse?

And a mouse may be small, but it can scare an elephant. Does this remind you of anything?

What is the mouse doing? How do you feel about it? How do you feel about mice in general? Why?

PANTHER

Panthers were believed by the ancients to have saved humanity from the dragon, the evil one. For this reason panthers often represent fierceness in battle, remorselessness, and fury. And panthers are excellent patient and silent hunters.

And since panthers were believed to have sweet breath, the early Christians used the panther as a symbol for the Breath of the Christ.

RABBIT

Rabbits symbolize softness, quiet, humility, and gentleness.

Rabbit is a lunar symbol representing fertility and associated with the Earth Mother and most moon deities, male and female.

But rabbit can also be a symbol of promiscuity, excessive and indiscriminate sexual behavior, and lust.

Rabbit may also be telling you that you are hopping around too much, jumping from one thing, person, or thought to another and not spending enough time on any one thing.

In some Native American cultures, rabbit takes the place of coyote as the trickster. It also symbolizes the Fear Caller, the one who attracts the very thing it claims to not want. Wearing a rabbit skin symbolizes putting on humility when in the presence of the Great Spirit.

Rabbit can be a good pun. Are you scared as a rabbit? Do you have the sexual morals or appetite of a rabbit? Has the rabbit just died (i.e., who's pregnant, and by whom and with what)?

SEAL

Seals are playful and have fun in the element of water; see WATER. Seals often also represent applause and being given credit for a good performance or show.

And seals make for good puns. Does some part of you feel like a trained seal? Has something in your life just been "sealed?"

SHEEP

Sheep symbolize trust, innocence, and a passive, blind willingness to follow others. Sheep can be trying to tell you that you are giving all of your own responsibilities to someone else, leaving your life and fate in the hands of those who protect you. And sheep, of course, were favorite sacrificial animals.

In many ancient cultures, and even today, sheep symbolize helplessness and blind and unintelligent following.

To the ancient Chinese, sheep represented retirement and were the eighth of the symbolic animals of the Twelve Terrestrial Branches.

To the early Christians, sheep were symbols of the faithful, the flock of the Christ and of the Apostles as followers of the Christ.

Sheep can also be a good pun. Are you a sheep being led to the slaughter? Is there a wolf in sheep's clothing in your life? Is some part of you trying to pull the wool over the eyes of another part? Are you feeling sheepish about something? And, "might as well be hung for a sheep as a lamb..."

What qualities do you think sheep have? What are these sheep doing? How is that the same as, or different from, the usual things sheep do?

Who would watch over these sheep? Why? Are they in danger of any kind? How is a sheep different from a lamb?

SNAKE

The snake or serpent is a very ancient and exceptionally complex symbol. It is one of the earliest celestial beings found in human cosmologies.

People of all cultures around the world dream of snakes entering their body, and in fact the snake is often referred to as "the Spirit Which Penetrates All."

It was not until fairly late in human evolvement that the snake or serpent was given its deep and complex psychological and spiritual interpretations.

But in general, snakes are seen as both killers and creator-healers. They can be male, female, or even completely self-created and androgynous.

Snakes are both solar and lunar, possess both wisdom and blinding passion, can poison and heal, and in general symbolize both the physical and the spiritual aspects of humankind.

While snakes most often represent wisdom and healing, they can also symbolize danger and treachery. Snakes and serpents also symbolize subtle cunning, power, knowledge, subtlety, darkness, lightning, and the force of water.

Snakes have also almost always been credited with the gift of understanding the speech of other animals.

But your dream snake is most likely symbolizing the awakening of your creative powers, your healing powers, and the energy and power of the Life Force deep within you. Snakes have always been a symbol of spiritual awakening and the continuation of spiritual growth.

And snakes symbolize the state of conscious dreaming (known as lucid dreaming, of being aware that you are dreaming while you are still dreaming; see Glossary).

Snakes can also represent your forgetfulness of your true cosmic or heavenly origins, reminding you of your immense unused energy source, and that you need neither legs nor wings to get you where you're going.

And since the snake or serpent possesses dual forces, it can also represent your boundaries or limits of consciousness, and the inner forces of earthly existence by which the growth of the Soul is achieved.

Snakes and serpents are the guardians of vast deeply buried treasures in virtually all cultures, and divulge wisdom to anyone brave enough to confront them directly, symbolizing the gaining of wisdom or knowledge by the courage to go deeply within and face your own monsters.

A snake is an ancient symbol for a mediator between Heaven and Earth, between Earth and the Underworld, and together with Earth, Sky, and Water represents the Cosmic Tree; see TREE/Cosmic Tree.

And the presence of a snake or serpent is universally associated with fertility and pregnancy. Snakes are frequently companions of female deities, especially The Great Mother, and often portrayed twining around her hands or feet.

In the Eastern part of the world, the serpent and dragon are in most cases interchangeable as symbols, the snake being viewed as nothing more than a small dragon.

Serpents and dragons are the Guardians of the Threshold, the guardians of the esoteric knowledge of all lunar deities, temples, and great treasures; see also Dragon above.

Serpents also symbolize storms and are master controllers of the waters; see WATER.

In many legends, the serpent is said to have a jewel in its head and to possess treasures and magic rings, which they guard jealously and ferociously (as does the toad).

And it is a rainbow serpent which intercedes for human beings in myths and tales in several cultures.

The serpent is the Primordial Ocean from which all life emerged and to which all life returns. A serpent supports and maintains the world, encircles it (usually symbolically shown as the Ouroboros), and therefore also symbolizes cycles. In many ancient myths, it is the Ouroboros who encircles both the Cosmic Egg and the Earth; see Ouroboros below.

Snakes are also strong symbols of self-creation and represent your generative and regenerative powers. Living underground, snakes are symbolic of underworld powers, magic, and hidden knowledge and potential through that knowledge, your "treasure."

Snakes symbolize the primordial and instinctual nature of humankind, the upward moving Life Force, the animating spirit, the Kundalini energy; see Kundalini below.

Snakes are also, of course, very strong phallic symbols. And worms and lizards are often symbols substituted for snakes, as are toads and frogs.

To the Native Americans, snake was often a thunder creature, the enemy of the Thunder Bird, and symbolized lightning, the spear of the war gods.

Snake also symbolized the rain-bearer and was lunar and full of magical powers.

Snake is a symbol of Eternity, and a mediator between human beings and the lower world.

In some Native American cultures, the Great Manitou took the form of a serpent with horns, with which it pierced the Toad, the Dark Manitou; see Horns below.

To the Buddhists, the snake represented anger when shown at the center of the Round of Existence, the Wheel of Karma.

In ancient China, the serpent was seldom differentiated from the dragon, but when it was, it was a symbol of malevolence, destruction, negativity, deceit, and evil. The snake is the sixth of the symbolic animals of the Twelve Terrestrial Branches.

As a symbol for the early Christians, snake is ambivalent and symbolizes Satan as the tempter and enemy of God. Satan is, in fact, sometimes referred to in medieval literature as the "Great Dragon." But the early Christians also used the snake to symbolize the wisdom of the Christ as a sacrifice on the Tree of Life; see TREE/Tree of Life.

Even Dante used the serpent as a symbol of wisdom when it entwined the Tree of Life, and as evil when entwining the Tree of Knowledge.

To the ancient Egyptians, the snake (especially the cobra) symbolized supreme royal and divine power and wisdom, knowledge, and gold. The two serpents on each side of the sun disk, Nous and Logos, symbolized the royal serpent goddesses who drove out the enemies of Ra, the Sun god. The serpent with a lion's head was a common ancient Egyptian talismanic protection against all evil; see Lion above.

To the Gnostics, the serpent symbolized the creator of Divine Gnosis. The winged serpent with a nimbus around it symbolized Knowledge and Illumination.

To the ancient Greeks, the snake symbolized wisdom, renewal of life and healing and was associated with Hermes, Aesculapius (a savior-healer god), Hippocrates, and Hygieia. The snake was sacred to Athene and Apollo. It was not until much later in their history that serpents became symbols of death and treachery, as symbolized by the hair of the Medusa for example.

To the ancient Hebrews, serpents symbolized temptation, evil, sexual passion, and the souls of the damned in Sheol. However, the brazen serpent of Moses was a homeopathic symbol, translated as "like heals like."

And to the Hindu, the snake is Shakti, Cosmic Power, Nature, Chaos, the Non-Manifest, the manifestation of Vedic Agni (fire). The dark serpent represents the potential of Agni. Vishnu sleeps on a coiled serpent on the Primordial Waters, symbolizing the unpolarized state of being before Creation from the Cosmic Ocean.

And the Naga and Nagina are serpent kings and queens and often share the symbolism of the Chinese dragon as rain-givers, fertility, rejuvenation, and the life force of the waters.

In Islam, the snake is symbolic of that which gives life, the giver of the life principle, not just mere existence. But to the Iranians, snake was "the throttler," the enemy of the sun deity.

Snake symbolism was widespread in ancient Crete, and there is some archeological evidence to suggest that there was a pre-deistic snake cult.

The Great Goddess as protector of the Cretin households is seen with snakes in each hand, and snakes were associated with all of the deities who later replaced her.

And to the ancient Celts, the serpent was associated with all healing wells and waters. And the snake was an emblem of Brigit as the Mother Goddess.

In ancient Rome, snakes were associated with any savior, fertility, and healing deities, and with Minerva, the Goddess of Wisdom. To the Sumerians, the Great

Goddess Ishtar was portrayed as a serpent, and the snake is associated with both the Earth Goddess or Mother and with her dying Son.

In Scandinavia, the god serpent Midgard was believed to encircle the world with the endless coils of the ocean. The serpent Nidhogg lived at the foot of the Cosmic Tree, continually gnawing at it, symbolizing the malevolent forces in the Universe.

So, as you can see, there is no easy, slick interpretation of snake. How you feel about snakes in general and how you feel about them in your dream or meditation will help you unravel the interpretation that best fits at the time.

Snakes can also be great puns. Is there a snake in the grass lurking somewhere in your life? And in the Orient, to refer to a woman as a snake is a very great compliment.

COMMON SNAKE SYMBOLS:

ANGRY SNAKES: An angry snake is an old symbol for the autonomous nervous system. Angry snakes or serpents also symbolize that the Self or inner you has become angry with the Ego, the outer you, for forgetting to relate to your deeper wiser parts.

BITING EACH OTHER'S TAIL: Two snakes or dragons biting each other's tail is a symbol that forces and things within the world of duality actually originate from the same source and principle, even though they may have the appearance of being in opposition to one another.

BITING YOU: A snake biting you in your dream or meditation can symbolize your creative or spiritual energy trying to break through in that particular part of your body.

Conversely, this can also be a symbol of the potential for danger or damage to the part of the body bitten. What does the biting snake remind you of that is going on in your life at the time of your dream? How does it feel? What will happen if the bite goes untreated? See also BODY, FEAR, PAIN.

AS A BRACELET, BELT, or GIRDLE: Wearing a snake as a bracelet, girdle, or belt is an ancient symbol for the eternal evolution of life and the natural cycles of dissolution and regeneration.

CADUCEUS: Two snakes wound around a staff with a ball or globe and wings at the top is the Caduceus, and symbolizes the homeopathic powers of healing and poison, illness and health, that "nature can overcome Nature," "like healing like."

The Caduceus is believed to be of ancient Greek or Roman origin, usually in the form of a rod, staff, or wand with two snakes entwined around it, crossing six times, and with a pair of wings and a globe at the top.

The winding snakes represent the six Chakras, the wings represent the Kundalini energy taking flight, and the globe represents the World.

This was an emblem used since early times to honor those who had earned royal office, and was often associated with the Greek god Hermes.

THE CELESTIAL or RAINBOW SERPENT: The rainbow or celestial serpent symbolizes the rainbow which forms the bridge from this world to the next. A rainbow serpent often intercedes for human beings in legend and myth. See also WEATHER/Rainbow.

CHILD PLAYING WITH SNAKE: A child playing with a serpent symbolizes Paradise found and regained, freedom from conflict, and the end of the material mundane world. The lion lying down with a lamb shares this same symbolism.

COILED or KNOTTED SNAKE: A coiled or knotted snake symbolizes the cycles of physical manifestation, latent power, and the dynamic potential available within each of us for either good or evil; see also KNOT.

COILED AROUND AN EGG: A serpent coiled around an egg symbolizes the incubation of the Vital Spirit, protection, and guarding the source of your being. This is one of the many forms of the Ouroboros; see Ouroboros below.

COILED AROUND A TREE: A snake or serpent coiled around a tree (or any other axial symbol)

represents the awakening of vibrant dynamic forces (Kundalini energy, for example), the innate genius of all growing things, and the cycle of existence.

COILED AROUND A WOMAN: When coiled around a woman, the snake symbolizes the solar Yang (male) qualities and characteristics, and the woman symbolizes the lunar Yin (female) qualities and characteristics. Together they symbolize the male-female relationship with all of its inherent potential for learning.

WITH AN EAGLE or STAG: A snake or serpent with either an eagle or a stag symbolizes Cosmic Unity, the Totality, duality through conflict, and any pairs of opposites. The eagle is often shown with the snake in its talons and the stag trampling on it, both actions symbolic of the victory of good over evil, light over darkness, the spiritual over the worldly; see also BIRD/Eagle, and Stag below.

EGGS: The eggs of the snake symbolize imminent rebirth, and the embryonic potential for rebirth.

FIERY SERPENT: The fiery serpent is symbolic of purification, solar energy, and forces that transmute and transcend the ordinary earthly state of existence; see also Dragon above.

FIGHTS: Snake fights or a battle between a snake and another animal considered to have a higher consciousness symbolizes the tensions between the autonomic and voluntary nervous systems. It can also be a symbol of the Higher Self battling the Lower Self, your higher nature fighting with your lower.

KUNDALINI: Snakes have represented Kundalini energy since the very earliest times. This energy is the vital life force energy in its purest form within physical Matter.

Ideally, Kundalini energy is symbolized by the White Cobra, representing the steady, cool, detached rise of this energy, but Kundalini energy can be represented by any type of poisonous snake.

The White Cobra is also often a reminder of knowledge of your previous births, so if it scares you to death, try to remember what exactly it was doing before you woke up screaming.

LIDLESS EYES OF THE SNAKE: The lidless eyes of the snake symbolize wisdom acquired by tireless, ceaseless watchfulness.

HOLDING AN HERB or FRUIT: A snake holding either fruit or an herb symbolizes immortality.

HORNED SERPENT: The horned serpent is usually a water spirit or deity, representing the fertilizing power of water.

The horned or ram-headed serpent represented the Celtic god of fertility and virility, Cernunnos.

ON A POLE: A single snake wound around a pole was the symbol used in ancient Alchemy to represent the subjugation of the Vital Force. This subjugation allowed the temporary use and rechanneling of the Vital or Life Force energy.

OUROBOROS: The Ouroboros is an ancient symbol representing that "my end is also my beginning," and "all is one." It also symbolizes self-sufficiency, the natural cycle of disintegration and reintegration, the Eternal Cycle, Time, the androgyne, the darkness before Creation, potential before actualization, Eternity, Wisdom, and Truth and Knowledge in One.

In ancient Alchemy, the Ouroboros represents the latent power of Nature and sometimes shares the symbolism of the Kundalini power.

PASSING THROUGH A CIRCLE: A snake passing through a circle of any kind was a symbol used in ancient Alchemy to symbolize the alchemical fusion. This is also a strong and obvious sexual symbol.

PLUMED SERPENT: To the Aztecs, Quetzacoatl was a combination of the Quetzal bird and the snake, symbolizing the Sun, the Spirit, the power of ascension, thunder and lightning, rain, wind, the breath of life, knowledge, the Eastern regions, Eternal Creation, Unending Time, and the intermediary between God and man. The plumed serpent was also a strong phallic symbol.

The plumed serpent was the White God from whose black bowels rain falls, the Sky God when Quetzacoatl was in his solar aspect. Coatlecue, Snake Woman, who wore a skirt of woven serpents, was the female counterpart of Quetzacoatl, representing his lunar aspect.

SNAKE WITH AN EAGLE or STAG: A snake with either an eagle or a stag symbolizes Cosmic Unity, Totality, duality through conflict, and pairs of opposites. The eagle is often shown with the serpent in its talons and the stag is often shown trampling the snake, both symbolic of the victor of good over evil, light over darkness, the spiritual over the worldly.

SNAKE WITH A PIG: When shown with a pig, the snake symbolizes greed, avarice, and ignorance.

SNAKE WITH A PIG AND ROOSTER: When all three animals are shown together, they symbolize the weaknesses and instincts which bind humankind to the World of Illusion and the Round of Existence, to the Cosmic Wheel of Karma.

POISONOUS SNAKES: All poisonous snakes are symbolic of the Kundalini energy. Dreaming of poisonous snakes can, of course, also be warning you about something in your life. What type of

snake is it? How does it strike? How does its poison kill? How long does it take? What color is it? What is it doing? If it could talk, what would it say to you?

SNAKE WITH A ROOSTER: A snake with a rooster symbolizes carnal earthly passions.

SNAKE AND THE TREE OF KNOWLEDGE: In this context, the snake or serpent was viewed in ancient mythology in its poisonous, dangerous, negative aspects within the world of physical manifestation.

SNAKE AND THE TREE OF LIFE: Within this context, the snake or serpent was used by ancient mythologists to represent beneficence and life-giving abilities.

TWO SNAKES BITING EACH ANOTHER'S TAIL: Two snakes or dragons biting each other's tails is a symbol that forces and things within the world of duality actually originate from the same source and principle, even though they may have the appearance of being in opposition to one another.

TWO SNAKES TOGETHER: Two snakes shown together symbolize the opposites of dualism which are always ultimately united.

TWO SNAKES AROUND A TREE or STAFF: Two snakes wound around a tree of staff symbolizes the spiral cycle of Nature, the Summer and Winter Solstice, the two fundamental forces of winding and unwinding.

TWO SNAKES WITH UPWARD AND DOWNWARD MOVEMENT: Two serpents with upward and downward movement symbolize the Divine Sleep and Divine Awakening in the nights and days of Brahma.

TWO SNAKES WOUND AROUND ONE ANOTHER: Two snakes wrapped around each other symbolize Time and Fate, the two great binding powers.

UNDULATING SERPENTS or DRAGONS: The undulating movement of both snakes and dragons symbolizes the cosmic rhythms and the power of the waters. This is also a strong sexual symbol.

WINGED SERPENTS or DRAGONS: Winged snakes or dragons are solar symbols and represent the union of Spirit with Matter, the union of the eagle with the serpent, the union of all opposites.

Winged serpents also symbolize a quickening of understanding, leading ultimately to wisdom.

WHITE COBRA: The white cobra is one of the most common symbols for Kundalini energy, especially in its cool, detached, steady rise.

The cobra blinds its victims before striking, so your white cobra may also be trying to tell you that it can be deadly if you are not consciously working with this energy.

The white cobra is also a symbol of your previous births into the world of Matter.

STAG: The stag was the natural symbolic enemy of the serpent, symbolizing the conflict of opposites, light against darkness, conscious against subconscious, etc.

And, of course, it was the stag which was chosen to draw the vehicle of Father Time, and later Father Christmas.

A STAG TRAMPLING ON A SERPENT or snake is an ancient symbol of the victory of the Spirit over Matter, and a special favorite in medieval times; see also ANIMAL/Snake.

TIGER
Another complex symbol, tiger is ambivalent, representing both the natural female and male forces, powers and energies, whether you are male or female.

Tigers also symbolize your strong but unaccepted fears. Tigers are both positive and negative symbols of wildness, strength, and the fierce warrior. They are often symbols of royalty and cruelty, as well as manifestations of the Earth Mother.

Since it can also find its way easily in darkness, the tiger represents inner light, the increase of light, or light after difficult or dark times.

As a predatory animal, the tiger symbolizes the dangerous powers inherent in your natural uncontrolled drives, passions, and instincts. In this context, your dream tiger may represent fear of your personal power.

But to the ancient Chinese, tiger was a protective spirit of the hunt and of agriculture.

To the Buddhist, the tiger represents spiritual exertion and the Spirit who is able to find its way through the jungle of Matter.

And tiger is one of the three senseless creatures of Buddhism, and in this context represents anger (the monkey represents greed, and the deer love-sickness). And the tiger is the third of the Twelve Terrestrial Branches and is often the emblem of gamblers.

In its Yang aspect, the tiger takes the place of a lion as king of beasts and lord of the land animals. Tiger is a guardian of graves and drives away evil spirits and the Lord of Wealth rides a tiger, who guards treasure, especially chests of money.

How do you feel about the tiger? What color is it? What is it doing? How is it different from other tigers?

Where would you be most likely to find this tiger? Why? What do you think the natural characteristics of a tiger are? Why? If this tiger could talk to you, what would it say?

A BLACK TIGER symbolizes water, Winter, and the North.

A BLUE TIGER symbolizes the East, Spring, and plant life and energy.

A TIGER FIGHTING A DRAGON or SERPENT symbolizes the natural conflict between opposites, and solar celestial power and energy.

A RED TIGER symbolizes the Element Fire, the South, and Summer.

TO RIDE THE TIGER, to "ride the tiger" symbolizes an encounter with dangerous, often elemental, forces.

A WHITE TIGER symbolizes Autumn, the Western regions, the Earth Element of Metal, and royal virtues and qualities.

A YELLOW TIGER symbolizes the Center, the Sun, and the Celestial Ruler.

TOTEM ANIMAL
A totem animal (or any totem object for that matter) often tells you that you are receiving a particularly strong message from your subconscious, your "other self," or from a guide or teacher.

A totem animal is often a direct message from one of your allies or teachers, giving you protection and guidance and reminding you that you are never, ever alone.

A totem animal can also be telling you something about your spiritual identity, where you are, and the lessons you are to work on at the time.

Many totem animals show up in your dreams, meditations, and waking experiences, and change as you change, so be sure to keep track of them and when and how they change.

TORTOISE

The tortoise is basically a land animal, while the turtle lives in water, although they can both live for a time in one another's environment. There are also amphibious tortoises which live in both environments, but all tortoises count on their shells to protect them from attack. Remind you of anything?

In general, tortoise carries much of the same symbolism of turtle, especially of long life and good fortune.

TURTLE

A turtle is a symbol of good luck, long life, strength through patience and perseverance, new life, and the ability to resist diseases and aging. And turtles move slowly, even in water.

As an archetype, the tortoise symbolizes the Waters, the Moon, the Earth Mother, the beginning of Creation, Time, immortality, and regeneration. It was believed by many ancient cultures to be an oracle. In some cultures, it is turtle who supports the Earth on its back.

To the ancient Chinese, the tortoise was one of the Four Spiritually Endowed Creatures (along with the dragon, the phoenix, and the ky-lin).

Turtle is also representative of the Earth and of the keepers of the Earth Elementals. Rattles are made from turtle shells in many cultures, and are used to call spirits during sacred singing and chanting.

Turtles symbolize both Heaven and Earth, the underside of the shell being Earth and the top representing the celestial heavens which cover all.

As an animal with access to both land and water, turtle is also an ancient symbol for one who is able to easily make the transition at will from one element or dimension to another. Turtles are often keepers of doorways and gateways for this reason.

Turtles have excellent sensing devices and are good survivors; they also have a sense of smell and can see some colors. Turtle in this context symbolizes your awakening senses, both physically and spiritually.

And turtle showing up in your dream or life may be a message that you have clairaudient abilities, that you should pay attention to what you pick up through vibrations.

Your dream turtle can also be telling you that you are protecting yourself too much, hiding in your shell. Or are you just plain moving too slowly? Or do you need to slow down? Or do you need to realize that you have everything you need for survival, right on your own back?

What kind of a turtle is this turtle? What actions is it carrying out? What color is it? How do you feel about it? What does it remind you of? Why? How is a turtle different from a tortoise?

TUSKS

Tusks and horns are symbols of spiritual power used in overcoming evil and ignorance.

So tusks by the side of the mouth symbolize the force of that which is spoken on the Higher Planes of Truth, Love, and Power.

WOLF

Probably the most common use of wolf is as a symbol of the free, untamed, natural, wild spirit.

Wolf is also a symbol of strength, loyalty to family and the family unit, guardianship, and your ability to survive "in the wild." Wolves have a strong sense of family and generally mate for life.

Wolves also symbolize fierceness and the Earth. Wolves see well in the dark and for this reason are often associated symbolically with light, the inner light that is a light within the dark.

Wolves are often found as companions of early deities, as are snakes and ravens.

But in many cultures the wolf is a symbol of aggression and war, and sometimes evil that inevitably overcomes and devours its prey. A wolf can also symbolize fear, especially fear associated with personal survival.

The ancient Celts believed that it was a wolf that swallowed the sun at night. To the Aztecs, the howling wolf was the God of the Dance.

To the ancient Alchemists, the wolf and the dog together represented the dual nature of the *nous*, the philosophical mercury, Mercurius.

The wolf was sacred to Ares/Mars, Apollo, and Silvanus, and of course a wolf was said to have nourished the founders of Rome, Romulus and Remus.

To the Scandanavian and Teutonic cultures, wolf was the bringer of victory and ridden by the god Odin. But Fenris, the Cosmic Wolf, was a bringer of evil.

And to the early Christians, the wolf symbolized evil, the devil, cruelty, stiff-necked people, gluttony, avarice, and heresy. However, the emblem of St. Francis of Assisi was a wolf, which legend says he personally tamed.

In some Native American cultures, wolf often symbolized the pathfinder, the innovator who brought new ideas to be taught.

Wolves are ritualistic animals and live by clearly defined structures. There is always an alpha female and an alpha male, for instance, but each wolf in the pack has its own special place and function. They have a complex system of vocal communications. It appears they even sometimes howl just for the sheer joy of it. Wolves are extremely tolerant of their young, and if a mother or father is unable to care for a pup, another pack member will adopt it. There are even wolf "babysitters."

It is believed that the wolf's sense of smell is over 100 times keener than that of a human. This trait is often used symbolically to represent a keen sense of discrimination, especially spiritually.

And, yes, wolves are predators, but their prey is mostly the old, sick, or very young. Wolves have great stamina for hunting and have been clocked running at 24 miles an hour.

Wolves often form quick and strong attachments, so your dream wolf may be telling you to either do the same, or to beware of doing so.

And wolves are extremely intelligent. They will go far out of their way to avoid any danger or trouble. Should you be doing the same?

Wolves also often have a playful relationship with ravens (see also BIRD/Raven). Does this remind you of anything?

And wolf makes a wonderful pun. Is the wolf at the door? Is there a wolf in your life (remember what happened to Little Red Riding Hood)? Are you wolfing something down? Or is it time to pay more attention to your family and your own pack?

What color is the wolf? How is it different from other wolves? Why? What is it doing? If it could speak, what would it say?

What do you think wolves are really like as animals? Who or what does it remind you of? How do you feel about wolves in general? Why?

ARGUMENT

Arguments often represent some struggle you are experiencing at the subconscious level with your own feelings, behavior or habits.

An argument can also symbolize the old you trying to hold back the new. Or, conversely, the new you convincing the older version of you of what it has to offer. Arguments can also represent your own unexpressed, even unrecognized, emotions and frustrations.

Remember that dreams are a safe place to release any strong feelings, harming no one, including yourself. So any dream arguments can be an effective way to work out conflicts in your feelings and actions by literally talking things over with yourself.

Who is having an argument? Who is the stronger; who will win? Why? How do you feel about the argument in your dream? What will be the outcome? How will things be different when one side has convinced the other? What does this remind you of that is going on in your life at the time?

See also EMOTION/Anger and any action(s) related to the argument.

ARTWORK

Art is always symbolic of something of value to someone somewhere. Art is a representation of the subject of the work of art, a symbol within a symbol. It is an artist's view of the subject, and since you are the dream artist, any form of art represents your views of the subject of the art form (i.e., a painting, sculpture, etc.).

But art can also symbolize traditional, abstract, or ancient views of life.

Who would want to own this type of art? Who would create it? Why? How valuable is it? What form does it take? What colors are involved? How would you like to own it?

How is it the same as, or different from, the works of art you are naturally drawn to at the time of the time of your dream? How would you like to spend time with the artist? Why, or why not? See also COLOR in artwork, PHOTOGRAPH, and any object that is the subject of the artwork.

ATTACK

Dream attacks most often symbolize your unrecognized or suppressed anger or fear. An attack can represent one part of you that is angry enough to literally attack another part.

An attack, of course, can also be a warning that your subconscious has picked up some data you should be paying closer attention to. Are you about to place yourself in a position or situation that has a potential for attack of any kind?

Being attacked in a dream or meditation can also be an early health warning, telling you that something is trying to attack your body (virus, bacteria, etc.), so you may want to begin taking evasive action, like getting more rest and watching your nutrition — or laughing more often.

Who is the attacker, and who is being attacked? What is the weapon? Why that weapon and not another? What caused the attack? What kind of person or thing would make such an attack?

How do you feel about the attack? What actions are you taking because of it? How are your dream actions different from actions you would take in the same situation when you are awake? Why? What is the result of the attack?

See EMOTION/Anger, Fear, GANGS (if present), INVASION, PAIN (if there is pain), RUN (if this action is taken), STRUGGLE, WAR, WEAPON used in attack).

B

BABY

Babies most often symbolize that any newly emerged parts of yourself, including ideas, talents, and habits, are still in the infant stage of growth and have no real-life practical experience yet.

And babies symbolize any of your unrecognized and therefore unused creativity, especially when pregnancy is involved; see PREGNANT.

A baby can also represent almost anything at all that is new and has just come into your life. The baby's stage of growth and development will tell you how far along any of this is at the time.

It is common for women to dream of babies just prior to, during, or just after menopause, especially of stillborn and dead babies, and some of these dreams can be pretty graphically gruesome. The theory here is that it is the body's way of mourning the children it now will not have — its "dead babies."

It is also common for both men and women from about the age of 35 onward to dream about gifted babies or "cosmic infants." Cosmic infants are babies or toddlers who can talk, walk, and act like adults, often more wisely than we do, and almost always show up to teach you something important at the time.

How big is this baby? Is it a boy or a girl? Why? How would the baby be different if it switched gender? Why?

Was the birth difficult? Is the baby healthy? Who are its mother and father? Who is responsible for its care and education? What does it look like? What is it doing? How is your dream baby different from other babies you have seen or dreamed? If it is talking, what is it saying?

How do you feel about the baby in your dream or meditation? How do you feel about babies in general? What does the baby remind you of that is going on in your life at the time? Who will it be when it grows up? See also FAMILY and FEMALE or MALE.

BELL

Bells most often symbolize a communication of spiritual symbols, a literal notice to attend (especially to what is being shown to you in your dream, meditation, or real life event). Bells are a call to the meeting, a call to attend class in order to learn, even a call to remember. Does any of this ring a bell with you?

As an archetype, bells are ancient symbols of the harmony and connection existing between Heaven and Earth, between God and humankind. Bells also symbolize Cosmic Harmony and the obedience of the human mind to Divine Law. To the ancients, bells were the echoes of Divine omnipotence, the physical manifestation of the voice of God. Bells had the power to drive away evil spirits, who presumably didn't like their sound.

Bells also issue warnings of impending storms, and were once believed to be able to act as barriers against misfortunes and evil of all kinds.

Bells are often rung in celebration of births, christenings, and weddings. But bells can toll for fallen leaders and those "lost at sea."

Bells are also good puns. Does something ring a bell with you? Are you getting the message? For whom is the bell tolling? Who is the belle of the ball? Has the starting bell rung? Are you about to be late for class? Who wants to come in, and why?

What kind of bell is ringing? What is the tone and sound of your bell? Why? What is it made of? What type of building would have your bell? Why is the bell ringing? Who or what caused it to ring? Who will hear and respond to your bell? How do you feel about bells in general? See also ALARM.

BIG

Anything big in your dream or meditation most often symbolizes the size of your emotional, mental, or spiritual feelings about the symbol itself. Something big or oversized is clearly telling you that this is BIG.

Big can also symbolize your current potential creativity, plans or goals, ideas, personal power, love, money, fear — anything your big symbol means to you.

And big can also be letting you know that you are letting something grow out of all proportion to its real size. Are you making a mountain out of a molehill? Have you created a monster? Or are you in danger of doing so?

FAT frequently symbolizes that you are trying to hide within what the symbol means to you, that you have a strong need to protect and disguise your emotional and vulnerable tendencies.

Being fat can also be a message from You to you that right now you are filling up with non-nutritional, false "food" (ideas and beliefs), and that it's now time to slim down, dump things no longer honoring you.

But fat also symbolizes prosperity and abundance, that you are guaranteed a constant "food" source and everything necessary for your survival.

What or who is fat? Is the fat person jolly, or disgusting to you? How do you feel about fat people in general? Why? How does it feel to be fat? What would you gain, or lose, if you were fat? If you feel you are too fat, what would you gain or lose by losing your "fat?" Who decides the difference between fat and thin?

BIRD

It is common for birds of one kind or another to pop up in your dreams or life at critical periods in your growth.

Birds symbolize freedom and the ability to fly above your ordinary everyday limitations and problems. Birds are supported by and trust their flight to the wind (Spirit).

They are symbols for thought, imagination, swift and easy movement, and for the spiritual growth process in general.

All birds bring messages and are almost always carriers of good news, messages of what is needed or helpful to your optimum survival at the time of your dream or experience.

At the highest symbol level, birds represent love, beauty, joy, and the human soul. Birds have symbolized the human spirit or Soul since the human beginnings.

And birds also often represent an out-of-body experience in your dream, but even here, they are symbolic. Why that particular bird, and not another? How does the dream change if the species of bird changes?

And birds are great puns. Are you being told to get a bird's eye view of something? Are you in danger of acting like a bird brain? Does some part of you feel too flighty? Do you feel a need to fly away? Do you eat like a bird (which roughly translated means double or triple your weight in food daily)? Have you or some part of you been caged or shot down?

What type of bird is it? What color is it? Does it sing? Can it fly? Why, or why not? What is it doing? How do you feel about it? If it could talk, what would it say to you? How would your dream or experience be different without it? Why? How is it different, or the same as, other birds of its species?

COMMON BIRD SYMBOLS:

BLUE JAY

Although the blue jay has a reputation for being a thief and bully, it is a strong symbol for using your powers wisely.

Blue jay is a reminder that we are of both this Earth and the realm of Spirit, and that our goal is to become masters of both worlds, not to become obsessed by one at the expense of the other. So your blue jay may be reminding you to stop playing with the subject of your dream or experience and get on with it.

Dreaming of a blue jay may also be a message that you are entering a period of expanded ability and adaptability, that you will be better able to see how to use the things around you more effectively.

Jays don't migrate and therefore symbolize the ability to stay in one place and make it through the long, cold winter, reminding you that you have tremendous natural survival abilities right where you are.

CARDINAL

Cardinals are old symbols of recognizing your own self-worth, just as you are at the moment. Cardinals remind you to accept who and what you are, without judging that or becoming arrogant because of it.

Cardinals don't migrate but generally stay in the same area all year, and so can also remind you that you can survive and thrive right where you are until Spring arrives.

Cardinals have loud whistles, reminding you to wake up and pay attention, especially to your inner voice. And since the female cardinal is less spectacular in color than the male, they are also reminders to bring out the Yin or female qualities, including your natural creativity and intuition.

Since cardinals were named for the cardinals of the Catholic Church, this one may be bringing you a message from that symbol as well. What is the function of a Catholic Cardinal? What stage of spiritual growth were they at

before they were made Cardinals? What does this remind you of?

CHICKEN

Chickens were one of the first birds to be domesticated by human beings. They are always associated with fertility because of their ability to produce so many eggs so regularly, so often.

Believe it or not, this is one of the reasons why chicken feathers were once used to stuff mattresses — to increase the fertility of those who slept on them — so now you've been warned.

Chickens have almost always been a common sacrificial bird; again, at least partly because of their symbolic link to sexuality.

Various forms of divination have also been attached to chickens, such as how many eggs a chicken laid, and even throwing feed to them. If the chickens refused the feed, the gods were angry and were refusing to listen.

Chicken is also an obvious good pun. Have you been lately? Are you running around like a chicken with its head cut off? Who's a dumb cluck?

CRANE

The crane is an ancient symbol for long life and immortality. It was once believed that the crane lived 1,000 years. The crane also symbolizes cleanliness, purity, vital life energy, Spring, love, and an intense zest for life.

In some cultures in Africa, the crane symbolizes language and thought, since it often gives the appearance of contemplating its environment. But in India, the crane is a symbol of treachery and betrayal.

CROW

Crows are ambivalent symbols, representing both good and evil in many cultures. Crows are often associated with magic, especially deeply hidden and secret magic.

While all birds are messengers, crow also carries memories, and not just yours, but memories of the entire human race, making crow a good symbol for the Collective Unconscious.

To the ancient Alchemists, the crow was symbolic of the first stage of Matter in the Great Work. And the crow was a sacred bird to the ancient Greek deities Athene and Apollo.

To the ancient Hebrew, the crow was a carrion bird symbolizing death and dissolution. To the Japanese, crows were symbols of misfortune, a bad omen, while in Shintoism crows can also be the messengers of deities, and for this reason are sometimes shown in front of the sun.

And to the early Christians, crows represented solitude and the devil in the act of blinding sinners, which is why you see them in so many even today in Hollywood horror productions.

To the Chinese, a black crow symbolizes evil, bad luck in business, and malice, but if the crow is red or gold, it symbolizes the sun, with all of its symbolism. And a black crow shown with a white heron symbolizes the Yin-Yang principles.

The ancient Egyptians often used a pair of crows to symbolize happiness in marriage.

Another good potential pun, what are you crowing about? Or is it time to eat crow?

DOVE

Doves and pigeons share much of the same symbolism. They are of major symbolic importance, from antiquity to our present time.

Doves symbolize Hope, Peace, contentment in love, the Soul, the Spirit of Light, purity, innocence, tenderness, simplicity, pure love, and chastity, especially the white dove. For example, in the ancient Babylonian deluge story, it was a white dove which was sent from the ark on the seventh day.

Doves are sacred to all Great Mothers and Queens of Heaven and symbolic of Her Divine power. For instance, in the Near East, the dove was a symbol of Ishtar and Astarte (Ashtoreth), the bird of sexual passion, and in ancient Greece was sacred to Aphrodite. A dove was also a symbol of the goddess Sophia, herself representing God's Wisdom.

In India, a dark dove was a symbol of bad luck, fear and death, and other doves were symbols of lust.

But in ancient China, doves symbolized marital fidelity and longevity since doves are usually found in pairs and the male and female share their parental responsibilities. They are also often a fertility symbol, probably because they reproduce and multiply so quickly.

Doves are sacred in Islam because it was one of the animals which protected Mohammed during his escape. And in the Hebrew sacred texts, it was three doves which were sent out by Noah from the Ark after the Deluge.

In ancient times, the dove was the symbolic opposite of the eagle and the raven, and in our time is still opposite to the hawk. For instance, peace keepers are said to be doves while those in favor of war are hawks.

Doves were also symbols of intimate, erotic love, probably due to their ancient connection to the various love goddesses. For example, doves were sacred to Adonis, Venus, Cupid, and Bacchus as the "First Begotten of Love." Doves were also associated with many forms of divination.

The Greek priestesses in the sacred grove Pleiades at Dodona were called *Peleiae*, meaning *doves*. And in the Orient, the Mystic Seven were the Seven Sisters, the Pleiades, whose Greek interpretation means "a flock of doves." They were daughters or rays of Aphrodite as Pleione, Queen of the Sea.

To the ancient Romans, the dove was sacred to Venus, and its eggs were believed to be strong aphrodisiacs. It was also believed that doves had no bile in their systems, which accounted for their peaceful natures, and that the herbs they ate made their flesh, blood, and organs especially therapeutic. Even dove and pigeon droppings were once used in poultices.

A BLACK PIGEON SETTLING ON AN OAK TREE is an extremely old symbol that a shrine should be built on that spot.

A PAIR OF WHITE DOVES is a strong symbol of love and fidelity, as is the turtle dove (it was once believed that a turtle dove died immediately after its mate).

A WHITE DOVE symbolizes the Holy Spirit in Christianity. For example, in Christian art depicting the baptism of Jesus, a white dove is above Him, symbolic of the saved soul of humanity, saved by the Holy Spirit.

The seven gifts of the Holy Spirit (wisdom, understanding, counsel, fortitude, knowledge, piety, and fear of God) are often represented by seven white doves, and white doves also frequently symbolize the newly baptized.

And a white dove is often used as a symbol for the Soul as it leaves the physical body, again, especially in art.

A WHITE DOVE WITH AN OLIVE BRANCH IN ITS BEAK symbolizes peace, forgiveness, and deliverance.

A WHITE DOVE WITH A PALM BRANCH IN ITS BEAK symbolizes victory over death and a guarantee of the resurrection.

DUCK

Ducks are ancient symbols of a mediator between the sky and the waters.

And ducks also symbolized marital happiness, fidelity, and beauty to the ancient Chinese and Japanese, and the duck was considered a Yin (female) symbol, while the rooster or cock symbolized the Yang (male) principle.

Ducks were associated with Isis in ancient Egypt, and to the ancient Hebrew represented immortality.

Conversely, ducks also symbolize useless chatter, deceit, and superficiality.

This one is also a good pun, of course. Should you be ducking? Does some part of you feel like a lame duck? Is there a quack in your life? Are you trying to tell yourself "if it looks like a duck, walks like a duck, and quacks like a duck...?"

EAGLE

All eagles are associated with solar deities and power by virtually every culture where eagle can be found.

Eagles symbolize great power, endurance, pride, and spiritual energy. They are universal symbols for the spiritual principle in humanity which is able to soar toward the heavens when it trusts to Spirit to carry it higher and higher.

Eagle has almost always been a symbol of the sun, Heaven, the sky, lightning and thunder. It is also a strong symbol of rebirth, and frequently a substitute for the ancient mythical Phoenix bird if legends.

Eagles are symbols of the power of faith, prayer (especially an ascending eagle), spiritual knowledge, and solitary contemplation.

To dream of an eagle or see one is often a message for you to learn to use your personal power and energy wisely, to learn to use the air currents (the energy of Spirit) whenever possible to lift you and sustain your flight. Effort and struggle is unnecessary when you learn to combine your natural abilities with the support of Spirit, and learn to trust in both.

Eagle also represents courage, freedom, independence, and responsibility. Eagles have strength, speed, and extraordinary eyesight, and are powerful and efficient hunters.

Eagles bring inspiration and symbolize ascension, victory, pride, contemplation, authority, royalty, release from bondage, the capacity to soar to great heights, exceptional perception, and the element Air.

As a symbol, eagles have been traced back to the ancient Hittites, indicating that this bird was probably a strong symbol long before that culture.

And an eagle is one of the vehicles of the Buddha. And in the ancient Egyptian alphabet, the letter A is in the form of an eagle, symbolizing the warmth of life, the day, and the Origin. In Vedic tradition, the eagle is an important messenger, bringing *soma* (the elixir of the gods) from the god Indra.

In some Native American traditions, eagle symbolizes connection with the Divine and the ability to leave the Earth in spirit while still remaining connected to both Earth and the Divine, so your eagle may be representing an out-of-body experience.

Eagle also represents Universal Spirit, and in some Native American cultures, the White Eagle symbolizes a man and the Brown Eagle a woman.

To the early Christians, the eagle was a messenger from Heaven, the spirit of prophecy, prayer rising to the Lord, and Grace descending to humankind. But the eagle was also given a position as one of the Seven Deadly Sins, the sin of Pride, while at the same time considered one of the four cardinal virtues, Justice.

In all cultures, eagles were believed to be able to fly higher than any other bird. Eagle was the bird of Jupiter, the storm bird, and is connected directly to lightning, thunder, and war by many cultures.

Aristotle believed that eagles had the ability to look directly into the sun and suffer no harm as they soared upward, adding to its symbolism of direct spiritual knowledge and the ability to carry it.

To Carl Jung, eagles were a father symbol, and eagles have been the symbol of kings since very ancient times. Even Dante referred to the eagle as the bird of God.

In some cultures, the owl is considered to be the opposite of eagle.

An eagle can also be a good pun. Are you being told to keep an eagle eye on something? Has your eagle landed? Will your eagle fly on Friday (payday)? Is it time to soar with the eagles?

THE EAGLE IN THE SYMBOL OF AQUARIUS, a man carrying a pitcher with an eagle over the man, symbolizes that even the gods need the water of the Uranian forces of life.

AN EAGLE CARRYING A VICTIM, human or otherwise, symbolizes the sacrifice of the lower animal instincts and energies to the higher ones.

CONFLICT BETWEEN AN EAGLE AND A BULL symbolizes the triumph of Spirit over Matter, the intellect over the physical; see also ANIMAL/Bull.

CONFLICT BETWEEN AN EAGLE AND A SERPENT, and an eagle with a snake in its talons, symbolizes the Celestial Powers of good and evil. Eagle in this context is also symbolic of Unmanifest Light, the serpent symbolizing Unmanifest Darkness. Together they are a Totality, the union of Spirit with Matter. This particular symbolism has been found from the Far East to Pre-Columbian America.

AN EAGLE DEVOURING A LION symbolizes the ability of Spirit to transform Matter; see also ANIMAL/Lion.

A DOUBLE-HEADED EAGLE represents all twin deities and is often symbolic of omniscience and power doubled.

EAGLE FEATHERS symbolize the Great Spirit, the Thunder Bird, Universal Spirit, and individual rays of Light.

PERCHED ON A PILLAR symbolizes various sun deities victorious over darkness.

A SOARING EAGLE symbolizes the liberated Spirit, and the power of faith and prayer.

AN EAGLE WITH HUMAN ARMS symbolizes worship of the sun, with all it symbolizes, and was the being who conducted Souls to immortality (a Psychopomp) in many cultures.

FALCON
A falcon is most often identified with the sun and all solar deities and qualities.

To the ancient Egyptians, a falcon was a divine symbol because of its strength, courage, beauty, and ability to fly high. It was sacred to Ra, and the god Horus often assumes the form of a falcon or is shown with a falcon's head. But other Egyptian deities also sometimes take the falcon form.

During the European Renaissance, a hooded falcon became a symbol of hope for the light which will illuminate the darkness.

FEATHER
A feather frequently symbolizes sacred or higher thoughts, a direct connection to Heaven and the Angels.

Feathers also represent lightness and the ability to fly or float easily, especially when carried by the air of Spirit.

In ancient cultures, a feather often symbolized the Truth which must and ultimately always will rise, lightness, dryness, the heavens, heights, speed, space, flight to other levels or dimensions, the Soul, and the elements of Wind and Air (especially as the opposite of the humid moist element Water).

To the ancient Egyptian, the feather symbolized sovereignty, truth, dryness, height, flight, and weightlessness. It was an emblem of the goddess Maat, the one who weighs the hearts of the dead against the weight of a feather in her role as Truth. In ancient Amenti, it was the god Osiris who weighed the hearts of the dead rather than Maat.

Deities with feathers were also symbols of attributes of ancient Egyptian solar deities: Amen Ra, Anheru, Osiris, Horus, Shu, Hathor, Amsu, Mentu, and Nefertium.

Pay attention to the type of feather it is, too. Is it a wing feather or one of the down feathers? Why? How are they different?

Feathers can also symbolize a graduation, promotion, or work well down, a feather in your cap.

Watch especially for the dream puns with this one. "Birds of a feather...," "light as a feather," etc.

What kind of feather is your dream feather? What kind of bird grew it? What color is it? Why is it in your dream? How does the bird who lost the feather feel about that? Why? Does losing the feather change the bird at all? What does any of this remind you of?

A CLOAK OF FEATHERS is an old symbol for one who journeys to other worlds and dimensions. For example, Celtic fairies often wear feather-trimmed garments and the Aztec kings and priests wore cloaks of feathers.

A CROWN OF FEATHERS symbolizes the sun and the direct connection to it, and all of its symbolism, by the wearer of the crown.

EAGLE FEATHERS symbolize the Great Spirit, the Thunder Bird, Universal Spirit, and individual rays of Light; see also Eagle above.

FEATHERED STICKS of any kind symbolized contemplation, prayer, and connection to Spirit, the Creator in most, if not all, early cultures.

OSTRICH FEATHERS are strong symbols of Truth, Justice, Equality, and Spiritual Law, since they are perfectly equal. If worn on the head, ostrich feathers symbolize "One who is a Master of Truth." And the Egyptian goddess Maat weighed the hearts of the newly dead on a scale balanced by an ostrich feather; see also Ostrich below.

PEACOCK FEATHERS are ancient symbols for an eye, especially the Eye of the Soul and the Eye of God; see also Peacock below.

THREE FEATHERS together symbolize the lotus and lily, the flower or flame of light and life, royalty, and the triple majesty of the deity wearing three feathers.

TWO FEATHERS together symbolize Light and Air, the two poles, and resurrection.

TO WEAR FEATHERS of any kind in any manner is to take on the power of the bird, and helps the wearer to connect to the knowledge of birds and all that they symbolize.

A WHITE FEATHER can symbolize clouds, sea foam, peace, and pure spirit. But a white feather is also an old symbol for extreme and inexcusable cowardice.

GOOSE
A favorite in many myths and legends, the goose has almost always been used as a symbol for an intermediary between Heaven and Earth. And the goose often shares the symbolism of the swan; see Swan below.

Goose is a strong symbol of love, marital fidelity, fertility, and vigilance. Geese mate for life and cooperate in raising their young.

In ancient Egyptian mythology, it was a goose who laid the World or Cosmic Egg, and the goose was sacred to Seb, the father of Osiris. Seb was the god of Time, the equivalent of the ancient Greek Kronos, and one of the first gods of Creation.

A bird sacred to Aphrodite and Juno, it was once believed that the flesh of a goose was an aphrodisiac, and that its bile enhanced a man's sexual potency.

Geese also symbolize someone who constantly makes too much noise, especially about nothing, and malicious spiteful gossip.

They are prime for puns. Who is a silly goose? Whose goose is cooked? What's sauce for the goose....?

FLYING GEESE are strong symbols for following a quest or purpose, of returning again and again to your true source or home. Flying geese can also be telling you about a deep subconscious longing to be on your way to new territories.

HAWK
The sound of a hawk's cry has the ability to pierce any state of awareness and consciousness, helping you to wake up and look for additional ways of being and doing. Hawks, like eagles, have an extraordinary overall view and perspective of events taking place on the ground.

And a hawk was often associated with Mercury, the ancient Greek and Roman messenger of the gods.

To the ancient Egyptians, the hawk was a symbol for the human soul, representing the potential for solar or divine transfiguration.

But to the early Christians, the hawk was a symbol for the evil mind of the sinner and was frequently used as a symbol of death. Conversely, the early Christian symbol of a hawk tearing a rabbit or hare to pieces symbolized the victory of the Spirit (the hawk) over lust and lasciviousness (the rabbit).

In some Native American traditions, hawk is a messenger who brings information from those who lived before. Its cry was often seen as a warning, to be aware. But the cry of the hawk was always a message to heighten your awareness, pay closer attention to your inner and outer environment.

HERON
The long beak of the heron most likely gave it its symbolism of curiosity and the ability to probe into hidden knowledge. Herons are also strong symbols of self-reliance and the determination to accomplish anything you set out to do.

To the ancient Chinese, the heron was a symbol of a long and happy life. And to the ancient Egyptians, herons symbolized the morning, and regeneration of life, and were one of the birds associated with the mythical Phoenix bird.

In ancient Greece and Rome, the heron was sacred to the sea god Poseidon/Neptune, and its appearance was always a good omen.

To the early Christians, it symbolized behavior to be imitated, a message to shun the places and food of the heretic, and to fear the storms of this world. In Christian art, herons are often portrayed devouring a snake, symbolic of the Christ's victory over the serpent. And because of the belief that the heron could shed tears of pain, it became a symbol for Jesus at the Mount of Olives.

A GRAY HERON is an ancient symbol of repentance or reflection on past actions, and a good reminder to look at old habits and ways of thinking.

A WHITE HERON is an ancient symbol of purity, and always a good omen.

HUMMINGBIRD

Hummingbirds can fly in any direction — up, down, forwards, backwards, even hover in one spot. No other bird can fly backwards, and it is probably for this reason as much as any other that hummingbirds have been seen as magical birds by many cultures.

Hummingbirds also symbolize achieving the seemingly impossible and recognizing your own unique brand of happiness and bliss. What makes you truly happy? When was the last time you played and laughed out loud without caring what someone else thought about it?

Hummingbirds spend their lives moving from one flower to another, bringing new life as they extract the nectar. Is it time for you to do the same? Or is this a message that maybe you do this just a little too much? See also FLOWER if your hummingbird is hovering over one.

An old legend assures us that hummingbird feathers open the heart, and without an open heart we will never taste the sweet nectar (essence) of life. Remind you of anything in your life?

Hummingbirds are adept at reaching and living on the "nectar of life." Hummingbirds could not live without the flowers, and many flowers count on hummingbirds to continue their species; see also FLOWER.

Hummingbirds are good homebuilders, and each home is unique. Should you be looking at your own architecture?

And they have the innate sense to slow down at night and get plenty of deep rest, although no one could fault them on their busyness during the day. How about you?

MAGPIE

A close cousin to the crow, the magpie symbolizes the appropriate use of intelligence, your natural inquisitiveness, and the correct use of magical, metaphysical, and hidden knowledge.

The magpie is one of the most intelligent of birds and highly adaptable to its environment and circumstances.

Magpies are also very good sneak thieves and will steal anything not too big to carry away. But while they are opportunists and scavengers, this is only one evidence of their natural intelligence; they are able to use anything convenient to reach a goal.

Magpies are seen as both lucky and unlucky, depending upon the culture telling the tale. They have a long connection to witchcraft in the Western part of the world, and it was once believed that they were spirits or familiars in animal form. Again, their intelligence is most likely to blame for this old belief.

So if you have dreamed yourself up a magpie, or are especially aware of them these days, are you telling yourself that you have intelligence and knowledge that you are afraid to use because of what others might think? Or is magpie warning you to be careful to whom you show your knowledge? Or is it telling you to look around you and use what's there?

OSTRICH

Its feathers being perfectly equal, the ostrich is an old symbol for Truth, Justice, and Equality.

However, in ancient Semitic cultures, the ostrich represented the dragon and was a demon.

And to the African Dogon, the ostrich symbolizes both light and water.

Ostrich also makes a good pun. Are you in danger of burying your head in the sand when you should be taking evasive action?

OSTRICH FEATHERS ostrich feathers are strong symbols of Truth, Justice, Equality, and Spiritual Law, since they are perfectly equal. If worn on the head, ostrich feathers symbolize "One who is a Master of Truth."

Ostrich feathers were one of the emblems of the ancient Egyptian goddess Maat, the goddess of truth, justice, and the law, who weighed the deeds of a person (symbolized by the heart) against the weight of a feather, almost always an ostrich feather.

AN OSTRICH EGG symbolizes the Creation, Life, resurrection, and spiritual vigilance.

OWL

Owls are ancient symbols for the wisdom which penetrates through the darkness of ignorance, and the talent for seeing clearly even with very little light or information available.

However, owl is another ambivalent symbol, representing both good and bad. For example, owl is considered to be the polar opposite of eagle in some cultures. And seeing or dreaming of an owl can be a warning of some kind, depending upon your dream content and how you personally feel about owls.

In ancient Egypt and India, the owl was the bird of death, night, cold, passivity, the realm of the dead sun, and believed to be "uncanny." In ancient China, it was associated with the lightning which lights up the night, the drum which penetrates the stillness of night, and the Yang (male) principle.

Athena, the Greek goddess of wisdom, is often shown with an owl perched on her shoulder to aid her in perceiving unseen truths, giving "light" to her blind side.

In some Native American cultures, owl sits in the East, the place of illumination. And owl medicine is associated with clairvoyance, astral projection, and both black and white magic, depending upon the culture you are in. Owl is often the medicine of witches and sorcerers, probably because of its ability to see and hear in the dark and to fly silently. Owls are efficient silent hunters.

PEACOCK
The peacock symbolizes the sun, and is the vehicle of various solar deities, including the Buddha. It was also sacred to the ancient Greek goddesses Hera and Juno.

In ancient Persia, the peacock's tail symbolized the Universe, the full moon, and the sun at midday. The peacock retained this symbolism in very early Christianity, but by the European Middle Ages had become the symbol for the sins of Pride and Vanity.

PEACOCK FEATHERS are eye symbols, most often as the Eye of the Soul and the Eye of God.

PEACOCK WITH A SERPENT IN ITS BEAK symbolizes Light defeating Dark, most likely because at one time the beauty of the peacock was believed to have been created by the transmutation by the peacock of the poison of the serpent.

PELICAN
The pelican is an ancient symbol of sacrificial parental love.

It was once believed that the pelican killed its disobedient chicks and awakened them after three days by feeding them its own blood from self-inflicted wounds. Because of this belief, in medieval times in the Western part of the world, the pelican was a common symbol for the sacrifice of the Christ.

And the pelican symbolized the Philosopher's Stone to the early Alchemists, the stone that could turn lead into gold.

PHEASANT
Because of its unusual song and dance routine, in many cultures the pheasant is a symbol of Cosmic Harmony. Its voice and the ritual flapping of its wings is also symbolically associated with thunder, rain, storms, and Spring.

And the pheasant is symbolic of the Yang (masculine) principle, but was believed to become Yin during the cycling of the seasons.

RAVEN
A raven is an old symbol for flight into the Unknown, especially the

unfamiliar and unknown parts of yourself. Raven is always a carrier of significant messages.

And since it was once believed that the raven preferred to live along, it symbolizes self-imposed solitude.

In many cultures, raven is both divine and solar, probably due to its intelligence. And since it is such a talkative bird, it has almost always been associated with prophecy.

But raven is one of the "unclean" animals of the Hebrew and Christian sacred texts, and the ancient Egyptians saw it as a symbol of destruction.

In Japan, however, raven is a messenger of the gods and a sun symbol, especially the red raven.

In ancient Persia, raven was sacred to the god of light and the sun. In Persian Mithraic tradition, raven represented the first level of initiation — to become the servant of the sun.

To the ancient Romans, raven was a symbol of hope. To the Chinese, it was one of the Twelve Terrestrial Branches, and symbolized power. While to the ancient Greeks, raven symbolized longevity and was sacred to Apollo. Raven was especially invoked at weddings to ensure fertility.

In some Native American cultures, raven often symbolized the bringer of magic, and appeared just before or at a change in consciousness. Raven also represents healing and is believed to be present at any healing ceremony.

Raven is also symbolic of a shape shifter, one who can appear to be almost anything at any time. And raven sometimes takes the place of coyote as the Trickster.

ROBIN
Robins are old symbols of new growth in many areas. Even though robins actually migrate only when there is a lack of winter food, they are traditional ambassadors of Spring; see SEASONS.

And all robins are especially sensitive to the color red. To the male robin, the color red translates as "This is *my* territory!," but any argument over territory is almost always by a battle by song, not flying feathers. So is your robin telling you to step up and sing your own tune, establish your territory by peaceful harmonic means, rather than through direct confrontation and conflict?

Baby robins are born from a beautiful powder blue egg and completely featherless, symbolizing the birth or activation of your ability to speak your own truth, even though that truth is still in its infancy; see Feather above.

SPARROW
Sparrows most often symbolize the past, getting together in groups, companionship, and the nobility of the common person or thing.

To the ancient Greeks, sparrow was one of the attributes of Aphrodite, also often identified with Lesbia, while to the Japanese, sparrow symbolized loyalty.

But to the early Christians, a sparrow symbolized insignificance, lechery, lewdness, and lowliness in general. But at the same time, the symbol of the Twelve Sparrows represented the twelve qualities within human nature which aspire to be reflections of the Higher Self.

And sparrows are often attributed to the apocryphal story of the child Jesus when he made clay birds on the Sabbath for the entertainment of his friends, and when chastised by his elders, caused them to fly away by clapping his hands, is symbolically interpreted this way:

Overhearing the conversation between old thought and the ego (represented by the adults and children in the story), Jesus immediately directs the attention of old habits of thought (i.e., not being allowed to do anything on the Sabbath) to a new and higher way of taking form (i.e., the clay sparrows), by making a deliberate physical effort (clapping his hands together), to give the new higher forms life and the ability to function differently (to take flight). The clay birds (the sparrows) are now free to develop in their own way at their own speed, allowing the spiritual evolution of the mind to proceed along its natural course.

SPARROWHAWK:

Since the female Sparrowhawk is often larger and stronger than the male, it was a symbol of a woman's domination in marriage.

And to the ancient Egyptians and similar cultures, the sparrowhawk was the bird of Horus and a sun symbol.

STORK

The stork symbolizes good fortune, long life, new birth and renewal of life, childlike gratitude, and philosophical contemplation. And since they migrate and return annually, storks also symbolize resurrection and Spring.

Storks were frequently a symbol of the enemy of evil, since they hunt and kill serpents. They were also sometimes used as a symbol for the Bearer of Souls, a common symbol for us even today.

Storks have long legs which allow them to wade in shallow water along shorelines, places traditionally associated with mythical fairy realms.

Conversely, a stork is one of the "unclean" animals in the Judeo-Christian sacred texts.

Storks are legendary for their devotion to their young and are protective parents. They often return to the same nests year after year, raising each generation in the same environment. So if you have dreamed or seen a stork, are you being nudged to go back to your beginnings, your home base, return to the nest? Are you going to receive a little surprise package?

SWAN

Swans are ancient symbols for awakening to your true self or nature.

Swans also symbolize exceptional sensitivity, grace, and beauty. At the same time, swans are powerful birds and have been known to break a human arm just by beating their wings.

Swans represent the mystic, poet, dreamer, and the child in us all. They are credited in many myths with the ability to connect different dimensions or worlds. A familiar myth embodying this message is the one of Leda and the Swan.

There are also many stories linking the swan to the fairy worlds, which strongly hint at the power and inherent dangers involved when being directly involved with Beauty.

And, of course, one of the best known legends of all is of the story of the swan's song. It was commonly believed that the swan sang its most beautiful song just before it died, leaving human beings with a poignant longing to know the mysteries of life and death.

TURKEY

Turkey is associated with thunder and rain, probably because it becomes so restless before a storm.

Turkey was the sacred bird of the ancient Toltecs and was a ritual food at festivals. In many Native American cultures today, turkey is the South Eagle, the Peace Eagle, incorporating much of the symbolism of Eagle itself. And, of course, this bird is prime for a pun. Are you?

VULTURE

In many ancient cultures, the vulture was a symbol for Fate. Vulture often symbolized one who knew the secret of the transformation of useless material (dead bodies) into gold.

Vultures are also symbols of purification, literally being picked clean of your former flesh (beliefs). They are also strong symbols of patience, of learning to wait till events bring you what you need for survival, just when you need it most.

In ancient Egypt, vultures were the protectors of pharaohs, and were commonly prominent on crowns and headdresses.

This bird was sacred to the ancient Greek god Apollo and other sun deities. And to the early Christians, since it was believed that the eggs of the female vulture were fertilized by the East wind, it was also a symbol of the Virgin Mary.

But to the ancient Mayan, vultures symbolized death. And in many Native American cultures in our country today, the vulture is a symbol of fire and the sun, and all that they symbolize.

WINGS

Wings often symbolize a desire to fly, to soar above, to reach new levels and heights, get above it all. Wings also symbolize freedom, especially freedom from the limitation of the heavy, mundane, material world.

But wings can also be telling you that you are being too heavy, letting something in your life weigh you down when you should be soaring or floating gently, and that it is now time to get a bird's eye view of the situation and lighten up. An old Scottish proverb tells us that "Angels can fly because they take themselves so lightly" — good advice anytime for anyone.

Wings are solar symbols, representing the power and ability to transcend. Almost all winged deities are solar gods.

As an archetype in the West and Middle East, wings almost exclusively symbolize the actual presence of divinity or supernatural beings.

Wings are attributes of all messengers of the gods and symbols of the ability of human beings to communicate with the gods.

But wings are often ambivalent symbols since they are also an attribute of many demons, fallen angels, and other evil entities.

WINGED CAP, WINGED SANDALS, AND WINGS ON CADUCEUS are symbolic of someone who is a Messenger of God or the gods.

WOODPECKER
Woodpeckers are symbolic of an awakening (especially one accomplished through the use of repetition and rhythm, like drumming and chanting), of prophecy, of good fortune (especially the green woodpecker), and were once believed to be excellent weather predictors. And in some cultures, the woodpecker was the symbol for lightning and thunder.

To the early Christians, the woodpecker was a symbol of prayer without end, and since it fed on worms was also a symbolic enemy of the devil, sometimes even symbolizing the Christ.

WREN
In the Western world, any type of wren frequently takes the place of the dove as a symbol of Spirit, and is sometimes dubbed the King of Birds. But wrens are also often associated with witches here in the West.

A wren was sacred to the Greek god Triptolemos and to the Celtic deity Taliesen. And in medieval England and France, wrens were killed at Christmas, hung from a pole, paraded through the town, and then buried as a symbol of the death of the old year, while in Scotland it was considered very bad luck to kill a wren.

Wrens also symbolize resourcefulness and adaptability, the ability to build your home anywhere. Are you using the resources you already have to your best advantage? Have you forgotten to trust in yourself?

BLOOD
Blood symbolizes Divine Truth, the element of the Divine as it functions and flows within the human body of Matter. Consequently, blood also symbolizes your vital life energy, force, and power.

Since the earliest of times, blood has been symbolic of the Seat of the Soul and of the Life Force. (In ancient symbolism, both blood and water can symbolize Divine Life and Truth).

But blood can be a message that you are draining yourself, losing energy through fear, anger, over-work, worry, frustration, loving too much, etc.

Dream blood can also, of course, be a clear health message of some kind, but keep in mind that you almost always receive dream health messages in plenty of time to repair anything.

Blood also symbolizes race and family, our connection to one another and those like us, and the character or nature of the personality (e.g., bad blood, cold blooded, bloodthirsty). See also RACE, HUMAN, and FAMILY.

"Pure" blood (usually the blood of a virgin) was at one time even believed to be able to restore beauty, health, youth, and heal fatal diseases like leprosy.

Among many primal cultures, blood is symbolic of a contamination, and this is the reason for isolating women during menstruation and during and after giving birth.

Blood was often seen as having magical supernatural powers, even the power to restore life, and was believed to be the life-giving food of various supernatural beings.

The ancient Aztecs believed that human blood helped strengthen the sun, which lost its power nightly because of its journey through the Underworld. Blood was therefore indispensable if the proper cosmic order was to be regained and maintained.

What area or part of the body is bleeding. Why? What color is the blood? Is there any pain? How much blood is being lost, or given? How do you feel about it in the dream? What will be the final result?

See also COLOR (of blood), any objects causing the blood to show (e.g., Knife), and the part of the BODY losing blood.

BLEEDING is often a symbol that you are losing far too much energy, or even some personal but favorite truth, symbolized by the area of the body suffering the loss of blood.

Losing blood is also a strong symbol of the heavy price some part of you is paying, or is willing to pay, for the actions taken in the dream or meditation which resulted in the loss of blood.

But bleeding can also be telling you that you have a particularly strong connection to life symbolized by that place on your body; see also BODY.

Which area of the body is bleeding and how you feel about it in your dream or meditation will tell you which interpretation might be right for your experience.

BRIGHT RED BLOOD often symbolizes new and vital energy being lost or wasted, or, conversely, that your life force is vibrantly healthy, depending upon how you feel about the blood at the time. Bright red blood can also be telling you that this is a recent wound which hasn't had a chance to heal yet, and could be warning you about a wound or energy loss that hasn't yet happened.

INTERNAL BLEEDING most often symbolizes a deep inner pain or injury, loss of vital life energy or force represented by the area bleeding. Internal bleeding can be a warning to stop wasting valuable energy before the bleeding becomes a physical reality.

DARK RED BLOOD often represents an old wound from the past, one that may not yet be healed. And dark red blood can also be a warning that you might be about to repeat past mistakes, mistakes which will end in this same kind of wound. What does the blood remind you of going on in your life at the time?

BODY

A common universal symbol, your physical body symbolizes the earthly desires in which your true Self is housed, and through which it manages to manifest these desires within the world of form and Matter.

Your body is the place where you live, the sensory vehicle that allows you to survive and function within the Third Dimension. It is literally your biological spacesuit.

In many cultures, the physical body is viewed as something that must be transcended, often by specific initiations, trials, and rituals. In these traditions, the body is believed to represent the seven states of consciousness that all human beings simultaneously function within. Each level or layer of your body (consciousness) is impacted by the actions of each other level.

And dreaming of your body can also be an early health warning of some kind, relating to your body as a whole or any part of it being emphasized in your dream. These kinds of dreams appear almost without exception in more than enough time to fix whatever's going wrong *before* it does, so don't panic — just fix it. See also HOUSE, VEHICLE.

COMMON BODY-RELATED SYMBOLS

ANKLE

In many esoteric traditions, the ankles symbolize the zodiacal energy axis poles within the Earth, the Hierarchy.

It was once believed that all evil intelligences directed their telepathic energies toward the ankles, the first axis — just one of the reasons why people wore ankle-bells (see BELL).

Ankles also symbolize the connecting point between the foot and the leg, how you are relating to their symbolism at the time of your dream, and how flexible you are in relation to them; see Foot and Leg below.

Is the ankle adorned, or bare? Has it been injured? How does it feel? Why? If it could talk, what would it say to you first? What is it doing, and what is its purpose in your dream or meditation?

ARM

Arms are ancient symbols of strength, of Action relating to Will as it acts on the Mental Plane of Existence.

They are almost always a symbol of strength, or lack of it, depending upon the context in which they are used.

A BENT ARM is traditionally a symbol of the inability of the Mind to act in perfect unison on its own, since it was believed that the Mind or Will could not find Truth without connection and flexibility.

BOTH ARMS RAISED WITH PALMS OUT is an ancient symbol for someone who comes in peace to help or teach, and one who in order to accomplish this mission relinquishes all means of self-protection and carries no weapons.

To the early Christians, upraised arms symbolized a plea for Divine grace and the Soul's opening to Divine influences. Raised arms can also symbolize surrender and giving up your power and right of self defense.

Arms raised, palm out, also symbolizes that you have absolutely nothing at all to hide, there are no hidden weapons or agendas with which to harm.

AN EXTENDED ARM or an arm reaching out traditionally symbolizes the power of Justice, specifically Justice being extended to you or the object toward which it is reaching.

An extended arm can, of course, also be telling you clearly that you are reaching for the subject of your dream or meditation. Or that you are being offered what is on the arm or in the hand attached to the arm. What has just been extended to you?

THE LEFT ARM, in general, symbolizes energy coming in or projected inward, even if you are left handed. This is universally the arm with which you receive and take in. The left arm is also generally the one representing the Yin (female) qualities. It is controlled by the right side of the brain. See also LEFT and RIGHT.

MULTIPLE ARMS on a person or other object is an ancient symbol for compassionate aid from a divine source, each arm and the symbolic object it holds representing various characteristics or qualities of that particular deity.

TO HAVE NO ARMS is an old symbol for intense feelings of helplessness, of inaction, your latent but unused talents or powers, and the inability or refusal to take action, to react, to defend yourself, or to be able to help others. How does it feel to have no arms? How did this happen? How would things be different with them? How did the arms get lost?

ONE RAISED ARM even today still symbolizes taking an oath, bearing witness to something, and a greeting or salute.

THE RIGHT ARM generally symbolizes outgoing energy, energy being assertively and forcefully projected outward, whether you are right handed or not. The right is also often considered to represent the Yang (male) qualities. And the right arm is controlled by the left side of the brain.

EAR
Ears often symbolize your spiritual hearing, or clairaudient abilities, a talent which is said to be older than spiritual seeing (clairvoyance).

And ears symbolize communicating by being the listener, obedience to what you hear, your receptivity to hearing, and your willingness to accept advice and guidance.

Ears can also symbolize your mind in its more passive contemplative aspects, showing you that you are now more receptive to new ideas and thoughts.

Ears are an ancient symbol, and since they have much in common with the spiral, the whorled shell and the sun, many myths tell us of births from the ear (most shells are a strong birth symbol; see SHELL).

But ears could also be telling you that you are relying too much on external guidance, that you are trusting in an authority other than your own at the time, that you are listening too much and maybe not speaking enough.

To the ancients, ears were the seat of memory, giving us even today the gesture of pulling your ear as the message "don't forget."

The ear hears the Word of Creation, and for this reason is almost always associated directly with the Breath of Life and the Logos, the Word.

For example, in ancient Egyptian symbolism, the right ear received the Air of Life, and it was the left ear which received the Air of Death.

Ears are also great puns. To what should you be lending an ear? Who is all ears?

BIG EARS are old symbols for psychic powers, especially the power of clairaudience. But, of course, big ears can also be telling you that you are eavesdropping too much about things which do not really concern you.

BROAD EARS are an ancient symbol for immortality, wisdom, judgment, and one who has a long history of psychic abilities; see Big Ears above.

ELONGATED EAR LOBES are ancient symbols for greatness and spiritual or royal authority (e.g., the ear lobes of the Buddha).

POINTED EARS are often associated with Pan, and are ancient symbols for the fool and the lower physical instincts and behavior.

ELBOW
Like knees, elbows most often symbolize your flexibility, your ability or willingness to bend. Elbows are midway between the hand and shoulder, symbolizing the mid-

point between these two symbols; see Hand and Shoulder below.

Traditionally, an arm bent at the elbow symbolizes the inability of the Mind to act in perfect unison on its own, since it was believed that the Mind or Will could not find Truth without connection and flexibility.

Another good candidate for a play on words, are you trying to elbow your way into something?

EYEBROWS

Eyebrows are effective, but silent, communication tools. They are one of the most expressive parts of the face. Eyebrows have been praised by poets for thousands of years.

RAISING ONE EYEBROW is a quick and effective nonverbal way to express doubt or disbelief, ask a question, convey curiosity, and request further information on the subject being discussed.

BOTH EYEBROWS RAISED together most often is a symbol of surprise, shock, even fear.

EYEBROWS MOVED IN TOWARD ONE ANOTHER indicates anger, frustration, complete puzzlement, even great pain.

EYE

The eye is an ancient symbol for one who can take the outside world into the inner, and one who can also project the inner world onto the outer.

As a universal symbol, the eye represents omniscience, the All-Seeing. The eye has almost always been a basic symbol of sun deities, representing their life-giving powers and watchfulness.

Eyes are symbols of our individuality and personality as the centers of perception on the Mental Plane, and within the realms of both higher and lower consciousness. Eyes represent mental perception, especially of feelings and ideas, as the external parts of consciousness.

Eyes also symbolize intuitive visions, enlightenment, knowledge, the mind, vigilance, protection, a never-sleeping watchfulness, and the Cosmic or Mystic Eye.

Dreaming of eyes can also be one of any number of puns, the most common substituting "eye" for "I," and sometimes represents self-centeredness and ego.

WHEN BOTH EYES ARE CLOSED, it often symbolizes your refusal to look at what is right in front of you, the subject of your dream or meditation.

Both eyes closed can also be telling you that you are trying to remain asleep when you need to be more alert, and to literally open your eyes.

But closed eyes can be showing you that you just need to rest more, stop being so visual, shut things out for a few hours.

WHEN BOTH EYES ARE OPEN, it frequently symbolizes either a need for further clarity, or that you are already clear on the subject of your dream or meditation, that you literally have "both eyes open." What do those open eyes see? How do you feel about it?

THE EYE OF THE HEART is an ancient symbol for the Spiritual Center.

THE EYE OF HORUS is an extremely complex symbol, representing among other things the Pole Star, Enlightenment, and the Eye of the Mind.

The Eye of Horus is often also associated with the moon, especially his left eye, picking up all the symbolism represented by the moon and the left.

THE EYE AND EYEBROW OF HORUS together symbolize tremendous power and strength, the strength and perception of the gods.

THE LEFT EYE to the ancient Egyptian symbolized the moon and Isis. In more recent times here in the West, the left symbolizes the eye of the moon, the intuitive faculties, the past, and the night. But in the Orient, this interpretation is reversed with that of the right eye.

ONE EYE is an ancient symbol for the Eye of God, the Wisdom of God, the Eye of Osiris, the Eye of Horus, and ever-expanding consciousness. Conversely, a single eye can symbolize monsters with de-

structive powers, like the Cyclops, devouring parts of your emotions with single-minded purpose.

ONE OR MORE EYES is an ancient symbol for judgment and understanding, no matter whose they are or how many there are.

PEACOCK FEATHERS are frequently called the "Windows to the Soul." See also BIRD/Peacock.

THE RIGHT EYE to the ancient Egyptians was symbolic of the sun, the Eye of Ra, and the Eye of Osiris. In more recent times here in the West, the right eye is the sun, the future, and the day. But in the Orient these interpretations are reversed.

THE THIRD EYE, most often shown in the middle of the forehead or between the eyebrows, symbolizes clairvoyant abilities in both the dream and waking worlds. This type of dream or scene in meditation often precedes your physical ability to consciously recognize and accept this talent. You will generally stop dreaming about a Third Eye when your natural ability has been consciously allowed to develop.

The Third Eye is sometimes called the flaming pearl or the shining spot, and also symbolizes unity, seeing things as a whole, transcendent wisdom, the crystallization of light, spiritual consciousness, enlightenment, and deliverance from duality.

A TRIANGLE WITH AN EYE IN ITS CENTER is an ancient symbol for the All-Seeing Eye of God.

TWO WINGED EYES symbolize the two divisions of Heaven into North and South, the sun and the moon.

FACE

Faces symbolize the outward or surface personality, the face shown to the world.

Faces also symbolize knowledge acquired either through the physical senses and life experiences or through intuition and inner learning, or by means of both. And faces symbolize the mental aspects of being.

As a universal symbol, a face is the expression of your own inner truth, your beliefs and consequent behavior — who you are always shows in your face.

Faces can also be good puns. Are you trying to put on a good face? Should you face the truth? Should you do an about face?

What expression is this face wearing? Why? When do you wear that expression?

THE FACELESS STRANGER is one of the most common universal symbols. The "faceless" or unknown stranger in your dream represents your own characteristics, characteristics with which you are not familiar — they have no clear identity yet.

Don't take these faceless people for granted. How are they dressed? What actions are they carrying out?

Why? How would your dream be different without them? Who do they remind you of? What parts of you might they be? How do you feel about each of them?

But faceless people can also be telling you that some part of you feels that it has "lost face," been humiliated in some way. Or that you yourself aren't yet secure in your own identity, not quite sure which face you should show.

MULTIPLE FACES is an ancient symbol for the different qualities, characteristics, and powers or functions of a being or deity.

Multiple faces can also, of course, be telling you that you are being two-faced, or showing a different face to different people, or even that you are confused about who you really are.

SEEING YOUR OWN FACE in a dream or meditation is frequently showing you very directly what your present character traits are, or some aspects of them. You may, of course, be seeing yourself as you wish you were, or as you may become; see also MIRROR.

SEEING THE FACE OF SOMEONE YOU KNOW in a dream or meditation is often showing you specific personality traits of that person, showing you how and why your subconscious is using them as a symbol. What is the owner of that face really like as a person? Be exceptionally detailed in your description; this is not about criticism or judgment, it's about getting to how your subconscious is using that person as a symbol.

What does this person remind you of? What part of you is like this person, or would like to be, or is afraid it will be?

FINGER
Finger sacrifices have been common since prehistoric times. And each finger has its own individual symbolism. See also Hand below.

A FINGER BY THE SIDE OF NOSE is an old symbol for keeping a secret, not telling what you see, hear, or know. Remember Santa?

THE INDEX FINGER is related to the ego and ego development, self esteem, and how you relate to the outside world.

The index finger is the finger of authority, judgment, of making a point, the one pointing to a solution represented by your dream or mediation. It can even give directions, point the way.

Consequently, the index finger represents Jupiter, Zeus, and all father gods, and is in general a phallic symbol.

THE INDEX FINGER RAISED is an old symbol for Divine Justice. A raised index finger is also often used to say non-verbally, "Wait just a minute," "I just remembered something," and of course can be showing you the number one.

THE INDEX AND RING FINGERS RAISED together, the first and fourth fingers, symbolize protection against the evil eye. But when pointed directly at someone they are a very, very big insult indeed, and can even be a curse.

THE LITTLE FINGER represents Mercury, the messenger of the gods, public speaking, communication, science, common sense in business, your mental powers, your intellect, memory, and even how diplomatic you are in expressing your thoughts.

THE MIDDLE FINGER represents Saturn, and is an ancient symbol for a strong sense of morality and responsibility. At one time, the middle finger also symbolized the Spirit and the Heavenly Mediator.

However, in its negative aspects, the middle finger represents depression, timidity, hidden agendas, and of course, when raised....

POINTING A FINGER at someone was once considered to have magical power, but today is just considered to be very bad manners.

Pointing a finger is also an act of condemnation or judgment. But in some Native American traditions, pointing a finger at someone else also means that you are pointing three back at yourself. And a pointing finger may be literally pointing you in a direction, showing you the way.

What part of you is trying to point something out to you? What does this pointing finger remind you of? What kinds of people point fingers?

FINGER RAISED IN BENEDICTION, either one, two, or three fingers, is an ancient symbol for the conferring or passing on of spiritual powers. For example, Christian ministers and various church officials raise three fingers when giving a blessing, symbolizing the blessing of the Holy Trinity.

A FINGER RAISED TO THE LIPS is a message to be silent, tone it down. This is also a symbol for a secret, for meditation, and can even a warning of some kind.

THE RING FINGER, the fourth finger, symbolizes creativity and money matters, and is the finger of success and popularity.

It is this finger which represents the sun, Apollo, and all other sun deities.

It is also of course the "marriage finger," especially when on the left hand, and does in fact connect directly to the heart.

THE THUMB is an old symbol for power and the transmission of power, just one of the reasons rings were once commonly worn by royalty on the thumb. Even today, the thumb is believed by some authorities on palmistry to be the key to the entire personality.

The thumb and the forefinger are both connected to ego development, learning to separate yourself from your culture and social system.

Thumbs are also a means of identification and are necessary to get a good grip on things.

And the thumb once represented Venus, Aphrodite, and Astarte.

A THUMB POINTED DOWN symbolizes extreme disapproval, that you have failed at something. And, of course, the Romans used it to signal death to a loser. So thumbs down almost always translates as "Not!"

A THUMB POINTED UP symbolizes good luck and good will, a signal to "go for it!," everything is now okay, YES!

TWO FINGERS RAISED together symbolize teaching or judging.

Ancient Egyptians bestowed blessings by raising two fingers, symbolizing help and strength united and the two fingers of Horus extended to Osiris to help him climb the ladder from this world to the next.

FOOT
The foot is related to the human will, how we step out into life, how we assert ourselves in our daily life and actions.

So a foot and feet often symbolize the foundation on which your body stands, and the way you get from one place to the next in daily your life; see BODY above.

A foot can also symbolize freedom of movement, humility, and a willingness to serve, depending upon the context in which you are using it.

Feet can symbolize your balance and stability, or how you feel about them at the time of the dream or meditation, and your foot is the part of your physical body most closely connected to the Earth.

Foot can also represent taking authority, responsibility, or possession of something. Do you now have your foot in the door?

Traditionally, the foot is the symbol of the lower (physical) activities during the journey and progress of the Soul.

In ancient times, the foot also symbolized the moral natural supporting the spiritual nature.

The foot was a symbol of physical actions taken by the Soul within Matter as it progressed, so feet themselves often became a kind of shorthand symbol for the Soul's progress.

Feet or a foot can also be one of many excellent puns. Are you putting your foot down, putting your best foot forward? Have you given someone a foot, only to have them take a mile? Is your foot in your mouth? What have you just stepped into?

What do the feet look like? Whose are they? What are they doing? If they could talk, what would they say? How would the context change if they changed action, if they skipped instead of walked, for instance?

THE ABSENCE OF FEET symbolizes extreme instability and insecurity and feelings that you have no base or foundation upon which to stand. How were the feet lost? How are people with no feet limited, or enhanced?

BARE FEET are old symbols of humility, trust, openness, and the freedom to be who you really are.

Bare feet are also great instant equalizers. Take off your shoes and see who you become. People in a group who remove their shoes become less inhibited and more cohesive within just a few minutes. Try it.

And, of course, this one is prime for puns. Who's barefoot and pregnant?

DEITIES WITH PEOPLE OR OBJECTS UNDER THEIR FOOT symbolizes the conquering of worldly passions, the control of the world of *maya*, illusion, and the complete mastery of the being over the object underfoot.

FOOTPRINTS are an ancient symbol for the succession of physical forms and personalities worn by the Ego during the Soul's development.

Footprints also represent a Divine presence, a visit from Spirit. And they often take on the same symbolism as the foot in its representation of the Soul's progress on its journey home.

Footprints can be showing you a blueprint to follow, that you are to walk in a particular person's footsteps or patterns of behavior. Footprints can also represent the steps you have already taken in your life or personal growth up to the time of your dream or meditation.

FOOTPRINTS GOING IN BOTH DIRECTIONS usually represent past and present or past and future, coming and going, movement back and forth.

KISSING THE FOOT is an ancient symbol for devotion to the person or deity, your willingness to bow and submit your own human ego and desires to a higher energy and purpose.

OTHER PHYSICAL FORMS REPLACING FEET is an ancient symbol that whatever the replacement is has now been incorporated into your being, is now under control, that you have adapted to the new element (e.g., a mermaid has control within the element of water and all that it symbolizes).

Replacing feet with other forms or objects can also symbolize mastery of the replacement form, or taking on the personality and characteristics of the form. And, of course, that you are now operating from a different base or foundation.

THE SOLE OF THE FOOT is an old symbol for the measurement of Time, or a particular segment or length of Time. This one would also make a great play on words, "sole" for "soul."

STAMPING YOUR FOOT is a universal symbol of frustration and rage. Or have you just smooshed something?

THE WASHING OF FEET is an ancient symbol of submission of the human ego to a higher energy, or a strong need or desire to perform a service for someone, someone you admire and respect.

Washing feet is also symbolic of a healing or cleansing of any or all of the things that feet represent to you.

WINGED FEET symbolize Spirit firmly attached to the Soul's progress through Matter, and, of course, very swift movement. Winged feet almost always belong to messengers of gods.

HAIR
Hair most often symbolizes your personal power at the time of the dream or experience, especially your spiritual power and energy as it flows from your Crown Chakra (see CHAKRA) — assuming the hair is on your head, of course.

In general, the longer, healthier, and fuller your hair, the more power you have for use at the time.

In many ancient cultures, hair was the symbol for strength and extraordinary power. Hair is also a symbol of your faith in the Divine, intuition of the Truth, and the highest qualities of the lower (physical) aspects of Mind.

What color is the hair? In what style is it being worn? What does that remind you of?

How would your dream, meditation, or life change if you changed the color and style of your hair? How is it this style same as or different from yours normally?

How healthy is it? How do you feel about it at the time?

See also COLOR of hair, and any geometric shapes into which hair may be styled or cut (a common dream symbol when you start to grow and stretch).

COMMON HAIR-RELATED SYMBOLS:

BALD: Baldness often symbolizes the Crown Chakra unadorned and no longer in need of hiding itself from you or the outside world.

Baldness also symbolizes the Initiate, one who is ready to begin in the instruction of True Reality.

If the baldness or bald spot is in a geometric pattern, the pattern will also have symbolic meaning; see GEOMETRIC SHAPE.

Baldness also symbolizes simplicity, humility, and acceptance of yourself with no pretenses or covering up being any longer necessary.

Conversely, a loss of hair can also symbolize a feeling of a loss of power. In general, the more hair you have in your dream or meditation, the stronger your energy and power at the time.

Baldness or loss of hair can also represent a feeling that no new thoughts are growing at the time, or a loss of positive thinking, which is absolutely guaranteed to cut your energy and power down.

How do you feel about the baldness in your dream? Why? What color was your hair before it disappeared? How do the other people in your dream react to the baldness? What do you think bald people are like? Why?

BEARD: Beards symbolize strength, especially masculine strength, and the Yang principle and qualities. Long beards are universal symbols for wisdom and knowledge acquired through life experience, and the power acquired through that wisdom.

How do you feel about the beard in your dream or meditation? Is it soft, or scratchy? What color is it? Why? Is it neat, or scraggly? Why? What kind of person usually grows a beard? How are beards different, and what does that mean to you?

BODY HAIR: Body hair often symbolizes a need for warmth and protection, and specifically on the part of the body showing the hair. Body hair can also represent various characteristics of your animal instinctual nature.

On what part of the body is the hair? Does it normally grow there the way you see it in your dream or meditation? Why, or why not? What does this remind you of going on in your life at the time?

How do you feel about the body hair in your dream or meditation? How healthy is this hair? Do you take any action to groom or remove it? Why, or why not? How is this different from actions you would take when awake? And what does this remind you of?

See also specific part of the body on which the hair appears and COLOR of hair.

BLACK, DULL: Dull black hair often symbolizes anxiety, fear, depression, and confusion, and can be an early warning of potential health problems caused by any or all of these unrecognized emotions.

It could also be showing you that you need to lighten up, brighten your thoughts, or even that's it's now time to get your energy and power into condition again.

BLACK, SHINY: Black shiny hair most often symbolizes the deep mysteries of the mind, the unknown, the deeply hidden secret.

Shiny hair of any color also symbolizes excellent health and great vitality.

BLOND: Blond hair often symbolizes light, spiritual thoughts, great happiness, and euphoric spiritual growth and progress. But how you feel about blonds in general will tell you how your subconscious is using this hair color.

Do blonds really have more fun? Are they all really air heads? Why, or why not? What does this remind you of?

BRAIDS: Braided hair frequently symbolizes neat and orderly patterns of thought or habit, but sometimes orderly to the point of total control.

Braids are an ancient symbol of the three-fold strength of an individual (body–mind–spirit) intertwined, a message that you have the support and strength you need at the time.

Braids make good puns, too. Are you upbraiding yourself about something? Twisting yourself up?

How do you feel about braided hair in general? What kind of person braids their hair? Why? How would you behave differently if you braided yours?

COMBING: Combing your hair often symbolizes getting your thoughts together or under control, a desire to tidy yourself up, make your thoughts more presentable to the outside world by untangling your ideas and energies.

Combing your hair also symbolizes the reasoning part of your mind. Are you having difficulty keeping your thoughts in order, are they flying away from too much static?

The comb itself was once a symbol for disentangling, and one of the emblems of Venus.

Why are you combing your hair? What will be different in your life if you comb your hair? How much electricity is your hair discharging?

CURLY: Curly hair often symbolizes unlimited, boundless, bouncy energy, your ideas and energy spiraling out, and a very, very active mind and imagination.

But curly hair can be a symbol that now is the time to straighten out your thinking, that you are feeling a little woolly-headed, all mixed up.

Is your thinking childish in connection with the subject of your dream or experience? Or do you need to be more childlike in your thinking, get back to basics?

How do you feel about curly hair? What kind of person has curly hair? And how do you feel about them? Why?

CUTTING HAIR: Cutting hair in a dream or meditation carries much of the same symbolism as baldness or hair loss. Cutting hair can be a clear and direct warning that you are in danger of cutting your power or energy.

But cutting hair can be telling you that it's definitely time for a trim. Are you being too assertive lately? Is it time to take control and shape your power for a special occasion or purpose?

Who is cutting the hair? Why? Into what style or shapes? How does it change the image of the person whose hair is being cut? How do you feel about it in the dream?

CUT INTO GEOMETRIC PATTERNS: Hair shaved or cut into any geometric pattern often symbolizes one of your special spiritual traits or patterns, a special trait represented by the specific geometric shape. See individual shapes (e.g., Rectangle, Square, Triangle, Circle, etc.) under GEOMETRIC SHAPE.

DIRTY: Dirty hair often symbolizes that it's time to clean up your thinking, or anything else hair symbolizes to you.

Dirty hair can also be telling you that you or some part of you feels that your thinking is "dirty," not acceptable, even downright shabby.

What kind of people have dirty hair? Why don't they care about their appearance — or do they?

Why is your hair dirty? How did it get that way? How will it come clean? How will your life be different when you hair (power/energy) is clean?

GRAY: Gray hair most often symbolizes maturity and the wisdom and knowledge accumulated and won through your growth and life experiences.

Conversely, gray hair can be telling you that you are losing energy through old-fashioned thinking patterns and beliefs. And it can, of course, be a symbol that you or some part of you is beginning to feel old and gray.

Do you need to let yourself have more fun, act a little more immature from time to time? How's your nutritional intake? How do you feel about gray-haired people? Why? How would the dream or meditation change if you suddenly changed the hair color?

GOLDEN: Golden hair usually symbolizes the highest aspirations of the mind in direct contact with the Divine.

Golden hair also symbolizes Divine Wisdom and Celestial Truth, a higher state of consciousness where Wisdom and Truth are clearly perceived and then correctly employed.

What shade of gold is it? Does it shine? Why, or why not?

LONG FREELY-FLOWING: Long, freely-flowing hair symbolizes freedom and extraordinary powers, especially psychic and spiritual powers and energy.

During the European Middle Ages, long, loose, flowing hair was a symbol of both the virgin and the whore, or "loose woman."

How does it feel to have long, flowing hair? How is that different from your own hair? What condition is it in? What kind of person wears this kind of hair style? Why?

LOSS OF HAIR: A loss of hair usually symbolizes a feeling of a loss of power or energy. In general, the more hair you have in your dream or meditation, the stronger your energy and power at the time, but see Bald above.

Loss of hair can also represent a feeling that no new thoughts are growing at the time, and a loss of positive thinking, which is absolutely guaranteed to cut down on your energy and power. What actions should you take to stop the loss?

RED: Red hair is a traditional symbol for extraordinary powers of

perception — in other words psychic powers.

Red hair also symbolizes the beginning of the spiritualization of Matter, and great energy and mental activity.

It can also, of course, symbolize anger, someone with a temper, a lustful nature, and any of the many uncontrolled physical human passions.

What are redheads like as people? Do you like red hair? Why, or why not?

RED, GOLDEN: Golden red hair symbolizes an extremely active mind, positive growth, and a deep permanent bonding of the spiritual with the physical. See also Golden and Red above.

SETTING HAIR IN CURLERS: Setting hair in curlers carries much of the same symbolism as combing hair, but also incorporates the symbolism of changing your style and how your image.

What will be the result gained from taking the time to set your hair? What kind of person does this on a regular basis? How do you feel about them? Why?

WHITE: White hair generally symbolizes purity, acquired wisdom, and the spiritual maturity of the sage and teacher.

HAND
Hands are the most common part of the human body to appear in symbols. Paleolithic cave paintings

are full of hands and outlines of hands.

As a symbol, hands are highly complex and ambivalent. They can hold or push away, caress or strike, carry or refuse to support. Hands are the expressive, tactile, kinesthetic parts of you. They are strong symbols of force, non-verbal communication, power, and taking action.

Hands are potent tools for self-expression, second only to the face, and used constantly not only for communicating but for creating, building, getting things done — or tearing things apart.

It is estimated that approximately only seven percent of all human communication takes place through the spoken language, and our hands certainly play a large role in the other ninety-three percent.

And, of course, hands can speak all by themselves through sign language, communicating in ways and in a language that would otherwise not be possible. Specialized hand signals were and are common among religious and other secret societies.

Hands also sometimes symbolize the strong desire to take some kind of action, to "get your hands on" something or someone, form it, use it, change it, reject it, care for it. So your symbol hands could be telling you to go ahead, it's already in your hands, or to reach for it.

In ancient cultures, the hand was a symbol of royalty and authority. And for a man to ask a woman to marry him is to "ask for her hand."

Hands can channel magical and spiritual power, bless, consecrate, heal (kings, for example, were once believed to have the power to heal with a single touch), and give pleasure or pain.

And in ancient times, any object which had been blessed was not to be touched by unblessed (unclean) hands.

Hands can also be one of several puns. Are you waiting for a handout instead of taking action? Do you need to lend a helping hand to yourself or someone else? Are you biting the hand that feeds you? Is something about to get out of hand? Will you make money hand over fist? Does one hand wash the other?

What does this hand look like? Whose is it? Does it belong to a male or female? Would you like to hold it? Why, or why note? What condition is it in? How do you feel about it? How are hands different from feet? What kind of a person would have this hand? Why?

COMMON HAND SYMBOLS:

A CLOSED HAND: A closed hand most often symbolizes secrecy, spiritual mysteries, unity, strength, or conversely anger, aggression, fear, or that some part of you is "tight fisted," ungenerous, or even ready to strike.

COVERED OR HIDDEN IN SLEEVES: Hands hidden or covered by sleeves is an old symbol for respect in the presence of royalty or authority, and acknowledgment of that authority.

EXTENDED TO YOU: A hand extended to you symbolizes that help is available if you just remember to ask for it, that you are getting a helping hand. Or is it time for you to extend a hand to someone or something else? What, if anything, is in the extended hand? Why?

WITH FINGERS SPREAD: The hand with all five fingers spread symbolizes disunity, an unwillingness to work together, and that you may be about to let something slip through your fingers. A hand with its fingers spread apart is also a common signal for "I don't know" or to show a feeling of helpless frustration.

But this symbol could be just as easily be telling you that there is nothing to hide, you're carrying no hidden weapons. How you are using it in your dream or meditation will tell you which version is most appropriate.

WITH FIVE FINGERS: The hand with all five of its fingers was used in many cultures to symbolize the five ingredients required to become a complete or civilized human being, ingredients which vary from culture to culture.

For example, in Islam these five requirements are proclaiming one's faith, prayer, pilgrimage, fasting, and generosity, while to the Chinese they are charity, courtesy, modesty, justice, and wisdom.

In other systems of belief, the five fingers represented the different aspects of their own particular cosmology; see Fingers above.

FOLDED HANDS OR RAISED: Both folded hands and hands raised palm out symbolize prayer, devotion, and pleading for the intervention of a higher power. Folded hands also represent calmness and strength through unity, especially through the unifying of opposites (the symbolic left with the right).

HANDSHAKE: A handshake is a universal symbol of sealing an agreement or bargain, and a gesture of friendship. Some authorities believe that this custom actually originated as a way of showing that no weapon was hidden in the hand.

INJURED: If the left hand, it may be telling you that you are not allowing yourself to receive whatever is represented by your dream or meditation, or anything else the left hand represents to you.

If the right hand is injured, it may be telling you that you are not giving, or releasing, as freely as you can, especially in connection with the subject of your dream or meditation, or anything else the right hand represents to you.

How did the hand get injured? Is there pain or blood? Why, or why not? What does this injury remind you of going on in your life at the time?

LEFT HAND: It is the left hand which is believed to receive energy, and the right to project it, and this may be true even if you are naturally left handed.

In the Orient, to sit on the left hand of an emperor or other authority figure is the seat of honor, except in times of war when this position is reversed. The left hand is Yin energy, and the right Yang.

Some systems of belief contend that the left hand is the hand of "black" or negative magic, while the right is "white" or positive magic, a belief giving us even today the phrase "taking the left hand path."

But in many other systems of belief, the left is the is a symbol for the passive, external incoming energy of the Soul. The left is almost always representative of the Yin (feminine) characteristics and qualities; see also LEFT.

OPEN HAND: An open hand symbolizes a friend, that there is nothing to hide, someone who comes unarmed and in peace. It is also a strong symbol of generosity.

And, of course, an open hand can symbolize someone in your life who is always expecting you to give, someone who is always asking for a handout of one kind or another. How you feel about the open hand and what action it is taking will give you your clue.

PLACING YOUR HANDS IN HANDS OF A TEACHER OR LEADER: Placing your hands or hand in the hands of another is an ancient symbol of your willingness to learn, your submission to a higher authority for the period of learning, and your acceptance of an initiatory training period. It is literally placing yourself in the hands of another, no questions asked.

Much of this same symbolism carries over to the marriage ceremony, where even today we use the phrase "giving your hand in marriage." you have literally placed yourselves in each other's hands.

RIGHT HAND: It is the right hand that is believed to project and release energy.

And in both the Middle East and the West, to sit on the right hand of a powerful person or being is the seat of honor. But in the Orient, the place of honor was the left, except in times of war where the importance of these positions was reversed.

In some systems of belief, the right hand is believed to represent "white" or positive magic, while the left represents "black" magic, thus the phrase "taking the left hand path."

The right generally represents Yang (masculine) characteristics and qualities.

RIGHT HAND WITH THREE FINGERS RAISED: The right

B

hand with three fingers raised, specifically the thumb, index, and middle fingers, symbolize the oath "As God is my witness...."; see also Fingers above.

HEAD

The head is a common symbol for that which distinguishes human beings from other life forms.

So the head most often symbolizes the mind, wisdom, control, intelligence, thought, the governing principle of a thing, and how you are interpreting life at the intellectual and thought levels. And Plato stated that the head was the image of the world.

The human head has been used symbolically for thousands of years, and almost always in some spiritual context. For example, in some esoteric systems, to "make a head" was a major spiritual achievement.

The head is the place of both wisdom and foolishness, and is the first part of the body to be both honored and dishonored.

And, of course, the Christ is the head of the Christian Church., the Church itself His body.

THE HEAD OF ANIMALS sym-

bolize the vital life force and fertility of the animal. The most common animal heads used in ancient times were the horse, boar, and ox.

For example, to the early Scandanavian peoples, the head of a boar symbolized prosperity, abundance, and fortune for the coming year; see ANIMAL.

BOWING THE HEAD is an old symbol for your willingness to subdue or lower your own life force or divinity before that of another in honor and in submission.

DECAPITATION often symbolized severing the body from the spirit and the intellect, a terrible punishment indeed. It was a common belief among ancient cultures that the head was the seat of the Soul or Spirit of any being.

In ancient Egypt, for example, the decapitated head of Set symbolized the mental elements of the desire-mind being removed, thus depriving evil of its intelligence.

The practice of decapitation has been traced back to Neolithic times.

FEMALE AND MALE HEADS JOINED together is an old symbol of the androgyne, the unification of opposites, the unifying of spiritual and earthly power. Images of kings and queens together have similar symbolic meaning.

THE FOUR HEADS OF BRAHMA are the source of the four Vedas.

HEADS ON A FOUNTAIN symbolize the power of refreshment and of speech, especially refreshment by Spirit; see also WATER/ Fountain.

THE HEAD OF HORUS ON TOP OF A POLE to the ancient Egyptians symbolized the aspiration and divinity of humanity directed at and dominate over the lower physical nature.

NODDING THE HEAD is an old symbol for pledging your life force, a gesture still used in auctions even today.

Nodding heads are also saying "yes," and of course may be simply nodding off.

HEAD ON TOP OF A PILLAR OR POLE, a popular symbol for the ancient Celts and other early cultures, was a strong phallic symbol representing fertility. But this symbol was also frequently used as a funerary emblem, symbolizing resurrection and rebirth. And, of course, much later became a symbol of shame and punishment for treason or other criminal actions.

HEAD WITH A RING IN ITS MOUTH is always a guardian of doorways, guardians of the Way.

THE HUMAN SKULL itself was often used to represent the heavens, most likely because it was used symbolically as a sphere, representing Oneness. It has this same meaning in ancient Egyptian hieroglyphics.

TWO-HEADED BEINGS are old symbols for all-seeing energies. This figure of course doubles the symbolism of the head itself.

Two-headed beings represent the beginning and the end, the natural dualities of life, the past and the future, solar and lunar powers, the choices presented at a any crossroad, the beginning and end of a journey, departure and return, opening and closing doors, destiny, judgment and discernment, cause and effect, seeing inward and seeing outward, the ability to look both ways and see both views of something, the Summer Solstice in Cancer (the door of humankind) and the Winter Solstice in Capricorn (the door of the gods).

Examples of two-headed gods or beings are Janus, the Sumerian god Marduk, and the Semitic El.

HEADS ON TOMBS AND BUILDINGS represent the life force or genius of the person or animal depicted, especially heads with wings attached. Heads with wings also symbolize supernatural forces and knowledge and the Soul.

A TRIPLE-HEADED DEITY or being symbolizes the three realms of existence; the past, present, and future; the three phases of the moon; and the rising, noon, and setting sun. Serapis, Hecate, Cerebus, and Cernunnos are often represented with three heads.

A VEILED HEAD is an old symbol of secrecy, inscrutability, hidden knowledge, and psychic knowledge and power. For example, the Oracle of Delphi was always veiled.

Heads of sacrificial victims were often veiled and decorated with garlands of flowers, most likely giving rise to our custom of veiled brides and nuns. Within this context, a veiled head is symbolic of dying to the old life prior to taking on the new.

The veil is also symbolic of protecting the inner life of the head and all that it symbolizes, as is the wearing of hats, head scarves, etc.

HEART

The heart most often symbolizes compassion, love, trust, openness, feelings, understanding, and the emotions.

In Islam, the heart is the symbol for the seat of spirituality and contemplation. In ancient Greece, the heart symbolized thought, feeling, and the will.

While in ancient Egypt, the heart symbolized the center of will, vital life energy, spiritual energy, and was the seat of the Source of All Knowledge. Ptah, the Egyptian god of creation and one of the three original great gods, first planned the universe in his heart and brought it into existence through his spoken word, the Logos.

In the Hebrew sacred texts, the heart symbolizes the inner conscience, the inner person, the truth about how you feel. And in Hinduism, the heart symbolizes the seat of Atman, the Absolute.

The ancient Aztecs believed that the sun lost its strength and vital energy as it disappeared over the horizon each day, journeying through the Underworld as skin and bones, and gaining new strength only from the blood in the hearts of ritually sacrificed victims each day. To them, the heart was the seat of the soul and of life.

Before cremation, a green jewel, usually jade, was placed in the mouth or heart of the body to ensure the person could revitalize the heart in the next world.

And in the West, beginning approximately the time of the Middle Ages, the heart was used as a symbol of romantic love and yearning, most often symbolized by an arrow piercing the heart, representing the sweet pain of love.

If you are having trouble with your heart in your dream, meditation, or waking life, it can also symbolize that you are losing energy through either too much empathy with someone, or by not having enough compassion or empathy, by not opening your heart to your own feelings. Is someone or something giving you a heartache? Do you need to take heart? To speak from your heart? Do you have a heart?

A heart can also, of course, be telling you something directly about the condition of your physical heart, but in plenty of time to see what's really going on there.

What is the shape of this heart? Is it shaped like a human heart, or like a valentine? What overall condition is it in? How does it feel? If it could speak, what would it say to you? How well do you treat it?

JAW

The jaw often symbolizes your ability to speak, your verbal eloquence. It can also symbolize your ability to chew things over, to take in information and break it into smaller parts in order to digest it more easily.

And a jaw can be a message from some part of you that you are talking too much, that you are jawing when you should be listening and digesting what you have already taken in.

Jaws also make great puns. Have you been jawing with the wrong people? Did you just get socked in the jaw by something? And, of course, just when you thought it was safe to go back....

CRUSHING JAWS often symbolize a strong feeling of being under enormous pressure, often by sources you feel are beyond your ability to control. Or are these the jaws of life, and actually saving you? What are the jaws crushing? What will be the end result?

A LOCKED JAW often symbolizes a strong desire to let out suppressed emotions by using sound (speech, singing, chanting, yelling, screaming, etc.), or that you might want to take in more information before you speak. What has locked the jaw?

KNEE

Knees often symbolize humility, strength, vitality, and the generative life force. But conversely, knees can symbolize a feeling of helplessness or slavery, of being a captive and being required to bend your knee to someone or something you don't like.

Knees are also one of the three axis points of the physical body and used symbolically in various initiation ceremonies.

And knees and the act of kneeling often have the same or similar symbolism.

Knees are good puns. Do your feelings have you on your knees? What has you weak in the knees? Are you using "kneed" for "knead" or "need?"

THE ACT OF KNEELING itself is an old symbol of moral strength, submission to the law or order of something, or personal progress by the act of restraining the lower activities (lower limbs) by slightly weakening them through an agreement to bend them to a higher will or authority.

Kneeling also represents respect and homage to a higher or superior person or idea. And it symbolizes supplication, submission, prayer, and acknowledgment of a position slightly lower or less than the object before which the person is kneeling.

To what are you kneeling? Why? How do you feel about it in your dream or meditation? Is it difficult or easy to kneel in the dream? What does it remind you of that is going on in your life?

PUTTING SOMETHING OR SOMEONE ON YOUR KNEE symbolizes recognition and acceptance of your close connection to the person or thing, usually in a parental or protective and supportive, even loving, role.

LEG

Legs of any kind usually symbolize your physical power and support. Your legs are the columns that support your body and are part of the means by which it moves through life. Not surprisingly, the symbolism of leg is usually related to that of the foot.

In Qabalism, the leg symbolizes splendor and firmness, and is associated with the symbolism of the pillar. In ancient Egypt, the leg symbolized lifting up, founding, and erecting.

In ancient times, a one-legged god or being symbolized the World Axis, or was a phallic or lunar symbol.

Legs can also be good puns. Are you being given a leg up? Should you shake a leg? Which leg of your journey are you on?

To what is this leg attached? What is it doing? How is it moving? What color is it? What type of covering does it have? Why? What kind of a person, animal, or object would normally have this kind of leg? Why? If it could talk, what would it say? How does it feel in your dream or meditation?

MOUTH

The mouth most often symbolizes verbal expression and communication, and how you are going about it at the time of your dream or experience.

Mouths are also the part of the body that take in nourishment, as well as air.

In ancient times, the mouth was considered to be the primary location which took in the breath of life. A mouth can also symbolize the power of Spirit and creativity, especially by inspiring the Soul and life. And in ancient Hindu tradition, all other gods came from the mouth of Prajapati.

Mouths are entrances to, ways in or out, and often used in legend and myth in just this way.

As an archetype, the mouth symbolizes the entrance to the Underworld, or to the inner world. It also represents the devouring aspects of The Great Mother.

And a mouth symbolizes sensual pleasures, especially if receiving food, so to close the mouth was used as a symbol for shutting down purely human desires and instincts.

There are also many symbolic connections between the mouth and the womb. In European medieval times, covering the mouth of a woman symbolized that she had died shortly after her husband and before his stone was carved.

A mouth can also be one of several puns. Are you down in the mouth? Being too mouthy about something? Does someone around have a foul mouth? Are you just giving lip service to something? How about "out of the mouths of babes?"

CLOSING THE MOUTH is an ancient symbol for closing or denying the lower (physical) human instincts and desires.

Of course, a closing mouth can be telling you just that — close your mouth!

AN OPEN MOUTH symbolizes speech, judgment, words of power, and the rise of the consciousness of the inner Self.

To the ancient Egyptians, the funeral ceremony which "opened the mouth" was symbolic of restoring life.

An open mouth can also be a symbol for another symbol, like the mouth of a river or mouth of a cave. Either way, within this context you are at the beginning of a new adventure.

And, of course, an open mouth may be telling you to open up, say what you mean.

A MOUTH SPEAKING is an old symbol for perception and consciousness, and often has the same symbolism as being reborn, to open your mouth and speak on a higher plane of existence.

Or is this mouth speaking when it should stay shut? Is somebody being too mouthy?

What is the mouth saying? In which language? Who would listen to what this mouth has to say? Why?

NECK
The neck most often symbolizes your vulnerability, your trust in the particular situation of your dream or meditation, and may be telling you about something which could be potentially dangerous to you in the long run.

The neck also symbolizes communication and perception, since the lower throat is believed to be the location of the 5th Chakra.

The 5th Chakra regulates not only speech, but your ability to hear and perceive correctly; see CHAKRA/5th.

The neck is an ancient symbol of the purification of the emotions, since it is the bridge or connection between the heart and the mind. The neck also houses the carotid arteries, sending the blood of life to the brain.

Necks make good puns. Who is sticking their neck out? Would you like to neck with someone? Is there a pain in your neck? Are you being stiff necked about something?

A NECK WITH A NECKLACE, especially a jeweled necklace, symbolizes the higher aspects of mind and the higher emotions, the bridge between your higher (spiritual) and lower (physical) natures.

The jewels themselves symbolize wisdom and the capacity to connect and bring about union with the true Self, that you are perceiving something of great value; see also WEALTH/Jewel.

What type of necklace is it? What is it made of? Who would wear it? Why? How valuable is it? See also RING.

NOSE
The nose is an old symbol for the ability to act independently and autonomously. It is an old, old symbol for free will.

Noses are also symbolic of the breath of life, a means by which the brain is able to activate the mind and give you control and better powers of discretion.

USING YOUR NOSE TO SMELL symbolizes that you are in the process of making choices or decisions, that you are "sniffing things out." What are the smells? (And remember that being aware of strong smells in your dream is often a signal that you are on some level of lucid dreaming; see Glossary/Lucid Dreams).

SKELETON

Dreaming of a skeleton is not, repeat NOT, a warning of death or dying. Remember that your dreams are symbolic.

Skeletons are ancient symbols of the emotional experience of disintegration experienced by the spiritual initiate during training. Within this context, skeletons represent the loss of your old ways of feeling, thinking, and experiencing, literally losing the weight and flesh of your former life, clearing the way to put on more appropriate flesh. Emaciated or scrawny figures carry much of this same symbolism.

For example, the alchemists used the skeleton to symbolize the purification stage of the Great Work, and the promise of resurrection and rebirth of Primal Matter, and for this reason was often colored black rather than white.

But a skeleton can just be trying to tell you that you are not in touch with your feelings, that you are only a framework or shell without substance, that you are not developing your ability to be fully human, or that you have even forgotten what it means to be a fully functioning human being.

The skeleton also symbolizes the structure upon which your physical body is built, the structure holding you together and allowing you to move through life.

Skeletons often also symbolize your personal belief framework, the structure on which your belief systems hang. Do you need to "flesh out" some of your ideas or beliefs?

In ancient times, the skeleton symbolized the moon and was associated with the gods Cronos and Saturn, and with the ancient Mayan god of death and the Underworld.

Skeletons are, of course, also symbols of human mortality, the vanity of worldly things, the inexorable passage of Time, and the transformation that comes through physical death.

Even today, skeletons are strong symbols of death and favorites in art, especially in showing us the Apocalypse and what awaits the unworthy.

STOMACH

The stomach is an ancient symbol for the appetite of the lower (physical) nature. Trouble with the stomach often tells you that you have taken in errors or illusions somewhere along the line and have not taken the time and energy to ingest true wisdom and knowledge.

The stomach is the area of your "animal wisdom," your physical intuition and hunches. It is the general clearing house for all personal power issues, which probably tells you everything you need to know about it.

The stomach is directly associated with the 3rd Chakra, the Solar Plexus or Spleen Chakra, which is believed to help control the spleen and gall bladder, as well as the physical stomach.

A malfunction in this Chakra is believed to result in stomach cramps, ulcers, heartburn, diabetes, and even cancer which began due to the repression of your natural assertive and very human feelings or reactions, feelings which have been misdirected, suppressed, and turned inward.

The 3rd Chakra is also associated with feelings of grief, depression, and the inability to relieve distress for one reason or another; see also CHAKRA/3rd.

Stomachs also represent a wish or need to control your many appetites. Stomachs are the places of assimilation of many different tastes and textures.

The stomach houses our feeling natures, our sensitivity, intuition, your gut feelings. It is the place where we instantly *know*, whether that knowing is rational or not. The stomach automatically, strongly, and instantly reacts to stress, shock, fear, anger, and excitement.

And in ancient esoteric systems of belief, it was through the stomach area that we left and re-entered the physical body during out-of-body travels.

The stomach also makes a great pun. What can't you stomach? Why?

TEETH

Teeth are ancient symbols of strength, physical virility and vitality, aggressive behavior and feelings, power, and competence or capacity for either attack or defense. Teeth can also symbolize how you feel about your sexuality at the time.

Primitive peoples all over the world adorned themselves with the teeth and claws of animals, symbolizing both their mastery of the qualities of the animal and their control of those qualities. It was also a common ancient belief that the teeth and bones of animals and human beings retained some of the essence of the being. For example, in many myths and legends armed warriors were grown from the lost teeth of a dragon.

And teeth frequently symbolize that you are beginning to come to a better understanding of the subject of your dream, meditation, or experience, depending upon the condition of the teeth and what actions they are taking.

Teeth are used to cut things into smaller pieces so they can be easily swallowed and digested. And so teeth frequently represent your wish or need to think things over, to discuss something, literally chew it over before swallowing, a message not to swallow it whole.

Dreaming of teeth can also be giving you direct health information about the current condition of your teeth. What condition are they in? When was the last time you visited your dentist?

Teeth can also be a good pun or play on words. Who is dressed to the teeth? Is someone or something very "toothsome?" What would you like to sink your teeth into? Do you love someone so much that you could just gobble them up?

To whom or what do these teeth belong? What are they doing? How do you feel about teeth in general? What color are they? If they could talk, what would they say about themselves and their function in your dream? Who or what would normally have these teeth?

BARING YOUR TEETH at someone or something symbolizes strength, determination, strong defensive action by warning, and aggressiveness, and can obviously be a clear warning not to get any closer to the subject of your dream or meditation.

And baring your teeth could be a good example of a symbol within a symbol, telling you that you are ready to come clean about what teeth represent to you, or what these particular teeth are doing.

BRACES are probably telling you that you are taking the appropriate discipline and action on some level to make sure you are straight with yourself and what teeth mean to you. Wearing braces can also symbolize a desire or need to restrict your speech or the way you speak, a possibility that you may

want to "straighten up" the way you break down information, even change or improve your image.

Have you ever worn braces? How did you feel about it? If you have never worn them, how would your life be different if you had or did?

CROOKED TEETH often symbolize a subconscious intention to deceive, maybe an intention that has by now even become a habit with you or the object in your dream or meditation.

But crooked teeth could also be a message to get straight about the subject of your dream or experience, that it's a little off-center or in the wrong position right now.

How do you feel about the crooked teeth? What made them crooked? What does that remind you of? What will it take to straighten them? Why do people have crooked teeth?

DECAYED OR DECAYING teeth are usually messages from some part of yourself to clean up your ideas and words, that you have been ingesting to much "unsuitable" things or even empty (but maybe sweet) ideas and illusions instead of solid healthier information or experiences.

Decayed or damaged teeth in a dream or meditation can also be an early warning about the state of your own teeth. When was the last time you had a checkup?

What kind of person has bad teeth? Why? What does this remind you of at the time? What causes teeth to decay? What does this remind you of going on in your life at the time?

A TOOTH EXTRACTION often represent the removal of useless or too long neglected ideas, beliefs, or nutritional intake. Which tooth was pulled? Why? Surely not your wisdom tooth?

FANGS: Fangs are ancient symbols of Divine Will, and the Power of the Word, the Logos. Fangs were called the Sword of the Spirit, while tusks and horns were symbols of spiritual power used in overcoming evil and ignorance.

GRINDING TEETH are strong symbols of stress, frustration, and sometimes anger. But in ancient China, it was a common belief that the gnashing or grinding of teeth kept ghosts away.

LOOSE TEETH can represent loose thinking, carelessness in the breaking down or assimilation of something going on in your life at the time. Or that you are not paying enough attention to yourself in the area represented by the loose tooth.

Loose teeth can also be telling you to go to your dentist, of course.

What caused the teeth to become loose? What will be the ultimate result?

LOSING TEETH is one of the most common dream symbols. To lose a tooth or teeth in a dream most often symbolizes a feeling that you are losing personal power to act in a particular situation, or that you are failing at something in your life.

Losing teeth can also symbolize that you are inhibiting yourself by not using your natural capacities, that you are losing your strength or anything else symbolized by this particular lost tooth.

Losing teeth can also symbolize that some part of you feels it is losing control of your words, that you are speaking without thinking it through, even that you are in danger of getting involved in meaningless chatter, again, depending upon where the tooth is and what it is normally used for.

And the ancient Chinese believed that dreaming of losing a tooth symbolized that you would soon lose a parent — which shows you how important teeth were to them.

ORAL SURGERY symbolizes a learned skill or discipline which can now be used to correct a serious fault that has been allowed to continue for too long for it to be corrected in any other way.

How did the surgery go? How did you feel? Why? What would have prevented its necessity? What does this remind you of?

THIGH
The thigh is most often a symbol of creative power, strength, and procreation. The thigh is a phallic symbol in many cultures.

For example, Dionysos was born from the thigh of Zeus, symbolizing that Dionysos was born with and from the creative strength and power of his father.

A SKULL AND CROSSED THIGH BONES symbolize the two vital sources of power, the head and the loins, of the person after death.

This symbol was once believed to possess strong magical powers and capable of drawing away the life force, giving it its current symbolism of death and poison, and most probably why it was adopted by pirates.

THROAT
The throat often symbolizes verbal expression, but it can also represent your ability to hear clearly and perceive correctly; see CHAKRA/5th.

Dreaming of any problems with your throat can also be a direct early health message, but all of the above symbolism can also apply, and even be the means by which you correct the impending health problem.

This one can also be a good pun. Does someone have you by the throat? What part of you would like to rip out your throat? Why? See also Neck above.

BEING CHOKED or strangled in a dream or meditation can be telling you that you need to verbally express the subject of the dream *immediately* before your internal imbalances become life threatening to you or some part of you.

Being choked or strangled could also be purely an early health warning that you have something unsavory trying to get you down; see ATTACK.

This is also a very good candidate for a pun. Whom would you like to strangle? Does someone or something have a choke-hold on you?

Who is choking whom? Why? What will happen if they don't stop? What would it take to make them stop?

LARYNGITIS has much of the same symbolism as being choked or strangled, but at a slightly milder level. Laryngitis almost always is telling you that some part of you wants to speak up and be heard, shout it out.

Conversely, laryngitis could be telling you to be quiet, to soften your words, even to stifle it. The context in which you are using this symbol will tell you which one applies to this particular situation.

A SORE THROAT may be a message from some part of you to communicate more clearly, or to take time to heal your 5th Chakra. Or is your perception not functioning properly?

A sore throat can obviously also be an early health warning that you are about to come down with a sore throat, so take evasive action.

Another potential pun, what are you "sore" about? What can't you do because of the sore throat?

A THROAT WOUND may be a message that you are losing energy through the 5th Chakra; see CHAKRA/5th.

How did the wound happen? Are you bleeding? Is there pain? What kind of weapon caused the wound? Is it life threatening? What does it make you think of?

THE THROAT CHAKRA, the 5th, is at the base of your throat. It is the one through which you not only speak your personal truth, but through which you hear and perceive. It is in fact often referred to as the Third Ear.

Dreaming specifically of the lower portion of your throat is almost always a message to pay closer attention to your life and what is going on in it at the time of your dream, to listen up, check your perception of the subject of the dream; see also CHAKRA/5th.

TONGUE
The tongue is a symbol for language and the expression of Truth, the active manifestation of the Logos on the many material planes of existence.

The tongue has almost always symbolized the Voice of God, and manifestations of any powerful voice.

And the tongue symbolizes preaching and teaching, and is often a substitute for the serpent or snake as a phallic symbol. Tongues are also often substituted for swords.

In ancient China, the tongue was associated with antlers as containing supernatural and magical powers. For instance, the Buddha was said to have an especially long tongue.

To the early Greeks, the tongue at first symbolized the Divine Word, and later changed to a symbol of fear and malevolence with the Gorgon. To the ancient Hindus, Agni's and Kali's tongues "touch the Heaven."

The ancient Egyptians believed that the Great God Ptah created the Universe by using his heart and tongue, thereby creating reason and language at the same time, and the god Bes (connected with healing) was often shown with a protruding tongue.

The early Christians believed that the tongue of an Angel contained the Angel's power. Early Christians also used the tongue as a symbol for martyred saints, whose tongues were often cut out before execution.

A FLESHY or FAT TONGUE is an old symbol for the negative, lower human instincts and emotions, and a strong tendency toward excessive sensuality.

STICKING OUT THE TONGUE: Sticking out the tongue is an old symbol for moving from darkness to the light, especially in the East. However, here in the West it is mostly just a symbol of disrespect.

A TONGUE PROTRUDING FROM AN ANIMAL symbolizes a prayer or plea for rain or water, the animals themselves often symbolizing the Life Force, vitality, fertility, and renewal. This is a common symbol on older statues and artwork.

WRIST

The wrist most often symbolizes flexibility, especially flexibility as it supports and connects to the symbolism of the hand; see Hand above.

This one is also a good pun. Have you just gotten a slap on the wrist? Is the action all in the wrist?

BOOK

Books most often symbolize information, knowledge, and wisdom that has been accumulated from many sources and experiences.

So dreaming of books often represents an important lesson or piece of information, or that you want to look for more knowledge or information.

Books also symbolize the Totality of the Universe, a unity composed of many individual letters, pages, and chapters. They symbolize the Ideal which contains all of the Laws of Divine Intelligence.

Books can also represent the knowledge, opinions, and experiences of others.

If you dream of books often, you can use them as a test to see if you are in a lucid dream (see Glossary/Lucid Dream). Find a book in your dream, read from it, turn away, and then turn back and read from the book again. If the text stays the same, you may be out-of-body; if you can make the text change, you are probably lucid, or "awake" in your dream.

What type of book is it? Who would write it? Who would pay money to own it? What kind of a cover does it have? Why?

Where is it located? Who wrote it? Who would want to read it? Why? What is its title? How will you change after you have absorbed its contents?

BOY

A boy frequently symbolizes the Yang (male) principle and qualities of your personality, qualities which are still in a young, growing and adventurous stage, whether you are male or female.

Boy (and girl) also symbolize the human mind in an early stage of development, a young mind, a mind still forming, and mental knowledge still being acquired through actual experience.

A boy can also represent you as a child at the age of the boy in your dream or meditation, again whether you are male or female.

Boy can also be a message that some part of you feels you are acting immaturely or childishly.

Conversely, your dream boy can be telling you that you need to become more childlike, play and explore more, take chances, use your imagination.

What is the boy doing? What does he look like? Does he remind you of anyone? Who are his parents? Where does he live? What does he like to do for fun? How is a boy different from a man? How do young boys generally behave differently from young girls? Why? How do you feel about young boys in general? See also GIRL, MAN.

BRIDE, BRIDEGROOM

Marriage is an ancient symbol of the union of Yin and Yang (male and female qualities), the merging of body with spirit, the Higher Self with the Lower Self, the physical with the non-physical, the passive with the assertive, mind with emotions, wisdom with love, creation with action.

Within this context, to be a BRIDE is to bring the feminine qualities into this merger; to be a BRIDEGROOM is to bring the masculine qualities into it.

Dreaming of either a bride or bridegroom can also symbolize the beginning of a new life, one with a better balance and sense of responsibility, a marriage between your mind and your emotions.

After a bride and groom have fulfilled the requirement of the wedding ceremony, they will be a third entity, the relationship or marriage itself. What does this remind you of going on in your life?

How do the bride and bridegroom feel? How are they dressed? What type of ceremony will they participate in? What kind of person enjoys being a bride or bridegroom? How do you feel about it? See also CEREMONY/Wedding; FAMILY/Husband, Wife; and MARRIAGE.

BRIDGE

Bridges almost always symbolize transitions of one kind or another; crossing from one place, level or stage to another; overcoming any natural obstacle; and a unity through connecting to something else. Bridges link things that are otherwise separated by chasms and obstacles or difficulties, things that otherwise might be inaccessible.

All bridges have to be crossed to move in the direction of or across the object the bridge spans. Bridges also symbolize a connection with or a safe and easy way over the subject of your dream or meditation.

Because of their deep archetypical meaning, in ancient cultures newly constructed bridges required special sacrifices. Bridges were also often tests mythic heroes had to cross in order to win their next symbolic prize.

In many tales and legends, the bridge to the next world is exceptionally narrow, and sinners will never be able to make it safely across. It was common for a special divinity or mythical being to guard bridges, again keeping the unworthy or impure of heart from crossing.

A bridge can also be a great pun. What is bridging the gap? What are you bridging over? Are you about to burn your bridges? Do you like to play bridge?

What kind of a bridge is this one? What is it made of? Who built it? For what purpose? How well is it fulfilling that purpose?

What is its overall condition? How do you feel about crossing the bridge? What will change once its been crossed? What type of vehicle is normally used to cross it? Why?

Where would you be most likely to find this bridge? Why? What kind of people would normally use it, and for what reasons? Does this remind you of anything going on in your life? See also CANYON, DOOR, WATER, and any other object spanned by the bridge.

THE BRIDGE OF HEAVEN is a worldwide symbol for the mediator between the Higher Mental Plane and the Buddhic or Heavenly Plane.

Rainbows and the Milky Way are often used as symbolic bridges of this type; see also WEATHER/ Rainbow.

And in the mineral world, the Opal is the Bridge of Heaven stone.

THE HIGHER SELF AS A BRIDGE is often symbolic of the connection between the personality and its Soul.

BUILDING

Buildings are almost always symbols of your personality and/or your physical body, and usually represent the various states of consciousness and awareness you inhabit at the time.

Buildings are manmade constructions, symbolizing the framework of your beliefs, your attitudes, how you are thinking at the time of the dream or event, and your

opinions caused by your beliefs. The type of building and where you are in the building will tell you how your subconscious is using this common symbol.

Remember that everything in your dream and meditation is a symbol and that nothing, absolutely nothing, is there just to fill in the picture. If you dream that your building has four walls and a roof, it is not just because most buildings you have experienced have these things. How are the walls and roof different from those you have experienced before?

What size is the building? Of what type of material is it constructed? How safe do you feel in it in your dream? Why? What is this building being used for? Is this the same as its normal use?

Who would own it? What kind of people would work or live there? Why? Where is it located? What type of furnishings does it have? How light or dark is it? How do you feel about it in your dream? How do you feel about it after you wake up? Would you like to go there when you are awake? Why, or why not? And, of course, what does this particular building remind you of that is going on in your life at the time?

BUILDING-RELATED SYMBOLS

APARTMENT
An apartment or apartment house frequently symbolizes a temporary state of mind, that you may be checking out your options before you take up permanent residence

in the subject of your dream or meditation. Apartment buildings can also represent the many different ideas and beliefs coming and going in your life at the time.

ATTIC
Attics often symbolize your higher mental qualities, your intellect, higher consciousness, your present spiritual perception or level, and both or either the 6th and 7th Chakras; see CHAKRA/6th, 7th.

Attics also represent your superconscious and the highest level you are on in your dream at the time.

Attics are also good puns. Do you have toys in your attic, bats in your belfry? What have you shut away in your attic that is forgotten, neglected and gathering dust? Is it stuffed with undiscovered treasures, or old discardable junk?

How do you feel about attics in general? How do you feel while you are in this particular attic? What do most people store in attics? What condition is yours in? Why? What does this remind you of? What kind of a person would store things in this attic?

BANK
A bank often symbolizes the Collective Unconscious, the sum total of human resources and knowledge at the time of your dream, meditation, or experience.

A bank also represents your own personal resources, your spiritual bank account at the time. Banks remind you that you have the right to withdraw any amount from your account at any time, up to the

amount you have socked away, of course.

Some accounts also earn interest on the original amounts deposited, a good reminder that you don't have to earn everything yourself and that your accounts draw interest, and remind you that you can draw from what you have earned in the past or from any past or parallel lives.

Or is your bank telling you that you are hoarding any of these things instead of spreading them around?

A bank also makes a good pun. What are you banking on? Have you just cut into your principle or ethical principals?

What type of a building is the bank? What kinds of people would want to work there? Who would own this bank? Is it open or closed? What kind of person would trust your bank with their assets? Why?

How do you feel about banks in general? What kind of valuables does a bank normally protect? Are you making a deposit, or withdrawal? Why?

See also WEALTH, and any objects in the bank.

BAR
This symbol often represents your search for strength from outside yourself, a strong desire or need for companionship and acceptance, a shot of courage and support from others or from some stimulant outside your usual environment.

Bars also represent a need or wish to relax, have some fun,

loosen up, get a little crazy once in awhile. Or are you ready to meet new people?

A bar scene can also, however, symbolize the beginning of a transformation of almost any kind; see ALCOHOL.

What type of bar is it? What kind of things go on there? What kind of people would frequent this bar? Why that bar and not some other?

How is this bar different from any bars you have been in when awake, or asleep? What kind of music is playing? What kind of beverages are served? What is the lighting? How is it decorated? How are the other people in the bar dressed?

How do you feel about bars and the people who frequent them in general? Why?

[NOTE: Remember that the sleeping brain believes everything it sees happening, so if you know someone who is working with an alcohol addiction, reassure them that dreaming of drinking is the next best thing to actually doing it, but without penalty or guilt. In short, this would be a good sign, not a bad one. Since the brain believes it has already had its alcoholic fix, they can just get on with their lives. It does not necessarily mean that they are in danger of going back into old behavior patterns. The same thing applies to any type of addictive behavior. Dreaming of it can be an excellent and very effective release of any built-up cravings.]

BARN

A barn frequently symbolizes your lower (translate that as "more physical") levels of consciousness, depending on what is kept in the barn and how you feel about it at the time.

Barns also make great puns. Who or what is as big as a barn? Is your barn door open? Are you trying to lock a barn door after its inner contents are already gone? What does this remind you of? Why?

What is housed in this particular barn? What activities are going on there? What is it made of? Who owns it? What condition is it in? See also FARM.

BATHROOM

When you begin to get serious about finding out who you are and why you are here, you will most likely find yourself dreaming more and more bathroom dreams, including some pretty graphic elimination scenes. Record them all and watch how they change as you change, because they most certainly do.

Bathrooms almost always symbolize a strong desire to cleanse and purify some part of yourself, or that it is now time to start this process.

A bathroom can also symbolize a desire to freshen up or change your image, change your clothes (i.e., the roles you play), get yourself together for public presentation.

Bathrooms also symbolize a need to be alone, a place to go where others do not usually interrupt or bother you (unless you're a mother, of course).

What actions are going on in your bathroom? Are you taking a bath or shower, grooming yourself, changing clothes, cleaning the room, using the toilet?

What are bathrooms generally used for? How do you feel about that? How is this bathroom different from other bathrooms? How do you feel in it? Are there others in there with you? Are they paying any attention to you? Who are they, and why are they there? How do you feel about that? See also WATER/Bath, Toilet below, and any objects in the bathroom.

BASEMENT

A basement or cellar often symbolizes you are, or want to be, working with your subconscious or "underground" feelings and emotions.

Basements also symbolize your sexual feelings and relate to the 1st and 2nd Chakras, and all they each represent; see CHAKRA/1st, 2nd.

Cellars and basements also symbolize the hidden treasures of the True Self, self-knowledge, or even your dark mysterious drives or knowledge. Within this context, they share some of the symbolism of the cave; see CONTAINER/Cave.

What type of lighting do you have in your basement or cellar? Why? What is kept there? How

does it feel to be there in your dream or experience?

What kind of a building would normally have this type of basement? Is it clean, dirty, cluttered? Why? See also UNDERGROUND and any objects in the basement.

BEDROOM

A bedroom often symbolizes rest, physical renewal, dreams, the subconscious in dreams, sexual satisfaction or frustration and any other sexual feelings, the night, and/or withdrawal from the symbolism of the other rooms in your dream house and what they each symbolize to you. How is a bedroom, for instance, different from a library? Why?

How is this bedroom different from most bedrooms with which you are familiar? Who sleeps there? How comfortable are you in this bedroom? What does the room itself remind you of going on in your life at the time?

CEILING

Ceilings often symbolize the upper limits you have placed on yourself at the time of the dream or experience.

But ceilings also symbolize protection, especially from the natural elements, the unknown, or anything that could fall on you suddenly from above.

How is this ceiling decorated? How solid is it? What color is it? What kind of a room would have a ceiling like this? Why? How is it different from, or the same as, ceilings you are most familiar with? Why?

CHURCH

A church, cathedral, or temple most often represents your strong yearning or desire to connect more intimately and directly to a power and a consciousness or belief system higher and more supportive than the one you have at the time.

They each, of course, also represent a desire to re-connect to what the image represents to you personally. The original meaning of the word religion, *religio*, is *to link back to*.

As an archetype, a church, cathedral, and temple symbolize the Inner Mind as it spiritually takes physical form within Matter.

Many cathedrals, temples, and churches are constructed over high energy power points. Does this remind you of anything?

Churches are also places of peace and calm, and were once sanctuaries for the persecuted, a safe haven open to everyone, no matter what the crime or infraction of the rules of society.

Dreaming of a church can also be a message that it is now time to stop relying so much on past beliefs or supports and the forms of spirituality which were perfectly appropriate to a past time in your life, but which you may have now grown beyond.

Conversely, this could be a strong message to link back to your spiritual beliefs, get back in the congregation.

And churches can also be a symbol that you are paying too much attention to the outward forms of religion and spirituality, and not enough to their inner essence, that your ideas about religion or spirituality are too structured and rigid, or in danger of becoming so.

How you feel about the church in your dream or meditation will lead you to which interpretation works for you at the time.

What does the church, cathedral, or temple look like? Why? How is it the same as or different from ones you go to or remember going to?

What kind of people would regularly go there? For what purposes? What kinds of priests, priestesses, ministers, and teachers would be connected to it? What sort of ceremonies are performed there?

How do you feel about these structures in general? Why? What would this church be used for when it is not being used for religious or spiritual purposes?

What sacred objects are in the church? What is it made of? What kind of lighting does it have? What does it smell like? Why?

See also CEREMONY, if one is taking place, and any objects in the church.

CLOSET

Closets are small very specialized rooms where you store all kinds of things, your stuff. What is in the closet? Why those things, and not others?

This one makes a wonderful pun. Would you like to be closeted with someone or something? Have you just put someone or something back on the shelf, or on a back shelf? What is coming out of your closet?

How do you feel about closets in general? Is this closet messy, or organized? Why? Which room is it in? Why? How would what it holds be different in a different room? See also any objects in the closet.

DINING ROOM

A dining room symbolizes companionship and social interaction with others, being entertained while at the same time being nourished, and formal or business relationships (depending upon the style of the dining room and the type of dining going on).

What kind of person would like this dining room? Why? Who is there? What is being served? What type of dining is this room normally used for? How is that the same as, or different from, what is going on in your dream or experience? Do you like dining rooms? Why, or why not?

DOOR

The symbolism of door is similar to that of bridge in that it both provides a method of transition and an access from one place to another.

In general, doors and windows both symbolize your current view of life or of a particular situation or relationship represented by the dream or meditation, and your choices or opinions available at the time.

Doors represent an opportunity, desire, or need for new discoveries, new knowledge, new approaches, new ways to look at things, new ways to enter or leave a the situation represented by the dream.

Doors can also symbolize the future or the past, and the different choices you have available at the time. Are you coming, or going?

Conversely, doors can symbolize a limited viewpoint or access, your unwillingness or inability to see or get into the total picture or more of the environment around you.

As an archetype, doors are entryways and gates, and most often symbolize the entrance to the Mind which enables Consciousness to perceive other dimensions of reality. They represent your Higher Mind or Higher Self's potential to enter and exit. What style of door is it?

What kind of a door is your door? What kind of a building would have such a door? Why? What color is it? What is it made of? How does it open? Does it lock? Why, or why not?

How are doors different from windows? What is on each side of your door? What will change when you walk through it? What would happen if you locked it forever or never moved through it? How do you feel about that? Why?

A CLOSED DOOR frequently symbolizes secret or hidden things, a barrier or prohibition, frustra-

B

tion, or feelings of futility and ineffectiveness, that some part of you may be feeling that this particular door is closed to you.

A closed door can also be showing you the completion of the subject of your dream or meditation, that it's finally finished and you've now closed the door on it.

What kind of door is it? What is it made of, what color is it? Why is the door closed? What is on the other side? What does this remind you of? Why? How would the dream change if the door suddenly opened?

A NARROW DOOR or doorway is an ancient symbol for the Higher Mind or Higher Self as the main entrance to any of the Higher Planes of Existence; see also Gate.

AN OPEN DOOR almost always symbolizes an opportunity that is right in front of you, or a challenge, even an "open secret" and that you now have access to the secret if you use this door.

ELEVATOR

Elevators generally represent smooth, rapid movement or change, usually through little effort of your own part. All you have to do is punch the right buttons and not get caught in the automatic doors.

Elevators also represent choices and desires, a way to escape quickly to other levels of doing and being.

But an elevator's movement is restricted to up and down; it cannot make lateral moves or move outside its own narrow pathway. Does this remind you of anything going on in your life at the time?

What type of elevator are you in? Is it an express elevator, a freight elevator? How fast does it move? How many floors does it stop at? Where will it take you? How many people are in the elevator with you?

What kind of building would have an elevator like this one? Who would habitually use it? Does it remind you of any elevators you use when you are awake?

See also NUMBER of floor, CONTAINER, DIRECTION/Up, Down.

FAUCET

Faucets frequently symbolize the ability to turn your emotions off and on anytime you feel like it.

Faucets and plumbing are also symbols for parts of your physical body, and can be a clear early health signal. What is going on with your faucet? Why?

Where is this faucet? What is the temperature and quality of the water coming out of it? Is the faucet turned on or off? Is it a new designer faucet, or an old one?

See also Plumbing below, WATER, and any object supporting faucet or coming out of it.

A LEAKY FAUCET often symbolizes that you may be or are in danger of losing energy through lack of control of your emotional life. A leaky faucet is also a great pun: is there a drip in your life? Is the slow, steady drop-by-drop impact of something making you nuts? (Remember the old Chinese water torture)?

FOUNDATION

A building's foundation most often symbolizes your support system, the foundation on which your life is built at the time.

A foundation can also symbolize your core or foundational beliefs, the structure upon which your emotions, thoughts, and actions develop and from which they take strength and form.

What is this foundation made of? What does it support? What kind of a building would have this kind of foundation? What sort of person would construct it? Is it solid, or done as cheaply as possible? How long will it last?

See also BODY/Foot, NUMBER/4, GEOMETRIC SHAPE/Square, Rectangle, etc.

FLOOR

Floors are specialized foundations, places allowing you to stand safely, and usually in well-balanced positions. So floors most often symbolize the ground you are standing on, in other words your principles and beliefs.

And the different floors of a building frequently represent the level of consciousness you are on in your dream or meditation.

Floors are great puns. Is your floor falling out from under you?

Who or what is now taking the floor? Has something just floored you?

Which floor are you on? What covers it? Why? What kind of building would have this type of floor? What does this remind you of?

A FLOOR FALLING APART is most often a symbol that your old beliefs, ideas, and life are in the process of changing dramatically, and that you are feeling understandably insecure about the whole thing at the time.

What kind of building is the floor in? What is it made of? What condition is it in, other than falling away? What does it remind you of?

THE GROUND FLOOR of any building almost always symbolizes your day-to-day life, actions, and beliefs.

It can also represent a wish to, or fear of, walking up to the next level of growth or consciousness, especially if you are almost always on the ground or first floor of the buildings in your dreams and meditations, or the upper floors are usually shadowy or even scary.

What activities are carried out on this ground floor? How do you feel when you are there? How do you feel about going to the next floor, and the next? And while we're at it, what's the difference to you between the ground floor and the main floor?

Another good pun, are you about to get in on the ground

floor? Or have you just been grounded?

THE MAIN FLOOR of any building is generally a clear message that you are in the main subject of your dream or meditation, and the primary or main level of consciousness you are on at the time.

How do you know it is the main floor? How is the main floor different from the second floor? What is on the main floor? How do you feel about being there? Why?

AN UNFINISHED FLOOR is generally telling you that the new ideas or life style you are constructing at the time are not quite solid or completed yet, and that some part of you is feeling just a little uneasy about it, needs to watch where it puts its weight and where it steps next.

A floor which has been stripped of its carpeting or paint most often symbolizes the process of doing away with old ideas and beliefs so that brand new ones can be laid down.

GARAGE

Garages are extensions of a house or other building built especially for the purpose of protecting and parking your vehicle; see VEHICLE.

Garages also symbolize a place to store or even hide your junk, some of the parts of you that you don't use very often or on any regular basis.

What is in the garage? Who would use it? For what purposes?

What kind of a building is it attached to? Why? How is it the same as, or different from, most of the garages you are familiar with? Why? How are the things stored in the garage different from the things stored in a basement?

See also, JUNK, VEHICLE, and any objects in the garage.

GATE

Gates are ancient symbols for access points between the worlds or dimensions. Gates are often guarded by fierce and terrifying monsters which must be defeated or pacified before passing through the gate.

What is on the other side of this particular gate? What is it made of? Is it guarded? Why, or why not? Who built it?

HALLWAY

Hallways are almost always symbols of pathways or passages to or through the subject of your dream or experience. What is at the end of the hallway? What does it allow access to?

They can also, however, be strong sexual symbols, representing the vaginal canal.

Where is the hallway? What is at either end? What actions are being carried out there? What type of building is it a part of? How would things be different without the hallway? See also ALLEY.

HOTEL

Hotels can symbolize your multiple personality traits and talents, and your choices in accessing them —

especially the parts of you that come and go or travel a lot.

Hotels also symbolize looking for a place where you can at least temporarily have little or no personal responsibilities, that its time to rest or take a vacation from your everyday life and let someone cater to you for a change, even if you have to pay for it.

Hotels can also be a message that you are in danger of becoming too impersonal in your interactions with others.

How do you feel about the other people in a hotel when you stay in one? Does this remind you of anything?

A hotel can also symbolize that you are in the process of moving or are or about to go on a journey and need a temporary place to stay. They are good reminders that you are just passing through, that you only came here to visit and experience, not to take up permanent residence.

How are hotels different from other buildings? Who is staying in the hotel? What kind of hotel is it? How much would it cost to stay there?

How do you feel about hotels in general? Why? What actions are taking place in it? What part of the hotel are you in, which floor?

What kind of people would pay to stay in this hotel? What kind of people would choose to work there? Who would want to own it?

HOUSE

A house most often symbolizes the Self and/or your physical body.

Houses are also symbols of Cosmic Order and the entire Cosmos with its many rooms and roles.

What style of architecture is the house? What does this remind you of? Why? What overall condition is the house in? Have you ever lived in a house like it? When? At what age? What was going on in your life at that time that had an emotional impact on you?

What kind of a person would like this house? What kind of a person would avoid it? Why?

INSIDE

When you are inside any building, you are often dealing with your internal feelings, thoughts, beliefs, and processes. Or it could be a message that you are inside the situation, a part of it, that you are not just on the outside looking in.

How do you feel when you are inside of a building? How is it different from the way you feel when outside? Why? What does this remind you of?

KITCHEN

Kitchens frequently symbolize transformations of some kind, often strong psychological ones. Kitchens, for instance, are often thought of as the heart of the home.

They can also symbolize your physical survival through proper sustenance, preparation of your "food," the nutrition that gets you through your day or life.

And, of course, kitchens eventually must be cleaned up. Does this remind you of anything?

What is happening in this kitchen? What do you use your own kitchen for when you are awake? How do you feel about that? What kind of equipment is in this one? Why? What kind of a person would like the kitchen? Who would avoid it? Why?

LIBRARY

A library most often symbolizes knowledge and information which has been accumulated over many years and from many cultures. Information held by libraries is easily accessible and retrievable by anyone willing to take the time and effort to do so.

A library can also symbolize your intellect or mind and a desire to learn more in depth, to explore consciousness, to dig deep and hit the books again.

What are you doing in the library? What section are you in? How do you feel inside it? Why?

How do you feel about libraries in general? What kind of a person would use your dream library? Why? What books are kept there? What kind of a building is it or what kind of a building is it in? Who owns it? Who would work in this library? Where is it located? See also BOOK and any objects in the library.

LIVING ROOM

A living room most often symbolizes your normal social interactions, entertainment or relaxation of some kind, and the comfort and safety to be yourself.

A living room is the place where you live, the place where you often publicly relate to your friends and family, or where you can comfortably sprawl in your favorite sweats.

What kind of furniture is in this particular living room? Who is there? Why? What interactions are going on? How is this the same as or different from what usually goes on in your living room? Does this remind you of anything?

MANSION

Mansions symbolize the tremendous potential available to you from within yourself at the time of the dream or experience. They show you how unlimited you are and to set your goals and thoughts high.

Mansions can also symbolize that you now are ready to expand on many, many levels, to move into new quarters, and upgrade your way of living and being, to take possession of your potential and birthright.

What type of a mansion is it? How many rooms does it have? How is it furnished? Who owns it? Which floor are you on? Which room are you in? Why? What are you doing while you are there?

Who would have the responsibility for caring for this mansion? How is this mansion different from your present living space? How do you feel about the mansion in your dream or experience? Why? What does this remind you of? What kinds of people normally live in mansions? How is that the same as, or different from, you? How do you feel about that?

OUTSIDE

When you are outside a building, you are often dealing with external influences and beliefs, beliefs or things imposed upon you by your culture or family and friends. Being outside can also be telling you that some part of you feels the subject of your dream or experience is beyond your control, outside your field of influence.

And, of course, being outside can show you deep unrecognized feelings of being an outsider.

PATIO

Patios symbolize relaxation, entertaining just for fun. They are symbols of an extended, outer and exposed part of yourself.

Some authorities believe that the back of a house symbolizes the past and the front, the future, but how you feel about patios in general will tell you whether this applies.

PORCH

Porches most often symbolize the part of yourself that is out in front, exposed to anyone passing by, that you cannot and do not have anything to hide from your neighbors.

Traditionally, a porch symbolizes your human sensory nature, one of the entrances into the lower more physical aspects of your consciousness.

Porches can also represent relaxation and a willingness to communicate and interact with others socially. They are a place to relax and just watch the world go by, so your porch may be telling you that it's now time for you to just sit and rock or swing for a while.

Some authorities believe that a porch or your front yard can also represent the future; see also Patio above.

PLUMBING

Plumbing of any kind usually symbolizes either the elimination or circulatory systems of your physical body.

Plumbing can also be symbols of how your various levels of energy are flowing or connecting at the time.

And dreams of any kind of plumbing are often early health messages. Pay close attention to the condition of the plumbing, especially if and where there are leaks or something is backed up. And remember that you always get dream health warnings in plenty of time to fix potential problems.

Where is this plumbing located? What kind of a building is it part of? Why? What type of material is it made of? Why? How efficiently does the plumbing system work?

If it could talk, what would it say to you? What is its overall condition? What was it originally constructed to handle? How well is it doing so?

In what condition is the material flowing through the plumbing? Does this remind you of anything going on in your life?

See also material the plumbing was built to take care of and type of building or room that houses the plumbing.

PUBLIC BUILDING
Any type of public building usually symbolizes your own culture's public or general opinions or ideas, the overall state or level of consciousness of your culture or society at the time.

Public buildings also represent cultural ideas that you don't, or won't, accept as really being your own, such as a particular social, racial or political opinion or attitude.

For what purpose was the public building ordinally built? How is it being used now? What style of architecture is it? Why that one, and not another style?

What kinds of people work there? How do you feel about the building. How is it different from other public buildings; for instance, if it is a police station, how is that different from a public library?

RESTAURANT
A restaurant is most often reminding you about the many ways there are to feed yourself. Restaurants point out the options to choose from you have available at the time in order to get the nutrition and energy you require to stay healthy. What's on the menu?

Restaurants also represent new ideas to put on your present menu, ideas you might want to taste just to see if you like them, new ways to put old favorites together, and new ways to serve them up to others.

Restaurants also represent supplying sustenance and essential nutrients to others, feeding or serving many at one time and all in one place, or even that it's now time to allow yourself to be served for a change.

A restaurant can also symbolize that some part of you feels a strong need to be sustained and nourished, paid attention to, fed, or maybe even that it needs companionship, to "eat" in the presence of others. Or are you being given food for thought?

Restaurants can also be a message from your real physical body that it needs the type of food normally served by the restaurant in your dream or experience. For instance, if you are eating ice cream, in addition to all of the things ice cream symbolizes to you, you might want to check your calcium intake.

For what type of cuisine is this restaurant best known? Who is serving the food? Who prepares it? How many people are in the restaurant? How are they dressed? What does the building look like? What actions are you carrying out in the restaurant? How is that the same as or different from the way you usually behave in restaurants? Who would be most likely to frequent this restaurant? Why? Who would never go there? Why? See also FOOD.

A WAITER OR WAITRESS symbolizes the female (Yin) and male (Yang) parts of you which serve, or would like to serve, others or yourself.

What kinds of people choose to be waiters and waitresses? Why? Does the waiter or waitress remind you of anyone or any personality trait of yours?

A WAITER OR WAITRESS FEELING RUSHED is frequently telling you that you are trying to handle too many things at one time, or feel that you are on some deep inner level. How are the people being served responding to the situation? Are they upset, or patient? Why?

A WAITER OR WAITRESS RUNNING BEHIND SCHEDULE could be telling you that you are not giving the kind of service you would like to, most probably to other parts of yourself; see also LATE.

SOMEONE MAD AT A WAITER OR WAITRESS is probably representing the part of you that feels it is not being treated equally, that you screwed up the order, or that some part of you feels it isn't being fed fast enough. Who is angry and why will tell you which part of you this may be. (Remember that anger in your dream is always directed first at yourself and then at the dream object).

ROOF

A roof most often symbolizes protection, safety, and security.

But since it is the highest part of any building, a roof also symbolizes your highest personal goals or ideals at the time of the dream or experience, or the highest level of consciousness achieved at the time.

Conversely, a roof can symbolize personal limitations you have put over yourself, a message that you or some part of you are afraid of being left exposed to "higher" things.

Traditionally, a roof represents the sheltering aspect of the Yin (female) principle and qualities.

What type of roof is it? What condition is it in? Is it sloped, or flat? What type of a building would normally have this kind of roof? Why?

How do you feel about the roof? Is it protecting you, or getting in your way, holding you back? Are you getting ready to jump off it? And if so, will you fly, or go splat! (And, no, you don't die if you do go splat in a dream or meditation).

ROOM

Each room in a building or house symbolizes a part of your personality, your individuality, and clearly indicates in which context your subconscious is communicating to you at the time. How you feel about the various rooms in your house, awake or asleep, can help you learn a lot about yourself.

Rooms have windows and doors connecting to other rooms or to the outside world, allowing a view of and passage to other realms of existence and ways of behaving or feeling. For example, how do you behave differently in your living room than you do in your kitchen?

A TOTALLY CLOSED OR SEALED ROOM is an ancient symbol for virginity and all of its symbolism.

The closed or sealed room is common in initiation rites, and often referred to as the "secret room." In this context, a closed room almost always represents the womb and/or a rebirth.

Conversely, a closed or sealed room can represent your feeling of being closed in, or out, or a fear of letting in the light, life, or the subject of your dream or experience..

What kind of room is this? What is in it? What colors are used in the room? What kind of building is it in? What kind of a person would like this room? How is it furnished? Why did you create this particular room in your dream or meditation, and not another kind?

SCHOOL

Dreaming you are back at your old grade or high school or college is common to most of us, usually surfacing when we are under prolonged periods of stress.

This dream is most often telling you that the subconscious feelings you have right now are the same ones you felt back then. Your subconscious has simply connected the way you are feeling now with the way you felt at that age. So what is going on in your life at the time of your dream that could make you feel the way you felt back then? Schools and universities also symbolize your most critical or important life lessons or issues at the time of your dream or experience. They represent the courses of study that you are in the process of learning, or ones that are coming up, or ones you have just completed, depending upon the context in which they are used.

A school can also be dealing with lessons from your past which still have a strong impact on you, especially when you are dreaming about a school you actually attended. At what age did you attend that particular school? And what was going on in your life emotionally then that is similar now?

Dreaming that you are back in school and taking a test is another common dream and, again, is often telling you that the way you felt when you took tests at that time in your life is the way you are feeling now, at least at the subconscious level.

On what are you being tested? What does this remind you of? What emotional things were going on in your life at that age? How did you handle tests then? How do you handle them now? How does that connect to what you are experiencing at the time of your dream?

What kind of school or university is it? What is it best at teaching? What level of education is represented by the school? What does this tell you about the subject of your dream?

What are the tuition and academic requirement to enter and to graduate? Who teaches there? What kind of people would normally attend this school?

Are you a registered student, or merely auditing the class? Which classes would have to be completed before you were allowed to attend the class you are attending in your dream? How do you feel in your dream? What does it remind you of that is going on in your life at the time? See also LECTURE, TEACHER, and TEST.

SHOPPING CENTER

Dreaming you are in a shopping center or mall usually symbolizes that you are beginning to shop around for new ways of thinking, behaving, acting, and living. You may also be shopping for new experiences, new people, new attitudes, or a new perspective or atmosphere.

A shopping center can also tell you that you are about to bring new parts of awareness or consciousness into your waking life, and the shops you go into will help you identify those parts.

Malls and shopping centers contain many smaller shops and make a wide selection of products much easier to find and purchase, even experiment with before buying. They are good places to try things on for size before you take them home.

Each individual shop in the shopping center is often showing you your inner potential and the variety of options and opportunities you have available to you at the time.

An individual store can also be pointing out a strong wish or need for the products sold by the store,

so pay particular attention to the various types of stores in the shopping center, which ones you go into, and which ones you ignore.

Which shops attract you in the dream? Which ones did you think about going into, but didn't? Why? Are you buying, or only shopping around? Why?

How crowded is this shopping center? What are the other people there doing? What kind of person would shop in this mall on a regular basis? How do you feel about being there? See also any objects in your shopping center, like CLOTHES.

STAIRS

Stairs or steps as symbols are found in virtually every culture on this planet.

Stairs often symbolize your step-by-step progress — emotionally, psychologically, and spiritually — as you move through the normal ups and downs of your life.

Stairs also symbolize your path in life and your skill in moving from one level to the next. In this context, stairs share the symbolism of the ladder; see LADDER.

Moving up or down stairs is also often a strong sexual symbol. In general, any rhythmic movement carried out in your dream can be a sexual symbol as well as all of its other representations.

In ancient Egypt, nine was the number of preferred steps, but in ancient Mithraic cultures only seven were needed to reach the top of the structure or the Self.

To the ancients, stairs symbolized the power of Ascension, the transcendence and movement to new levels of existence. This was especially true of stairs on any sacred building or sacred mountain; see also PYRAMID.

In fact, stairs often became symbols of other symbols, such as mountains, trees, rainbows, ladders, and even ropes.

Steps are often used in myths and legends in just this way, showing us the power of the heroine or hero to break through and open the way for communication for the rest of us between one world and the another.

Which step or steps are you about to take? What level of the building are you on? Where will you be after you have used the stairs?

What are the stairs made of? Why? What kind of stairs are they? Where do they lead? What is at their foot, and what is at the end? What is their general overall condition? What color are they?

Are there objects lying on the stairs? If so, who is responsible for removing them, and who put them there? Why?

Is your ascent or descent easy, or difficult? How much energy does it take? How well are you doing?

What kind of a building would normally have these stairs? What kind of a craftsman would build them? What kind of people habitually take the stairs? How are stairs different from elevators; see also ELEVATOR above.

THE INDIVIDUAL STEPS of any stairway are frequently symbolic of your ability to break through various levels of existence, your attainment of a goal, and stages of personal development.

STAIRS LEADING UNDERGROUND are ancient symbols for the ability to break through the barriers of the Underworld, the Unconscious.

It was also a common practice to name each one of the steps, and this is just one of the ways the ancients left clues for us about the steps to be mastered in order to attain the goal. For example, the stairs of Solomon's Temple led to the Middle Chamber, symbolizing the unknown future.

SPIRAL STAIRS are frequently used to symbolize the spiral movements of the stars and the sun and moon, the continuity in your own spiral progression, the Veil of The Great Mother, fertility, storms, the many dimensions of existence, and the wanderings of the Soul and its ultimate return to its Source or its Center.

Spiral stairs also symbolize the mysterious and unknown, and the conscious exploration of what you are moving toward at the end of the spiral stairs. See also GEOMETRIC SHAPES/Spiral.

THE STAIRWELL AND LANDING often symbolize that you have reached a plateau, a place to rest for a short time before you continue your climb, either up or down; see direction/Down, Up.

SUPERMARKET

Supermarkets and markets of any kind most often symbolize that you are shopping for new ways to feed yourself, new energy sources, especially in relation to practical, everyday, down to earth physical things.

Literally, everything you require to sustain your physical body can be found in a supermarket. And if you are shopping for a particular food group or food item, check your diet to make sure you have included it or what it represents to you.

What type of supermarket is it? What kinds of people regularly shop there? Why? What are you shopping for? Who works there? Where is the supermarket located? Is it old, or new? Clean, or shoddy? What type of products does it carry? How do you feel when you're in it? Why?

TENT

Tents almost always represent highly temporary, short-term states of mind or consciousness. A tent is a shelter from the elements, a place to rest for short periods of time before you continue on your journey.

Tents are also used for recreation and places of shelter while enjoying nature. Do you need to?

Tents are also great puns. Are you "in tense?" Which tense do you live in most often — past, present, or future? Is it time for you to fold up your tent and slip away?

How do you feel about tents? Why? What type of tent is it? What are you doing there? Where is it?

How long will it be okay to stay there? What kind of people like to stay in tents? How are tents different from houses?

TOILET

Dreams of toilets, urination, and defecation are extremely common. This is just one good example of why it is important to separate your feelings *in* a dream from your feelings *about* the dream after you wake.

Toilets are containers for holding and then disposing of things you have already processed, the minerals, vitamins, and fluids not utilized or taken in by your system, waste materials that can now be disposed of or recycled.

Toilets also symbolize the process of elimination and cleansing, or your need for it. This is one of the reasons why bathroom dreams are so common when you begin the journey toward self-discovery and self-mastery.

And, of course, toilets in a dream can be direct messages from the brain to the body to eliminate real waste materials, so toilets can also be pretty direct health messages.

In what condition is this toilet? Is it modern, or primitive? Is there water, and if so what color? Is it overflowing? How do you feel about toilets in general? Why?

EXCREMENT itself has a long history for symbolizing riches containing the power of the person, and at one time was a common symbol of wealth and abundance.

TOWER

Towers are ambivalent in their symbolism, representing both the Yin (feminine) principle, chasteness, and virginity, and the Yang (masculine) principle, especially as a phallic symbol.

Towers in general, however, are ancient symbols for a place of Spirit, a place from which to gain a better perspective of the view, a place from which you can see the whole picture or landscape.

And towers can symbolize a safe, tamed, remote, orderly, and structured nature or personality. The legendary professor in his or her ivory tower is an example of this symbolism.

Towers also tell you that some part of you is feeling separated from ordinary life and other people, that it is being kept imprisoned by some other part of you.

Towers are places of refuge, protection, vigilance, or of imprisonment, depending entirely upon how they are used by their owners. The context within which you are using tower in your dream and how you feel about it will lead you to your interpretation.

Traditionally, towers symbolize vigilance, and ascent to a higher place. In this respect, towers share some of the symbolism of ladders and pillars; see also STAIRS above.

Towers are also good puns. What have you shut away in an ivory tower? Who is a tower of strength? Is something towering over you?

What kind of a tower is it? Does it stand alone, or is it attached to another building? What is it generally used for? How is it different from, or the same as, the way the tower would be used in waking life?

Who built it? Who maintains it? What is it made of? Who lives in your tower on a regular basis? Why? How do they feel about it? See also MOUNTAIN.

A TOWER HOLDING VIRGIN OR PRINCESS is an old symbol for the "Abode of the Soul," for Paradise, and for the Soul itself and the qualities cultivated by it up to that time. Within this context, a tower with a princess or virgin inside it has the same symbolism as the closed or walled garden; see FLOWER/Garden.

AN IVORY TOWER is an old symbol for the inaccessible, self-imposed or culturally-imposed virginity, and being closed off from common everyday life and experiences and day-to-day reality.

Even today, we use this symbol for someone who is so far removed from everyday reality and how things work that they have no way to relate to the rest of us.

So an ivory tower can be telling you that you are spending too much time with theory and study and not nearly enough testing out those theories or putting your studies into practice.

WINDOW

Windows most often symbolize your view or perception at the time of what can be seen through the window.

Windows also symbolize your ability to see beyond the situation represented by your dream, to literally see through the wall or object blocking your vision.

While windows cannot themselves give light, they allow light to flow through. Windows let you see in two directions at once. They can also symbolize your openness and vulnerability to outside influences.

A window can also represent your desire to be more outside of yourself, your problems, or anything that is outside of the window. Are you on the inside of your house when you really want to be outside participating in the action?

Are your windows wide or narrow, barred, curtained, shuttered? What kind of framework holds your window? What shape is it? Why? What would the view be through a different shape?

Are there blinds on your window; are they open or closed? Are you looking in your window, or out of it? What is the view from your dream window? What type of building would normally have windows like these? Why?

YARD

A yard symbolizes an outside extension of yourself, specifically your areas for personal growth and self expression.

What is growing in your yard? What objects are there? Who takes care of it? Why, and how? How healthy or well-kept is the yard?

What kind of a building is the yard around? How would the yard change if the building changed?

BACK YARD: Some experts believe that back yards are symbols of the past. But keep in mind that all of your dreams are about current feelings, even when you are dreaming about the past.

A back yard can also be telling you that you want to or should be private and a little less open about the subject of your dream or meditation at the time.

FRONT YARD: Some experts believe that front yards represent the future, but keep in mind that dreams are about your feelings right now, even if you are dreaming future wishes and things.

A front yard can also be telling you that you are up-front and out in the open about the subject of your dream or meditation, or that you are ready to go public with an idea, belief, etc.

C

CANDLE

Candles are (as are oil lamps) ancient symbols of the relationship between the individual Soul and Matter. The Soul is represented by the flame which consumes Matter (the wax or oil). The burning of incense has a similar symbolism, with the added symbolism of scent.

Candles also represent light with the power to eliminate the darkness, but by the use of a gentle persistent power of the flame rather than the more violent potentially destructive force of a full-blown raging fire.

Candles also symbolize Illumination itself, the light within the darkness of ordinary life, and the revitalizing power of the sun.

And candles symbolize the fragility of human life and how easily it can be extinguished. This is one of the reasons why in many fairy tales and legends, Death has power over a burning candle, to symbolize Death's power over human life.

What color is this candle? Is its flame steady and strong, or flickering? Where is it? What is it sit-

ting on or in? What is its purpose? At what stage of burning is it, new or almost burned out? What kind of a person would choose this kind of candle? What was used to light it? What is it made of?

How would your dream or experience be different if the candle went out? Why? See also COLOR of candle and FLAME.

A CANDELABRA or any kind of candle holder symbolizes spiritual light and salvation. The number of branches on a candelabra has always had mystical symbolism in virtually every culture on this planet.

A CANDLE ON EACH SIDE OF THE CROSS OR ALTAR symbolized the dual nature of the Christ, the human and the Divine to the early Christians.

THE MENORAH, the seven-armed gold candlestick of Judaism, is believed by some authorities to correspond at least in part to the ancient Babylonian Tree of Life. It is also associated with the seven heavens and seven planets.

However, today, the Menorah symbolizes the presence of the Divine, with the fat of the candles symbolizing a sacrifice to Jahveh; see also Candelabra above.

A SINGLE CANDLE is an ancient symbol of the individual life within the Universal or Cosmic Life.

THREE CANDLES together represent the Trinity. And to the ancient Qabalists, three candles joined together represented the trinity of Wisdom, Strength, and Beauty.

CANYON

Canyons frequently symbolize new unexplored parts of your own personality or Inner Self.

Canyons can also symbolize the territory (experiences) toward which you are moving at the time.

Dreaming of a canyon often tells you that there will be specific lessons or situations ahead that must be mastered through understanding before you can move up and out of the canyon again.

And in many cultures, canyons are sacred places, so your canyon could be clearly telling you to reconnect with your own places of power, to re-enter your sacred places and time.

Dreaming of a canyon can also represent a strong desire to go exploring, to get back to the power of Nature in the raw, discover new simple natural things, get away from the concrete and glass. Have

you become buried in manmade schedules and material things, or are you about to be?

What type of a canyon is it: open or box canyon? What kind of rock is it made of? How was it formed? What colors are there? What grows or lives in your canyon? Is there water in it? Is the canyon dangerous, hidden, restful? How do you feel about being there? What actions are you taking? Why? See also MOUNTAIN, VALLEY.

CEREMONY

Ceremonies of any kind usually tell you that you have graduated and are about to move to the next stage or phase of growth.

A ceremony can also be telling you that an initiation into a new phase or a transformation of some kind either has or is about to take place.

What type of ceremony is being performed? Who is attending? Why? How are the attendees dressed? How are you dressed? Why? What is the overall emotional tone of the ceremony? Why? How do you feel about either attending or performing ceremonies in general? Why did human being create ceremonies? How is this particular ceremony different from, or the same as, ceremonies you actually do attend?

COMMON CEREMONIES:

AWARD CEREMONY: An award ceremony usually symbolizes that you have just completed a lesson or phase of growth, and with honors. What type of award is being given? Who is attending? What must be accomplished and completed before such an award can be given? How long does it normally take to earn this award?

BAPTISM: Any baptism symbolizes that you, or the object being baptized, are discarding your old behavior and actions, and that you are now consciously committing to a different and higher way of being. Some form of anointing or baptism is common at many initiation ceremonies, for instance.

Baptism also symbolizes your connection with your source of spiritual strength, or your own internal source and nature, and that you are now willing to change your present behavior and habits in order to gain access to and experience something better.

A baptism can also symbolize a spiritual awakening of some kind, a birth into new life and new beginnings, dedicating yourself to your true spiritual nature, becoming the Initiate.

And baptism can symbolize a purification by Spirit (the water or oil used in the baptism) of the basic and lower (physical) qualities of your Soul, a purification now made possible by your decision to be willing to take the right action (being baptized). Within this context, a baptism symbolizes your willingness to dedicate your physical life to your spiritual one.

Into what belief system or organization are you being baptized?

Who is performing the ceremony? Who is attending? Are you an infant, child, or adult? Male or female? Why?

What element is being used to perform the anointing? Are you being sprinkled, or fully immersed? What kind of a person would choose to be baptized in this way?

How do you feel in your dream or experience? What types of organized belief systems believe it is important to baptize their members? Why, what does this accomplish? What does this remind you that is going on in your life?

BIRTH CEREMONY: A birth ceremony symbolizes the newest facet of your total Self, which has now been born and is being welcomed by those around it into its new existence. Who is attending the ceremony? What part of you are they?

Birth ceremonies are also sometimes called naming ceremonies or christenings. (See also BABY).

CHRISTENING CEREMONY: A christening ceremony symbolizes the launching of a totally new life, that a part of your total Self so new that it still must be named has been born. Christening also symbolizes that the person or object being christened or blessed is gaining a new identity in a new form.

Christenings are a welcoming into the culture or level of society of which you have just chosen to be a part, and that you are being accepted by those who are already a part of this society. Christening dreams are often acknowledgments of your initiation into a specific belief or level of consciousness.

Have you just received a new "name?" Have you just dedicated yourself to a new belief system? What does a christening remind you of that is going on in your life at the time? Who or what is being christened? Why?

FUNERAL CEREMONY: Dreaming of funerals and death is almost never precognitive. *It is extremely rare to dream of your own death.*

Any dream funerals almost always symbolize a death of one or more of your outgrown habits, and ways of acting and thinking, and that you are beginning the internal process of letting go of them.

A funeral ceremony is telling you that you are beginning to be at peace with this loss, that you are putting certain internal conflicts to rest, but that mourning this loss is not only perfectly acceptable, it is preferable to ignoring it.

A funeral can also represent any unacknowledged and leftover feelings about your past that you haven't quite worked through yet, a reminder to go ahead and have the funeral, bury it, leave it behind.

And a funeral may also be a ceremony in recognition of your movement into the next phase of existence. Mock funerals were very common in ancient spiritual initiation training.

Funerals can, of course, also be one of the best ways to work through leftover grief concerning the loss of anyone or anything close to you that actually has died. Remember that the sleeping brain believes what it sees, and so will go about releasing all the right chemicals to help you work through grief.

And don't forget the puns. Who or what will soon be "dead and buried," or what do you wish were? What has "passed away" from your life? Would you like to throw dirt in somebody's face?

Who is at the funeral? Whose funeral is it? What kind of funeral is it — sad and somber, or a rowdy wake? What kind of a person would be given a funeral like this? Why? What are you feeling in the dream or meditation? What colors are there? See also DEATH, EMOTIONS/Mourn, GRAVE.

GRADUATION CEREMONY: Graduations symbolize pretty much exactly what you think they do — that you have successfully completed a stage or phase of growth and learning. If you're lucky, you may even get a break between semesters.

From what are you graduating? What courses must be mastered before you receive the diploma? Who is attending the graduation? How will life be different after graduation? What's the next step? How do you feel about that See also BUILDING/School.

INITIATION CEREMONY: An initiation ceremony of any kind symbolizes your acceptance into a new system of belief, a belief which when mastered will dramatically and totally change who you are.

Initiations also symbolize your willingness and commitment to work through the levels or stages of this new belief or knowledge new or additional knowledge.

And an initiation can also be telling you that you have just been accepted by a new group or social level. What will be the result of the initiation? What changes?

SACRIFICIAL CEREMONY: Sacrifices of any kind often symbolize a need or wish to sacrifice some part of you to gain a greater goal, including the sacrifice of limiting thoughts, behavior, and beliefs.

Conversely, a sacrificial ceremony can also be telling you that you or some part of you may be actually enjoying playing the part of the martyr. What kind of a person becomes a martyr? What does this remind you of about yourself?

Sacrifices are carried out to honor and appease a deity or powerful being. Does this remind you of anything going on in your life?

Who or what is being sacrificed? Why? Who is performing the ceremony? What instruments or symbols are being used? Is there any blood or pain involved? How do you feel in your dream? See also BLOOD if present, MARTYR, PAIN (if present), SUICIDE, VICTIM.

WEDDING CEREMONY: A wedding most often symbolizes a merging of the Yin-Yang (feminine-masculine) qualities and prin-ciples of your True Self, a merger made in order to form yet a third and stronger entity, the relationship.

Historically, when a man gives a woman his name in marriage, he has given her power over him; see also Naming Ceremony below.

To dream of marrying a former lover or friend usually symbolizes a strong desire to integrate the positive aspects of that person into your own personality. Or it may be a message that you miss those qualities in your present relationship.

Dreaming of past loves rarely means that you really want to go back to that love, and could also be showing you that there are some lessons still left out of that relationship which it is now time to complete before you move on to the new relationship.

Why do human beings have weddings? Who is the bride? Who is the groom? Where is the ceremony taking place? Are they happy about the merger?

How are they dressed? Who is performing the ceremony? Who is attending? Does the ceremony go well? Why, or why not? What does this tell you about yourself? How do you feel in your dream? How do you feel about weddings in general? Why?

CHAKRA

The word *chakra* is an ancient Sanskrit word meaning *whirling vortex (or wheel) of light.*

Chakras are energy dynamos, centers through which energy is

taken in, dispersed, and released. They are each a specialized meeting point for the physical and the spiritual.

Chakras are believed to be pure energy, centers of consciousness symbolically represented by the emotions housed and controlled by the individual chakra.

Chakras are also memory centers, storing physical and Soul memories, including those from any past or parallel lives.

They are believed to be responsible for the brightness or dimness of the various layers of your aura, the energy fields surrounding your physical body.

The various schools of thought and Chakra systems do not agree on many points, including whether or not Chakras physically exist or whether they are merely symbolic. Different belief systems don't even agree on the order or connection between the seven main Chakras within the human body.

For instance, in the ancient Tibetan and Edgar Cayce systems, the positions of the 6th and 7th Chakras are the reverse of the 6th and 7th in other systems. For purposes of this guidebook we have kept to the more familiar system, but if you disagree, just reverse the symbolism of the 6th and 7th Chakras as given below.

To "open" or "close" a Chakra, think of the lens of a camera or a flower opening and closing. Each Chakra is also opened and closed by using specific colors, and we have included this information for you here.

Many teachers, however, recommend that you let each Chakra open and close on its own, that you "let the rose unfold" naturally, on its own. This does not mean that you cannot actively work on or with your Chakras, just that you should do so with knowledge and respect for the energy involved, and there are many excellent books and teachers to help you do just that.

Certain minerals are believed to not only open and close specific Chakras, but to help align them and keep them in peak working order (see list below).

It is generally held by most systems that the Chakras are "attached" to the physical body at the back of the spine, although they are really not attached in the way we normally use that term at all. Each Chakra meets or converges at a specific point on the physical body, whirling and expanding outward both front and back to create the "energy vortex" or wheel of light.

When a Chakra is functioning correctly, its color is a very pale shade of its primary color, although all Chakras contain some degree of all colors, including white. The pale color simply tells you that that particular Chakra is operating at a very fine high rate of vibration.

If a Chakra is not in balance or harmonized (i.e., malfunctioning), its color will be dense, darker, sometimes even muddy.

The ability to see Chakras or auras in no way implies that you are on a "higher" spiritual or metaphysical plane than someone who doesn't have this talent. The truth is that anyone can learn to "see" auras and Chakras, in one way or another.

Each of the seven major Chakras are related to the endocrine system of the physical body and influence the corresponding endocrine glands.

Each Chakra also responds to a specific musical note or tone and we have included this corresponding tone in the Chakra description below.

In general terms, the four lower Chakras (Chakras 1 through 4) integrate with your normal psychological-spiritual energies as they are able to exist within ordinary physical matter. They are symbolically thought of as the four Earth Elements: Earth, Water, Fire, and Air, in that order.

Additionally, the four lower major Chakras represent the Yang (masculine) qualities, or the left brain functions of the physical body (your assertive, protective, intellectual, linear-creativity, etc).

The three upper Chakras (5 through 7) primarily aid in the integration of your physical being with your Soul, with your true spiritual nature. And the three upper Chakras represent the Yin (feminine qualities), and the right brain functions (your intuition, sensitivity, non-linear thought and non-linear creativity, etc).

Chakras 8 through 12 are generally believed to have no attachment within your physical body as we understand it, but serve largely

to further your spiritual evolution by providing secure established routes for you to experience higher dimensions of existence while still functioning within a physical body.

And many systems today believe that new Chakras are being created or gaining prominence. This includes a Chakra between the 4th and 5th, and Chakras above the 12th.

It is important to remember that one of the primary functions of the Chakras is to keep you operating at maximum spiritual capacity while living within the physical dimension — no small feat, you'll have to admit.

As we said earlier, not all spiritual systems agree on the placement of the Chakras. For instance, while most contemporary metaphysical information place the 6th Chakra slightly behind the eyebrows (the Brow Chakra, or Third Eye), the ancient Tibetan and Edgar Cayce systems place it at the top of the head, with the 7th Chakra at the brow.

Diagramed, this placement would take the form of the Ancient Egyptian and shepherd's crook, a potent symbol on its own.

We recommend that you try any Chakra exercises both ways, and then work with which one feels most appropriate for you personally at the time. The truth is that these two Chakras are so closely tied together that for practical purposes it will not make much difference to you over the long haul which one is where. Your experience is *your* experience, no matter what anyone else says, including us.

Many authorities now believe that the human Chakra system is going through a transitional phase as we expand our awareness. A secondary Chakra system, literally on top of and interfacing with the current seven main Chakras, is believed to be in process even as we speak.

This phenomenon is believed to be due to an event to occur in the near future which will assist in the birth of the "new" Earth and the emergence of the Blue Star, our second sun.

Within this belief system, the traditional Chakra system will stay attuned to our present sun, while the secondary one will attune to the Blue Star, our second sun.

Changes in your own Chakra system will normally be extremely subtle, building bit by bit on a daily basis, in order to prepare your current physical body and nervous network for the upcoming energy changes.

The bridge or transitional colors are believed to be mauve (4th Chakra), salmon (5th Chakra), and crimson (6th Chakra); see COLOR.

1ST CHAKRA – THE BASE, ROOT, SURVIVAL CHAKRA:

The 1st Chakra is located at the base of your spine and is most often associated with the color red.

Symbolically, the 1st Chakra represents the human physical body which is not yet awakened, developed, or sensitive to the existence of its own Soul.

The roots of the 1st Chakra are considered symbolically to be the actual points in time and space where the Soul manifests within the physical body. In other words, it is both the meeting place and boundary of the body and the Soul within physical matter.

This Chakra is directly connected to your fear of or for your very physical existence. It is the Chakra giving you your most physical connection to life and the Earth's environment, and represents your very first spiritual step into physical reality.

The 1st Chakra is stabilizing and grounding, helps you keep both feet on the ground, and directly influences your desire to be comfortable with the concept of settling down here on this very scary planet Earth — or just in a relationship.

The 1st Chakra also houses the fight-flight and other survival mechanisms connected with your physical body.

This Chakra directly takes in and magnifies the energy that enters your physical body through the Chakras in the feet.

In other words, the 1st Chakra represents your first step into the scary world of Matter, the *physical* process of spiritual learning. It represents the very beginning of the spiritualization of Matter.

This is the first of the Chakras to become conscious of physical life, and what that means to you personally. This is where many of your core beliefs are stored and where you can access your core identity, and often your core lessons.

When properly harmonized, the 1st Chakra increases your capacity for receiving inspiration of all kinds, and helps you release any inability to coordinate and harmonize with the other Chakras. (This coordination is often called "being aligned").

The 1st Chakra is connected directly with the gonads of the endocrine system and with the kidneys. Most systems hold that stimulation of the 1st and 3rd Chakras together helps ease disorders of the lower extremities, particularly in thigh muscle tissue and circulation in the feet.

Traditionally, the 1st Chakra is also believed to be associated directly with muscular deterioration and many nervous system disorders. And disharmony in the 1st Chakra is believed to facilitate imbalances in the pancreas and spleen. Disorder in this Chakra is also believed to be associated directly with the mood fluctuations generally associated with blood sugar levels.

Some systems attribute male sexuality to the 1st Chakra and female sexuality to the 2nd, but in either case malfunctions of the 1st Chakra are believed to be directly related to disorders related to impotence, frigidity, and its opposite, obsessive sexuality.

Imbalances within the 1st Chakra are also believed to impact urinary functions, often related psychologically to an over-strict early physical training of some kind, which leads to compulsive or obsessive behavior patterns of many kinds.

Imbalances are also related to any "over-domestication" symptoms, in general having the effect of weakening your natural survival instincts. So if you're basically a couch potato, you might want to look at what's going on in your 1st Chakra.

Working with or on the 1st Chakra is believed to help ease disorders associated with disorientation, deeply buried subconscious fears, an inability to focus on the really important issues in your life (a definite symptom of prolonged stress), and over-riding concerns for your immediate survival, rational or not.

Working with or on the 1st Chakra is also believed to help ease problems of, and associated with, the adrenal glands, heart diseases, and most kinds of stress.

The key negative emotion associated with the 1st Chakra is long-term or chronic stress, almost always accompanied by deep feelings of insecurity, whether they are conscious or not.

Some of the key indications of these imbalances are chronic anxiety, hyperactivity, being a compulsive work-a-holic, and an uncontrollable restlessness.

It is widely believed that cramping in this area of the physical body is related directly to your inability to "let go in public," symbolizing literally the restriction of the inner human animal, and your inhibited natural creativity.

In India, the 1st Chakra is called *Muladhara*, meaning *root support*. Within this system it is associated with the White Elephant or the White Horse, and often symbolized by a four-petaled lotus.

The 1st or Root Chakra is the dream body manifesting itself into Matter, and the very beginning of individuation, of becoming a self-reliant individual, so it's no wonder it houses our insecurities.

Both the 1st and 6th Chakras are considered Master Controllers of the physical body's metabolic systems. It is believed that excesses and prolonged imbalances in the 1st and 2nd Chakras will eventually weaken the actions of the both 6th and 7th Chakras. (The 1st and 2nd Chakras are often spoken of as one and work together closely, just as do the 6th and 7th).

The color red opens the 1st Chakra and the color blue closes it. It resonates to the musical note middle C and the musical tone *do*.

2ND CHAKRA – SPLEEN OR NAVEL CHAKRA: The 2nd Chakra is located approximately three inches below your navel and is most often associated with the color orange.

Symbolically, the 2nd Chakra represents the subconscious mind and the first level of experience of the subconscious within the physical world, your first experience of non-ego and of being more than you seem to be on the surface.

This Chakra is connected to physical sex, your personal relationships, natural creativity, and the proper development of your personal sexuality and creativity.

Some systems attribute the actions of the 2nd Chakra to female sexuality, and male sexuality to the 1st Chakra, but in any event the 2nd Chakra allows you access to your memories and experiences, and beliefs about human sexuality and all that it carries with it.

Traditionally, the 2nd Chakra is believed to help adjust all fluids of the physical body, and to help the body regain its balance after any overexposure to Earth's natural radiation fields.

This Chakra is believed to help govern the ovaries, gonads and testicles, and is connected to the endocrine glands which produce lyden. It is believed to aid directly in increasing personal creativity, initiative, and self-esteem.

Work with the 2nd Chakra is believed to help ease sexual disorders, including infertility. It is linked to imbalances of the male and female hormonal systems due to the improper assimilation by the body of proteins.

Work with the 2nd Chakra is also believed to aid in the integration of your physical emotions at the cellular level, and to increase your ability to allow intimacy, even with yourself.

Working on and with this Chakra is also believed to help you achieve a balanced, healthy attitude toward sexuality in general, and your own in particular. This is where you store or release both sexual and creative tensions.

It is believed that a properly functioning 2nd Chakra aids in effective detoxification, especially of the urinary tract system.

Traditionally, disorders in the 2nd Chakra are believed to be linked to arthritis, especially in men.

It is also associated with all psychosomatic disorders, and directly connected with stress caused by unexpressed and internalized anger and rage.

This Chakra is often associated with emotion, but emotion of a deep physical nature rather than of a more purely feeling one. For instance, the deep physical feeling of love instantaneously transforms the energy of the 2nd Chakra.

In India, the 2nd Chakra is often referred to as the Six-Petaled Lotus and is called *Swadhistana*, meaning *whole*. It is sometimes referred to as the fluid Chakra and Water Chakra, and is believed to be the actual fluid center of the physical body, corresponding directly to the kidneys and adrenal glands.

Some systems state that the more you stay within only normal everyday consciousness, the more the energy of the 2nd Chakra becomes "negative." This type of imbalance is often symbolized as a devouring fish or whale.

An imbalance or malfunction of the 2nd Chakra is often symptomatic of holding onto your past. Some of the physiological problems that may surface because of any holding on are uterine problems, prostate problems, bladder and/or kidney disorders, and a general overall lack of fluidity in the body, sometimes experienced by heat flashes, and arthritic-like symptoms.

People suffering from a malfunctioning 2nd Chakra often feel hemmed in, caged, and trapped by social and personal obligations, weighed down by the "shoulds" in their lives.

The 2nd Chakra is associated directly with what are usually termed the mental and emotional energy bodies (don't ask — it's a whole book on its own).

The color orange opens the 2nd Chakra, and the color turquoise closes it. It resonates to the musical note D and the musical tone *re*.

3RD CHAKRA – THE SOLAR PLEXUS OR SECOND MIND CHAKRA: The 3rd Chakra is located in the solar plexus or stomach area, and is most often associated with the color yellow.

Symbolically, the 3rd Chakra is often represented by fire and lightning.

The 3rd Chakra is the general clearing house for all personal power issues — which should tell you pretty much everything you really need to know about it.

This Chakra is directly connected with all of your emotions and often experienced as "butterflies in the stomach." It houses all of your personal feelings; emotional rather than cellular anger, hostility and rage; and your ability to express or act on your free will and personal ambitions.

This is the Chakra dealing most directly with your lessons of personal control and intellect. The 3rd Chakra is the general area of your "animal wisdom," your "gut feelings," your physical intuition. It is the area from which most of your will power and determination comes.

This is also, of course, the center for the beginning of the chemical breakdown of food before further assimilation by your physical body, a good symbol all on its own.

When functioning properly, the 3rd Chakra increases your sensitivity, clarity, and understanding of visionary and revolutionary experiences. A properly functioning 3rd Chakra also dramatically increases your sensitivity and natural intuition.

A malfunction in the 3rd Chakra is most often symptomatic of emotional problems of one kind or another. This is the great clearing house for grief, depression, and the inability to effectively release emotional distress of just about any kind.

The most notable emotional problem exhibited by anyone with a malfunctioning 3rd Chakra is what was called in older systems an "affliction of character"; many of the people we like to avoid are suffering from 3rd Chakra malfunctions, and probably have lousy digestion, too.

The 3rd Chakra is believed to directly integrate the emotions, and to be especially effective at integrating any emotions connected to lessons to be learned through your association with your mother, or any mother-figure symbol.

The 3rd Chakra is linked directly to the mental energy body. It is also connected with instinct, impulsiveness, and even violence. This is, in fact, the psychological center for blatant violence when inner signs are either incorrectly heard, ignored, or not heard at all.

The 3rd Chakra also deals directly with personal courage, the use of power on a personal level, your intuition, and your self esteem.

The 3rd Chakra reacts instantly to your mind's directions, completely overriding or ignoring the physical consequences to your body.

A split between the ego and the 3rd Chakra is recognized most often in this area of the body by unconscious groans and sporadic deep breaths or sighs.

In India, the 3rd Chakra is referred to as the Ten-Petaled Lotus and is called *Manipura*, meaning *the lustrous gem*. Its symbol is the ram, the symbol of the East Indian god of fire.

Physiologically, the 3rd Chakra is believed to be directly associated with problems of the spleen, stomach, and gall bladder.

Stomach cramps are often related to a malfunction in the 3rd Chakra, as are ulcers, heartburn, diabetes, and even cancer, all of whose originations stem from the repression of your quite natural assertive feelings or reactions to life in general. But when these natural human reactions or emotions are shut off and stuffed down, they turn inward as destructive anger aimed against the body.

The 3rd Chakra controls the adrenal glands of the endocrine system, including the concentration of minerals in the body.

The colors lemon, gold, yellow, and white open the 3rd Chakra, and the color brown closes it. It resonates to the musical note E and the musical tone *mi*.

4TH CHAKRA – THE HEART CHAKRA: The 4th Chakra is located behind the breastbone in the area of the lungs, and is most often associated with the colors green and pink. Within the New Earth system of belief, the 4th Chakra is also associated with the color mauve.

The 4th Chakra is often symbolized by a gazelle, an ancient symbol for psychosomatic problems and disorders. And it is an ancient symbol for the place where God or the Divine reaches down to and connects directly with humanity.

Working with and on the 4th Chakra directly aids in aligning all of the other Chakras. It is for this reason that the Heart Chakra is often called "The Great Balancer."

It is only when the 4th Chakra is functioning properly that the quality of Divine Love is able to come into it. It is from this Chakra

that you deeply yearn to connect to all life.

The 4th Chakra is directly related to love, harmony in and of all things, and all Soul issues and lessons. In fact, some ancient systems believed that the Soul actually lived in the physical body within this Chakra center.

This is the energy center most often connected with love and the harmonization of the Yin (female) and Yang (male) qualities and characteristics. The heart center is actually androgynous, however, being neither male nor female in its actions.

The 4th Chakra is the one dealing directly with all interpersonal relationships (see also 2nd Chakra above).

The 4th Chakra affects all nutrients, all pre-physical conditions, all childhood diseases, the physical heart and blood and circulatory systems, and the entire immune system. In fact, it is widely believed that the 4th Chakra symbolizes our mastery of the immune system and thymus, particularly within the first seven years of our physical existence on this planet.

Traditionally, this Chakra has always been connected to the thymus gland of the endocrine system which, among other things, does indeed control the body's immune systems. This Chakra has also traditionally been linked directly with the process of tissue regeneration.

Malfunctions of the 4th Chakra often show themselves by imbalances that can lead to blood disorders (including leukemia), various heart diseases, and thymus and immune system disorders.

Malfunctions within the 4th Chakra also often surface as hypochondria, over-excitement, chest cramps, and arrhythmia (the heart "skipping a beat"— another interesting symbol on its own).

The 4th Chakra is believed to be directly connected with the astral, emotional, and spiritual energy bodies.

In India, the 4th Chakra is referred to as the Twelve-Petaled Lotus and is called *Anahata*, meaning *place of unstruck sound*, the place where God reaches down to humanity.

Within this system, it is believed that the unconscious reaches down to conscious life, and may be heard and controlled in this area of the body through the breath.

The colors emerald green and gold open the 4th Chakra; the color orange closes it. It resonates to the musical note F and the musical tone *fa*.

5TH CHAKRA – THE THROAT CHAKRA: The 5th Chakra is located at the base of the throat, and is most often associated with the color blue.

The 5th Chakra connects thinking with feeling, and is links directly with all matters dealing with the integration of the spiritual body into the physical one.

This Chakra is connected with communication, personal expression, judgment, perception, hearing, and the ability to make wise choices and decisions.

The 5th Chakra deals directly with all illnesses resulting from suppression of the true self.

This Chakra is directly connected with disorders of the immune and neurological systems, throat disorders, disorders of the upper bronchial systems, psychosomatic illnesses, and even throat cancer.

In fact, in some systems the 5th Chakra is believed to control the entire endocrine system. But in any case, it is directly connected to the thyroid gland, which among other things controls the body's metabolic rate.

A properly functioning 5th Chakra keeps your interest in spiritual affairs at maximum and amplifies your ability to then allow this interest to flow outward to stimulate others in the same way.

The 5th Chakra deals directly with self-expression and the perception of your own personal reality. When you want to really listen well, open your 5th Chakra, your "third ear."

Indications of a malfunctioning 5th Chakra are an introverted or moody person who is unable to express emotions appropriately, if at all.

Additional typical indications of a malfunctioning 5th Chakra are chronic depression, extreme stubbornness, a strong need to assert personal wishes even at the expense of others, and speech and throat problems.

In India, the 5th Chakra is referred to as the Sixteen-Petaled Lotus and is called *Vishuddha*, the *purification center*. It is often symbolized by air, wind, the ether, and "the door that swings back and forth without cause." This Chakra is sometimes also symbolized by an elephant.

Your voice (which comes directly through the 5th Chakra) is easily impacted by your ego, the part of your personality usually in charge at the moment. Your voice also, of course, can be used to manipulate others. But because the 5th Chakra is the center for purification, your voice and the sounds it makes can be fairly easily cleared of any false unproductive impact it might have on others, through working directly with this Chakra.

The colors blue and turquoise open the 5th Chakra, and the colors red, yellow and orange close it. It resonates to the musical note G and the musical tone *sol*.

6TH CHAKRA – THE HIGHER MIND CHAKRA: In the ancient Tibetan and Edgar Cayce systems, the 6th Chakra is located at the top of the forehead, the crown, and is most often associated with the color indigo.

However, all other chakra systems place the 6th at the brow and the 7th at the crown. We suggest that you experiment and see which one feels most correct for you personally. And if you feel that the 6th chakra is the crown chakra and the 7th is the brow, simply reverse the definitions for the 6th and 7th given below.

As a side note, placing the 6th chakra at the crown and the 7th at the brow forms a perfect shape for the shepherd's and pharaoh's crook, an interesting symbol all on its own.

But no matter where the 6th Chakra is located, this one *forcefully* projects its energy out into the world, and is the one used most often in visualizations and affirmations; to mold your thought, ideas and feelings into your physical reality.

The 6th Chakra symbolizes idealism and the desire for a genuine spiritual nature. This is the "If you can dream it, you can do it" Chakra.

The 6th Chakra is often referred to as the "Third Eye" and is believed to connect directly with questions about your spiritual nature, your inner dreams, all philosophical issues, your inner visions, insight and understanding, and the expansion of inspiration and intuition. It deals directly with symbolism.

This Chakra helps to dissolve grief, and chase away nightmares. The 6th Chakra is also connected with fantasies of all kinds, including daydreams.

Malfunctions in the 6th Chakra lead to a retreat from reality by creating patterns of extreme visual intensity similar to autistic-like behavior, and this is one of the major symptoms indicating an imbalance in the 6th Chakra.

Another symptom is what is usually called "delusions of grandeur," especially spiritual delusions. This is probably just one of the reasons why Amethyst Crystal has always been associated with the 6th Chakra; Amethyst helps tone down spiritual arrogance.

A serious imbalance in the 6th Chakra also leads to inflated ideas of your spiritual nature and purpose, usually caused by an inability to correctly understand your true spiritual reality and lessons and how you are actually connected to and interact with Spirit.

Working with and on the 6th Chakra is believed to help you better understand the true nature of God and how God manifests on physical levels. It is linked directly to the interpretation of visions and symbols — and dreams.

This is the Chakra of the "higher mind," the Christ or Buddha Consciousness.

The 6th Chakra is the most reliable center for holding Soul memories of past or parallel lives simply because when it is functioning properly your emotional nature is better understood and correctly interpreted.

In India, the 6th Chakra is referred to as the Two Petaled Lotus and is named *Ajna*, meaning *the seat of thinking*.

Your personal sense of time, represented by the flow of mental images and internal dialogue, awaken here first. This is the point where Time and Timelessness come together, the center containing the "winged seed," itself symbolizing a point when thoughts are stopped and inspiration seems to come from nowhere, but in reality come directly from the Self.

The 6th Chakra is Command Central where you can learn to control the flow of images and visions, cancel time, and experience freedom by "emptying the mind."

It is linked to the pineal gland of the endocrine system located in the center of the brain, and was in ancient times called "the seat of the Soul."

The 6th Chakra links directly to the 2nd when functioning at optimum capacity. And both the 1st and 6th Chakras are Master Controllers of the physical body's metabolic systems.

The color indigo opens the 6th Chakra, and the color scarlet closes it. It resonates to the musical note A and the musical tone *ti*.

7TH CHAKRA – THE CROWN CHAKRA: Within the ancient Tibetan and Edgar Cayce systems, the 7th Chakra is located just behind the forehead slightly above the eyebrows and is most often associated with the colors violet, pure white, and gold.

However, all other chakra systems place the 6th at the brow and the 7th at the crown. We suggest that you experiment and see which one feels most correct for you personally.

But no matter where it is located, the 7th Chakra is your direct link to a clearer understanding of God (however you personally interpret that), a place of blending your inner life with your outer life, of discovering your Divine purpose in this life, and even seeing into the future.

The 7th Chakra is the one that aligns you directly with any truly "higher" forces or energies.

This is the Chakra where spiritual healing takes place, and from where it is dispersed to the other Chakras.

The 7th Chakra is connected to both the spiritual and soul energy bodies.

It is believed that a properly harmonized and functioning 7th Chakra automatically annihilates all negativities.

Physiologically, the 7th Chakra is linked directly with the cells of the physical brain, and both the pineal and the pituitary glands but primarily the pituitary, the Master Gland of the endocrine system.

Working with the 7th Chakra allows a fusion of body and spirit, and activates the process of "becoming one with the Infinite." Focusing on the 7th Chakra directly activates and expands your understanding of just about everything, in fact, and not just spiritual things. It has the capacity to "spiritualize the intellect" and has always been associated with the perceptual reality of God.

The 7th Chakra symbolizes your personal ability to integrate with God through the framework of your own unique personality, and is directly related to how you integrate with all higher energies.

This is also where experiences of a sense of fulfillment and completion originate. The 7th Chakra is directly connected to the soul energy body and is where true

Illumination occurs within the physical world.

Excesses in the 1st and 2nd Chakras will eventually weaken both the 6th and 7th Chakras.

In India, the 7th Chakra is referred to as the Lotus of the 1,000 Petals and is called *Sahasrara*.

Kundalini energy has its true awakening within this Chakra, often accompanied and identified by parapsychological phenomena. Kundalini is often experienced in the 6th or 7th Chakra as heat or pulsations at the top of the head; see ANIMAL/Snake, Kundalini.

Mental stimulation or subconscious materials struggling to be born into their own consciousness also frequently create pressures here. But pressure in the area of the 6th and/or 7th Chakras can also simply be related to ordinary and limited attitudes and a message that its now way past time to release or change them.

The 7th Chakra is the "Mythical Marriage Chakra" the true point of "I Am." It is here that you will receive your most intense experiences of Oneness, timelessness and formlessness.

It will most likely be hard to verbalize any 7th Chakra experiences, since things experienced through the 7th Chakra leave the personal human realm and connect directly to Universal or Cosmic Truth. In other words, your experiences may not always "make sense" to you.

Most Chakra systems hold that no negative emotions of any kind are, or can be, associated with the 7th Chakra at any time. This stems at least partly from the belief that all human emotions are believed to extend only to sensory reality and perception, and 7th Chakra experiences transcend all of these.

The symbol of the serpent being carried off by the eagle symbolizes the experience of transformation of knowledge or matter into the Soul, and has been associated with the 7th Chakra for thousands of years, by many different cultures.

The colors pure white, violet, magenta, and gold open the 7th Chakra, and the colors dark blue and blue-black close it.

It resonates to the musical note B and the musical tone *do*, bringing us full circle on the musical scale back to where we began, but at a slightly higher frequency or rate of vibration.

THE HIGHER CHAKRAS: The Chakras above the 7th are generally referred to as the Higher Chakras.

They are believed to be intersecting points for all of the subtle energy bodies, and are for this reason sometimes referred to as the Channeling Chakras.

The soul body is not believed to be directly connected to the upper three Higher Chakras, but to a Chakra located within your aura but not situated at any one stationary point.

It is believed that the pure metals gold, silver, and platinum begin the opening and balancing process of Chakras 8 through 12.

8TH CHAKRA: The 8th Chakra is believed to be anywhere from a few inches to a few feet above the top of your head.

The 8th Chakra must be properly opened and harmonized in order to enter and truly experience the higher spiritual realms or dimensions. This is the center from which you receive the purest information about the "invisible world."

The 8th Chakra helps coordinate the etheric and emotional energy bodies, and aids directly in the transformation of the purple and violet energy frequencies and the violet energy of the 6th Chakra.

The 8th Chakra activates the power necessary to bring energy from one level of existence to another. In the West, the 8th Chakra is most often associated with the color purple.

9TH CHAKRA: The 9th Chakra is believed to be outside the atmosphere of Earth. It connects the emotional and mental energy bodies, and reminds you that you are one of the caretakers of this planet.

The 9th Chakra is generally associated with the color peach, the combined colors pink of the 4th Chakra and the orange of the 2nd Chakra. It is likely that the 9th Chakra is also connected to the "new" Earth through this peach or salmon color.

10TH CHAKRA: The 10th Chakra is believed to reach through our entire solar system, and coordinates the mental and astral energy bodies.

The mineral green tourmaline helps to open the 10th Chakra. The 10th Chakra is generally associated with silver in its pure metal form (pure in this context meaning unalloyed).

11TH CHAKRA: The 11th Chakra connects to our entire galaxy, not just the solar system, and unifies the astral and causal energy bodies.

This Chakra is directly associated with the near-enlightened or near-perfected state of being, and unconditional love at the Universal level.

The 11th Chakra is generally associated with gold in its pure metal form.

12TH CHAKRA: The 12th Chakra reaches outside our galaxy and is your information highway to the entire Universe.

It is responsible for the consolidation of the causal and fully-integrated spiritual energy bodies.

The 12th Chakra encompasses all colors, and for this reason is most often associated with the color pure white.

MINERALS RELATED TO CHAKRAS:

TO OPEN:

1st   Red Aventurine
       Red Jasper
       Black Obsidian
       Ruby

2nd   Red Aventurine [opens 2-5]
       Red Carnelian
       Red Garnet

3rd   Natural Citrine
       Yellow Carnelian
       Golden Tiger's Eye

4th   Emerald
       Green Aventurine
       Hackmanite [Pink
          Sodalite]
       Kunzite [all colors]
       Pink & Green Marble
       Rose Quartz
       Rhodochrosite
       Rhodonite

5th   Blue Aventurine
       Blue Topaz
       Chrysocholla
       Turquoise

6th   Amethyst
       Ametrine
       Azurite
       Blue Sodalite
       Calcite
       Iolite
       Kyanite
       Moonstone [all colors]
       Natural Pearl
       Natural pure Silver
       Opal [all varieties]
       Sugilite
       Selenite [esp. Wands]

7th   Apophyllite [all colors]
       Ametrine
       Diamond [all colors]
       Gem Silica

Natural pure Gold
Phenachite
Selenite
Sugilite

Blue Calcite opens, heals, soothes, and helps unblock all of the main 7 Chakras.

8th   White Diamond
      Pure Gold
      Pure Platinum
      Pure Silver

9th   Blue Diamond
      Pure Platinum

10th Green Tourmaline
      Pure Silver

11th Pure Gold
      Yellow Diamond

12th Pink Diamond

TO CLOSE:

1st   Blue Tourmaline
      Sodalite

2nd   Blue Fluorite
      Blue Tiger's Eye
      Turquoise

3rd   Brown Jasper
      Brown Sandstone
      Brown Tiger's Eye

4th   Carnelian
      Orange Calcite

5th   Carnelian
      Citrine
      Yellow Calcite
      Yellow Carnelian

6th   Brown Jasper

7th   Brown Jasper

Brown Jasper instantly closes and protects all Chakras. Brown Jasper, in fact, prevents cording.

TO ALIGN AND BALANCE:

1st   Black Jade
      Scheelite

2nd   Black Jade

3rd   Black Jade

4th   Aragonite

5th   Aragonite

6th   Aragonite

7th   Sugilite

Muscovite instantly aligns all Chakras, anytime, anywhere.

CHASE
Whether you are being chased or doing the chasing, this symbol often represents that you are running from something you do not want to face at the time, that you

are taking evasion action and avoiding or dodging something in your life or personal growth at the time of the dream or experience.

But it also may be telling you that you are making a great effort to catch up to the object being chased.

Who the pursuer is and what or who is being pursued will lead you to the right interpretation of your dream chase. (Remember that on the first level of your dream you are playing all of the parts, so even when you are being chased, you are also the one who is pursuing).

Chasing or being chased can also symbolize that some part of you feels it literally has to chase you down and corner you to get you to listen to what it has to say.

What part of you is chasing which other part? Why? Is a man or woman being chased? Is a man or woman doing the pursuing? Why? Is the pursuer animal, human, or something else altogether?

What happens when the object being chased gets caught? How will the life of the pursuer be different once he/she/it has caught what it is chasing? How do you feel in the dream? Why? See also EMO-TIONS, RUN.

CITY

Cities are ancient symbols for Divine Order. A city is a large gathering of individuals with the ability to produce experiences not usually otherwise supplied by Nature such as products, entertainments, support, education, and protection

Cities also represent excitement, intellectual opportunities and stimulation, creative inspiration, enormous energy and productivity made possible through the pooling of interests, resources, and ideas.

For instance, people who live in cities do not often have to grow their own food or weave their own cloth. However, because of the large number of different individuals contained within them, cities are also dangerous, treacherous, challenging environments.

Dreaming of cities could also be a message that you need to slow down and get in touch with your true nature or needs, to get back in touch with Nature.

Conversely, dreaming of cities may be a message to contact some of your creative, curious, hard working, hard playing capacities.

Where is the city located? What country is it in? What is happening in it? What is it best known for? How do you feel in it? How do you feel about cities in general? What condition is your the city in?

What time of day is it, what time of year? What's the lighting in the city? Why? What time period is it in?

What kind of buildings and vehicles are there? What is its main industry? What type of person would be drawn to live and work in your dream city? Why? How would you like to visit it? Why, or why not? How is a city different from a small town or a farm? And what does any or all of this remind you of?

CLIMB

To climb anything you must use your personal physical efforts. Most climbs require some amount of concentration and caution, no matter what direction you are climbing.

What are you climbing? Is it rough, steep, difficult? Is the ascent or descent smooth, or frightening, to you? Why? Is anyone with you? Why, or why not? What does this remind you of?

Why are you making the climb at all? What type of person would normally want to make this climb? Why? Where will you be when your climb is over? How do you feel about that?

See also any dream object you are climbing, MOUNTAIN, HILL, DIRECTION/Up, Down, LADDER, HOUSE/Stairs.

CLIMBING DOWN is often telling you that you are, or feel you are, retreating. Climbing down can also be a message that you are about to go back over thoughts or feelings you have already covered, that you are returning to what appear to be safer more solid emotions or experiences.

But climbing down could just as easily be telling you that there is nothing for you in the direction you are climbing at the time. How you are using this symbol will tell you which definition might best apply at the time.

CLIMBING UP often means that you are going in the right direction, depending upon the circumstances of the climb and the overall content of your dream or meditation.

Climbing up, for instance, might tell you that you are trying to run away, get away from it all, or just view things from a higher perspective.

How you feel about the climb, how you feel during the climb, and what you are climbing will help you determine which of these possible interpretations apply at the time.

CLOTHES

Clothes most often symbolize the roles you create for yourself and the uniforms you are wearing at the time.

Whether you are awake or asleep, your clothes are highly symbolic and tell those around you a great deal about you. In effect, all of your clothes are uniforms, worn for specific occasions or to help you accomplish certain goals or tasks, or make certain statements.

Clothes are symbols of your levels of social, economic, and other achievements. Clothes can also symbolize your current opinions and beliefs.

And clothes also reflect your feelings and attitudes about yourself at the time of your dream or meditation.

Clothes tell you how you feel about your physical body, how modest or shy you feel, how restricted you feel. Are you covering up too much, or not enough?

Clothes also represent protection from the elements of Nature, and from invasion of your privacy by others. Are you feeling exposed, or underexposed to the natural elements of your life?

How are these clothes different from the clothes you normally wear? How do you feel about the clothes in your dream or meditation? Why? What kind of a person would choose to wear these clothes?

CHANGING YOUR CLOTHES in a dream or meditation almost always is telling you that now is the time to change your self-image, your thoughts and beliefs, your way of behaving, the way you accomplish certain things, or even that its time for some R&R, get out of uniform, depending upon the clothes you are changing from and into.

From what kind of clothes are you changing? Into which ones? Why? How will you behave differently after the change of clothing? Why?

CLOTHES DIFFERENT FROM THE ONES YOU USUALLY WEAR may be telling you that some part of you feels that you're not being yourself right now, especially in the area of your life or emotions represented by your dream or meditation.

It can also symbolize that there is something about yourself that you are trying to ignore or deny, and that the way you are dressed in the dream or meditation is how you really feel.

Or clothes different from your usual ones could be trying to tell you that some part of you feels it would like to change its style, play dress-up, change the role it is now playing.

But this can just as easily be a symbol that it is time to make a change and be the way you really are or want to become.

What kind of person would wear this type of clothing? For what purpose? How do you feel about those kinds of people? How are these clothes different from the ones you usually wear? What do they remind you of?

CLOTHES FROM ANOTHER TIME PERIOD is believed by many experts to represent a past or parallel life memory of some kind. However, this generally just means that the roles you are playing at the time are the same ones you played then, that your feelings at the time of the dream or meditation are the same then as they were in that lifetime. It can even be telling you about a lesson you didn't complete in that lifetime, or warning you about a pothole you feel into last time.

How were human beings different in that particular time period from how they are now? Why did they choose the style of clothing they did? How is it different from yours? What does that tell you about the connection to your roles then and now?

SHOPPING FOR CLOTHES is almost always symbolizing the part of you that is or wants to look for a change in style, that you are shopping around, looking at the possibilities and options available at the time, usually in the role or roles you normally play.

Shopping means just that — that you are looking for new ways of expressing who you are and who you would like to be. How will your behavior change when you change your style? Why? See also BUILD-ING/Shopping Center.

WHITE SHINING CLOTHES or ones glowing and radiating light of any kind are ancient symbols for the victory of the Spirit over the physical body and earthly things and desires, victory over your lower or physical nature

Are you wearing the clothes? If not, what is the person like as a person who is? What actions are being carried out? How do you feel at the time? Why? What kind of clothes are they? What do they remind you of?

COMMON CLOTHING SYMBOLS:

CAPE: A dual symbol, a cape or cloak represents both dignity and a veil which conceals your true form from the world.

Capes are also ancient symbols of wholeness, and total confidence in self-expression. Cloaks and capes are also symbols of removing yourself from the everyday natural instinctive influences of general humanity; e.g., the cloaked oracle, sage, and mage.

The position of the cloak on the body and what it is doing are important clues to interpreting its significance.

A CAPE FLYING IN THE WIND LIKE WINGS symbolizes the presence of Spirit (the wind) and the ability to merge with it, the ability to merge the fixed principle (Matter) with the volatile, activating principle (air/wind/Spirit).

GLOVES: Historically, gloves were symbols of sovereignty and the law. Gloves can also symbolize a particular station or level you have attained in life; for example, gloves were once worn only by the aristocracy.

And gloves can symbolize that you are covering up, even protecting, some of the talents and abilities you should now be using, specifically in connection with the use of your hands, or what hands symbolize to you.

Gloves also show you that you may feel a need to protect your hands and what they symbolize to you at the time, or that you should be; see BODY/Hand.

Who is wearing the gloves? Why? What are they made of? Are they decorated, or plain? What color are they? Are they appropriate for the climate?

How do you feel about gloves? What kind of a person likes to wear gloves? Do you often wear them? Why, or why not? How are gloves different from mittens?

WEARING DIRTY GLOVES often symbolizes you feel a need to improve your performance, or that you are in danger of getting your hands dirty concerning the subject of your dream or life experience. Or even that you believe you can keep your hands from getting dirty by wearing gloves.

HAT: Since it covers the head, a hat has a long history of symbolizing thought, opinions, and beliefs.

Hats also symbolize your personal viewpoint or perspective, your talents or occupation, even your self-image.

And hats were once very strong symbols of the status or class of a person.

A hat can also symbolize your mental condition at the time of the dream or experience, your mental attitudes.

Hats are also great puns. Are you tossing your hat in the ring? Is something old hat? Are you being told to keep in under your hat?

What material is the hat made of? Why? Who is wearing it? How is it being worn? What condition is it in? Is it fashionable, or out of date?

Would you like to wear this hat? Why, or why not? What kind of a person normally wears this kind of hat? Why? See also COLOR of hat, BODY/Hair, Head.

CHANGING YOUR HAT is symbolically the equivalent of changing your mind, your roles and position in life, and any specialized group you might like to join; e.g.,

fireman's hat, bishop's miter, nurse's cap, etc.

SHOES: Shoes most often symbolize authority and control. In ancient times, shoes were symbols of a free person since slaves usually went barefooted.

Shoes were also a symbol of the Yin (female) principle in its fertility aspect, the foot itself being Yang (male). Shoes are still often strong sex symbols and are used in many myths and fairy tales to show the true power of the female.

Shoes also symbolize something that protects you as you continue your journey or path through life.

And shoes can be a message that you now have enough protection to move ahead, take action, and that you are protected specifically by what the style of shoe represents to you.

Shoes can also be a good pun, as in "don't judge another until you have walked a mile in his shoes," "the shoe is on the other foot," "barefoot and pregnant," or even "shoe" for "shoo!" Or are you ready to give someone or something the boot?

What type of shoes are they? What color are they? What are they made of? Who would normally wear these shoes? Why and for what occasion?

What action is taking place in the shoes, or because of them? How would you like to wear them when you are awake? Why, or why not? How are shoes different from boots or sandals? See also COLOR of shoes, BODY/Foot, and VE-HICLE.

TAKING OFF YOUR SHOES BEFORE ENTERING SACRED SPACE symbolizes leaving your earthly characteristics and thoughts outside or behind, and that you are entering the sacred space in a submissive and reverent attitude by taking off negative thoughts and feelings, that you are literally taking off your "lower" physical nature and leaving it outside in the world where it belongs.

IF YOU ARE MISSING A SHOE, it can be a message that you are over-exposing yourself or that you are in danger of misplacing your protection related to your movement through your life at the time.

But the style of shoe and how you feel about it makes all the difference in your interpretation of how you use it. How do you feel about the missing shoe? What kind was it? How critical is it that you find it? Why? See also LOST, MISSING.

UNIFORM: A uniform of any kind generally symbolizes how you see yourself or how you show yourself to the people around you at the time, literally the surface personality you wear.

A uniform can also be telling you to loosen up, get out of uniform once in a while, be who you really are and not what others or you think you should be.

But a uniform can be a message that you actually need to be more organized and professional in some areas of your life, more uniform, to do it by the book, accept authority once in a while.

What type of uniform is it? Who would normally wear this uniform? What are they like as people? How is this uniform the same as, or different from, the same uniform in waking life? What material is it made of? How do you feel about the uniform? Why?

COLOR
As with all other personal symbols, each of us has our own unique color reference chart, a personalized way we see and interpret colors.

We recommend that you use the following possible interpretations only as a reference point. Your personal color index may or may not be the same. No two people ever physically see exactly the same color or interpret its symbolism in exactly the same way.

AMBER: The color amber relates directly to the life force energy of planet Earth, especially ancient and nearly forgotten energy.

To dream of or be especially aware of the color amber could be a clear message about your energy as it connects to our planet. The overall content of your dream or experience will tell you which area of your life you are connecting with, or that some part of you would like to connect to at the time.

AQUAMARINE: Aquamarine symbolizes peace, calm, protection (especially protection associated with water and all it symbolizes), psychic development, and clear verbal expression.

Aquamarine is said to be one of the true Angelic colors, most often associated with the Order of Cherubim.

BEIGE: Traditionally, beige symbolizes idealism and neutrality in feelings and actions. However, some authorities see beige as a "negative" color. How do you feel about the beige at the time? What colors need to combine to make the color beige? What does this remind you of going on in your life?

BLACK: The color black has symbolized deep knowledge and wisdom, the Unknown, the Unconscious, and Great Mystery, Nothingness, and Non-Being since the earliest times.

Black is considered to be Yin (female) energy, while Yang (male) is white. It is a color of great dignity.

To the ancients, black represented the presence of the indwelling living Spirit and the expression of the potential of the hidden spirit within the Soul.

Black is the polar opposite of white, containing all colors, but by absorbing rather than releasing them, making black a strong symbol for the capacity to hold all of the answers, and for the unconditional acceptance of all things.

Conversely, black can also represent the absence of Light. So the color black can represent darkness, an unwillingness or inability to see clearly, and any and all negative or "dark" feelings or emotions.

The color true black reduces the activity in any Chakra; see CHAKRA. True black is a tremendous absorber of any negative energies, and has been used by metaphysicians and mystics for generations to deflect "evil" or unwanted energies and influences.

In some Native American traditions, black is one of the four power colors. And to the ancient Egyptian, black represented both the abundance of life (fertility) and its total emptiness.

But black also symbolized the rebirth of the Spirit. The original meaning of the phrase black magic, in fact, is believed by some authorities to refer to ancient Egyptian magic, magic that came from the Black Land of Egypt.

BLUE: Blue symbolizes Peace, spirituality, compassion, communication, healing, perception, Truth, and the 5th or Throat Chakra (see CHAKRA/5th).

Blue is the first truly higher (translate that as "faster") vibration on the color spectrum, and said to be one of the primary Angelic colors, especially Sky Blue.

Blue represents the Higher Mental Planes of existence, and the Higher Mind or Higher Intellect.

Blue opens the 4th (Heart) Chakra and the 5th (Throat)

Chakra, and closes the 1st, the Root Chakra. Blue cools, while red warms.

Blue also symbolizes spiritual transparency (i.e., the absence of pollutants of any kind), the immaterial, Divine Truth, and fidelity accomplished by steadfastly clinging to Truth.

And in the Orient, blue symbolizes protection against evil. Blue is also symbolic of the fantastic and the unreal.

Blue also makes a good pun. Are you feeling blue (which, by the way, wearing too much blue will do for you)? How about "blue" for "blew?"

BLUE-GRAY: Blue-gray symbolizes analytical behavior and attitudes, probably one of the reasons why it's still used at West Point.

BLUE-WHITE: The color blue-white symbolizes the Eternal and the Divine.

BROWN: The color brown symbolizes earthiness, conservative feelings or attitudes, physical satisfaction, being grounded and connected to the Earth, and comfortable stability.

Conversely, brown can also symbolize illness, strictness, your immediate problems, and overwork, as in "browning out." Brown may be a strong message that you need to take a break, focus on something entirely different for a while.

It can also be telling you to get back in touch with the physical aspects of your life, connect with Nature, acknowledge that you live in a physical world in a physical body.

Brown is the color of Earth and of Autumn. The color brown closes all Chakras.

CANARY-YELLOW: The color canary-yellow symbolizes curiosity, a naturally inquisitive nature, and light-hearted happiness.

CHARTREUSE: Chartreuse or a sickly green color frequently symbolizes envy, deliberate malice, lies, hate, and potential illnesses caused by storing or refusing to acknowledge any or all of these feelings. Remember the old expression, "Pea green with envy?"

CRIMSON: The color crimson symbolizes the vital dynamic quality of your life energy, a healthy circulatory system, and health and energy in great abundant. Crimson also symbolizes honesty, command of your ego, and very, very passionate love.

Crimson is one of the bridge colors, providing an interim connection for the shift in human consciousness now taking place. Crimson is strongly connected to the 6th Chakra.

EMERALD GREEN: Emerald green symbolizes an initiation, a purification, and a spiritual assistance or teaching.

Emerald green opens the 4th or Heart Chakra and is said to be one of the primary Angelic colors. It is especially connected with all teaching orders of Angels.

GOLD: The color gold symbolizes Purity, Divine Light, Divine Consciousness, Enlightenment, the Soul, the Higher Self, heavenly light, and the 7th Chakra.

Gold in a dream or meditation is often a cue that your experience has more than its usual spiritual content.

Some authorities connect the color gold with the ancient civilization of Lemuria.

The color gold opens all of the Chakras, including the ones above the 7th (see CHAKRA).

The ancient Egyptians believed that the flesh of the gods were made of gold, while the bones of the gods were made of silver. To the ancient Aztecs, gold was literally the "feces of the gods."

The metal gold is durable, but extraordinarily soft, especially in its purest form, which interestingly enough has a chemical formula of *Au*.

Gold also represents unchangeableness and something of great value, esoteric and precious knowledge, and the highest spiritual state attainable while in a form.

Gold was used to symbolize spiritual things long before it had any commercial value. It has always been considered the most noble of metals and colors by every culture in which gold it is found.

Since it cannot rust, the metal gold has often been used as a symbol of morality. It is associated with the sun and all sun deities worldwide.

GOLD-WHITE: The color gold-white symbolizes the level immediately next to All-That-Is, to God. Gold-white often symbolizes the Buddhic or Christ Light and level of existence.

GRAY: The color gray often represents loss of energy, fear, depression, sadness, or a need to rest, to withdraw. Are you walking around in a fog? Are you beginning to get into gray areas of thinking or feeling?

But gray also symbolizes meditation, the intermediate planes of existence, and compensation accomplished through the workings of true justice.

Gray consists of nearly equal parts of black and white, taking on the symbolism of these two combined or merged. Gray also represents the physical brain, your "gray matter."

To the early Christians, gray was the color of the cloak the Christ will wear at the Last Judgment (see CLOTHES/Cape).

In some metaphysical systems, gray is the color of the various levels of the Astral Plane, while in other systems these Planes are believed to be green.

GRAY, DARK: Dark gray often symbolizes physical and spiritual discipline through the determined use of will.

GREEN: Green often symbolizes an awakening to life, abundance, longevity, immortality, freshness, cyclic or annual renewal, healing, peace, hope, new or continued growth, prosperity, money, physical balance, life, growth through intense desire, and the 4th or Heart Chakra.

Green is a neutral color, the mediator between the yellow of emotional feelings and the blue of perception (the 3rd and 5th Chakras); see CHAKRA).

Green is said to be one of the primary Angelic colors, especially emerald green or shimmering green.

Green opens the 4th Chakra and is believed to have no adverse side effects — ever, under any circumstances.

In some metaphysical systems, green is the color of the Astral Plane, while in others its various levels are believed to be gray in color.

In Islam, green symbolizes both material and spiritual salvation, and the wisdom of the prophets. It is a symbol of illumination, the "green light" that is often seen at the rising and setting of the sun.

In ancient China, the color green was associated with the symbolism of thunder and lightning, and the Yin (female) principle.

The ancient alchemists saw the "secret fire" (the living spirit) within the color green, and believed this color to be capable of dissolving the metal gold. This secret fire was often symbolized as a translucent crystal.

Green in your dream or meditation may also be a straightforward message to GO!, you have the green light.

GREEN, DARK: Dark or forest green often symbolizes peace, healing, and Nature. It also frequently signals the beginning of a teaching dream. See also Emerald Green above.

GREEN, LIGHT: Light green symbolizes shyness and your psychic sensitivities.

It can also represent low energy levels, especially related to what green symbolizes to you. See also Pale Colors below.

INDIGO BLUE: Indigo blue symbolizes the Higher Life Force energy, spirituality, divine protection, psychic consciousness, and the 6th Chakra.

Some authorities suggest that to see indigo blue in connection with yourself or anyone else tells you that you have been accepted by a Master Teacher.

Indigo blue opens the 6th Chakra and closes the 2nd (see CHAKRA).

LAVENDER: Traditionally, the color lavender symbolizes mother-consciousness, mother love, and working yourself out of a karmic situation.

MAGENTA: The color magenta often symbolizes the realm where fantasy and reality blend — in other words, living on the edge.

Magenta also represents creativity made tangible, building something out of thin air.

This color can also be telling you that you either have, or should find, your own original viewpoint about the subject of your dream or experience.

MAUVE: Mauve is one of the transitional colors, bridging the vibrational differences between Earth colors and to the "new" or second sun, the legendary Blue Star. Mauve is strongly related to the 4th or Heart Chakra.

MUDDY COLORS: Traditionally, muddy colors of any hue symbolize one of the four lower astral levels of existence.

Muddy colors can also be symbolic of depleted energy and confused or muddy feelings, emotions, and thinking. Are you unclear about something symbolized by the color?

Muddy colors can also be a message to not get stuck, or that you are in danger of being stuck by or in what the muddy color symbolizes to you.

NAVY BLUE: Navy blue symbolizes discipline in thought. It relates to the planet Saturn (see PLANET/ Saturn), and closes the 7th Chakra (see CHAKRA).

ORANGE: Orange symbolizes energy, warmth, change, sociability, creativity, self-esteem, security, "gut-level" intuition (often associated with the 2nd Chakra), and the

releasing of traumatic feelings and memories.

Orange closes the 5th Chakra and opens the 2nd (see CHAKRA).

ORANGE, DEEP: The color deep orange symbolizes personal pride, family pride, racial pride, possessiveness, lust, and most strong emotions.

ORANGE, GOLDEN: The color golden orange symbolizes invigorating positive energy, warmth, a healthy focus on life, your life energy in general, the sun and all sun deities with all of their symbolism, and a healthy and balanced 2nd Chakra (see CHAKRA).

PALE or PASTEL COLORS: Pale or pastel colors often symbolize neutrality, or a balance in the emotions represented by the color.

Pale colors can also be telling you that you are ready to enter a new experience, to add something to that particular color and what it symbolizes to you.

Conversely, pale colors can be warning you that your energy is getting very low and scattered. Are you running in too many directions at once, taking on too much at one time?

Pastel or pale colors can also be a signal that you are beginning to take the intensity out of the feelings and emotions represented by the color. Or are you becoming "just a pale reflection of yourself?" The overall content of your dream or experience will tell which interpretation applies.

PEACH or PINK-ORANGE: The color peach or pink-orange symbolizes the connection of your emotional and mental qualities. Peach helps connect the 4th Chakra with the 2nd, and Peach is the dominate color of the 9th Chakra (see CHAKRA).

This is the color most often associated with the Buddhic or Christ/Messianic Plane of existence. See also SALMON below.

PINK: The color pink has a long tradition for symbolizing the heart, Peace, serenity, Love, spiritual innocence, the innocence of children, devotion, tenderness, sensitivity, chastity, reverence, and the 4th or Heart Chakra (green also symbolizes the Heart Chakra; see CHAKRA).

PURPLE: Since purple combines the colors blue and red, it is an ancient symbol for Wisdom and Knowledge.

And purple symbolizes Divine protection, the nobility or a member of a royal family, healing, telepathic capacities, and the 7th Chakra (the colors white and gold also symbolize the 7th Chakra; see CHAKRA). At one time, wearing purple was restricted to royalty.

Conversely, purple can also symbolize arrogance (especially spiritual arrogance), the misuse of psychic powers, and someone who is almost totally ego-centered.

For most of us here in the Western part of the world, the dominate color of the 8th Chakra is also the color purple (see CHAKRA).

RED: Red symbolizes strong passions, excellent health and life energy, spiritual energy, physical survival, sexuality, lust, and the 1st or Root Chakra. And in ancient times, red symbolized protection from danger.

Red opens the 1st Chakra and closes the 5th (see CHAKRA).

In some Native American traditions, red is one of the four power colors. To the ancient Egyptians, red symbolized destruction and evil, but was considered a positive color when used on the crown of Lower Egypt.

To the Romans, red was the color of nobility, of power, fertility, new life, warmth, and was worn by all high ranking judges.

And to the alchemists, red was the color of the Philosopher's Stone.

Red also means STOP! and may be a warning of some kind about the subject of your dream or experience.

ROSE: The color rose symbolizes mystical love, safety, nurturing, empathy, affections, the heart, and the 4th or Heart Chakra.

ROSE-RED: The color rose-red is symbolic of the highest personal expression of love possible to a human being, and of True Love, or God's love. For instance, the color rose-red in your dream is often present when you are receiving a communication from a teacher, a guide, or saint.

Rose-red is often used to heal excesses of emotional love by substituting the qualities it symbolizes for the excesses.

ROYAL BLUE: Royal blue symbolizes a blessing, and a promise of importance and major expansion or growth. Some authorities suggest that royal blue can only be seen in dreams or a meditation by someone who is in alignment with "higher" mental qualities.

RUBY RED: Ruby red symbolizes trust, respect, integrity, authority which has been earned, protection against evil, spiritual honors, and the approval of a teacher or guide.

SALMON: The color salmon is one of the bridge colors allowing easier access to the changes in consciousness occurring at this time. Salmon is strongly connected to the 5th or Throat Chakra.

SCARLET: The color scarlet often symbolizes unpredictable willfulness, immaturity, an out-of-control temper, one who constantly accuses, an agitator, irresponsibility, someone without a conscience, and intense sexual energy.

Scarlet closes the 6th Chakra and opens the 2nd (see CHAKRA).

SILVER: The color silver symbolizes spiritual protection, Truth, Purity, wealth, mystical powers, initiation, Light, self-knowledge, and something of value.

Silver also symbolizes the moon and all moon deities and energies.

Silver seen in your dream or meditation often indicates that you

are beginning initiation into the proper use of the 6th Chakra, but the color silver itself is usually related to both the 3rd and 6th Chakras.

And silver opens the 7th Chakra and is often the dominant color of the 10th Chakra (see CHAKRA).

Silver is a highly reflective metal when polished and can function as a mirror, a secondary reflecting source, when you are not quite ready to face or come in contact directly with the real thing (see MIRROR)

The ancient Egyptians believed that the bones of the gods were made of silver, while their flesh was made of gold.

SKY BLUE: All variations in shades of the color sky blue are said to be used almost exclusively by Angels, and specifically the Order of Cherubim, as a message that you are aligning with them.

This color is used to give hope, support, and assurance that you are on the right path at the time of your dream or experience.

TURQUOISE BLUE: Turquoise blue symbolizes protection, the presence of a carrier of ancient wisdom and knowledge, psychic gifts, communication, speaking your personal truth, and rewards you have earned.

Some authorities connect the color turquoise blue with the ancient civilization of Atlantis.

The color turquoise opens the 5th or Throat Chakra and closes the 2nd (see CHAKRA).

VERMILION: Vermilion is an old symbol for excesses of racial pride, in other words that there is the potential to become bigoted about the subject of your dream or experience.

VIOLET: The color violet symbolizes Wisdom, Knowledge, the death of the ego-self, the falling away of physical desires, the power to transmute matter into energy and energy into matter, mastership, openness to Divine influences, miracles, immortality, divine protection, someone of a true spiritual nature, and the 7th Chakra.

Violet opens the 7th Charka and closes the 3rd (see CHAKRA).

VIOLET-PINK: The color violet-pink symbolizes healing, restoration, faith, wisdom, humor, understanding, and one who is a giver of life.

VIOLET-WHITE: The color violet-white symbolizes the integration of Spirit and Truth at its highest level.

WHITE: White almost always symbolizes Purity, spiritual perfection, Spirit itself, transcendence, Peace, Truth, true insight, chastity, and the 7th Chakra (but in fact all of the Chakras contain some degree of the color white).

White opens all Chakras. White deflects all colors, refusing to hold any color other than itself.

YELLOW: The color yellow symbolizes intellectual activity, energy, happiness, emotions, and the 3rd or Solar Plexus Chakra.

Yellow also is an ancient symbol for the Center of the Universe, Eternity, kingship or supreme rulership, supremacy over the lower physical human nature, and transfiguration.

Yellow also symbolizes the emotional impact of your intellect, especially yellow tinged with either orange or red.

Yellow opens the 3rd or Solar Plexus Chakra and closes the 7th (see CHAKRA).

To the Buddhists, yellow symbolizes the "robe of fire," the Ego liberated from the lower human nature, especially yellow robes or clothes.

But to the ancient Egyptians, yellow was the color of envy and disgrace.

In some Native American traditions, yellow is one of the four power colors.

Yellow in your dream or meditation may also be telling you to "proceed with caution," to heed the yellow light. Or does some part of you feel "yellow," cowardly?

YELLOW, CLEAR: Clear yellow symbolizes lucidity, a pure and clear intellect, honesty, and integrity. Clear yellow is especially effective at opening the 3rd or Solar Plexus Chakra (see CHAKRA).

YELLOW-GOLD: Yellow-gold symbolizes humility, spiritual power, respect, and reverence.

YELLOW-GRAY: The color yellow gray often symbolizes exhaustion, doubt, even melancholy.

In some metaphysical systems, yellow-gray is believed to be a warning of the presence or attempt of another person or energy to attach to you and your energy.

CONTAINER

Containers are any object with the capacity to contain or hold something else inside of them. The most common ones in symbolism are: box, cup, glass, vase, bag, sack, bottle, jug, pitcher, dish, cage, well, cave, pot, purse, vehicles, and wallet.

Containers will obviously have a variety of symbolic interpretations, depending upon the type of container in your dream or experience, what it is being used for, and how you feel about it.

Containers represent protection, a place of storage and safety, a place to hold or keep. They also very often symbolize the womb and places to incubate new life or growth.

Containers are also symbolic of a place to conceal or hide something, or many things at once, they can even be places of imprisonment.

Puns are often associated with containers. Do you feel boxed in? Are you brown bagging it? What's in a bottleneck? Are you hiding your light under a bushel? Is it time to come out of your cave? Is your cup running over?

BOWL: A dish or bowl is an ancient symbol of a container of the Spirit.

A bowl is also a symbol of your present limitations or boundaries. Bowls were often used by beggars, students and disciples during certain initiation periods, for instance.

A dish or bowl can also be a pun, as in "she's quite a dish," "dishing it out," "bowled over."

What is this bowl or dish being used for? What is in it? What kind of a person would own this dish? What does it remind you of that is going in your life?

BOX: Boxes are dual symbols, representing both specialized containers for holding special or precious objects, and places of great stress and captivity.

Of course, this one is prime for a pun. Does some part of you feel boxed in? Who or what would you like to box?

What kind of a box is it? What is it made of? What was it built to hold? How does it feel? If it could talk, what would it want to say?

CAVE: A cave is an ancient symbol for the Universe and the place of the union of the True Self with the ego personality.

Caves were once places of initiation and rebirth ceremonies. They almost always represent the Yin or female qualities, the womb, and the meeting place of the divine with the human.

Sometimes, the cave is also associated with the heart as a spiritual center and both the cave and the heart are often depicted as a downward-pointing triangle.

And caves, of course, are strong symbols of the Underworld and a place of vague happenings and, in the Platonic sense, a safe place to hide from Reality, things as they really are. Caves are passages to other worlds, especially unfamiliar worlds or realities.

CUP: Cups symbolize the spiritual heart, your capacity to hold and give real love.

Cups are very old symbols for the Soul as the container and a vehicle for the Higher Self.

Cups are also ancient symbols for openness, having a receptive nature, immortality, abundance, and initiation.

The cup and cupbearer have been spiritual metaphors for thousands of years. The Holy Grail, the legendary cup from which Jesus drank at the Last Supper, and the Sufi Cup of Jamshi representing the Mirror of the World, are good examples of using the cup symbol as spiritual metaphor.

Cups also symbolize your emotions. And they can represent an overflowing of abundance and the good life.

Cups are containers capable of holding nourishment, refreshment, intoxicating substances — or poison.

What kind of a cup is it? What is it made of? Who would like it? Who would buy it? What's in it? Is it full, or empty? For what occasion or purpose is the cup being used?

DRINKING FROM A CUP symbolizes that you are participating or drinking in what is in the cup, or what the cup is being used for.

MORE THAN ONE PERSON OR OBJECT DRINKING FROM THE SAME CUP is symbolic of the union of dualities and the end of a solitary existence. This metaphor is still in use today at many wedding ceremonies.

AN OVERTURNED CUP is an old symbol for carelessness and emptiness caused by heedlessness, and sometimes through vanity.

It might also be telling you that something is over, or concealing something else. What was originally in the cup? Has something been lost, or gained? After all, the cup must be empty before it can be filled again.

A CUP ON TOP OF A PILLAR or column symbolizes one who offers himself or herself to Heaven, and one who in return receives Heaven's grace.

VASE: A vase and a pitcher have the almost the same symbolic interpretation, both representing The Great Mother, the Cosmic Waters, the matrix, the Yin (female) principle and qualities; e.g. fertility, acceptance, and the qualities of the heart.

Vases are often associated with the Tree of Life. See TREE/Tree of Life.

To the ancient Chinese, a vase was a symbol of harmony and longevity. To the ancient Egyptians, a vase symbolized the heart, the waters, and the life-giving attributes of Nature. It was a common emblem of both Isis and Osiris. And to the ancient Hindu, a vase was the power of shakti.

A vase or pitcher can, of course, also be representing the astrological sign of Aquarius. Is there an Aquarian in your life?

FLUID FLOWING FROM A VASE OR PITCHER is an old symbol for a beneficent female deity or The Great Mother pouring out the waters of life and fertility onto the world. But if the vase or pitcher is in the hands of a male, this symbol represents an offering to a deity.

A FULL VASE OR PITCHER symbolizes a man of knowledge, one who is full but needs to make no noise about it. Or it could be telling you that you are already full, and that before you can take on more, you need to pour some of this stuff out.

It could also, of course, be telling you that you are just a little too full of yourself, to lighten up a little.

A VASE OR PITCHER OF WINE is an ancient symbol for Divine inspiration; see also ALCOHOL.

COOK
Cooking in a dream or meditation often symbolizes putting together,

mixing, or blending of some of the ingredients currently in your life.

Cooking can also be a wish or need to provide nourishment or sustenance to and for others, or for yourself, to prepare the good things in life, to taste life more fully, spice it up, add or try new ingredients.

This is also a favorite dream pun, as in "you're really cooking now," "too many cooks spoil the broth," "if you can't stand the heat...," "what are you cooking up now?" Is somebody's goose about to get cooked?

Who will receive the benefits of your cooking? How do you feel about cooking in general? Why? What kind of person likes to cook? What kind of person hates to? Why? See also BUILDING/Kitchen, FOOD.

COSMETICS
Dreaming of cosmetics in general, putting on makeup, or grooming yourself by using any type of cosmetics (and this includes shaving guys) symbolizes your personal image, especially your public personal image, the face you show the world.

So if you are sprucing yourself up, are you in the process of changing your image? How are these cosmetics different from the ones you would normally use?

Cosmetics can also be telling you that some part of you feels that you are wearing a mask, hiding your true face.

The original meaning of the word *glamour* meant to place a

spell on someone, to make them see you as more enticing than you really are, or even as a totally different form of life than you really are. Does this remind you of anything going on in your life?

How do you feel about yourself without using cosmetics? How do you feel when you use them? Why? Are you applying cosmetics in your dream, shopping for them, or removing them? Are you being made up?

What are your these particular cosmetics normally used for? What kinds of people use this kind? What colors are being used or applied? Are you ready to present a new face to the public? How do you feel in your dream? See also COLOR of cosmetics, BODY/Face.

CROWD

In dream interpretation language, a crowd is at least three people other than your own image (even though in the first layer of your dream everything and everyone technically is you).

A dream crowd often symbolizes that you have decisions to make, or that you have just made a decision and need to look at your options one more time. The number of people in your dream crowd, how they are dressed, and what actions they are carrying out can show you your options or choices.

Crowds also symbolize your character traits. They can also be a message that you should get out more, socialize, become one of the crowd.

Crowds can, and often do, also represent your spiritual guides, teachers, or partners, and how they are dressed and how they are acting becomes even more important to you.

A dream crowd can also be a pun of some kind. Are you feeling crowded? Are you hanging with the wrong crowd? Feeling lost in the crowd?

What kind of people make up your crowd? What are they doing? Why are they there? What kind of a person would normally be motivated to join this crowd? Why? How do you feel about the crowd in your dream? See also CLOTHES worn by the crowd, GANG, and STRANGER if you don't recognize your crowd.

D

DANCE

Dancing in a dream symbolizes extraordinarily light and fun-loving feelings, an exceptional enjoyment of the subject of your dream or meditation. Dancing can also symbolize strength, physical and emotional activity, and even sex.

Dancing is an ancient symbol for the creative energies of the Cosmos, the transformation of Space and Time, the natural rhythms of the Universe, and human imitation of the Divine Play of Creation.

CHAIN DANCES represent the linking of male and female, Heaven and Earth, or the linking of any polar opposites.

THE DANCE OF SHIVA in Hinduism represents the eternal movement of the Universe. Shiva dances on the defeated monsters of Chaos, Matter, and Ignorance, symbolizing that they have been overcome and representing the enormous joy of release when the illusions caused by these monsters

have been destroyed. It is only when Shiva dances alone that he becomes solitary and destructive. Does this remind you of anything in your own life?

DANCING AROUND AN OBJECT also symbolizes creating the magic circle and protecting and strengthening the object within the circle.

THE RING DANCE or dance in the round symbolizes the dance of the Angels around the Throne of God in many early religions. And in very early Christianity, the ring dance symbolized the 12 Apostles dancing around the Center, Jesus, symbolizing the Mystery, the Christ.

Any dances performed in the round also symbolize the sun's rhythmic movements, again enclosing a sacred space. And dancing in the round symbolizes the cycles of existence and their encircling by the Spirit.

Whirling Dervishes dancing in the round symbolize the whirling of a planet on its own axis around the sun., a good example of a symbol within a symbol. The rapid whirling also produces an altered state of consciousness.

DAY (Times Of)

Each segment of a 24-hour period carries its own unique symbolism. But in general, day (as contrasted to night) is a symbol of clarity of perception and vision, of openness and sincerity, of a time of great activity and the potential for productivity.

The four times or phases of day are also sometimes equated symbolically with the four seasons of the year. And days were used by the ancients to symbolize long periods of time.

Day is also a good pun. Have you finally seen the light? What is some part of you trying to bring into the light of day? Are you doing the same thing day after day, after day, after...?

What time of day is it? Why that time and not some other? Why is it day and not night? What does it remind you of that is going on in your life at the time? How you feel about the specific time of day will lead you to your personal interpretation. See also SEASONS.

COMMON DAY SYMBOLS:

DARK: As an archetype, darkness symbolizes the Primordial Chaos and the power of Chaos out of which all Matter took form. Darkness implies the existence of dualities; for instance, there can be no darkness without its opposite, light, and vice versa.

Darkness is not necessarily negative or evil in itself, as it is from darkness that the light originally emerged. Used in this context darkness becomes Unmanifest Light.

Darkness also precedes new physical birth, and for this reason as much as any other is a major component of most initiation rites. Germination and creation both take place in darkness, and at the physical level all things must return to the darkness.

And Darkness and Light are the dual symbols of The Great Mother, and the principles of the symbolism of Yin (dark) and Yang (light).

Darkness represents a place to rest and retreat, a place to hibernate before beginning a new phase or cycle of life and growth.

In some metaphysical systems, darkness represents the "dark night of the Soul," which symbolizes the deep spiritual crises often experienced during important periods of growth. Used in this context, the darkness experienced before the dawn symbolizes the next step in the transformation of the individual at the Soul level.

Darkness in your dream or meditation can also obviously be telling you that you are not yet enlightened enough in the area or situation being shown to you, that more facts still need to come to light, and that there is more there than meets the eye.

In general, when you are in a dark place or area in your dream or meditation, it represents a place where you are basically still unenlightened or have a shadowy interpretation of events, and may even be pointing out something you don't want to look at yet. Are you deliberately keeping yourself in the dark? Are you resisting turning on the lights because you're afraid of what you might see?

How do you feel about the darkness in your dream? Why is it dark? What lives in this dark? Why? What would happen if light suddenly intruded into the dark? How would things change?

DAWN: In general, the dawn is a symbol of hope, renewal and regeneration, new beginnings, illumination, the clear Light of the Void, a new life, and that literally the whole of a brand new day is in front of you.

To the ancient Greeks, dawn in the persona of the goddess Eos was the sister of the sun Helios and the moon Selene. The Romans personified dawn as the goddess Aurora, the "rose-fingered one."

This one makes another good pun. What has just dawned on you? Do you know anyone named Dawn?

LIGHT: Light almost always symbolizes wisdom and intelligence, especially Higher and Divine Wisdom and Intelligence.

In general, all forms of radiance symbolize new life received from a divinity.

Light can also represent enlightenment, illumination, and the actual manifestation of Divinity as direct knowledge.

And light symbolizes the source of all goodness and life, Truth, spiritual freedom, joy, the True Self, Pure Spirit, the Word or Logos, and the manifestation of non-being into being.

Light also represents energy, power, and the ability to see and understand clearly. Even a small light allows you to see more clearly in the darkest times.

To the ancients, to experience light was to experience Ultimate Reality, the Absolute, to experience God. Light is also connected with the Beginning and the End, and is the dual aspect of The Great Mother as Life and Death, Creation and Destruction.

And light is often associated with rain, symbolizing the Divine descending from Heaven.

Light is the essence of all matter, indestructible in its original state, but still capable of dividing and forming itself into other shapes and forms, textures and sizes, all with varying degrees of consciousness, awareness, and intelligence.

What causes this light? What is its source? How do you feel about it? What color is it? How bright is it? What might cause this light to dim or go out? How would your dream or experience be different without this light? Why?

THE LIGHT OF THE SUN symbolizes direct knowledge as

opposed to indirect, intuitional (or lunar) knowledge.

And the straight lines drawn in a sun symbol generally symbolize Light itself, while wavy lines symbolize the heat of the Sun. See also PLANET/Sun.

MIDDAY or NOON: Midday and midnight each carry much of the same symbolism in that they are both turning points and high points of the cyclic flow of the Yin (feminine) and Yang (masculine) qualities, the high points of a cycle.

As an archetype, midday is the time when no shadow is cast, the time when the spiritual sun is at is physical zenith. Noon is the brightest, hottest time of day. What does this remind you of?

Another good pun, are you about to experience your own high noon?

MIDNIGHT: Midnight and midday (noon) carry much of the same symbolism since they are both turning points or high points of the flow of the natural cycles of the Yin and Yang qualities, and the high point or zenith of a cycle before transition.

As an archetype, midnight is the time when the spiritual sun stands at its spiritual apex, and is therefore associated with deep contemplation, initiation, spiritual insight, knowledge, and the time of mysterious happenings.

So, of course, midnight is the witching hour, the time when according to many legends contact with spirits, ghosts, and demons is most easily achieved.

NIGHT: Night frequently symbolizes that you are not seeing things in as clear a light as you could, that maybe you need to turn up the light a little.

Night can also be telling you that you have deliberately turned off the light, turned your face away from the sun or light source, and that as a result some part of you now feels in the dark about the subject of your dream, meditation, or experience.

If you are in the dark in your dream or meditation you are likely telling yourself to put more light on the subject.

But dreaming of night can also be a message that you need to rest, sleep, relax, have some nighttime fun, maybe even dream and remember your dreams more, especially if you are a night owl by nature.

Night also symbolizes the Great Mystery, the Unknown, the irrational, and the subconscious or unconscious mind. Night symbolizes the darkness which precedes light and rebirth, and the Dark Night of the Soul.

According to the ancient Greeks, night was the mother of the gods, the all-enveloping aspect of the female powers, most often symbolized by a woman with a starstrewn veil holding a child on each arm, one black representing death and one white, representing the sleep before rebirth.

Night can also be a good pun, reminding you to hang in there, that it's always darkest before the dawn.

How do you feel about the night in general? Why? Is it comfortable in your dream or meditation, or making you uneasy? What has caused it to be night? How would your dream or experience be different with a little more light on it? Why? What does this remind you of going on in your life? See also COLOR/Black, Dark and Midnight above, and any objects inhabiting your night.

TWILIGHT: Twilight and dusk frequently symbolizes the beginning-of-the-end of the subject of your dream or experience.

Twilight is also a time for putting away the work and cares of the busy day, a time to relax and wind down before the new day begins.

Your twilight may also be telling you that you need to spend a little more time thinking about your real life, not your twilight existence. Or is it simply time to see the subject of your dream or meditation in a softer, gentler, quieter light?

DEATH

Dreaming of death is often a symbol of the total withdrawal from whatever form or object is dying in your dream or meditation. *Dreams of death or dying are almost never precognitive, and dreaming of your own death rarely symbolizes your physical death.*

Dream death is often a symbol for the withdrawal of the life force from a particular stage of growth or development, almost always related to a characteristic or habit of your ego-personality. This happens most often when a particular stage or level has already served its purpose and now is no longer necessary, and may even now be getting in your way. You are in effect jettisoning your booster rockets, stage by stage.

So death dreams most often symbolize a dying out or passing away of your obsolete personality traits, relationships, or the situation represented by your dream.

Dreams of death and dying can also be warnings that some part of you is about to pack it in, maybe a part that you would really rather not lose right now. How you feel in the dream or meditation about the death will tell you which definition fits best at the time.

Death dreams can also, of course, be early health messages, telling you very clearly that if you don't fix what is represented by your overall dream that, some type of death can be the result.

As an archetype, death is a symbol of the perfecting of the lower (physical) nature of the Soul, a death necessary for the birth of the higher Soul nature. Death to an earthlier life and behavior always precedes any birth of the spiritual life, a common theme and ritual acted out symbolically in many initiation ceremonies.

Death also symbolizes the unseen aspects of life, initiation into the Unknown, moving to another level of consciousness, or into another dimension of being.

The King of Death is often shown as a skeleton with a sword, scythe, sickle, or hour-glass. Other common ancient death symbols are ashes, a drummer, a dancer (often a beautiful girl), and crossing a river or sea. See also CEREMONY/Funeral, GRAVE, and any of the symbols listed below.

COMMON DEATH SYMBOLS:

Keep in mind that each of these symbols carries many, many other meanings in addition to symbolizing a death.

- Any movement in the direction West, the place of maturity and completion.
- Going toward an intense cool bright white light.
- Dying plants.
- Crossing rivers, oceans or other large bodies of water, especially in a boat or raft.
- Regrowth on old dead plants.
- Crossing bridges, especially bridges over water.
- Marriage, especially when a veil is used.
- Newborn infants of any species.
- A serpent, a lion, or a scorpion.

DESERT

Deserts are ambivalent symbols, viewed as both positive and negative. For example, many sacred texts describe the desert as both a punishment experienced by separation from God and being at the mercy of temptation by demons, and as the place where God can show Himself with extraordinary clarity and intensity.

As an archetype, deserts are often symbolic of the infinite magnitude of formless matter and the primordial chaos, a symbol of the place where the mind is unable to penetrate and thus incapable of totally comprehending.

Deserts also represent freedom from the morality and structure of the external world. Deserts have their own survival requirements, requirements which might be totally inappropriate in a lusher landscape. They can be very unforgiving to the uneducated and careless. Remind you of anything in your life?

DESTRUCTION

Any form of destruction, including any dream or meditation object capable of generating mass destruction (like a bomb or tornado), symbolizes massive power.

So destruction in your dream or meditation often symbolizes fear of a loss of control of your most powerful feelings and emotions, ones so forceful they almost seem beyond your control.

Any type of destruction can also represent fear of your true personal power, itself symbolizing who and what you really are. It is this fear of your true power, in fact, that is at the bases of many nightmares.

This type of dream can also be a clear warning of the suppression of any of your emotions which are leading you at the time toward a potentially "lethal" explosion of energy.

If you know this is your present interpretation, take immediate physical action to release the building pressure — talk to someone you can trust, beat the stuffing out of pillows, throw rocks at the moon, go someplace where no one can hear you and scream and yell till you can't yell anymore — whatever it takes to release the buildup of the potentially destructive energy bottled up inside of you.

Destruction dreams can also, however, be telling you about the awakening of what is generally called the Kundalini energy or power; see ANIMAL/Snake, Kundalini. Again, pay attention to your dream message and consciously work with this energy, preferably with someone who can show you how.

Kundalini energy is exceptionally powerful and should be consciously worked with to direct its safe movement. It is not an accident that this kind of energy is often represented by a white cobra; the cobra blinds its prey before striking.

What has caused, or will cause, the destruction? What has been destroyed? How will things be different after the destruction? Were

people or animals injured or destroyed? How do you feel in your dream or meditation? Does this remind you of anything going on in your life right now? See also EXPLOSION, FIRE, STORM, WEAPON and any object which caused the destruction.

DIRECTION
Each direction carries its own symbolism, and these do vary from culture to culture.

While our modern societies talk about four directions, the ancients saw six — east, west, north, south, up, and down.

Dream or meditation directions can also be good puns. Do you need to think about changing your direction? Who gives you direction? Are you upside down, or right side up?

DEEP: Depth often symbolizes the mysterious, the unknown or unfathomable, the areas of darkness, the descent into self-knowledge, going deep within the subject of your dream, meditation, or experience. How do you feel about the depth at the time? How deep are you? In what? See also UNDERGROUND.

DOWN: Down is the direction of the physical levels of existence and the Earth, the place of the mineral, animal, plant, and human life forms.

Down often, but certainly not always, symbolizes that you are headed the wrong direction; however, if you immediately move back up it is probably a symbol for the natural highs and lows of everyday life, and how smoothly you are adjusting to or moving with them.

But treasures are hidden deep down within the ground, and descending is a strong symbol for the search or quest for wisdom or knowledge, mystic rebirth, and even immortality.

Down is the direction taken in many initiatory rites and ceremonies and by virtually all dying deities.

Going down can also symbolize that you are working with deep subconscious matters, or that you are being gently nudged to do so. Down can also be a good pun. Are you feeling down? Has someone put you down, led you down the garden path? Are you about to go down?

How do you feel in your dream or experience? What is it you are going down? Is the way easy, or hard? Why? Would it be harder, or easier, to go up instead? Why?

EAST: The East is often a symbol for the direction in which the True Self appears.

The East also symbolizes birth, rebirth, the spiritual door through which we all enter, the direction in which your true spiritual strength lies, renewal, things yet to happen, youth, the rising sun, dawning new life, Spring, the place of lucidity and inner wisdom, and the place of mental healing.

In many cultures, it is the East toward which worship is to be oriented. Most rituals with themes of death and resurrection emphasizes the direction East and the sunrise as birth and resurrection, and West as the direction of the sunset and death.

The animal most often connected with the East in our Western world is the Golden Eagle, but different cultures associate different animals with this direction.

For example, in China the East is a green dragon, in Egypt a man, in Mexico a crocodile, and in Tibet a man-dragon.

HIGH: Height often symbolizes that you now have new opportunities to reach up, to grow toward the light or thing that is high. It also often shows you the level of growth already reached, or one you could be achieving with just a little more patience and effort.

Height also symbolizes your moral or spiritual level of development, how "high" you are at the time.

If you are on the edge of a cliff or mountain, it often symbolizes that you are ready to make a leap forward into new, unexperienced territory, even if being on the edge frightens you.

Height is also a good pun. What are you high on? Where are you in your dream or meditation? What actions are you carrying out? Why? How do you feel about the height? How do you feel about height in general? How did you get to this height? See also CANYON, CLIMB, FLY, MOUNTAIN, and any dream object that is high in your dream.

NORTH: The North symbolizes Winter, renewal which takes place naturally during sleep or rest, maturity, enjoyment of things saved and stored (things already learned), a time of personal healing, and old age and the Elders.

North is the most physically magnetic direction on our planet, and many authorities recommend that you always sleep with your head pointed North for optimum benefits from sleep and dreams.

The animal most often associated with the direction North in the Western part of the world is the White Buffalo; see also ANIMAL/Buffalo.

SOUTH: The direction South symbolizes the Lower Planes of Existence, or the Astral Planes. It is considered to be the most psychically magnetic direction.

The South also symbolizes Summer, your emotions, trust, accelerated growth, psychic information and experiences, young adulthood, emotional healing, examination of your actions, emotional understanding of experiences, humor, and love.

The animal most often connected with the South in the Western part of the world is the Wild Turkey, often called the Eagle of the South or Peace Eagle; see also BIRD/Turkey.

UP: Up is the direction of Spirit, the Oriental Seven Heavens, the place of our ancestors or those who came before, the place of all elemental beings, the place of all beings of Light, the place of spirit guardians, teachers, and the Angels.

Up often, but by no means always, symbolizes that you are moving in the right direction. See also Height above.

WEST: The West symbolizes the place where the cycle of life begins again. The West also symbolizes an inner seeking or quest, the direction we must face in order to find our path in life, the death of the old and any form of dying or passing away, maturity, the accumulation and enjoyment of past experiences, introspection, rest, contemplation and meditation, the end of a cycle, and the place of changes.

The animal most often connected with the West is the Bear, who hibernates each year to rest and digest what he has accumulated during the seasons just experienced. See also ANIMAL/Bear.

DITCH

Ditches most often symbolize diversions of some kind.

But ditches by the side of your road or path can symbolize a safe place for emotional runoff, a preparation for future heavy rainfalls (emotions), even a place of safety during a tornado or cyclone.

The overall emotional content of your dream, meditation, or experience will help you find the interpretation that fits best at the time.

Ditches are also another of your subconscious' favorite puns. Are you about to make a last-ditch effort? Who or what are you about to ditch?

What type of ditch is it? What is it constructed of? Who made it? For what purpose? How well is it fulfilling that purpose? Where is it located? Where would you normally be most likely to find this ditch? Why? How do you feel about it? Why? What does it remind you of? See also ALLEY, CONTAINER, ROAD, and any objects in or near the ditch.

WALKING OR DRIVING NEAR A DITCH may symbolize that you are in danger of falling into a diversion represented by the ditch, that you need to keep to the road or path, watch your step, pay more attention to where or how you are moving.

WATER RUNNING IN A DITCH symbolizes that your emotions are, or are in danger of, diverting you from your present path or road. Conversely, water running in a ditch beside you may be telling you that you are supported by your deep inner feelings, by Spirit, or even by some aspect of your own consciousness. What color is the water? How do you feel about the water-filled ditch? How did it get full? What makes it flow? See also WATER.

DIVORCE

Divorce is an archetype symbol of the separation of Love from Wisdom, Emotion from Action, Goodness from Truth, Spirit from Matter, and Emotion from Reason.

Divorce is the conscious decision to end a relationship and the conscious and willful dissolving of a bond, contract, agreement, or partnership.

Dreaming of a divorce can, of course, also be showing you unrecognized feelings about your current relationship, or some issues you may still have outstanding concerning an actual divorce or separation, even if the divorce was by death of one of the partners.

A dream divorce can also be a pun. From who or what are you divorcing yourself? Why? How do you feel about it?

How do you feel about divorce in general? What kinds of people generally get divorces? Who usually gains the most from a divorce? How will your life be different after the divorce? See also MARRIAGE, FEMALE, MALE, and LAW.

DRAW

Drawing in your dream or meditation is often symbolic of your ability or desire to define your boundaries, to outline your plans more clearly, or to become clearer about what is being drawn in your dream or meditation.

Drawing also represents your creative, artistic, intuitive nature and abilities. You are literally giving form to something, but in a safe two-dimensional reality before creating it in the third dimension.

And drawing can be a good pun, as "drawing from your own experience," "drawing a conclusion," "drawing to a close." Do you need to draw yourself a picture? Where are you drawing the line? What are you drawing toward you?

What is being drawn? Who is doing the drawing? In what medium? Are colors involved? What will your dream drawing be ultimately used for? How do you feel about it in the dream? See also ARTWORK.

DREAM

To dream that you are dreaming is to be experiencing some level of lucid dreaming (see Glossary). In other words a part of your mind and consciousness is aware that it is dreaming *while* it is dreaming.

When you become aware that you are dreaming in a dream, you can begin to take control of your dreams and use them to directly work out problems, experiment with new ways of doing things, and even gain more information and knowledge — all before you get stuck with any unwanted consequences.

Your conscious everyday mind is asleep and for the most part off duty when you are dreaming, and your subconscious mind does not deal in linear time or space, or logic. So be awake in your dreams supplies you with unlimited options.

Dreams are not often rational and do not need to make sense. Anything at all is plausible, possible, and easily accessible to your sleeping consciousness, especially so when you are in a lucid dream. The whole Universe becomes your amusement park — literally. You can go anywhere, do anything, be anyone. And since the sleeping brain believes everything it sees — well, you begin to see the implications.

After you have worked with interpreting your dreams for a while, it is common to begin interpreting them as you are dreaming them, to dream within your dream.

Dreaming that you are dreaming can also be telling you that you are "asleep" even when you think you are awake. Do you need to be more aware of what is actually going on in your life, and stop dreaming about it? Is it time to wake up and take action?

What is the dream within your dream? How does it relate to the rest of your dream? What would cause your already dreaming self to have this dream within its original production? What is this part of you trying to tell you?

DRIVE

Driving in your dream or meditation often symbolizes how in control of yourself and your life you feel, how well you direct your vehicle (your body), your life, and/or your emotions and feelings.

Driving is also a good pun. Do you feel driven? Is something driving you crazy? What is the driving force in your life? Are you in the driver's seat?

What direction are you headed? What type of road are you driving on? Who is with you in the vehicle? What type of vehicle are you in? How is it the same as, or different from, the vehicle you normally drive? Are there obstacles in the way? Is there heavy traffic? How in control of the vehicle are you? How do you feel about driving in general? What does this remind you of? See also DIRECTIONS, VEHICLE.

E

EAT

Symbolically, eating allows the qualities of that which is consumed to be metabolized by the one doing the consuming. So eating in a dream or meditation frequently symbolizes a need or desire to take in the nourishment or sustenance symbolized by what is being eaten, and not always food by any means.

Eating a specific food can also of course be a very specific message from your body to you that you physically need the food being eaten, or some food similar to it.

The lower (physical) Soul states change as Truth is taken in and assimilated, literally causing what was insubstantial to take on substance. Within this context, your food represents the truth or knowledge that is to be ingested, digested, and assimilated for storage and later use; see also FOOD.

To eat or to feed someone or something else symbolizes taking in and integrating what is being eaten. Either one of these actions can represent the acquisition of the object being eaten or fed, or just the acquisition of knowledge in general. Being fed is also often symbolic of being given truth, the nourishment gained from good things, and receiving feeding instructions from Soul to the Mind, or from a teacher to a student.

Eating is also a great pun. Are you eating your words, eating crow? Is something being forced down your throat?

What are you eating? Where are you eating it? How does it taste, smell? Is it something you would normally eat? If not, how is it different? What kind of people would eat or want to eat what is being eaten in your dream? Who is being fed? Why? Do you like to eat? Why, or why not?

CHEWING itself symbolizes breaking information and knowledge into smaller bites so you can digest or assimilate the nutrition it has to offer, that you are thinking something over, that you want to take time to literally chew things over.

If you are chewing something that is too tough or too big to swallow, this may be telling you about something you are not willing to handle at the time, or some stress or problem that may not be yours in the first place.

Have you just bitten off more than you can chew? What is being chewed? Who or what is doing the chewing? How does it taste? How is it impacting your dream? Does this remind you of anything going on in your life right now? See also BODY/Teeth.

EMOTION

Any emotions you experience in a dream are doubly important because your dreams are all about feelings anyway. So when you encounter strong emotions in your dream, you are giving yourself a reinforced signal that is clearly saying "Hey, you up there!! This is where we are and this is how parts of us feel about it."

Try to keep your feelings ABOUT the dream separate from the emotions you experience IN your dream. They are often quite different, not what you would expect, and flashing neon arrows pointing to the meaning of the feeling.

What are the major feelings in your dream or meditation? What are the feelings of each person and object? What has caused these feelings?

How would your life change if you had these same feelings when you are awake? How would your dream or meditation have been different if you had experienced the opposite feeling? What would you have to do to change these emotions? How do you feel about all of that?

COMMON SYMBOLIC EMOTIONS:

ANGER: Any dream anger is always directed first at yourself or some part of you, and at your dream object second.

When you or anyone or thing in your dream or meditation is angry, it is always, at the first level of meaning, showing you that some part of you is angry at some other part, even when the anger is directed at someone or something else. (We know; we didn't like that one either, but it's still true).

Anger represents your unexpressed emotions or frustrations, and experiencing them in a dream or meditation is creating a safe place to release these feelings that might otherwise damage you or the others around you.

Since the sleeping brain believes what it sees and experiences whether it is awake or dreaming, dream anger can be one of the healthiest ways for you to release these suppressed emotions, especially the petty ones the awake you feels you should have grown beyond by now. Denying that you feel anger only intensifies it, and it then has a tendency to pop out at the most inappropriate and damaging times.

On a purely spiritual level, dream anger symbolizes the fear of your lower self-centered nature directed against your higher spiritual nature, which your human personality often does not understand and consequently fears. To hide that fear, this part of you chooses to get angry.

The human part of you often subconsciously feels that your spiritual nature is its enemy, out to annihilate it, especially when you first begin to wake up and grow. This kind of anger often shows itself as some type of "divine" anger or wrath, symbolized by any strong authority figure, divine or secular. It also often manifests as some kind of monster or nameless dread.

Who is angry? Why? How does it feel in your dream? Does it remind you of anything going on in your life right now?

What form does the anger take? What will happen if you express the same kind of anger when you are awake? Why?

What actions could you have taken to disarm or transmute the anger? What actions are you able to take in your dream or meditation that you would not allow yourself to take otherwise? What is this telling you? See also ARGUMENT, STRUGGLE.

CRY: Crying in a dream often symbolizes a powerful release of emotional pain at a very deep subconscious level.

Dream tears can also represent a healthy way to balance your energy and release any unrecognized built-up tensions.

Tears can also be telling you that you are beginning to awaken spiritually, since it is common to feel sad for no apparent reason when you begin the process of growing and changing. It's more than just okay to mourn for old habits and ideas that you have now outgrown, it's necessary.

And remember that the sleeping brain is not able to differentiate between its experiences when you are awake and when you are asleep, so crying in a dream can release all of the right chemicals and hormones, just as crying when you are awake — good news indeed.

Tears and crying can also be good puns. Are your tears real, or false crocodile tears? Are you ready for someone to cry you a river? Is this a cry for help from some part of you? Do you have something in your eye, irritating it; see BODY/ Eye.

Have you allowed yourself to mourn when you needed to in your waking life? What causes the tears? Are they tears of happiness, or sadness?

What actions caused the tears? How does it feel in your dream? Does this remind you of anything emotionally taking place in your life at the time?

DANGER: A feeling of danger in your dream or meditation often represents a change or shift in your personal growth of which you are not consciously aware at the time, and that some part of you is feeling threatened by this change.

Danger also often means that new, totally unknown, and as yet unexperienced personality traits or talents are beginning to come into your conscious awareness, and that as a result your life will change in some way.

Danger can also be a direct message from your subconscious that there is a very real potential danger to you in your waking life, and that it may be close or moving closer. How you feel in your dream or experience and the overall content of the dream will give you your clues about what your feelings of danger is trying to show you.

What has caused the feeling of danger? Is it seen, or vague and in the shadows? Would the same situation give you the same feeling of danger in your waking life? Why, or why not? See also ATTACK, Fear below, and any objects causing the feeling of danger, i.e., ANIMAL, WEAPON, etc.

FEAR: You are almost always afraid of some part of yourself when dealing with dream fear. Fear in a dream is usually a message that changes are going on in your life at the time, and the bigger the change, the bigger your fear.

Feeling fear can also symbolize that you are very close to a particular part of your own personal truth, and that some part of you does not want to face this truth directly.

Fear also symbolizes your active resistance and refusal to meet the unknown, unfamiliar, unexplored parts of yourself.

And fear can symbolize a present hidden lack of willpower at the intellectual level. Fear is only possible to parts of your "lower" physical, ego-based nature; your spiritual nature can never be truly frightened. The ego is often afraid when it is going through changes of any kind, large or small, because by and large it doesn't like change — period.

And if none of the above applies to your fear, it's a sure bet that the fear you are feeling is fear of your own personal power, fear of your own true self.

What is the cause of the fear? Are you struggling, running, chasing, too paralyzed by the fear to move at all? Is someone or something trying to get into your house or vehicle?

How are you reacting to or handling your fear in your dream? Does it remind you of anything going on in your life right now? If your fear could speak, what would it be saying to you? See also CHASE, MONSTER, RUN, SHADOW, and any symbol causing or related to the fear.

MOURN: Mourning in a dream generally symbolizes your reluctance or inability to release some part of your personality that is passing away, or that you are hanging onto the past, specifically in the area covered by your dream.

Mourning can also be a symbol that this is a time of exceptionally deep transition for you. A part of you will almost always mourn the loss of an outgrown but still comfortably familiar part of you.

Who is mourning? Why? What does this feeling remind you of that was going on in your life at the time? How are your mourners dressed? Why? Is the mourning ritual, or genuine? Why do human beings mourn at all? See also CEREMONY/Funeral, DEATH, GRAVE, WIDOW/ER.

ENEMY

Enemies generally symbolize an unknown part of yourself, some part you fear because it is totally foreign to your conscious personality, a part you feel is uncontrollable and dangerous, maybe even totally unacceptable — the Enemy. Often your enemy will also be foreign or an alien, showing you how far removed this part of you is from your conscious awareness.

Enemies can also be clearly telling you that you are at war with yourself in the area your dream enemy symbolizes. A dream enemy can also represent certain qualities of your personality that are robbing you of the chance to reach your potential, or, conversely, unrecognized talents or strengths that are trying to forcefully come out.

In purely spiritual terms, an enemy symbolizes your "lower" more human emotions, while a friend symbolizes your higher spiritual ones; see also FRIEND.

Dreaming of enemies can also of course be a message that your subconscious has picked up information about a real-life enemy of

some kind, even a virus that is trying to invade your body, a common meaning of many attack dreams.

Who are your enemies? Are they wearing uniform? What kind? What weapons are they using? What country or territory do they come from?

Why are you enemies? Why do your enemies want to harm you? What would it take to placate the enemy? How do you feel about that? See also ATTACK, FOREIGN, WEAPON if one is used, and WAR.

ESCAPE

Dreams and daydreams of escape almost always symbolize your attempt to run away from some part of yourself or a situation in your life, or a strong desire or even need to do so.

Running away in slow motion can be telling you that before much longer you will be confronted by whatever you are escaping from if you don't stand and face it or deal with it now.

But escaping in slow motion can also simply be the body's attempts to carry out the action physically. Remember that in REM sleep your physical body is paralyzed, and since the sleeping brain believes what it sees, it may just be trying to wake; see Glossary/Stage Three Sleep.

And dreaming of escaping or trying to escape can be a message that you are trying to, or are about to, escape from an old level of thinking and behaving into a newer one. How you feel during your escape will give you your clue.

How important to you is the escape? What does it remind you of going on in your life at the time?

From what are you escaping? Why? Toward what are you moving to seek safety? Why? What has been keeping you in bondage or a captive?

How do you feel about the escape? What will change once you have escaped? How does the person or thing you are escaping from feel about all of this? See also RUN, VICTIM/Captive.

EXPLOSION

Explosions of any kind almost always symbolize the imminent explosion of deeply suppressed emotions and feelings.

But explosions can also represent strong suppressed desires to break free of a restrictive or constricting situation, person, lifestyle, attitude, job, or behavior. How you feel about the explosion in your dream or meditation will tell you which interpretation is yours at the time.

But no matter what interpretation you feel is the correct one, dreaming of explosions is always a strong, clear warning that too much emotion is being suppressed, and that this needs to be corrected — fast. Don't take this message to yourself too lightly. Explosions always cause damage, even ones you plan.

What is exploding, or about to? How much destruction will there be? How else could this explosive energy have been released? What does this remind you of that is going on in your life at the time of the dream? See also Anger above, DESTRUCTION, WEAPON/Gun, MOUNTAIN/Volcano, and any object exploding or causing the explosion.

F

FAIRY

Fairies and elves were originally included among the Angels as beings of Light. The word *El* itself translates as *light*.

Fairies most often symbolize the super-normal powers of human consciousness. Their magical powers themselves symbolize the sudden discovery of your own latent potentials carried with you at all times.

Fairies and elves are almost always seen as paradoxical beings, conferring magical gifts with one hand and playing nasty tricks with the other.

They were believed to bring extraordinary gifts to newborn babies (remember Sleeping Beauty?), to be able to cause wonderful things to appear from out of nowhere, and to heap hidden treasures (symbolizing hidden wisdom) on humans who had earned it.

Fairies are also strong symbols for the stages of development in the spiritual life of the human soul. They are dubbed White Ladies, Green Ladies, and Black Ladies in myth and legend for this very rea-son, in the same way the various orders of medieval knights were, and for much the same reasons.

Fairies were also known as the Lady of the Fountain, the Lady of the Mountain, and the Lady of the Lake, again symbolizing the stages of development of the human soul.

Fairies are famous for causing sudden and complete transformations in people and things, and, as with most mystical magical beings, can behave in both good and evil ways.

And fairies who are unwise enough to fall in love with and marry humans don't fare very well, a symbol of the very human tendency to take our "magic" for granted, which causes us to lose it.

Elves have symbolized mischievousness and playfulness for virtually every culture on earth. Elves are the tricksters, the little people who bring gifts in exchange for what was taken by them.

Dreaming of elves or fairies (or experiencing them in some way) can also simply be telling you that you need to lighten up and connect with the playful, magical side of yourself. Or maybe you need to just believe in magic a little more?

What do your elves or fairies look like? What are they doing? How do you feel about elves and fairies? Are they real? Why, or why not?

How would you like to meet one? Why, or why not? How would your life change if the fairy or elf in your dream or meditation were really in your life? What does this remind you of? See also ANGEL, BIRD/Wings.

FALL, TO

Dreams of falling are common and most often represent a strong feeling that you are either already out of or are about to lose control of the subject of your dream. Falling can also symbolize your fear of falling into or away from the subject of your dream or meditation.

Falling can also represent your fear of failing at just about anything. This fear is often, but not always, related to your work or personal performance in some area of your life at the time.

To dream of falling can also (but rarely) indicate you have made a bad landing coming back into your physical body after an out-of-body dream.

As an archetype, it was through "the fall" that the human species moved from the passive dependence of an infant on an outside source to take care of all of its needs to consciously accepting personal responsibility.

This movement in consciousness carried the human being to the level of one who understands the differences between higher and lower morality. This "knowledge of good and evil" propelled humanity into the learning phase of the struggle between these polar opposites. It is this internal struggle within each of us, and the knowledge gained through it, that helps us develop the qualities necessary for our next level of growth; see also TREE/Tree Of Knowledge.

And falling makes a great pun. For what or whom are you falling? Did you fall for that old one again? Are you about to hit bottom? Are you afraid you will fall flat on your face or backside?

From what or from where are you falling? Where will you land? Will it be a soft or hard landing? How do you feel while you are falling?

What caused you to fall? Were you pushed, were you careless, or did you jump? What will happen after your fall? Why? How do you feel about that?

[NOTE: Never assume you went splat! unless you actually see this happen in your dream. Where your falling dream ends can be important to your final interpretation of this symbol. And it is not true that if you see yourself hit the ground that you will die. Lots of people hit bottom, get smooshed flat, and then get right up again].

FAMILY

Family symbolizes the complete and incomplete facets of your existence, the aspect of your Spirit or

Soul as it interacts in many ways with Matter in this world. In other words, your family symbolizes the lessons you are learning or would like to learn.

This is especially true in your dreams or meditations where the other people walking through your movie are all symbolic parts of you first and themselves second.

What parts of your family are asking you to notice them? Does it remind you of anything going on in your life at the time? How do you feel about the members of your family? Why?

Families also symbolize the various roles or functions your personality plays or performs, and how it feels at the time about those roles: mother, father, brother, sister, wife, husband, cousin, step-parent, child, baby, adopted child, etc.

Family can also be symbolic of some qualities of you or someone in your life which have a fairly close relationship to one another, but which in reality are attached to a single center, the family. Who or what is the heart of this particular family? What does this remind you of?

Dreaming of family can also be telling you something about the interpersonal relationships in your own family and how you feel about them at the time. Your relationships to your dream family members will change as you change, so keep good track of them.

What is a human family? What is its purpose? How is your dream family different from your waking family? Is any family member act-ing out of character in your dream or meditation? How?

What is your dream family doing as a whole unit? What actions are each of them carrying out? Why? Do the actions of any member cancel out the actions of any other? How would this family change if the members switched roles?

How is your family interacting, or not interacting? What does this remind you of? How do you feel about this family in your dream?

How do you feel about the concept of family at all? Do you need one? Why, or why not?

FAMILY MEMBERS AS SYMBOLS:

BROTHER: Brother symbolizes your Yang (male) qualities and characteristics, whether you are male or female.

As an archetype, brother symbolizes the individual, the personality, the Causal Self, the one who acts and who is on its way to autonomy. Brothers also represent unconditional platonic (brotherly) love. And a brother is often symbolic of your kinship to all of humanity, as is a sister.

Brothers lend support in times of trouble, help move heavy objects, repair things, borrow money.

Brother can also symbolize some characteristic of your real brother that you see in yourself, or that you would like to incorporate into yourself (or get rid of).

Dreaming of your brother could also, of course, be showing you something important about your subconscious feelings about your real brother.

How is your dream brother different from your brother? How is he dressed? What is your brother like as a person? (Be very specific and honest so you will understand how your subconscious is using him as a symbol; this is not about judging or labeling, it's about understanding the unique way you are using this person as a symbol).

How do you feel about your brother in your dream or meditation? Why? Why is he in making this appearance at all? How would your dream, meditation, or life be different without him? What are brothers supposed to do for the other family members? Why? See also MALE, SISTER.

DAUGHTER: Daughters symbolize the Yin (female) part of you, whether you are male or female.

Daughters, like sons, are products and result of the merging of their mother and father.

As an archetype, the phrase "daughters of men" symbolizes the lower physical emotions and affections created by the mind as they merge with human desires.

And daughter can represent qualities you project onto your own daughter or qualities in the relationship between you as they exist at the time.

How is this daughter different from your own or one you know? What is she like as a person? How does it feel to have a daughter? How does it feel be a daughter?

How is this daughter different from either of these feelings?

FATHER: Father symbolizes your own mature, masculine, protective energy — the wise old man, the shaman, the teacher, the protector, the disciplinarian — whether you are male or female.

The archetypical Father symbol represents respect for man-made laws, while Mother in this context represents respect for natural laws.

Dream fathers can also represent any authority figure in your life. Father can also, of course, symbolize your real father. What is your father like as a person? How do you feel about him? How is your dream father different from your real father?

Who is your dream father and what is he father of? How would you like to have a father like your dream father? What are fathers like and what are their functions? Why? See also MALE.

GRANDFATHER: Grandfather and grandmother symbolize the wiser more mature parts of yourself in their male and female roles.

Dreams of grandfather and grandmother often carry important messages from You to you, and can even be messages from your guides or teachers.

How does your dream grandfather or grandmother look? What actions are they carrying out? How are they different from your real grandfather or grandmother? Would you like to have a grandfather or grandmother like your dream one? How would your dream be different without them? If you could sit down and chat with them, what would they want you to know? See also FEMALE, MALE, YOUNG.

HUSBAND: Husband is a symbol for the mind and your mental-nature, whether you are male or female. Husband is symbolic of the Yang principle, especially the qualities of Yang that you project onto the cultural role of husband.

Husband is also symbolic of strength, responsibility, and protection, the head of the family. A husband and wife are usually the first two members of any family.

Dreaming of an ex-husband often relates directly back to any unresolved emotions related to a past love relationship, or how you feel about marriage in general.

What do you believe the role of a husband is? How are they supposed to act? Why? What are their responsibilities?

What does your dream husband look like? Who does he remind you of? What part of you is he? How is he dressed? What actions is he carrying out? Or, how do you feel about being a husband in your dream?

INCEST: Incest in a dream rarely has to do with a hidden wish for, or fear of, incestuous behavior. Dream incest most often symbolizes a strong desire to blend certain characteristics of yourself with

other parts; for example, the adult part of you with the child, the brother with the sister, the father with the daughter, the mother with the son, etc.

Carl Jung believed that dream incest represented the longing for union with the essence of your true self, a longing for individuation. He believed that this was one of the reasons why ancient deities often created their children through incestuous relationships, to symbolize reinstatement of the Original Unity after having the experience of individuation.

The key to your analysis of this symbol will be how you feel in the dream or meditation. Remember that guilt is not an issue here. Even if you have been involved in some type of incestuous behavior, incest in your dreams can still be purely symbolic in nature and not relate to the incestuous event itself. Your subconscious simply picked the strongest feeling and image it could to get the message across to you, to get your attention. Dreams are also an extraordinarily safe place to work through deep subconscious emotions related to any actual incestuous experiences.

Who are the actors in your incest movie? How are they dressed, how do they look? What is their relationship to one another? What parts of your personality do they represent? What particular form of incest took place? Why? How do you feel about the incest while you are in your dream?

See also RAPE, SEX, and any objects, including people, involved in the incest.

MOTHER: Mother symbolizes your more mature, wiser, Yin qualities, even if you are male.

Mother represents wholeness, or your potential for wholeness, as it relates to what woman means to you. Mother symbolizes one who gives life to the individual personality.

The mother symbol also frequently represents the church or any spiritual belief which supports you at the time, with all of its own symbolism attached.

Any negative or positive feelings about mother most often represent your feelings about your own Yin qualities and characteristics, and not how you feel about your real mother.

But dreaming of your mother can, of course, be showing you something that you subconsciously feel about your own mother, or feelings you project onto a mother-figure.

What is your mother like as a person? Be very specific in your description so you can uncover how your subconscious is using the image of your mother as a symbol for you.

As an archetype, Mother symbolizes Nature, the Queen of the Immortals, The Great Mother, the single manifestation of all gods and goddesses that are, ever were, or ever will be. She symbolizes fertility, creativity, abundance, harvest, the origin of all life, the "opener of the way," perpetual renewal — the list is literally endless.

The Great Mother has been worshiped in many aspects by virtually every culture on our planet at one time, and in places still is. Mother in this context also represents respect for natural laws, while the archetypical Father symbol represents respect for man-made laws.

The Terrible Mother is symbolic of physical death and the devouring, cruel, indifferent side of Nature and natural laws. In some cultures, the phrase "To return to the Mother" was used to express the death of someone. The Terrible Mother usually comes into being as your symbol when she refuses to "cut the cord," to allow her children to become independent of her.

COMMON ARCHETYPE EARTH-MOTHER SYMBOLS:

- water, especially large bodies of water like oceans
- stones and rocks
- caves and caverns
- the night
- any great depth
- trees
- Spring
- gardens of any kind
- gentle, helpful animals, often a cow (e.g., the ancient Egyptian goddess Hathor).

How is your dream mother different from your real mother?

How do you feel about her in your dream? What would you like to say to her? How do you feel about mothers in general? What do you believe a mother should be like? Why? See also FATHER above, and FEMALE.

RELATIVE: A relative symbolizes various parts of your personality, not always the relative you dream about. A dream relative usually represents qualities in that person you either admire or dislike.

Dreaming of a relative can also be a good pun. What is relative, and to what? Are you kissing cousins?

What is related to what or whom in your dream? How close is the relationship? How did the relative become your relative?

SISTER: Sister symbolizes Yin (female) qualities and characteristics, and often the female aspects that are closest to you at the time, whether you are male or female.

A sister can also symbolize the qualities in yourself that you project onto your sister, or that you might like to incorporate into your personality, or even qualities you want to get rid of in yourself.

Sister can also be a message about your perception of one of your sisters or a sister-substitute figure in your life at the time of the dream.

As an archetype, sister represents one who is on the way to becoming willing to share, support emotionally, one who is beginning to understand the interrelation-

ships of life and their consequences.

And sisters can represent your connection to all humanity, as does a brother.

What does it mean to be a sister? How are sisters different from brothers? What are sisters supposed to do? How do you feel about your dream sister? What or whom are you sister to? See also Brother above and FEMALE.

SON: Son symbolizes the masculine Yang part of you, whether you are male or female. Sons, like daughters, are products of their fathers and mothers.

As an archetype, son is a symbol of the Higher Self incarnated as a human being in the image of his father, his Source.

Son also symbolizes the double, the living image of the father, the alter ego of the father.

The phrase "Son of Man" symbolizes the Soul in the stage of being made perfect by working with its lower physical nature, a Soul not yet completely evolved. (The Son of God represents the fully perfected Soul).

A son can also represent qualities you project onto your own son, or qualities in the relationship between you and your son.

How is this son different from your son or one you know? What is your son like as a person? What would this son like to say to you if he could rewrite his own lines? What are his parents like? What or whom is he a son to? See also MALE.

WIDOW, WIDOWER: Dreaming of a widow or widower often symbolizes that some of your Yin (female) or Yang (male) qualities have died, or are in danger of doing so from lack of attention or outright repression.

It is common, by the way, for widows and widowers to continue to dream about their mates for the rest of their lives, so if you are a widow or widower, it becomes even more important that you ask yourself what your mate was like as a person so you will understand how your subconscious is using him or her as a symbol.

How did this person become a widow or widower? What kind of death was it? What does this remind you of going on in your life at the time?

What kind of a mate did he or she have? How do they feel about the loss? How will their life be different now than it was before?

What was the mate like as a person? How does the dead mate feel about the whole thing? And what does this remind you of that was going on in your life at the time? See also CEREMONY/Funeral, DEATH, EMOTION/Mourn, Husband, Wife, and GRAVE.

WIFE: Wife symbolizes the emotions bonded or strongly allied with the mind.

Husband and wife are symbolic of mind (husband) and emotion (wife), your mental-nature now united and bonded to your emotional-nature within your Soul.

Dreaming of a wife also symbolizes your Yin (feminine) qualities and characteristics, whether you are male or female.

Dream wives can also represent something about how you feel about either being, or having, a wife.

If you have a wife in your waking life, your dream can also be showing you something in relation to your wife and any unrecognized feelings you have about her.

What is the function of a wife in a relationship? What are their responsibilities? Why? What are wives not supposed to do? Why? How good is your dream wife at portraying this definition?

How do you feel about wives in general? How is your dream wife dressed? What is she doing? Why? See MARRIAGE, DIVORCE, FEMALE, and Husband above.

FAMOUS

Famous people who make guest appearances in your dreams or meditations often represent a quality of the famous person that you admire and want to incorporate into your own personality, or that you would like to find in someone around you. How would your present life change if you really had this famous person in your life?

Dreaming of a famous person can also relate to the importance of a problem or situation represented by your dream, or the type of problem or decision confronting you at the time. In other words, some part of you wanted to make sure you would remember this dream.

A famous person making an appearance in your dream can also, of course, simply symbolize a wish or fantasy of some kind to interact with this person.

The appearance of a famous person in your dream can also represent a guide or teacher, someone of "star quality." Your teacher may have taken the form and personality of the famous person to symbolize something of importance in order to get through to you more clearly and to help you remember the dream. But even then, there is a symbolic reason why your teacher took this particular form. This star has a special symbolic significance to you at the subconscious level. What is it?

Dreaming of famous people is also often a favorite pun or play on words. For example, dreaming of Cher could be a message to "share," and Sting would be...?

What is the famous person like as a person in waking life (or how do you imagine he or she would be)? What actions are they taking in your dream? How are you reacting to or interacting with the famous person? How would you like to meet this famous person when you are awake? Are you the famous person? Why? How does that change your life? See also PEOPLE, STAGE, MOVIE.

FARM

A farm symbolizes production through direct personal effort and labor, or a goal that is deliberately being cultivated. Farms also represent physical security, a nurturing environment, food, and the growing and active cultivation of your latent talents and abilities.

And farm can symbolize a planting of almost anything, caring for, and then harvesting the results of what you have planted, and that you can make a profit from it — or at least have enough to live on for a while.

What is this farm growing? Why? In what stage of growth are the crops or products? What does this remind you of that is going on in your life?

A farm is also a good pun. Are you farming something out rather than doing it yourself? Have you just bet the farm on something? Has someone or something bought the farm?

What does the farm look like? Are you a good farmer, or an indifferent one? What crops or animals are being cared for? What actions are taking place on the farm?

What kinds of people choose to be farmers? Why? How do you feel about farms in general? What kind of people would want to work this farm? Why?

See also ANIMAL if there are any on the farm, FOOD if grown, PLANT, TREE, and any other objects on your farm, including people.

FAST

Moving fast in your dream or meditation generally symbolizes that your life is very busy and you have a lot of ground to cover in a very short time, that there is much for you to learn and do or finish at the time.

But going fast can also be a message to slow down and be more aware, that you are trying to move too fast which is causing you to miss something important in the scenery or process of movement; see also ACCIDENT.

Dreaming that YOU ARE ON A FAST may be telling you that it is time to purify and cleanse your body, mind, and belief systems. When carried to an extreme, however, fasting is damaging to the physical body, so pay close attention to your overall physical condition and feelings in the dream or meditation.

This one also makes a good pun. Who is fast? To whom or what would you like to hold fast? Is something getting away from you?

How do you feel in your dream or meditation? How does it feel to move this fast? What will happen if you slow down? See also any vehicle in which you are moving fast; e.g., BUILDING/Elevator, and any object that is fast or causing you to move fast.

FEMALE

The way either gender shows up in your dreams and meditations often tells you how you feel about the masculine and feminine qualities within yourself, as well as what you feel about that particular gender.

When all of the characters in your dream or meditation (other than you) are of the opposite sex, this is probably trying to tell you something about a problem you subconsciously have, either with that particular sex in general, with a particular person of that sex, or with a quality within you that is traditionally attributed to that sex.

But in general, a female symbolizes your intuitive, receptive, nurturing characteristics, your natural Yin nature and qualities, whether you are male or female.

A female also represents the Earth Mother, the Goddess, The Great Mother, and the planet Earth herself, with all of the attendant symbolism of each.

Who is the female? Who or what does she remind you of? What does she look like, what is she wearing, what are her most noticeable actions and emotions? What does this tell you about this part of yourself? How do you feel about her? Do you interact with her at all? Why, or why not? See also GIRL, MALE.

FENCES

Fences generally symbolize some kind of barrier or deterrent in your way, some limitation holding you back, or some part of you which feels it is being kept in or out by something.

But a fence also protects and preserves what it surrounds, and keeps out undesirables or things that don't belong there.

The type of fence is a strong clue to its meaning for you. For instance, a concrete block fence will most likely have a totally different meaning to your subconscious than a barbed wire fence or a wooden fence.

What the fence is surrounding will also change its symbolism. How is a wooden fence around a house different from an electronic fence around a military installation?

Fences also make excellent puns. Have you just fenced a hot item? What is fencing you in, or out? Do you need to fence with someone instead of tackling them head-on?

What material is the fence made of? Who built it? For what purpose? How well is it serving its original purpose?

Are you inside or outside the fence? Did you build it, or was it imposed on your territory? Is the fence restricting your view of anything? How do you feel about the fence in your dream? Is something fencing you in, or keeping you from moving in? Why?

What kind of person would build this fence? Where would you normally find a fence like it? Why?

FIRE

Fire is a universal symbol for purification and a means of rebirth to a higher level, no matter what level you are on at the time. This is just one of the reasons why fire has always been sacred to humanity since the year dot.

Fire also symbolizes the Life Force, both within and outside, and the Living Spirit; see also FLAME.

And fire represents intense, all-consuming passion and drive, and deep and potentially explosive anger.

But fire can also symbolize that you are being too cool at the time, that you need to show more warmth and energy in your feelings, behavior, and interaction with yourself and others.

Fire can also represent some fear that is holding you back in your present growth, a barrier that keeps you from your true desires and full potential. For instance, it is not uncommon to dream of a great teacher surrounded by a raging fire, fire that keeps you from getting too close, symbolizing that you still have lessons to burn away before you can connect with that teacher.

Fire is also one of the symbols for the 3rd Chakra, the "second mind" (see CHAKRA/3rd).

Fire or dream heat of almost any kind can also be a strong early health message. What part of the body is affected by fire or heat? How does it feel in your dream? What does it remind you of? What would cool the heat?

To the ancient Egyptians, fire symbolized the sun and was associated with vibrant life and health. It also represented control, superiority, all sun deities, and by this time in human history had developed into a clear symbol for spiritual energy.

To the ancient Alchemists, fire was the symbol for the agent causing transmutation. It was the seed from which each life was reproduced. Fire was the Element which operated in the Center of all things. In this aspect, fire was the mediator between forms which disappear and forms which are recreated, giving fire within this context much in common with the symbolism of water. Alchemical fire is symbolized by an upward-pointing triangle; see GEOMETRIC SHAPE.

Fire was a symbol for the earthly form of the gods, just one of the reasons why it was related to the symbolism of gold and lightning. It was an especially strong symbol of the triumph of Light over Darkness.

Fire can also, of course, be a first rate pun. Is something getting too hot to handle? Are you playing with fire? Are you in danger of fiddling while Rome burns? What are you on fire for? Or are you just burned up about something?

What is on fire in your dream or meditation? What started it? What will it consume? How big or hot is the fire? What could put it out? What color are the flames? How do you feel about your dream fire in your dream? What does it remind you of? See also FLAME, HOT, SMOKE, and any object that is on fire.

FISH

Fish are ancient symbols of abundance, life, fertility, immortality, regeneration and renewal, wealth, and harmony. Fish is also an ancient symbol for life brought up from the depths of the subconscious mind.

Fish is an old symbol of a psychic or mystical being who is connected to Cosmic Consciousness. In fact, in their broadest representation, fish were considered to be psychic beings capable of retrieving higher information from the deep, basic, original levels of existence.

And since fish are automatically associated with water, they have been sacred in some form since the very earliest times.

And fish can represent forms of sustenance and nutrition, especially spiritual nutrition.

Fish inhabit what is to most of us an unseen and unfamiliar world, and are able to move freely in, through, and under this world. They can go to great depths and travel great distances when they are immersed in their natural element. Does this remind you of anything in your life?

Fish can also symbolize your future potential. And fish are symbolic of humankind's physical being.

On the psychological level, fish symbolize the beginning of new consciousness. In this context, fish are important carriers or messengers of your new or awakening consciousness. And no less an authority than Carl Jung believed fish symbolized the various parts of our splinter consciousness.

Fish also symbolize the awareness which occurs when ordinary consciousness is quieted, as in meditation, during illness, by the use of certain drugs, and, of course, in dreams.

But fish also represent vague ideas and distorted intuitions, fantasies, and semi-conscious or incomplete plans. Is something fishy?

In ancient times, fish represented the Higher Self as the supreme manifestation within the Ocean of Reality (Cosmic Consciousness). Since they were associated with oceans and seas, fish were often sacred beings in and of themselves.

In ancient Egypt, most fish were thought to be sacred and holy, but also "uncanny" and to have extraordinary powers. Fish were strong procreative, fertility, and phallic symbols, representing the power of renewal, the powers of the waters and the origination of life.

Fish were also symbols for disciples and other spiritual seekers as the seekers swam through the waters of life on their quest for food, their spiritual nutrition.

And fish were the emblem of several deities, including Isis, Poseidon, the Buddha, Kwan-yin, the Christ, Vishnu as Savior of the World after the great flood, Ea, Tammuz, Frigga, Venus, Neptune, and Typhon. They are even today an emblem of Christians.

Your fish can also, of course, be a good pun. Have you, or some part of you, gone fishing? Are you feeling like a fish out of water? Would like to tell someone to go fish? Would you like to cut bait and run? Who is a cold fish? Would you like to fish in new waters?

What kind of fish is it? What color is it? What condition is it in? What is it doing? What kind of an environment is it living in? Why? If it could speak, what would it say to you? How do you feel about fish in general? Why? See also ANIMAL, SHELL, WATER.

COMMON FISH SYMBOLS:

CARP: The carp is an ancient oriental symbol for literary prominence, perseverance in your struggle against difficulties, love, and courage during adversity. To the ancient Chinese, the carp was capable of leaping over the Dragon Gate, and by doing so transform itself into a dragon, a high celestial being (see ANIMAL/Dragon).

To the ancient Japanese, the carp was a symbol of Samurai courage, dignity, personal resignation to one's fate, good fortune, and the capacity to endure.

TWIN CARP are often used to symbolize the union of lovers.

THE COSMIC FISH: The Cosmic Fish is an ancient symbol of the whole of the physical universe.

For example, archeologists have discovered an ancient Sythian Cosmic Fish made of solid gold. On its upper body above a heavy horizontal line are four beings representing the superior stage of animal —

the mammals: a horse, a stag, a boar, and a leopard. Below this line are beings of the lower stage of animal — the fishes and sirens, beings of the deep.

The Cosmic Fish's tail has two branches in the form of sheep's heads. In the middle of the tail is an eagle with spread wings. Its eyes resemble an octopus.

This Sythian Cosmic Fish is a representation of the progress of the physical world out of a sea of unformed realities, or of worlds dissolved or as yet unformed — the primordial seas.

CRAB: The crab is associated with the moon, and represents a mediator between the world of form and the world of the formless.

The crab is the emblem of the astrological sign of Cancer, which Orphic teachings saw as the threshold through which the Soul enters upon its incarnation.

DEITIES RIDING ON DOLPHINS OR OTHER FISH: A deity or mystical figure riding on dolphins or any other fish were strong symbols of independence and freedom of movement within the element of water and all that water symbolizes; see WATER.

DOLPHIN: Dolphins traditionally symbolize Truth and Wisdom, and the Ego of humanity. Dolphins also symbolize Spirit actively involved with Matter.

To the ancients, dolphins were Psychopomps, the guide of souls across the waters of death. They were also strong savior symbols, especially saviors of those in danger of being shipwrecked or drowned.

FISH CAUGHT IN A NET: Fish caught in a net symbolize the successful harvesting or netting of abundance (or anything else fish can represent to you).

Conversely, this may be a symbol of the imprisonment of some of your deepest feelings now being brought to the surface of your conscious awareness, which are now in danger of dying from lack of what they need most — the water of spirit, or anything else water represents to you at the time.

FISH SCALES: Fish scales are ancient symbols for protection, armor, and the Lord of the Deep. They were often worn by priestesses of The Great Mother, Controller of the Waters (i.e., of Life and Consciousness).

FISH SERVED WITH BREAD AND WINE: This is a very old sacramental holy meal common to many mystery religions. Fish meals and sacrifices were also associated with the rituals of all water, love, and fertility deities, who were often just the same being in different aspects. For example, this meal was sacred to Ichthys, the Sacred Fish and son of Atargatis, and to the ancient goddesses Ishtar, Nina, Isis, and Venus. Their sacred day was Friday, and fish was eaten in their honor on this day.

FISH SWIMMING DOWNWARD:
Fish swimming down symbolize the
involution of Spirit into Matter.

FISH SWIMMING UPWARD:
Fish swimming up or toward the
surface symbolize the return of
Spirit to its true Source.

OCTOPUS: The symbolism of the
octopus is related to that of the
dragon, spider, and spirals, and its
image is often seen in association
with a swastika; see GEOMETRIC
SHAPE/Cross.

Octopus is often associated with
the astrological sign of Cancer, the
Summer Solstice, and very deep
waters. See also NUMBER 8.

OYSTER: Oysters are symbolic of
the womb and the creative Yin (female) forces. They also symbolize
birth and rebirth, cosmic life, fertility, the sacred qualities of the
moon, initiation, and the mystical
powers and aspects of water; see
WATER.

In our own time, oysters are often credited with aphrodisiacal
powers. See also SHELL.

SALMON: Both salmon and trout
are associated with sacred wells,
symbolizing sacred knowledge,
precognition, the divinatory powers of the gods, and the wisdom of
the "other world."

Salmon, of course, are also famous for persevering through almost insurmountable trials to get
back to their origins in order to
ensure the continuance of their
species.

SEA URCHIN: The sea urchin
symbolizes the seed of Life, and all
latent forces and powers.

STARFISH: The starfish is symbolic of Divine Love in its Yin
(female) aspects, and the inextin-
guishable power of love.

To the early Christians, the star-
fish was a symbol of the Holy
Spirit, charity, and the Virgin
Mary.

STRANDED FISH: Stranded fish
symbolize your ordinary subliminal
conscious impulses which will dry
out and die if not refreshed by
deeper consciousness (the water of
the ocean or sea).

Stranded fish often tell you that
you are not recognizing or supporting your personal dreams,
your creative imagination, and the
creativity of your True Self. What
part of you have you left stranded
and gasping for air?

SWORDFISH: In general, the
swordfish carries the same symbolism as the Unicorn — that of chastity, purity, virginity, supernatural
being and qualities, and the Word
of God. See also ANIMAL/Horns,
SWORD.

**THREE FISH WITH ONE
HEAD:** Three fish with one head
is a very common ancient symbol,
found in Celtic, Indian, Meso-
potamian, Egyptian, Persian,
French, and Burmese symbolism,
and represents a trinity, especially
a mystical or spiritual trinity.

THREE INTERTWINED FISH:
Three fish intertwined symbolize a
trinity, and the strength contained
with that trinity.

TROUT: Both trout and salmon
are associated with sacred wells,
symbolizing foreknowledge and
the divinatory powers of the gods,
the wisdom of the other world, and
sacred knowledge; see also WA-
TER/Well.

TWO FISH TOGETHER: Two
fish shown together are symbols of
earthly and spiritual powers, and,
of course, the astrological sign of
Pisces. Two fish can also symbolize
the creative principle itself, and
the bliss inherent in true creative
union.

**TWO FISHES TOUCHING
NOSE-TO-NOSE:** This is an ancient symbol of the Yoni, the female creative principle.

WHALE: The whale is an old, old
symbol for the evolutionary process and cycles through which the
Soul passes.

As an archetype, a whale represents cosmic and personal regeneration and the power of the
Cosmic Waters.

The BELLY OF THE WHALE
is both a place of death and rebirth.

And a whale symbolizes your
natural intuition and perception,
and your ability to navigate and
communicate while "in deep water"; see WATER.

Whales also symbolize the enormous power and energy you have
at your disposal at the time of your
dream or experience.

And whales symbolize the world,
the body, and even the grave (remember Jonah?), and in ancient
times was considered a symbol of
containing and concealing what it
contained.

A devouring whale is also often
used to symbolize a malfunctioning
2nd Chakra; see CHAKRA/2nd.

In early Christianity, the whale
often represents the Devil, its jaws
symbolizing the gates of Hell, and
its belly, Hell itself.

In more modern times, the
whale has taken on the symbolism
of the area of the intersection of
the circles of Heaven and Earth, an
intersection which both constitutes
and holds the opposites of physical existence.

A whale can also be a great pun,
as in "a whale of an idea," or "as
big as a whale." Are you about to
have a whale of a good time? See
also BIG.

FLAME

A flame is an ancient symbol for
the Light of God, spiritual knowledge, spiritual awakening, and the
Bearer of Spirit. The brighter the
flame, the more spiritual consciousness is present at the time.

But flames can be calling attention to suppressed or ignored anger, anger that is now only a small
flame but which has the potential
of growing into a roaring inferno,
back draft and all.

Or a flame may be telling you that you are trying to contain the fire of your own energy, creativity, or anger, keeping it a small harmless flame.

Flames can also represent human love. Is this a new, or old, flame? Another good candidate for a pun, who or what is a flaming what?

What color is the flame? Where is it? What is its source? How do you feel about it? How hot is your flame? What contains it? What feeds it? Does it cause any smoke?

How would your dream be different if the flame became a raging inferno? If it could speak, what would it say to you? See also CANDLE, COLOR (of flame), FIRE, HOT, LAMP, SMOKE and any object aflame.

THE CONTACT POINT OF THE FLAME AND THE LIGHT is an especially strong symbol. In this context, the flame represents transcendence and the power to transcend, and the light represents the effects of transcendence upon the immediate environment.

THE FLAME OF A CANDLE or lantern generally symbolizes hope and a light within the darkness in addition to the above; see also LAMP.

FLOAT

Floating often tells you that you are in the natural flow of your life, just floating along, taking life as it comes.

Floating can also represent a desire to float or coast in the situation that is represented by your dream or experience.

Another good pun candidate, do you need to float a loan, or anything else?

Who or what is floating? On what is it floating? Where, and above what? How does it feel in your dream? What is the difference between floating and flying, or floating and swimming?

FLOATING ON AIR generally symbolizes that you are in direct contact with your own true spiritual nature, that you are ready to soar to literally float into new levels of awareness. Floating on air also symbolizes deep feelings of lightness and of rising above the mundane physical world, and the power of fairies and other beings of light.

FLOATING ON WATER generally symbolizes that you are floating above or on your emotions, your life, your consciousness, or all or any combination of these.

And floating can also symbolize a passive nature or time, literally a wish to return to a time when you had no responsibilities, to go back to an embryo-like existence where all your needs were met with no effort. So floating on water could be a message that you are just floating or treading water rather than taking the action implied by swimming or rowing.

But floating on water can also be telling you that you have a deep strong desire to be supported and carried calmly by what water represents to you at the time.

And it was once believed that witches could not drown, that they floated on water and would never be submersed.

FLOWER

Flowers are almost always a symbol of one or any combination of the following:

- Life
- Growth
- Happiness
- Peace
- The Soul opening to Spirit
- The Center of Being

Flowers are also sexual symbols, representing the female Yin principle, especially one unfolding.

Flowers are also symbolic of the fragility and transitoriness of beauty, of life, of youth, innocence, childhood, and Spring.

Each variety of flower also has its own meaning, and flowers in general are symbolically separated into two distinct forms: the flower in its essence, and the flower in its ?????????? MISSING TEXT HERE To the Buddhists, flowers symbolized the transitoriness of the physical body. To the ancient Celts, they symbolized the Soul, the Sun, and spiritual flowering.

In many ancient cultures, specific flowers were believed to have been created by specific gods. For instance, the ancient Romans believed the hyacinth grew from the blood of Hyacinthus, the violet from the blood of Attis, and the red rose from the blood of Adonis.

Deities were also believed to have emerged from flowers, the lotus having a particularly strong connection to this belief.

To the early Christians, the red rose grew from the blood of Christ, and both the rose and the lily were symbols of the Virgin Mary.

To the ancient Alchemists, a meteor or comet was the Celestial Flower, and a flower was for them symbolic of the "work of the Sun." A deeper symbolism was then further interpreted by the flower's color. And they often called a comet a flower.

What type of flower is your flower? How many are there? What color are they? Are they healthy, and if not what are they lacking? How are they being used? Are they growing, or have they been picked? If they could talk to you, what would they say?

COMMON FLOWER SYMBOLS:

BASKET: A basket of flowers symbolizes a long and happy life.

BLUE FLOWER: Blue flowers are old symbolize for the unattainable, the fabulous, the impossible, the Mystic Center, and the flower of the Wise which grows from the Cosmic Egg. This one was a special favorite of the Alchemists.

BUD: A flower bud symbolizes the potential with which a Soul is innately endowed, and which will eventually blossom when exposed to the Light of Spirit.

CAMELLIA: Camellias symbolize beauty, good health, physical and mental strength, steadfastness, and, conversely, sudden unexpected death.

CARNATION: The carnation symbolizes different aspects of human love, the type of love dependent upon the carnation's color.

The RED CARNATION is a symbol of admiration, passionate love, and marriage.

The PINK CARNATION symbolizes the tears of The Great Mother and motherhood in general.

The WHITE CARNATION symbolizes love in its purest form, and a YELLOW CARNATION symbolizes rejection in love.

CHILD RISING FROM A FLOWER: The image of a child rising from a flower is an ancient symbolize for the birth of a deity or magical being, the birth of a new day, the beginning of a new life, and the dawn.

CHRYSANTHEMUM: The chrysanthemum symbolizes Autumn, to retire in leisure, scholarship, long life, happiness, wealth, harvest, and that which survives the cold of hardships and perversity.

DAISY: The daisy symbolizes purity, innocence, freedom, simplicity, and the eye of the day.

FIVE-PETALLED FLOWER: All five-petalled flowers (e.g., the rose, the lily, etc.), symbolize the Gardens of the Blessed, and the Microcosm of humankind within the realm of the five physical senses.

GARDEN: A flower garden is an ancient symbol of Paradise, the Abode of Souls (see also GARDEN).

GARLAND: A flower garland was used by the ancients to symbolize dedication to a thing, holiness, honor, distinction by setting apart, good luck, and a happy fate.

GOLDEN FLOWER: Any golden flower symbolizes Divine Wisdom, Spiritual Perfection, Non-Being, the Light, the Tao, the crystallization of Light, transcendent power, the attainment of immortality, and spiritual rebirth.

GOLDENROD: Believe it or not, the much maligned goldenrod is an ancient symbol for spiritual discipline. Which makes this a very interesting symbol in light of so many allergic reactions to it, doesn't it?

GROWING or UNFOLDING: This is an ancient symbol for coming near to the completion of a goal or cycle of growth, the development of the spiritual potential of humanity. This one is also a strong Yin symbol.

IRIS: The iris symbolizes the power of Light, hope, grace, affection, beauty in solitude. The Iris was the mark of Iris, the feminine Greek messenger of the gods and a Psychopomp (guide of Souls). The Iris is also sometimes substituted for the lily in symbolism.

LILAC: Lilacs of all colors are symbols of first love.

LILY: In the Western part of the world, the lily symbolizes purity, peace, resurrection, royalty, the fertility of the Earth Mother, innocence, regeneration, and immortality. It was an emblem of virtually every virgin goddess, the One Who Is Many.

In short, both the lily and the rose carry the same symbolism in the West as the lotus in the East.

LOTUS: The lotus is a universal symbol, both lunar and solar, representing spiritual unfolding. With its beginning literally in muck and slime, the lotus grows upward through water and flowers in the light of the sun (see DIRECTIONS/Up, WATER and PLANET/Sun).

In the Eastern part of the world, the lotus is the "flower that was in the Beginning, the glorious lily of the Great Waters." The lotus is the Cosmos rising from the waters of Pre-Cosmic Chaos. It is the Flower of Light, the result of the creative interactions of the fire of the sun and the lunar energies of water,

thus symbolizing both Spirit and Matter. The lotus has been attributed to the Buddha, Horus, and Brahma.

Since the lotus opens at sunrise and closes at sunset, it also symbolizes immortality, renewal, opulence, fertility, and the perfection of beauty.

The lotus is also a symbol of superhuman or divine birth, and deities springing from the lotus represent the physical world arising from the primeval waters of chaos. It is also a strong symbol of the androgen, one who is self-born and self-sufficient, and can and does therefore exist in sexual purity.

In some systems the human Chakra system is described in the symbolism of the lotus; for example, the Crown Chakra is often called the Thousand-Petalled Lotus.

MARIGOLD: The marigold symbolizes fidelity. To the ancient Chinese, the marigold represented longevity and was the "flower of 10,000 years." To the Hindu, it is the flower of Krishna.

ORANGE FLOWERS: Both orange and yellow flowers carry all of the basic symbolism of the sun (see PLANET/Sun).

PEONY: The peony represents the Yang (masculine) principle, and is one of the few flowers to carry this symbolism. It also represents good fortune, riches, the

Spring, youth, happiness, light, glory, healing, fertility, and love.

In China, the peony is an Imperial flower, partly because it was believed to be untouched by any insect other than the bee; see INSECT/Bee.

RED FLOWERS: Red flowers symbolize the rising sun, the dawn, passions, life, being physical, blood, desire, beauty, passionate love consummated, and the relationship to and with animal life, blood, and gold.

RED & WHITE FLOWERS: Red and white flowers symbolize the harmonious joining of the spiritual and the physical, but each still maintaining its individuality. The red represents Fire and the white Water, which together symbolize the unity and harmonizing of these opposites.

ROSE: The rose is a highly complex symbol, but most often is used to represent true innocence, Divine Love, Perfection, natural beauty, and the gentler aspects of romantic love.

The rose has been a spiritual and mystical symbol since the earliest of times. In the Orient, the mystic rose is often replaced by the Lotus, which shares this symbolism.

Roses symbolize mystic rebirth, the mystery of life, the point of unity, completion, and the heart-center.

In ancient times, a rose was used as a reminder to the seeker not to blurt out secrets while in a spiritually intoxicated state. Later, roses were often hung in council chambers as a signal to those attending that the matters discussed at the meeting were secret and a need for discretion on the part of the attendees.

To the early Christians, the rose symbolized secrecy and discretion and was often connected with the symbolism of the cross.

To the ancient Alchemists, the rose symbolized Wisdom, the rebirth of the spiritual after the death of the worldly, and the Great Work.

To the ancient Chinese, the rose represented prosperity and sweetness in times of desolation and hopelessness, and the lotus flower then carried most of the purely spiritual symbolism.

To the ancient Egyptians, the rose was sacred to Isis and symbolized pure love freed from the carnal passions. Roses were used as symbols in the mysteries of both Isis and Osiris.

To the ancient Greeks and Romans, roses symbolized triumphant love, joy, beauty, desire, and respect for the dead, and were the emblem of Aphrodite, Venus, Dionysos, Aurora, Helios, and the Muses. Roses were grown in Greek and Roman gardens to symbolize resurrection and eternal Spring. The red rose was believed to have been grown from the blood of Adonis, a symbol later taken up by the early Christians.

To the ancient Hebrew Qabalists, the center of the rose

was the sun and its petals were the infinite harmonious diversities of Nature. It is a rose which grows from the Qabalistic Tree of Life, representing resurrection and regeneration.

To the Rosicrucians, the Rose-Cross is the Mystic Rose, taking on the symbolism of both the rose and the cross. The rose symbolizes the Divine Light of the Universe, and the cross symbolizes the pain and sacrifice of the physical world. A rose in the center of the cross symbolizes the four Elements and their point of unity.

THE BLUE ROSE symbolizes the impossible and the unattainable.

A FOUR-PETALLED ROSE symbolizes the four-square division of the Cosmos.

A FIVE-PETALLED ROSE symbolizes the Microcosm.

A ROSE GARDEN is a universal symbol for Paradise, and the place of the mystic marriage of the union of polar opposites.

A GARLAND OF ROSES represents heavenly bliss, and, to the Christians, the Virgin Mary as the Rose of Heaven.

A GOLDEN ROSE symbolizes Perfection, especially Spiritual Perfection.

A RED ROSE symbolizes desire, passion, joy, beauty, and love con-

summated. It is the flower of Venus, and grew from the blood of Adonis, representing martyrdom.

A RED AND WHITE ROSE symbolizes the union of Fire and Water, the union of opposites in perfect harmony with one another.

THE ROSE OF SHARON is a symbol of the Christian Church, the Church of the Christ.

THE ROSETTE is a representation of the rose (or lotus) as seen from above, and carries all of the symbolism of the both the rose and the lotus.

A SIX-PETALLED ROSE symbolizes the Macrocosm.

THE THORNS OF A ROSE originally symbolized the horns of the Crescent Moon. And to the early Christians, the thorns of the rose represented mankind's sin, sorrow, and the Fall.

THE THORNS AND ROSE TOGETHER symbolize the duality of pain and pleasure, joy and suffering, and the piercing sweetness of beauty.

SCENTED: Scented flowers were once believed to help the dead depart safely, and represented continuing life in the next world. Scented flowers are found in and on graves in virtually every culture, even today.

THE SIX-PETALLED FLOWER:
Any six-petalled flower is an ancient symbol of the Macrocosm.

TULIP: The tulip symbolizes perfect love.

VIOLET: The violet symbolizes hidden virtue, beauty, modesty, and humility. In Greek mythology, the violet grew from the blood of Attis and is the flower of Io and Ares.
The WHITE VIOLET is an emblem of Mary and Saint Fina.

YELLOW FLOWER: Yellow flowers symbolize the intellect, in addition to reinforcing all of the basic symbolism of the sun.

WHITE FLOWER: White flowers symbolize Purity in its aspects of the Higher Mind, innocence, virginity, love in its purest form, silver, and Peace.

FLY (TO)

Flying dreams are some of the most common of all dreams in any culture.

Dreams of flying generally mean that you are, or wish to, fly above your troubles or your ordinary day-to-day life, but flying has many interpretations beyond and in addition to the obvious.

Flying and flight is symbolic of transcendence, the release of Spirit from the limitations inherent in Matter, the release of the Soul at death, passage from one plane or dimension of existence to another, moving from the conditional to the

unconditional, and that you now have access to a superhuman ability and quality.

Many sages and spiritual teachers are credited with the ability to fly, a symbol of their release from the mundane world and their omnipresence. In fact, any flying object in your dream or meditation (human or otherwise) is often a symbol for an ascended teaching master.

Dreams of flying are also often the first signal that you are entering a lucid dream. Some authorities believe that all flying dreams are lucid on some level; see Glossary for brief explanation of lucid dreaming.

Flying dreams are also often symbols of magical or wishful thinking. And flying dreams can be purely sexual, especially if you are aware of pleasant physical sensations associated with your flying.

And flying dreams can be actual out-of-the-body experiences, but these usually have a slightly different feel and quality from your other dreams. For instance, the things around you will seem extraordinarily real or intense, because in a sense they are real. However, while colors will be clearer and brighter, smells and tastes will often be weaker; see Glossary/OBE.

Even with any, or all, of the above, flying dreams can also be a great pun. Are you flying high? Are you flying against all odds, flying in the face of adversity? Have you sent someone or something flying — or would you like to? What just flew off the handle?

Where are you flying? How is it going? Are you alone? Why have you decided to fly rather than walk or drive? What are you wearing? Where are you going and where have you been? How do you feel? How do you feel about flying in general? Are you in a vehicle, or flying solo on your own power? Why? See also any dream object or vehicle used in the flight.

FOOD

Food often symbolizes Truth, the Real and the substantial which gradually takes the place of illusion.

The lower Soul states change as Truth is assimilated, literally causing what was previously insubstantial to flesh-out. Your food represents the truth or knowledge that is to be ingested, digested, and assimilated for storage and later use.

In general, food represents nutrition and sustenance of all kinds — physical, emotional, intellectual, spiritual. Dreaming of food may also be a signal from your body that it needs the food in your dream. Food can also be a dream pun, as in "food for thought".

What type of food is it? Who is eating it? Who is preparing it? How does it taste? What colors are in it? What kind of people would like your dream food? What kind of people would never eat it? Why? See also COOK, EAT.

COMMON FOOD SYMBOLS:

APPLE: The apple often symbolizes awakening consciousness and insight, and is connected with the nourishing spirit or aspect of the Earth Goddess. Apples were sacred to Artemis, Venus, Nemesis, Freya, Diana, and later to Apollo.

In early times, to give someone an apple was a declaration of love. An apple also symbolizes the dream body (the Etheric Body), which nourishes the waking life and body.

Conversely, an apple can also represent deceitfulness and death.

An apple is an ancient fertility symbol and also represents love, knowledge, wisdom, divination, luxury, totality and unity, the Golden Age, the fruit of the Tree of Life. Because of its round shape, it is also often a symbol of perfection, spiritual knowledge, unity, and Eternity.

The apple is an ancient symbol for the link between this world and the fairy world, often growing from the Silver Bough. Apples were symbolic as the fruit of the Other World in many cultures. And apples are symbols of remembrance of a former existence.

Apples at Halloween are symbolic of the death of the old year or cycle. And, of course, your dream apple may be telling you that the subject of your dream is "forbidden fruit."

THE APPLE BLOSSOM itself is symbolic of beauty, peace, and awakening love; see also TREE/Apple.

APRICOT: The apricot is an ancient symbol of self-fertilization and the androgyne. However, to the ancient Chinese, the apricot symbolized timidity and death.

BREAD: Bread is an ancient symbol for Spiritual Truth, the spiritual food of both Soul and body, the bread of life.

Bread also symbolizes the union of the many within one substance, doubly so when the bread is then broken and shared with others.

Bread can also be a health message that you either need the type of bread or nourishment in your dream or that you are getting too much of it, depending upon the context in which your subconscious is using the symbol.

And bread is a great pun, using "bread" for money, or "bread" for "bred."

What kind of bread is it? What kind of people would make and buy the bread? Where would you be most likely to find the bread? How is it different from the bread you usually like? Do you like bread? Are you allergic to it or any of its ingredients? Why?

THE BREAKING OF BREAD is an old symbol for sharing, communion, and the death of a victim of sacrifice. Breaking bread also symbolizes providing food for the souls of the dead, and the union of the many within one. And to break bread with someone is a common gesture of hospitality and friendship.

BREAD AND WINE together are old symbols for the blending of liquid with solid, Spirit with Matter, male with female, man and divinity, the balance of humankind's efforts and skills within the material world. The wine symbolizes Divine ecstasy and intoxication, and the bread symbolizes the visible manifestation of Spirit which dies and rises yet again to nourish all who partake of it.

BREAD WITH FISH AND WINE was a sacramental holy meal in most mystery religions.

EGG: The egg has been a symbol for new or as yet unborn life since the earliest of times. In our own time cycle, it has also come to symbolize a re-birth.

Egg represents the germ of life, the totality of all creative forces. Egg symbolizes perfection, containing the inner nourishment necessary to fuel all possibilities. Egg also symbolizes the capacity to give birth from within the self.

Conversely, eggs can also mean that you have put yourself in a protective shell, or that it's may be time to break out, leave the safety of the nest and learn to fly on your own.

The YOLK OF THE EGG symbolizes the sky and the WHITE OF THE EGG represents the earth.

To the early Christians, the egg symbolized the Resurrection. To the ancient Alchemists, the egg symbolized silver and gold together.

An egg can also be a great pun. Do you have egg on your face? Is there a rotten egg in the basket? Is someone egging you on? See also GEOMETRIC SHAPE/Oval.

FRUIT: Fruit usually represents one or more of the following: Earth's abundance, health, energy, fertility, well-being, nutrition, and sustenance.

Fruit also often symbolizes that it is now time to harvest what you have planted and nurtured, enjoy the fruits of your labor.

Fruit can also symbolize ripeness and completed personal development. Dream fruit can, of course, also be a direct signal from your physical body that you should eat the fruit you're dreaming about. Or is one of your projects or plans about to bear fruit?

What type of fruit is it? Which part of its growth cycle is it in your dream? What color is it? Is it real or synthetic? Ripe or deteriorating?

On what does your fruit grow? Who would harvest it? What kind of a person or animal would normally like this fruit? Would you like to eat it? Why, or why not? How would you prepare it? See also particular fruit in your dream; e.g, Apple.

ICE CREAM: Ice cream often symbolizes a special treat of some kind, including a treat to be shared with others. Ice Cream is a "frozen delight," a special, delicious, sweet food frozen for future consumption and pleasure, but ultimately intended for integration into the body.

What kind of ice cream or frozen dessert is your dream ice cream? What flavor? Who is eating it? Who made it? What kind of a person would buy your dream ice cream? Why? How is it being served? Who is serving it? How do you feel about ice cream in general? See also WEATHER/Cold, Snow.

MILK: A very ancient symbol, milk represents life itself and was used in many different initiation rites. Milk symbolizes Divine nourishment, food for the newly born, the fluid of life, the Logos, the simple teaching given to the seeker before initiation into the mysteries and before being given the wine of Spirit.

See also ANIMAL/Cow or other animal giving milk.

PEACH: A peach symbolizes spiritual perfection, peace, harmony, longevity, and was one of the attributes of the Buddha. See also COLOR/Peach, TREE/Peach, CHAKRAS/9th.

STRAWBERRY: Strawberries are symbols of the fruit of good works, the fruit of the Spirit, the righteous human being. The red fruit of a strawberry also represents a readiness for marriage and parenthood.

Because of its leaf, the strawberry also symbolizes the Trinity. And because of the way it grows (low to the ground, surrounded by straw), it symbolizes humility and modesty.

Conversely, the strawberry also symbolizes a strong desire for the pleasures of this world.

FOREIGN

Anything or anyone foreign in your dream or meditation often symbolizes new and unfamiliar feelings, differences, and anyone or anything who is "other than" yourself — something totally unknown and foreign to your nature as you understand it at the time.

Foreign also symbolizes that you are or wish to travel to another state or level or stage of development, growth, behavior, and being.

Anything foreign can also symbolize that new and totally unrecognized, unfamiliar parts of yourself are coming forward, or would like to. How are you interacting with the foreign object or person? Why?

What is foreign? Are you in a different country? What kind of people would live there? Are the people in your dream foreigners? How do you feel about foreign people and things in general? See also STRANGER.

ALIENS and alien craft often means that you need to pay more attention to a part of yourself that you are holding back by denying its existence, that it is literally alien to your conscious mind, and therefore probably frightening.

Aliens can also represent a source of extraordinary, not-of-this-earth powers and perceptions. What type of alien is it? What is the environment into which you have brought the alien? How does the alien make its presence known to you? What is it saying or doing? Why?

What are your feelings and reactions to it in your dream or experience? Are you one of them? Why, or why not? How do you know? How are you interacting with the alien? How would you like to meet this one when you are awake? Why, or why not? What does all of this remind you of?

FRIEND

Dreaming of a friend almost always is showing you qualities in your friend that you admire, or that you may not like, as those same qualities apply to you.

A friend symbolizes trust, support, and companionship. In spiritual terms, a friend symbolizes your higher emotions, while enemies often symbolize your lower ones.

In some philosophies, the symbol of the Friend is a representation for the Companions of God.

What is your friend doing? Does he or she remind you of anyone you know? How would you like to have a friend like this friend? Why, or why not? What action is your friend carrying out? See also ENEMY.

FURNITURE

Furniture and furnishings symbolize your beliefs, your ideas, attitudes, desires, and your opinions at the time of the dream, meditation, or experience.

What style of furniture is it? What material is it made from? How would its function be different if it were made from a totally different material? Why is the furniture there at all? What is its function?

What kind of person would pay good money for this furniture? What condition is it in? How much would it cost? Why do human beings use furniture? What would change in your dream if you changed the style of furniture? Why? For instance, if you are in an old house with heavy dark Victorian style furniture, how does the house change if the furniture becomes Early American? See also type of BUILDING containing the furniture.

COMMON FURNITURE SYMBOLS:

BED: Beds most often symbolize rest, security, sanctuary, shared intimacy, and a desire or need to sleep.

How do you feel about the bed? How are the actions being carried out on the bed the same as or different from the activities usually carried out in your bed when you are awake? Why? What is on the bed? What colors are the covers? Where is it located? What does it remind you of?

CHAIR: Chairs generally symbolize your present position and your attitudes in life, literally how things

sit with you at the time, how comfortable you are about the subject of your dream or experience. Chairs also represent comfort, rest, and security in that rest and comfort.

Conversely, chairs can be uncomfortable, restrict your movement, and even kill or be instruments of torture (e.g., electric chair).

What kind of chair is it? How is it being used? What is it made of? Does it remind you of anything? What kind of person would own your chair? What kind of person would not be interested in it at all? Why? How would it feel to actually be your chair?

CURTAINS: Window coverings of all kinds are ambivalent symbols since they both protect from prying eyes and obscure views.

Curtains, drapes, and blinds frequently share the same symbolism as veils, a strong symbol of separation.

These are also good puns. Is it curtains for someone or something? It is time to close the blinds and retire for the night? Has the curtain come down, or is it being raised?

What kind of a room would normally have these window coverings? Who would like them? Who would not? Why?

What material are they made from? Why? How are they different from other window coverings? What is the view from the window? Do the curtains call attention to it, or obscure it? What does this remind you of? See also BUILD-ING/Window.

CLOSED: Closed curtains, blinds, or drapes frequently represent your fear of the unknown or of outside influences, especially things over which some part of you may feel you have no control.

Drawn curtains, drapes, or blinds can also symbolize a fear of being seen by others as you feel you are on the inside.

But closed curtains can also simply be telling you that you need to draw the blinds and rest, shut out the people and bright lights for a few hours. This may be a clear message that you are just plain tired.

How do you feel about the closed window coverings in your dream? What would happen if you opened them?

OPEN CURTAINS, drapes, or blinds frequently represent new opportunities and the ability to see beyond your present situation.

They also symbolize that you are now ready to look out at your present emotional landscape, but from a safe introspective point of view. And open curtains can be telling you that you are beginning to open up to the situation represented by your dream, meditation, or experience.

PARTED CURTAINS, drapes, or blinds frequently symbolize a first small step toward understanding, your initial penetration of the mysteries, that you are ready to see what is behind the curtain.

CURTAINS THROWN OVER SOMETHING often symbolize that you are trying to hide whatever it is the curtains are covering.

But this symbol could be telling you that you feel unprepared and not quite all moved in, organized, or finished yet. Or it could be telling you that you're just not ready to expose your unfinished work to the public at this point, that now may not be quite the right time.

What object are your curtains draped or thrown over? Why? Are they hiding the object, or protecting it? What would the scene look like if you removed the curtains from the object?

PILLOWS: Pillows generally symbolize rest, comfort, and support for the head and neck (and what they each symbolize during times of rest and renewal; see BODY/Head, Neck.

Pillows are also a symbol of reliance on your Higher Self in its position within your Soul, that you may rest the symbolism of your head and neck on the energy of your Higher Self.

A pillow can also be a signal that you need to rest, sleep, slow down, catch some ZZZ's.

What type of a pillow is it? Who is using it? How? What color is it, what material is it made of, what is it stuffed full of?

TABLE: Tables most often represent your day-to-day actions, habits, and thoughts. This is where you often interact with your family, friends, guests, business associates, and take any other actions normally taking place at a table.

A table can also be a signal to table something until a later time. Or to put everything out on the table concerning the subject of your dream or meditation.

What is the activity occurring at the table? Is food being eaten or served? Is it a conference table, a coffee table, a dining room table, a table used for some type of healing or relaxation procedure? How many legs does it have, or what is it support?

What kind of person would like this particular table? Why? What kind of person would not be interested in it at all? Why? How is it the same as, or different from, the table you usually use? What does this remind you of?

G

GANG

Gangs most often symbolize the uncontrollable, rebellious parts of your own personality, parts you might be consciously or unconsciously suppressing through fear of the strength of your feelings and the behavior that might result from releasing them.

Gangs also symbolize fear of thoughts, attitudes, or beliefs at the time. And a gang can also be a dream crowd (see CROWD).

Gangs make good puns. What or who is ganging up on you? Where is your old gang now? Do you feel like one of the gang?

Who is in the gang? Are the members male or female? Why? How are they dressed? Do they remind you of anyone you know? How do you feel about the gang in your dream or experience?

Are you one of the gang? Do you feel threatened, or powerful? What kind of people do you think belong to gangs? What is the purpose of this gang; why have these energies banded together? What can the gang accomplish as a whole that none of its members could individually? What does the gang remind you of that is going on in your life at the time?

See also ATTACK, EMOTION/ Anger, Fear, etc. if you feel threatened, and any object used by the gang; e.g., WEAPON/Knife.

GARDEN

Gardens are ancient symbols for both earthly and heavenly delights, Paradise, and the cosmic natural order of all things.

Gardens also represent specialized training grounds, especially an orderly, disciplined training.

WALLED or ENCLOSED GARDENS often symbolize lessons to be learned, and difficulties or obstacles to be overcome, before attaining higher levels of spiritual or personal development; see also BUILDING/Fence.

What is growing in the garden? Who takes care of it? What kind of a person would like the garden? Are there any pests in it? Is there enough water for the plants? Do you like gardens in general? Why, or why not? See also FARM, FLOWER, PLANT, TREE, and any object growing in the garden.

GEOMETRIC SHAPE

Geometrics, both in shape and in their mathematical formulas, have held symbolic significance for thousands of years, and in fact is often taught in the form of sacred geometry.

Each shape carries its own special symbolism, and any colors associated with it add to its significance and interpretation.

COMMON GEOMETRIC SHAPES:

CIRCLE: With perhaps the exception of a line or a dot, the circle is one of our oldest symbols and shares its meaning with that of the zero; see NUMBER/0.

Circles are symbols of wholeness and the experience of unity through perfection.

Circles are ancient symbols of the Absolute, the One. They represent the Sky or Heavens (Earth and Matter are the square), Spirit, and all sky or solar deities.

The circle is one of the primary symbols used in all magical practices from the earliest times, and the more concentric circles within this symbol, the deeper the protection goes. This protection was believed to be even more powerful if other geometric forms or symbols were inscribed between each concentric circle. The Seal of Solomon is a good example of this form of protection and binding of forces or energies.

In almost every culture on our planet, the circle has represented the drive and need for becoming a distinct, autonomous individual, and having the space to accomplish that necessary part of growth.

The circle is also an ancient symbol for the passage of the spiritual egos (the monads) through their various cycles of manifestation. It is also a symbol of the all-embracing principle of Divine perfect manifestation, which includes everything and wants nothing, absolutely time-less and sex-less.

The circle almost always represents the higher planes of existence. It is impossible to tell just by looking at it where a circle begins and where it ends.

"Experiencing the circle" is an old phrase used to indicate that you have just completed an important cycle of growth, or that you have a strong desire to do so.

Circles are endless lines, symbolizing Time and Eternity, always leading back to itself. Circles also often represent the number zero and the number 10 Circles also represent movement, especially circular movements.

By its implication of continuous movement, the circle also symbolizes that which brings into being, activates, and gives life to the energies involved in any giving process, including any forces which would otherwise act against one another; e.g., a prayer circle.

Circles are also protective of anything held within them.

A circle also symbolizes perfection, completion, Heaven, the ultimate union of Oneness, and sometimes Eternity itself. Almost all representations of Time have some form of the circle involved. And both the circle and the sphere have always symbolized the All, the Totality of Being.

A circle is also an ancient symbol for the evolution of the soul-personality until it reaches the human stage, where the human personality begins its long journey upwards to the stage of perfection and the ego is liberated from the lower qualities and born into the higher ones.

And a circle also represents the line drawn between good and evil (especially when used in ceremonies or initiations), usually called the sacred space or sacred circle. Where the circle is placed and what is within or around it also takes on specific symbolism.

But a circle can also tell you that you are going in circles and need to break out of a certain pattern and get on with your life. Are you spinning your wheels, running around in circles? If you are dreaming a lot of circles, you may also be telling yourself that you need more space right now.

A BLACK CIRCLE symbolizes the Yin (female) principle, passive energy, and the intuitive understanding of the Great Mystery.

A LARGE CIRCLE is an old symbol for the sun, any solar guardian or deity, the sustaining and generative power of love, the Yang (male) principle, and often for the color yellow.

AN OVERLAPPING OR DIVIDED CIRCLE is the *Fu Hsi* pattern, the ancient Chinese Yin-Yang emblem. The Yin-Yang pattern is a circle divided into overlapping positive and negative (white and black) halves, each section containing a dot of color from its opposite. It is a symbol of the Absolute which contains the seeds of its own opposites.

THREE INTERLOCKING CIRCLES symbolize any trinity or interrelated threesome, especially any spiritual or mystical trinity.

Interlocking circles tell you that there is great inter-connectedness and therefore great strength through this interlocked connection.

A SMALL CIRCLE often symbolizes change and growth, the moon, any lunar guardian or deity, the enormous potential for the power of growth and expansion at the time, the lessons inherent within power and growth, the Yin (female) qualities, and the power of perception.

A WHITE CIRCLE is an old symbol for energy, the presence of celestial influences, Heaven, and the active dynamic Yang (male) principle.

A CIRCLE WITH A CROSS IN CENTER symbolizes the Wheel of Change, the Wheel of Fortune, any sacred space, the four dimensions within the Cosmic Circle and the totality of the Great Spirit, and the Cosmic Tree extending horizontally over the Earth and touching Heaven through its vertical axis or pole; see TREE/Cosmic Tree.

A CIRCLE WITHIN A SQUARE is an ancient symbol for the mystic union of the four Earth elements, especially when enclosed within a sacred space or building.

It is also a symbol of the final realization of unity, the transformation of Heaven (the circle) into the square of Earth or Matter, and the Divine Spark (the circle) hidden within all Matter (the square).

A CIRCLE'S CIRCUMFERENCE symbolizes the acceptable and appropriate limitation of the precise and regular boundaries of the world of form.

It also symbolizes the inner unity of Matter, and universal harmony. And the circumference of a circle symbolizes Time, especially when it takes the form of a dragon or serpent swallowing its own tail (the Ouroborous).

The circumference represents all cyclic movements of any kind, including that of human destiny, growth, and evolution.

CONCENTRIC CIRCLES usually symbolize the highest level of enlightenment attainable, and the harmony of all spiritual powers.

A CIRCULAR BOX AND DRUM (and other circular containers) are often used as a symbol of the cycle of incarnations necessary in order to evolve and learn to act from your God-Self, from higher your emotional qualities.

The vibrations of the drum remind the inner nature to return to its true Self.

CRESCENT: The crescent is also called the *Apas*, and always drawn with its points facing up like a cup. The symbolism of the crescent in this form is "that which is used to reach the subconscious mind," just one of the reasons it is often associated with clairvoyance, dreams, ESP, and intuition.

Since the crescent moon changes from a full circle to a crescent sliver and then back again, the crescent shape symbolizes change within the world of form and matter, the passing away and promise of continuation and rebirth.

Crescents also symbolize the newly born, the Ship of Light which carries the Soul through the darkness into the light of a new dawn, the primordial element of water, and magical powers that have the ability to transform other shapes.

THE CRESCENT WITH A STAR is an ancient symbol of absolute sovereignty and Divinity, and in ancient times was an emblem of Ishtar, Astarte, Isis, Aphrodite, Venus, Selene, and almost all lunar deities, female and male. Today, it is still an emblem of Islam.

CROSS: The cross has been a universal symbol from our earliest times, and is considered by some authorities to be THE greatest of Cosmic symbols.

It is a highly complex symbol, but a small sampling of its many and multi-dimensional interpretations is:

- The point of communication between Heaven and Earth.
- The Cosmic Axis, the Tree of Life, the Supreme Identity.
- The Tree of Nourishment, and the Tree of Knowledge.
- The union of opposites.
- The descent of Spirit into Matter.
- Humanity at its fullest stretch.
- The Four Cardinal Directions.
- The Four Earth Elements, unifying at their fifth point, the center.
- The human physical form.
- The balance of perfection.
- Acceptance of death, or suffering, or sacrifice.
- The expansion of Being.
- Perfect communion between all states of being.
- Universal humanity capable of infinite expansion on both the horizontal and vertical Planes of Existence, and thus the attainment of Eternal Life.
- Union of the spiritual nature of the human Soul within the duality necessary for a full life experience.

THE ANKH CROSS was also known as the *Crux Ansata*. It is an Egyptian pre-dynastic symbol which combines the signs for male and female and represents the union of the sexes, and all that implies.

The Ankh also symbolizes the union of Heaven and Earth, life, immortality, eternal life, the life and time that is to come, hidden wisdom, the key to the mysteries of life and knowledge, the Tree of Life, the sun rising over the horizon, good health, and the union of Isis and Osiris, to both of whom it was a sacred emblem.

And the Ankh is often used as a key in legend and myth.

A CROSS IN A CIRCLE is a common symbol for the Wheel of Change, the Wheel of Fortune, a sacred space, the four dimensions within the Cosmic Circle, the Cosmic Tree extending horizontally over the Earth and touching Heaven through its vertical central axis or pole. It is found in virtually every culture on our planet.

A DOUBLE-BARRED CROSS is an ancient emblem of all solar deities, including Zeus, the Buddha, and the Christ. Today, it is also an emblem of Catholic Archbishops, while the triple-barred cross is reserved for the Pope.

A CROSS WITHIN A SQUARE is a symbol of stability, the Earth, and the Earth standing within the protection of Heaven.

A CROSS WITH WHEEL AT ITS CENTER is a common symbol for the Chakras, the energy vortices within the human body; see CHAKRA. It is also symbolic of concentrated power, and a dynamic solar symbol.

A CROSS WITH EQUAL ARMS, the equidistant or equal-armed cross, symbolizes the relationship of a thing, balanced connection, and integration. It is also a plus sign, so it may be telling you to go for it.

THE ROSE CROSS symbolizes the heart, harmony, and the Spiritual Center. This symbol, of course, encompasses the symbolism of both the cross and the rose. It is a common emblem of Rosicrucians.

THE CROSS OF ST. ANDREW is in the shape of an X and symbolizes perfection through perfect balance, martyrdom, suffering, the balance of equals, and the number 10; see also NUMBER/10 and X.

A SIX-RAYED CROSS symbolizes the six days of Creation and the six phases of Time, and the span of life of the physical world.

THE SWASTIKA is a very ancient form of the cross, so ancient that no one is even sure when or where it originated.

The swastika is basically just a cross with the added ability to spin from its center, its spinning arms often representing Light flowing outward.

The swastika has been, and still is, used virtually by every culture on our planet. For instance, the swastika was and is a strong Hindu, Buddhist, and Native American symbol, and prevalent in Tibetan cultures and art.

The origin of the word *swastika* comes from the Sanskrit *su*, meaning *well*, and *asti* meaning *it is*.

In general, before the Nazis grabbed it (or more likely, the reason why they appropriated it), the swastika was a symbol of the sun, life, regeneration, and powerful thought forms. One of the oldest beliefs about this shape is that any thought form projected through it doubled as it was repeated. This increase in power continued each time the same word or phrase was sent through the swastika. Think about Hitler's speeches in connection with that one!

THE TAU CROSS is in the shape of a capital T and symbolizes the Tree of Life, regeneration, hidden wisdom, Divine power, thunder and lightning, fertility, the hammer of the gods, and Thor's Hammer in his role as The Avenger.

CUBE: The cube has eight sides and contains all of the symbolism of the number 8; see NUMBER/8. It also symbolizes the Life Ether within the Etheric World. The cube is believed to vibrate to the color violet; see COLOR/Violet, and has become one of the major symbols of the New Age. And, of course, the Islamic Ka'aba is a cube.

DOT: A dot symbolizes the point of beginning.

A DOT IN A CIRCLE is sometimes called the *Adi*. This shape is found in Sanskrit and symbolizes the Beginning, or the First. It is sometimes also used to represent the Law of Center or Law of Totality, especially in Buddhism and some Native American traditions.

A dot in a circle also symbolizes an embryo, the Center from which all Creation began. And a dot within a circle symbolizes union, a bond, marriage, the extended family, universal friendship, and the Yin-Yang principles, the dot representing the seed (male) and the circle representing the Yin (female) which holds and nourishes the seed.

A LINE OF DOTS in a dream or meditation often symbolize these beginning points, which if followed will ultimately form the path you are to take — literally that you should follow the dotted line. And dots make good puns, as in "follow the dotted line" or "cut along the dotted line." What image appears if you connect the dots?

LINE: All lines in general represent a division, a measurement, and boundaries. Lines also often represent the path you are taking through your life at the time.

The line is often associated with the cord or rope as a tool to limit

or bind, the possibility of endless extension and freedom, and that which both limits and leads humanity to its destiny.

Lines are also good puns. Where have you drawn the line? Are you making a beeline for something? Do you have to hold the line? Who may be still holding on your line?

A HORIZONTAL LINE often symbolizes the physical world and the passive aspect of the object incorporating the line. It can also be telling you to look at your horizon. Is the horizontal line straight, wavy, broken? Why? How would the scene change if the line changed?

A STRAIGHT LINE usually symbolizes infinite Time from a point in which it is possible to go indefinitely either backward and forward. A straight line also symbolizes the indefinite in its very simplest form.

And straight lines represent an unswerving commitment or behavior. And, of course, it can be telling you to go straight, or straight ahead, or even to back up a little.

AN UNDULATING OR WAVY LINE almost always symbolizes smooth regular rhythmic motion, often the motion of the sun, or water, or any celestial body and what it symbolizes.

A VERTICAL LINE or lines is an old symbol for the spiritual world and the active aspect of the object, the ancient Cosmic Axis. A vertical line can also be telling you to stand up straight and tall. Or should you be more straight-up in your words and actions, more up-standing?

MANDALA: The word *mandala* comes from a Sanskrit word meaning *essence*. So mandalas represent the essence of a concept or thing, enclosed sacred spaces, Totality, the Macrocosm, cosmic intelligence, integration, the Spirit, and the whole of existence.

Mandalas represent a time when light, color, sound, and form itself appeared in the mind in a rhythmic and harmonious pattern.

Mandalas of any shape or pattern are symbols for and of your Higher Self, which is now emerging into the consciousness of your personality-self, your essence becoming more visible.

Mandalas are mystical diagrams of the Cosmos, often created from various geometric shapes attributed to a specific deity or entity.

In most cultures, Mandalas represent specific patterns of existence, and are a system upon which to base meditative exercises.

Which geometric shapes make up your mandala? Is it still, or moving? What colors are used? What is its overall pattern, and does its pattern remind you of anything in your life right now? What is the purpose of this mandala? What power does it have? How is it being used? See also COLORS and various geometric shapes within the mandala.

OCTAGON: In general, the octagon shares the symbolism of the number 8; see NUMBER./8. Octagons represent regeneration, renewal, rebirth, transition, perfection, and perfect expression.

After completing the first seven steps of initiation, the eighth step allows the Initiate to regain Paradise by entering as a new person.

In sacred architecture, an octagon was often used to support the dome (a circle), symbolizing the transition from the square of its foundation (the world of Matter) to the circle of perfection. In some temples, for instance, the dome is supported by eight pillars on a square base, a very efficient way to "square the circle" (see Circle In A Square above).

These eight pillars, or eight sides of the octagon, are the Eight Doors in Hindu mysticism, and form the baptismal font in many Christian churches.

OVAL: An oval is sometimes called an ELLIPSE and symbolizes the Cosmic Egg and the yogi. The two sides of the ellipse or oval represent the ascent and descent, involution and evolution.

An oval also symbolizes the potential for the manifestation of absolutely anything you desire. It is a very old symbol for the mystery of life, the container for thought and Matter. Space itself was at one time referred to as the Cosmic Egg, a symbol common in many cultures.

Ovals are also strong symbols of immortality, a symbolism used even today by our own Easter eggs; see also FOOD/Egg.

Ovals are also strong symbols for the original abstract idea of what is contained within the oval.

PARALLELOGRAM: This is a symbol for a willingness to learn and grow, the power to emerge from your present position, and a person who has the flexibility to accept new ideas.

When the parallelogram LEANS TO THE LEFT, it symbolizes achievement of your goals. When it LEANS TO THE RIGHT, it symbolizes that you are becoming inspired by the subject of your dream, meditation, or experience.

PENTACLE, PENTAGRAM: The pentagram, or pentacle, is in the shape of a five-pointed star, and is an ancient symbol of the human Microcosm.

This shape is sometimes called the Shield of David, its five points representing Spirit, Fire, Air, Water, and Earth.

Like the circle, the pentagram and pentacle has a long history of possessing the power to bind evil and all of the Elementals.

In its REVERSED form, the pentagram and pentacle is almost always a symbol of the reversal of humankind's true nature, of its perversions, just one of the reasons it is often associated with and used in black magic ceremonies.

RECTANGLE, HORIZONTAL: A horizontal rectangle represents the power of repetitiveness, many lessons in relation to one subject, and a person who needs to experience many lessons in one subject before they can move to the next phase or stage.

RECTANGLE, VERTICAL: A vertical rectangle symbolizes humanity as a whole. It also symbolizes the power to concentrate, the power of your physical abilities, self-sufficiency, and your focus and intent at the time. And, of course, a vertical rectangle could be showing you a door or doorway.

SPHERE: Spheres are circles (see Circle above), symbolizing the Spirit, the cyclic movement of growth and renewal, the elimination of Time and Space, the sum total of possibilities within the limitations of the physical world, and the Cosmic Egg.

A sphere can also represent the first level of the atmosphere, air, and heat which gives warmth to humankind (especially when associated with the color red), and the line drawn between good and evil (especially when used in ceremonies or initiations), usually called the sacred space or sacred circle. Where the circle is placed and what is within or around it also takes on specific symbolism.

This one also makes a good pun. What or where is your sphere of influence?

What is the sphere made of? What is its purpose or function? What is it doing in your dream or meditation? How would your dream or experience be different without it, or if your sphere were a square or octagon? If the sphere could talk, what would it say to you? See also NUMBER/0, 10, and Circle above.

SPIRAL: Spirals are a form of the circle, but a highly specialized form. All spirals represent the Center of Power. Spirals have been used since at least early Paleolithic times, and have been found on ancient artifacts from pre-dynastic Egypt, Crete, Mycenai, Mesopotamia, India, China, Japan, Columbian America, Europe, Scandinavia, Britain, and all Oceanic cultures (with the exception of Hawaii).

Spirals symbolize, in general, the process of growth and evolution, the process of returning again and again to the same position but at a slightly different level. Spirals also symbolize both solar and lunar powers, as well as air, water, rolling thunder, and lightning.

Spirals are symbolic of a vortex, itself symbolizing enormous creative forces and energies. Spirals are also symbolic of any expanding and contracting energies, such as birth and death, fertility and harvest, etc.

Spirals are often used to represent the energy of Nature, the weaving of the web of life, and the Veil of The Great Mother.

Spirals also symbolize the various dimensions of existence and being, and the wanderings of the Soul as it journeys through its experiences on its way back to its Source.

A DOUBLE SPIRAL symbolizes the alternating rhythms of all dualities — the two Earth hemispheres, the two poles, night and day, Yin and Yang — showing that these alternating rhythms are just parts of a continuing and natural cycle.

Double spirals are also symbols of thunder and lightning, and sometimes fire.

And most storm and whirlwind deities have double spiral headdresses or braids; see WEATHER/Whirlwind.

SQUARE: The square has almost always been used as a symbol of stability, balance, foundation, security, partnership, the Yang (male) principle and qualities, and has a long history of talismanic use.

For example, four-square was a common talisman, usually created by squaring the circle or circling the square, symbolizing the mystical union of the Four Elements, the attainment of unity.

A square also symbolizes earthly existence, Matter, integration, God manifest within Creation or Matter, honesty, integrity, morality, fixed perfection, straightforwardness, and the static or unmoving.

Squares are ancient symbols for the Four Earth Elements of Fire,

Water, Air, Earth, and of the Four Cardinal Directions of East, West, North, and South.

But squares can also symbolize limitations through form and boundaries, and the non-movement of your energy or ideas.

In sacred architecture, the square symbolizes transcendent knowledge and the archetype which controls all works of form.

To the Buddhists, the square represents the Earth Plane of Existence. In ancient Greco-Roman symbolism, the square represents Venus and Aphrodite as feminine reproductive power, a Yin form rather than Yang. And to the Pythagoreans, the square was the perfect symbol for the Soul, not the circle.

If you are dreaming or are aware of a lot of square-shaped objects these days, you may be telling yourself that now is the time to build, to put your plan into action, to manifest your dream, that you have the information, foundation, and stability to build.

A square also makes a great pun. Is some part of you feeling boxed in? Who or what is a square? Do you feel like a square peg in a round hole? Are you squaring off against someone or something? See also Cube above and NUMBER/4.

THE CELTIC TRIPLE SQUARE symbolizes the part of the mind that relates to the physical world through the senses (the outer square), the part of the mind that is receptive to both the physical world and the spiritual one (the middle square), and the unconscious mind which communicates with the other worlds, dimensions, and gods (the inner square).

A SQUARE SURROUNDING A CIRCLE symbolizes the mystical union of the Four Earth Elements of Air, Earth, Wind, and Fire, especially when found within a sacred space or building.

A circle within a square also symbolizes the transformation of Heaven into the square of Earth, Spirit manifesting within form.

A SQUARE WITHIN A CIRCLE symbolizes the transformation of the form of Matter into the sphere of Heaven or Spirit. Ancient Chinese money coins, for example, employed this symbol.

TRIANGLE: Triangles are the First Plane emblem, and are a symbol for the fundamental representation of the surface of a thing.

A triangle symbolizes the threefold nature of the Universe: Heaven, Earth, and Humankind. It also symbolizes any threesome: mother, father, child; body, mind, spirit, or body, soul, and spirit; Love, Truth, Wisdom, etc.

Triangles represent triads, any threesome which work in harmony or cooperation together. (Triads are not trinities; trinities are three-things-in-one).

Triangles also symbolize self-discovery, and often represent your goals, aspirations, visions, and dreams. So if you are dreaming or aware of a lot of triangles lately, you may be telling yourself that you are extremely focused and to keep at it, follow your dream, and pay particular attention to them.

All cone shapes, including triangles, are believed to generate a field of energy in their centers, and this is the original reason for having a student sit under the triangular cap — to stimulate brain activity through the active life force principle, the triangle of the cap. See also NUMBER/3 and PYRAMID.

THE EQUILATERAL TRIANGLE symbolizes completion and perfect balance achieved through cooperation of the three.

A TRIANGLE POINTING UP symbolizes Life, the Element of Fire, a flame, heat, solar powers and energies, the Yang (male) principle and qualities, the Linga, royal splendor, and the spiritual world.

To the ancient Hebrew Qabalists, the upward pointing triangle was the *Binah*, symbolizing the Supreme Triangle of Reason, Necessity, and Liberty. It also represents the triad of Love, Truth, and Wisdom.

The upward pointing triangle also represents the Number 3; see NUMBER/3.

TRIANGLE POINTING DOWN symbolizes the matrix, the Yin (feminine) principle and qualities),

the waters, cold, the natural world, the body, the Yoni, The Great Mother, and lunar powers and deities.

TRIANGLE IN A CIRCLE symbolizes the Plane of Form held safely within the Circle of Eternity. The area within the circle is sometimes in fact called the Plane of Truth.

A DOUBLE TRIANGLE is one of the images for the Seal of Solomon, a double triangle forming a six-pointed star, and symbolizes "As Above, So Below" and "Every true analogy must be applied inversely."

As the Seal of Solomon, the double triangle also represents the Preserver, and was once believed to have complete power over Matter and all Elementals.

The double triangle also represents the union of opposites, especially when the upper triangle is colored white and the lower triangle is colored black.

TWO HORIZONTAL TRIANGLES TOUCHING AT THEIR APEX is an ancient symbol for lunar powers, especially the power generated by the various phases of the moon.

This symbol also represents the Eternal Return, life and death, dying and resurrection. In fact, the point where the apexes touch is called the "point of dying," representing the death of the mundane or worldly to the birth of Spirit.

THREE INTERWOVEN TRI-ANGLES is an ancient symbol for the unbreakable strength and unity of any trinity, any three-in-one combination, but especially of spiritual trinities.

GIFT

Receiving or giving a gift in a dream or meditation often symbolizes a reward or recognition of some kind, a pat on the back for a job well done.

Gifts were at one time offerings to deities or rulers, tokens of homage.

Gifts also make good puns. Are you being told that you are gifted? Do you need to learn to give, or to receive?

What is the gift? Who is giving it? Who is receiving the gift? How is it wrapped? What does this remind you of?

Remember that even if you are the one giving the gift, in a dream you are also the one receiving it. Which part of you is bringing which part the gift? How do you feel about giving and receiving it? How do you feel about giving and receiving gifts in general?

GIRL

A girl generally symbolizes the female part of you, your Yin qualities (whether you are female or male), especially your younger, more sensitive, naive, innocent female qualities and characteristics.

Girl also symbolizes the early stages of Yin development — emotional, psychological, mental,

physical, and spiritual. The age of the girl will let you know where you are in this development.

Similarly, girl can represent knowledge being acquired through experience by the immature and still forming mind and emotions.

Whether you are male or female, dreaming of a girl may be a message that you need to play more or get in touch with the open, intuitive, more naive sides of yourself.

This can also be a message that you still have some issues to resolve in connection with what the girl represents to you, or issues related to the time period represented by the age of the girl in your dream or experience.

Describe the girl in detail. How will the same girl look and act as a grown woman? Would you like to have a girl like her as a friend?

This can also be a good pun. Is this your "dream girl?" How do you feel about the girl? How do you feel about girls in general? Does the girl remind you of anyone you know? See also BOY, YOUNG.

GRAVE

Graves symbolize a place of a long and deep rest, and the hope and promise of rebirth into a new form and life. Graves also symbolize being tended to and cared for, and a necessary preparation for your next stage of development — deep and complete rest before moving on.

Dreaming of a grave almost never symbolizes an actual death, yours, or anyone else's. Dream graves are most often about feelings buried in your past, or feelings which you wish were already dead and buried. How deep is the grave? How new or old is it?

Like funerals, a grave can also represent a ceremonial, ritualized way of getting rid of parts of your personality or beliefs that no longer are necessary or productive in your growth, a clear message that they have outlived their usefulness to you, and that it is okay to mourn their passing.

And grave can symbolize the extremely limited space you have created or allowed yourself, or are in danger of creating at the time. And dreaming of a grave can also be a symbol that you are unwilling or unable to take action to keep yourself from "being buried" by the subject of your dream or meditation.

Graves are also great puns. What is now dead and buried, or what do you wish were? Have you just dug your own grave? Or are you about to? Is the situation grave?

How do you feel about grave? Who or what is it intended for? What colors are around it? What kind of person would normally be buried in this grave? Where is it located? How well tended is the grave? Are their flowers? If so, see FLOWER. How do you feel about graves in general? Why? See also CEREMONY/Funeral, DEATH.

GUARD

Guards of any kind often symbolize protection, both physical and emotional. And guards symbolize divine protection of some kind; the type of protection is symbolized by the uniform or type of guard.

A guard can also be giving you the coded message to be more guarded in your behavior and speech concerning the situation of your dream or meditation, to be on guard about something.

Is your guard really a guard, or is it a guardian? What is the difference between these two concepts?

What is this guard guarding? Why is it necessary? How does the guard feel about all of this? What will happen if the guard goes to sleep? What objects does the guard use or need to perform his or her function adequately? How do you feel about the guard?

How is he or she dressed? How are you interacting with this guard? What does this remind you of? See also CLOTHES/Uniform, JAIL, and VICTIM/Captive.

A PRISON GUARD may be telling you that a part of you that is keeping the rest of you imprisoned and under guard. But then prison guards often serve more time than the prisoners they guard. Who is doing time, and why?

A SECURITY GUARD might be trying to tell you that some part of you feels your security needs guarding. What is the main purpose of hiring security guards?

What kind of a person feels it necessary? What does this remind you of going on in your life at the time? How are security guards different from the police?

GUEST

Your dream guests usually symbolize the parts of yourself that you do not allow to visit you on any regular basis. They are literally your guests, feeling they must be on their very best behavior to even get a chance to interact with you.

Dreaming of guests can also be telling you that some part of you feels like a guest, either welcome or unwelcome, in connection with the situation represented by your dream.

As an archetype, guests symbolize the higher more spiritual emotions visiting the lower more human ones.

What is the guest doing there and what does he/she have to tell you? How is the guest treated? Are you the guest, or the one visited?

Do you "feel like a guest in your own home," your body? How would you like to have a guest like this one?

Why is the guest visiting at all? What main action is the guest performing? What would the guest like to tell you if they could speak their own thoughts? What kind of person would normally welcome this guest? Why? What kind of a person would never let this guest in? Why?

H

HANDICAP

Any type of physical handicap experienced in a dream or meditation most often symbolizes an exceptionally strong limitation felt by some part of you.

Handicaps can also represent the lesson or lessons you are working on at the time, or ones you might want to consider working on.

And a handicap symbolizes the area in which the Universe or your spiritual energy is cutting you some slack, giving you a handicap, shaving points off of your total score for the moment.

What is the handicap? What caused it? How do people with this handicap usually feel about themselves? Why?

How do you feel about handicapped people in general? Why? How do you like being around them (be honest with yourself on this one; there are no right or wrong answers, just symbolic ones).

See also part of the BODY that is handicapped.

HANG

Hanging often symbolizes a strong need or unspoken desire to verbalize your feelings, that some part of you feels it is being choked off.

Hanging can also symbolize a warning of your potential for self-destruction through feelings of guilt or remorse at the time of your dream or meditation.

Hanging can also be one of several great puns. Are you in danger of choking on your words? What is hanging you up? What are your hang-ups? Is something hanging by a thread, or by the fingernails?

Who or what is hanging? What caused the hanging? What was the object used to accomplish it? How do you feel in the dream or meditation?

See also BODY/Neck, Throat, CLOTHES if clothes are being

hung, DEATH, KILL, ROPE if used in the hanging, and VICTIM.

COMMON HANGING SYMBOLS:

CLOTHES: Hanging up clothes often symbolizes that you are ready to or are in the process of straightening out and organizing your life, maybe even making sure what the clothes represent to you is protected from your environment.

If you are hanging laundry, it often symbolizes you have cleaned up some parts of your personality represented by the various articles of clothing, and that you will soon be ready to go public. Or it could be some part of you telling you to begin this process.

But hanging up clothes can represent your hang-ups, symbolized by the article of clothing you are hanging up. What kind of clothes are they? Where are they being hung? In what condition are they? See also specific CLOTHES being hung.

THE HANGED MAN: The hanged man is an ancient symbol and an extremely complex one. Any suspension in space is symbolic of the mystical isolation and suspension between Heaven and Earth of the person or deity suspended or hung. This symbol is also often associated to levitation and out-of-body experiences.

All hanged man legends are about ordinary human beings with extraordinary magical powers, Odin being just one of those.

The hanged man in the tarot teaching system is a highly complex symbol, but a common interpretation is that of someone who does not live the ordinary life, but instead chooses to live in the world of mystical idealism, "myself offered to my Self in order to gain my Self."

The hanged man usually hangs by one foot from a yellow gallows, symbolizing his intense concentration of thought and the light of intellectual perception. The two trees or pillars between which he hangs are related to all of the symbolism of the number two and the symbolism of pillars or columns, as well as trees.

The hanged man's clothing is usually red and white, symbolizing the alchemical mystical colors of the two-headed eagle. His arms are tied together behind him, and gold coins are falling from partially opened bags or pockets, symbolizing the spiritual treasures available for the person who performs this self sacrifice to the Self.

The Hanged Man card in the tarot deck is usually the twelfth card, this twelfth position itself symbolizing mysticism, continuance, self-denial for the sake of greater gain, and sacrifice in order to gain a more direct connection to the Divine.

The inverted position of the hanged man has always symbolized a self-imposed purification of some sort, since it inverts the natural earthly behavior or order of the human being.

The noose itself is an ancient symbol for Knowledge and the love of Truth and Right Action. A noose also symbolizes transmutation of the lower Soul qualities which have now been sacrificed for Truth; see also ROPE.

SWINGING WHILE HANGED: According to Carl Jung, this image symbolizes your unfulfilled longing and intense expectations, that you are suffering, probably unnecessarily, because of your intense desires.

HEAVY

Anything heavy in your dream or meditation often symbolizes that you feel you are carrying too much responsibility or weight, depending upon how easily you are managing the heavy object.

Heavy can also be an early health warning symbolized by the heavy object and what it means to you.

And heavy objects make great puns. Do you need to lighten up? What have you just experienced that is "heavy?"

What is heavy in your dream or meditation? How do you know it is heavy? Can you lift and carry it? Why, or why not? How would the same object or person be if they were light rather than heavy? Are you being dragged down by something? See also the object that is heavy; e.g., BAGGAGE, FURNITURE, ROCK, etc.

HIDE, TO

Hiding often symbolizes a fear of dealing with the situation represented by your dream, that you are not being entirely honest with yourself about the subject of your dream or meditation.

But hiding can also be a symbol that you simply need more solitude and rest, that you need to withdraw from everyday life for a time and hide out.

Who or what is hiding from what or whom? Why? How have you chosen to hide? How effective will this tactic be? Who or what has hidden the object or person? How do you feel about hiding in your dream?

What might you be trying to hide from yourself? What will happen if the hidden becomes seen? See also CHASE, EMOTION/Danger, Fear, and any object hiding or being hidden.

HILL

A hill often symbolizes your opportunity for upward movement and growth at the time, usually related to your personal inner and spiritual growth.

A hill can also be a good pun. Is your present goal or task "no hill for a climber?" Are you in danger of making a mountain out of what is really only a small hill?

What kind of terrain is the hill a part of? Why? What is your vehicle for getting up or down the hill? Is it easy, or difficult? Why? What is on the other side of this hill?

How is this hill different from a mountain or from other hills? What does this remind you of that is going on in your life? See also CANYON, CLIMB, MOUNTAIN, ROAD (if one goes up your hill).

HOMOSEXUAL

Being physically attracted in your dream or meditation to your same gender almost always is symbolic of a strong desire to become more aware of your own sexual feelings and nature, the inherent natural behavior of your own sex.

How do you really feel about the members of your own gender? Why? How much attention are you paying to that part of yourself lately? Are you consciously or subconsciously rejecting the integration of the Yin and/or Yang qualities within your present nature?

How do you feel about the homosexual in your dream, meditation, or experience? Why? How do you feel about the experience after you wake up? Why? What kind of a person is homosexual? How do you feel about the whole issue in general? Be exceptionally honest when answering this question. This is not about judging or labeling; it's about finding out how your subconscious is using this symbol.

What does all of this remind you of that is going on in your inner life right now? See also FEMALE, MALE, SEX.

HOT

Heat often symbolizes your anger, usually deeply hidden suppressed anger. The hotter the source (fire, stove, volcano), the more intense your anger. Heat also represents strong passions or emotions of any kind, not just anger.

But heat also represents deep and often intense purification and cleansing, spiritual or otherwise.

And hot can also be an early health warning of illness which may include a fever. How's your blood pressure? Are you drinking enough water?

Hot or heat can also be a wonderful example of a pun. Are you about to have a heated argument? Are you burning up about something or someone? Or are you about to get into hot water, or burned? What's heating up in your life? How about, "if you can't stand the heat, get out of the kitchen?" Is something getting too hot to handle?

What is the source of the heat? Does it have a color? How do you feel about the heat at the time? What things are normally hot rather than cold? What does this remind you of?

See also EMOTION/Anger, FIRE, FLAME, FUEL, MOUNTAIN/Volcano, and any object affected by or causing the heat.

HUNGER

Hunger often symbolizes your unconscious or unexpressed desires or needs at a very deep core level. Hunger also symbolizes a strong need for the intake of nutrition or food of some kind — physical, emotional, intellectual, or spiritual, or all of these.

Hunger can also, of course, be your body's message that it is really hungry for the food or nutrition causing the hunger.

For what are you hungry in your dream or meditation? Why? What causes this hunger? What will satisfy it? How do you expect to be fed? How does it feel to be this hungry? What does this remind you of in your life?

How will your life be different when you no longer feel this hunger? And how do you feel about that? Are you still hungry when you wake up? What does this remind you of that is going on in your life at the time?

See also FOOD and any object causing or satisfying the hunger.

HUNT

Hunting often symbolizes that you are looking for parts of yourself or your own nature. Dream hunting can also symbolize any goal or aspiration you have set for yourself. And it can represent your intense hunt for spiritual goals, your personal spiritual quest.

What kind of hunting is taking place? What or who is being hunted? By what or whom? Why? How do you feel about hunting in general? And, of course, why?

What will happen when the hunted object is found? Or are you simply hunting for something you feel you have lost?

See also ANIMAL, LOST, MISSING, any object being hunted or doing the hunting, and any weapon being used.

HUNTING AN ANIMAL often symbolizes a wish to get rid of that particular animal's qualities, and to admit to yourself that you have them. To hunt an animal can also symbolize that you wish to hunt down and overcome your pure and untamed animal behavior.

But hunting an animal can be a strong symbol that you wish to acquire the natural qualities of your hunted animal. How you feel about the animal will give you your best clue.

What kind of animal is being hunted? What does this remind you of about yourself?

IF YOU ARE BEING HUNTED by someone or something, it often symbolizes a part of you that is literally trying to track you down. The bigger the thing hunting you down, the more power available at the time?

What kind of a trap has the hunter built to catch you? What sort of weapon is being used? Why? How do you feel about it? What does this remind you of? What happens when the hunter finds what it is hunting?

I

INSECT

Insects or bugs most often symbolize the very small things in your life that are bugging you, buzzing around in your head, getting in your way, distracting you from what you want to focus on or accomplish.

Most insects are not dangerous, but they are annoying and distracting, wasting your time and energy to avoid or exterminate them.

What type of insect is this? How is it different from all other insects? Can it fly? Can it sting? What action is it taking? What color is it? How do you feel about it in the dream or meditation? Where does it usually live? Who does it usually bother? Why? What does this remind you of? What is the natural enemy of your dream insect?

COMMON INSECT SYMBOLS:

ANT: Ants have almost always symbolized hard work, dedicated and cooperative industriousness in carrying out a necessary task, the temperament and ability to function in an organized community of individuals for the good of all, preparing for the future, fertility, and continual persistent movement and activity.

Ant can also be a play on words, substituting the insect ant for "aunt."

What are ants like? How are they different from other insects? What do they remind you of? Why?

BEE: Bees have a long history as symbols for a bringer of messages from the gods (a particularly interesting symbol in view of the killer bees now moving northward).

While each bee is an individual, it is also part of a greater whole, helping to create, feed, and protect the hive.

Bees extract pollen (symbolizing the Life Force) by touching without destroying the life of the blossom itself., symbolizing one being touched by the gods or Spirit; see FLOWER.

Bees are industrious and work in harmony with one another for the good of all and with total unquestioning devotion to their queen, their center and reason for living.

Bees also represent productivity, especially creative productivity, intense diligence, support through and by the many, and cleanliness.

But bees can sting without warning when disturbed by outsiders. They are great defenders of the whole, sacrificing themselves without hesitation for the others and for the queen.

To the Chaldeans, bees were symbols of royalty. To the ancient Egyptians, bees were associated with the sun and symbolized the Soul.

To the early Christians, bees were symbols of hope because of their untiring, selfless work. They were also symbols of the Christ, their honey representing the Christ's gentleness and sweetness, and their stinger His judgement.

And during the European Middle Ages, bees symbolized the Immaculate Conception since, according to ancient traditions, bees did not hatch their own young but collected them from blossoms.

The HONEY itself symbolizes divine ecstasy, wisdom, the sweet words of inspired poetry, intelligence, natural sweetness, the change of the personality upon spiritual initiation, the Higher Self, self-improvement, and Divine Inspiration.

Bees can also be a wonderful pun. Are you busy as a bee, buzzing around like a bee, have a bee in your bonnet about something, smarting under someone's stinging words? Is something bugging you? Will it sting? Do you have too many thoughts buzzing around in your head? And are they potentially painful or dangerous?

What is the bee doing? What color is it? What kind is it? How is it different from other bees?

BUTTERFLY: One of the symbols for the Soul and immortality in many cultures, butterflies symbolize the final stage of self-growth, that you have received your celestial wings. Butterflies also symbolize joy, leisure, and resurrection.

Butterflies were an emblem of The Great Mother, and the ancient Greek Psyche is often depicted as a butterfly.

Conversely, a butterfly can also represent vanity and fickleness or something that does not live very long.

A BUTTERFLY ON A CHRYSANTHEMUM is a common symbol in Oriental art and most often symbolizes beauty in old age.

A BUTTERFLY AND A PLUM symbolizes longevity in the Orient.

A WHITE BUTTERFLY often symbolizes a spirit of the dead, especially in old legends and tales.

A PAIR OF BUTTERFLIES is an ancient symbol for happiness in marriage.

DRAGONFLY: Dragonflies share much of the symbolism of butterflies, and represent regeneration and immortality. But the dragonfly also symbolizes the whirlwind, great activity, swiftness, and Summer.

Conversely, the dragonfly can represent someone of weak character who is irresponsible and unreliable.

FIREFLY: Fireflies often symbolize the superficial or the kind of shallow knowledge that is incapable of maintaining enough sustained light to keep away the darkness.

But how you feel about fireflies or lightning bugs will tell you how you are using this insect symbol. They could just as easily be reassuring you that there are all kinds of light, even in the blackest night, and that even a very small flickering light is better than none at all.

FLY: Flies have almost always symbolized corruption and putrification, evil deities or spirits, and are often credited with supernatural powers and abilities.

Fly can also be a good play on words. What in your life is drawing flies? How long has it been dead? Is it time for you to fly? What's bugging you, won't leave you alone, keeps coming back and buzzing around your head?

SCORPION: Although the scorpion is an arachnid, not an insect, we have included it here for the same reasons we included spider.

A scorpion frequently symbolizes dangerous thoughts or remarks, stinging deadly comments.

So scorpions can be a direct message to watch your thoughts, words, and actions, or to be cautious of the words and actions of those around you, that things are not as they appear on the surface.

Scorpions are feared by every culture where they live, and as a universal symbol are often representative of painful death, disaster, destructive forces, and darkness.

Scorpions can also be a message about some physical danger from a potentially lethal but hidden source.

And a scorpion is the only animal that can work itself up into such a frenzy of anger that it will sting itself to death when it can't reach anything else — scorpions are not immune to their own poison, a powerful symbol on its own.

Even as a purely spiritual symbol, scorpions are often used to represent one of the lowest aspects of the human emotional nature. Are your unrecognized emotions in danger of poisoning you?

The scorpion was a strong symbol to the Egyptians long before the kingdoms were united under Menes, and appear to have been at one time associated with magical healers. The scorpion was an attribute of Set and Selket as protectors of the dead. And seven scorpions accompanied Isis on her search for Osiris.

Scorpions were also associated with the goddess Ishtar (Nina) in Babylonia. And the ancient Mayan black god of war Ek-Chuah was always portrayed with the tail of a scorpion.

In the Sumero-Semitic world, scorpion men guarded the Gateway to the Sun, the Mountains of the East, and the Twin Gates to Paradise.

To the early Christians, scorpions symbolized demonic powers. Dangerous anti-Christian sects were represented by scorpions, but conversely scorpions also were used as symbols of logic in connection with the seven liberal arts. In medieval art, the scorpion was also often used as a symbol for Africa.

Dreaming of a scorpion can be a subconscious symbol for someone born under the astrological sign of Scorpio, the eighth sign of the zodiac. Any Scorpio people in your life? Anything significant in your life that occurred between October 23 and November 21?

The sign of Scorpio traditionally has been associated with male sexuality, the occult (hidden knowledge), the mystical, illumination, destruction, resurrection, and healing. Scorpions within this context are a quick and sure source and means of change.

If you could sit down and chat with this scorpion, what would you talk about?

SPIDER: Even though spiders are arachnids, not insects, we chose to include them under this category simply because many people think of them more as insects than as animals.

The spider has eight legs, symbolizing perfect expression, balance, Cosmic Consciousness,

Infinity, and abundance, among other things; see NUMBER/8. After all, spiders do trap flies (see Fly above).

But spiders are definitely ambivalent symbols, thought of both as treacherous and deceiving and of announcing that good fortune is on its way, even that the prodigal son is returning home.

In many cultures, the spider was a symbol of the Soul, and it was believed that the Soul of a sleeping person could leave and return to its body in the form of a spider, attached to the body by its thread.

And spiders often are a clear message that it is you who create your reality, spin your own webs, weave your own designs.

Your spider may also be telling you that you are in danger of being caught in your own web, or that you are trying to control or trap others. How you feel about the spider in your dream or experience will help you find the way you are using this symbol.

In ancient Egypt, the spider was one of the symbols of the sun, a being who produced its threads and connection to its world through its own efforts, its inner strength, and powers of manifestation.

To the ancient Mayans, the spider symbolized the eternal spinner of the illusions of the physical senses.

In the Upanishads, the spider symbolizes self-liberation, represented by the spider's ability to climb up its own threads which it has spun from within itself from its own resources.

But no matter what their symbolism, spiders have always been seen as gifted weavers and spinners, and even today are still used as symbols of Fate.

Spiders can also be good puns. Is something giving you the crawls? Who is inviting you into their parlor, little fly? Are you in danger of getting tangled up in your own web? How do you feel about spiders and webs in general? Why? What does this remind you of going on in your life? See also NUMBER/8.

A COBWEB often symbolizes the talents and personal qualities you have not used, talents which may be in danger of gathering dust through neglect and non-use. Cobwebs can also obscure clear vision. What is the web hiding from view?

Cobwebs have also been used as symbols of protection, providing hiding places from predators and enemies. For example, a cobweb helped to hide Mohammed from his enemies during the Flight.

And cobwebs may be telling you about something very old, unused, outdated, something from the long ago past. Cobwebs have usually been abandoned by their original creator.

How do you feel about cobwebs? Why? How old are these? What originally built them? What do they remind you of?

A SPIDERWEB is both the home of the spider and its means of feeding and nourishing itself. And all spiders are instantly aware of anything that touches any part of their web, symbolizing your most sensitive intuitive faculties.

Different spiders weave different patterns. What does this one look like? Does it remind you of anything? What will be attracted to it?

What kind of a spider would weave this web? What does it expect to catch? See also any object caught in the web, and any object supporting the web; e.g., BUILDING, TREE.

INVASION

Invasions of any kind often symbolize a fear of being overwhelmed by your feelings or life events, especially if the invader is masked, a foreigner, stranger, or an alien being.

For example, if your invader is an animal, your dream might be showing you that you are afraid of your own feelings which the animal represents to you.

Invasions also often symbolize a strong need for privacy and time alone, that you feel invaded at the time.

Dream invasions and attacks are also very often early warning messages that germs or viruses of some kind are trying to invade your body; see also ATTACK.

Who or what are the invaders? What are they invading? Are they successful, or is something blocking their invasion?

How are they dressed? Are they carrying weapons? What is the purpose of the invasion? Is the invasion mechanized or personal? How do you feel in the dream? See also ENEMY, FOREIGN, GANG, WAR, and any emotion, weapon, clothing, or other object used by the invaders.

ISLAND

Islands are self-contained, surrounded entirely by water, often have difficult and limited access to them, and in general symbolize perfection and something special, unique.

Islands symbolize a place which can only be reached in a daydream, when "your ship comes in." And they can represent your carefree, unrestricted feelings, thoughts, and behavior, a strong desire to sail away to an island and away from our modern society and responsibilities.

Islands can also represent an wish to dodge or come to terms with some part of your life. Islands are isolated from other land masses by water (your emotions). Are you isolating yourself from a particular situation or feelings?

To Carl Jung, islands were places of safety from the continual assault of the unconscious mind (represented by the sea or ocean).

These are good puns. Are you shipwrecked on the island of broken dreams? How about "No man is an island?" Have you just landed on Fantasy Island, or would you like to?

What type of an island is it? How did you get there? Who lives on it? What kinds of plants and animals live there? What type of water surrounds it? Is it calm, or agitated? What kind of fish live in the waters surrounding the island?

How do you get on and off this island? How do you feel about islands in general? Would you like to visit this one when you are awake? See also WATER, and any objects on or around the island.

J

JAIL

Dreaming you are in a jail or prison most often symbolizes the restrictions, boundaries, and barriers you have accepted and which are now at a point of taking away your ability to think and act for yourself. Jails and prisons represent a deep inner feeling of having no personal control of your life, that you are a number with no name or identity.

A jail or prison can also symbolize your feelings of guilt, and that some part of you feels you should be punished, or even that this particular part is punishing you at the time. What do you think of when you think of a jail?

Are there guards in the jail? Are you the only prisoner? What type of jail or prison is it? What type of prisoner does it usually incarcerate? How do you feel about those kinds of people? How did you get in this jail? What was your crime? How was it committed? Why? Who was the victim? How do you feel about it?

What was your sentence? How much time do you have left to serve? What would it take to escape?

What kind of people get put in jail? What does this remind you of that is going on in your life at the time? See also CLOTHES/Uniform, GUARD, VICTIM/Captive, ZOO/Cage.

JUMP

Jumping often symbolizes a need or desire to make a leap into new space, new thinking or new ways of feeling or behaving. Or this may be a signal that you are about to jump into something.

A jump can also be a great pun, as in "look before you leap," "from the frying pan into the fire," "he who hesitates is lost." Who or what would you like to jump on? Or is it time to bail out?

Where is the jump taking place? What are your surroundings like? Is anyone with you? Does your jump require special equipment of any kind? How do you feel about the jump? How easy or difficult was it?

Where will you land? Why? Why would anyone want to make this kind of a jump? What does it remind you of that is going on in your life at the time? See also FALL, FLY, and any object being jumped from, over, or on.

JUNK

Junk generally symbolizes your worn-out and used up ideas, attitudes, feelings, and beliefs, any or all of which you now can dump.

But one person's junk is another's treasure. Are you about to junk something that may still be of value to you or someone in your life?

What objects are included in your junk? Are you throwing it out, or storing it? How do you feel about this junk? Would you keep it if you really owned it? Why, or why not?

What kind of person accumulates junk? Why? How long would it take you to pack it if you were moving it? How much storage space would it take? How is junk different from garbage? See also GARBAGE.

KEY

As an archetype, a key symbolizes Truth, Wisdom, and the next step on your path, that you have attained a certain level and mastered key lessons.

A key also sometimes symbolizes the threshold of consciousness, that you now have the key to move through the doorway, to unlock the treasure chest.

Keys are ancient symbols of the ability to control, confine, or to free power. In some mystical systems, a key is a symbol of attaining a certain status or office related to a particular power.

In many ancient texts, the tongue is referred to as a key. And to give someone the keys to a town or city was a symbolic gesture of surrender, or recognition of sovereignty over it. Do either of these things remind you of anything?

Keys were also once symbols of a woman's right to rule her own home and have access to the household's goods, a strong symbol of her status in life.

And keys symbolize mastery, loyalty that has been proven, and trust from your "master."

All keys have the power to either open or release, or to secure and lock away. And a key can represent safety, protection from the dangerous and unknown, or your feeling of being locked out, not having the right key to the subject of your dream, meditation, or experience.

Keys also can symbolize your inner awareness or intuition, your key to open locked doors. Keys symbolize the solution to a problem, a sure way in or out of something.

A key can represent an initiation of some kind and that you are being granted the authority to participate in the initiation, to become a member, to hold a key.

But a key can also represent restriction, being locked out or in, being kept away from or secluded, a feeling of imprisonment.

In many ancient legends and myths, keys are strong symbols of various deities, symbolizing a task to be performed or a mystery or riddle to be solved, and the means, the key, to accomplishing it. For example, the Key to Knowledge has a long history of being associated with the month of June, which represents healing.

In Japan, keys often symbolize good luck because they open doors to locked storerooms, allowing access to hidden treasures, including higher consciousness and spiritual treasures.

And your key can also be a pun. Are you being shown your key to success, your key to happiness, being given the key to the city? Who has the key to your heart? Are you receiving a key message? What is the key to decoding it? Or are you being shown one of your key symbols?

Which lock will this key fit? Is it used to lock something in, or out? What does the key look like? Is it T-shaped, an Ankh, a door key, the key to an ignition?

What kind of a person would use this key, and for what purpose? What will happen if the key is used? What will happen if you lose the key? See also COLOR (of the key) and any objects the key will lock and unlock.

AN ANKH AS A KEY is most often used to symbolize the Key to Eternal Life, the key that can open the Gates of Death through which immortality is obtained, the key to the very secrets of life and death.

FINDING A KEY frequently symbolizes your stage of growth just prior to the discovery of something of great value, or a solution to a problem which has been or is about to be found through your perseverance and trust, often after many frustrating delays.

A GOLD KEY, in general, a gold key symbolizes spiritual power, power over the Greater Mysteries or spiritual laws, while a silver key symbolizes power over the Lesser Mysteries, the physical laws.

GIVING or RECEIVING A KEY is symbolic of receiving full control and authority over the object to which the key belongs. Today, there are still ceremonies giving someone the "key to the city."

A SILVER KEY, in general, a silver key symbolizes physical, worldly power, power over the Lesser Mysteries, while a gold key symbolizes power over the Greater Mysteries, the spiritual laws. A silver key also symbolizes insights revealed through psychological and physical understanding.

THREE KEYS together are ancient symbols of the three secret rooms or containers always crammed full of treasure.

The first key is often silver, symbolizing things that can be revealed through psychological or physical knowledge; the second key is often gold, symbolizing things that can be revealed through philosophical or spiritual knowledge; and the third key is often diamond, symbolizing the power and authority to act from the total of knowledge acquired through the proper use of the silver and gold keys.

KIDNAP

Kidnaping often symbolizes that there is a part, or parts, of yourself which you are trying to take away and hide, or even do away with altogether, and that you are willing to use force to do it.

For instance, if a child is kidnaped, it might mean that you are not paying attention to the childlike or childish parts of yourself, that you may be holding parts of yourself hostage to other parts represented by the child.

Who is being kidnaped? How old are they? Why? Which sex? Why? What does this remind you of going on in your life at the time? Who is the villain, and who is the hero?

What are the circumstances surrounding the kidnaping? How was the kidnaping accomplished? Is there a ransom being asked? What is the real purpose of the kidnaping? How do you feel about the kidnaping? See also EMOTION/ Danger, Fear, VICTIM/Captive, and any objects used in the kidnaping.

KILL

To kill someone or something in a dream or meditation most often symbolizes that you are killing a part of yourself. This can be old beliefs, attitudes, habits, people no longer appropriate to your growth or progress, or, conversely, parts of you that are trying to come forward to aid in your growth at the time. Any of these will be represented by the person or object being killed.

For example, if you are killing your boss, it might be telling you that you are getting rid of the parts of you that your boss symbolizes, or that you have a deep desire to do so.

But any killing might be warning you about parts of you that are in danger, characteristics or talents which you might not want to let get murdered.

Is a male or female being killed, a child or parent, a pet or wild animal, a monster or an angel? Why? How do you feel about the killing in your dream or meditation?

Which weapons are being used? Why is the killing happening? Who ordered it? Why? How will your dream change if the killing is successful? Why?

The interpretation of kill will depend entirely upon the total context of your dream or experience. Remember that you can never take a symbol away from the overall context of the dream.

See also BLOOD if blood is present, DEATH, EMOTION/ Fear, PAIN if there is pain, any object used in the killing, any parts of the BODY involved, or any other symbol being killed or doing the killing.

IF YOU ARE BEING KILLED in your dream or meditation, especially if you are bleeding, it can be telling you that you are either losing energy, or conversely that you are very strongly connected to life through the areas that are bleeding. How you feel during the experience will help you find your interpretation.

What part of you is killing off what other part? Why? How do you feel about the killing? What happens once its over? What will be lost? What will be gained?

KILLING A CHILD frequently symbolizes that you are destroying a childlike part of yourself, but it can also represent that you are getting rid of the more infantile childish parts of you.

Killing a child can also be a message that you need to lighten up a little, that you are destroying important trusting and playful sides of yourself. Do you need to be more child-like, innocent, or trusting right now?

COMMITTING SUICIDE often symbolizes that you should look deeply into yourself for deep unconscious and dangerously destructive feelings at the time, just to make sure they aren't really there.

But dream suicide most often tells you that you are killing off a creative or vital part of yourself.

The method of suicide should tell you which part of you this is.

Or is some part of you feeling so neglected, bored, and unappreciated that it feels like committing suicide, forgetting the whole thing and moving on?

Suicide can also be a symbolic warning that you are avoiding a problem or lesson that needs to be handled before it becomes dangerous enough to damage you or some part of you.

KILLING A PARENT almost always symbolizes that you are forcefully getting rid of beliefs and attitudes you originally got from your parents.

While killing a parent can, of course, also clearly highlight unresolved and unacknowledged issues with your real parents, it almost never means that you would actually like to kill your parents off. This kind of dream is particularly likely to surface during early adolescence when the child is striving for autonomy and freedom from the restrictions imposed by parents. So within this context, it's more likely to be a good thing rather than a bad one.

KISS

Kisses symbolize a direct connection to what is being kissed, and a spiritual union with who or what is being kissed. Kisses also symbolize submission, surrender, or devotion to the one being kissed.

Ancient traditions tell us that a kiss represented the transfer of

Spirit, life, and power, and it is likely that kissing probably originally symbolized the transfer of the breath of the Soul.

However, some scholars believe that the act of kissing originated with mouth-to-mouth feeding, and from there eventually found its way into love play.

Kissing was originally most common in European countries, where it implied a bond among members of a clan or family, that they were kissing cousins, so to speak.

Symbolically, kisses are almost always seen as life-giving, not life threatening, although there are a few symbolic exceptions.

A kiss also symbolizes a sincere, strongly felt emotion for the object being kissed, including love, warmth, friendship, trust, sensuality, and reconciliation.

A dream kiss can also be a wonderful pun, as in the kiss of death, or "you have to kiss a lot of frogs to find a prince (or princess)." Have you been trying to "send a kiss by messenger?" Would you like to tell someone to kiss off?

Who is kissing whom or what? How does it feel? What kind of a kiss is it? Would you like to kiss or be kissed in that way when you are awake? Why, or why not? Why do human beings kiss? What does it remind you of that is going in your life? See also BODY/Lips, Mouth.

KNOCK

Knocks generally represent a signal from You to you to pay closer attention to what you are doing and what is going on in your life

at the time. Knocks also symbolize your yearnings and desires, that you are "knocking at the door."

In some metaphysical belief systems, a knock is a sound heard during a seance. A medium is believed to have the ability to spontaneously produce a knock, which some of the other people in the room or house can hear.

This is a psychic skill called percussion, and is usually used to convey a message to the medium by reminding them they have forgotten something, telling them that something is about to happen, that what they just thought or said was correct, for instance.

It is also fairly common to be awakened by knocking or the sound of a bell when you are in the beginning stages of new growth. But pay particular attention to how you feel when this happens, and then you'll know whether or not to answer that knock or doorbell at the time.

A dream knock can also be a great pun, as in "don't knock it till you've tried it," "knock and the door shall be opened." Did you just get some hard knocks? Knocking could also be a dream knock-knock joke. Who's there?

What is being knocked on? Who or what is doing the knocking? How does it sound? How many knocks are there? What happened in your dream or experience after the knock? How did it make you feel? Why? What does it remind you of? See also BELL, BUILDING/Door.

KNOT

A knot is an ancient extremely complex symbol, but most of its interpretations include some concept of a tightly knit or closed link, a pure and strong interconnection to something or someone.

Knots are even symbolic of another symbol, the spiral; see GEOMETRIC SHAPE/Spiral.

The symbol for Infinity, a horizontal figure 8 (and the number 8 itself) are knots, representing the unending, unbroken connection of a knot to the manifestation of Infinity.

Nets, loops, braids, cords, chains, necklaces, bracelets, and rings often share the same symbolism of binding, connecting to, or shackling, representing an unchanging psychic situation, no matter how unaware of the situation the dreamer or experiencer is.

Knots also symbolize bonding to, continuity, Fate, that which binds us to our destiny and our intentions, the inescapable, and linking to and connection with protective powers and energies of all kinds.

They can also symbolize complications or obstacles and problems. Even today, we sometimes talk about having a knotty problem.

Knots were extremely important elements in magical practices of many early cultures. How the knots were made and of what was vital, the sorcerer or sorceress literally weaving a spell through weaving or tying the knots.

In ancient Egypt, knots symbolized life and immortality, as in the Knot of Isis. In Islam, knots symbolize protection, but cannot be worn on a pilgrimage to Mecca. And the three knots on a monastic monk's belt symbolize the three vows of chastity, poverty, and obedience.

A knot can also be a good pun: a knotty problem, tying the knot, getting your knickers in a twist, tying the knot, or the substitution of "knot" for "Not!"

CUTTING A KNOT frequently symbolizes excessive impatience, the inability to wait for the gentler but slower method of untying. For this reason, it was an old symbol for taking the short and steep path to Realization.

Cutting a knot also symbolizes disassociating and freeing yourself from what the knot was binding. "Cutting the knot" is still a phrase we use today.

THE ENDLESS KNOT is one of the eight Emblems of Good Luck in Chinese Buddhism, symbolizing longevity, the power to keep out evil, the flow of life, Infinity, and Eternity. The lemniscate, a horizontal figure eight, is an example of the endless knot.

A KNOTTED CORD symbolizes a protective enclosure and is often used in ancient magical procedures for just this purpose.

A SLIP-KNOT is often used to symbolize oaths, journeys, and sometimes dishonor.

UNTYING A KNOT often symbolizes opening yourself and committing to act on the situation represented by your dream or meditation. It also represents a symbolic death, and that you are releasing yourself from the world and concern with its mundane, worldly things.

L

LADDER

Ladders symbolize your step-by-step progress, both up and down, achieved by means of your own personal skill and effort. And they represent your potential for access to True Reality, the Absolute, through your own effort and courage at the time, including the ability to keep your balance during your climb.

A ladder is an ancient symbol for the connection between Heaven and Earth. Ladders can reach up into the Heavens, and down into the Middle Earth. Ladders are used to climb into and out of kivas, for instance, and often represent the uniting of Heaven with Earth.

Ladders can also represent safety, since they can be pulled up out of reach after you have climbed to a safe place, leaving whatever is chasing you behind.

As an archetype, ladders symbolize the passage from one Plane of Existence to another, a breakthrough to a new level. Ladders are strong World Axis symbols.

Ladders are also an ancient symbol for the rainbow, itself symbolizing the relationship between God and humanity; see WEATHER/Rainbow.

And ladder is a good pun, as in climbing the ladder of success, or climbing Jacob's Ladder, a symbol of communication from Jacob to God and back again through the use of angelic energy and support.

Is your ladder leaning against something or does it stand by itself? Why? What is it made of? What condition is it in? Is it safe, or unstable? Why are you climbing a ladder instead of using another method for going up or down? Is the ladder heavy, or easy to handle? See also CLIMB, STAIRS.

CLIMBING DOWN a ladder can symbolize that some part of you feels that it would like to be on solid more familiar ground. Climbing down can also be your way of telling yourself that you are moving the wrong direction at the time.

This is not a given, however, and how you feel about climbing down and why you are doing so will help you determine whether or not this interpretation is right for you. For instance, you may be climbing down because the way up is too unstable, or blocked, or has too many dangers for you right now.

CLIMBING UP a ladder frequently symbolizes that you are climbing to the next level or levels of growth. Climbing up can also be telling you that you are headed in the right direction.

But, as we said above, your interpretation will depend entirely upon where your ladder is, where it leads, and how you feel about the climb, why you are making the effort to hold on and climb up. For instance, you could be climbing up just to avoid dealing with something, to get away.

THE RUNGS OF A LADDER are an ancient symbol for the power and ability of human consciousness to ascend and pass through all levels of existence as a result of our own personal efforts.

Rungs also represent the different levels of initiation, especially if there are seven, nine, or twelve rungs on the ladder.

THE TWO SIDES OF A LADDER are anzcient symbols for the left and right Pillars of the World, and the Two Trees of Paradise, connected, unified, and balanced by the rungs of the ladder.

LAMP

A lamp of any kind frequently symbolizes your inner light, the light inside your own home (your body and self), the light by which you are currently seeing.

Lamps also symbolize your personal spiritual light and the light of spiritual beings.

Lamps are an ancient symbol of both life and death. To extinguish a lamp is symbolically equivalent to extinguishing life, the light of the spirit.

A lamp can also represent the light of spiritual clarity, the light of divinity, immortality, wisdom, the human intellect, moral or spiritual guidance, the stars, love, and remembrance of things or people from the past.

Lamps are very old symbols for intelligence and Spirit, and the lamps of the ancients were shaped in accordance with their intended functions and to suit the nature of the god to whom they were dedicated. A pottery lamp, for instance, symbolized humanity, while a golden one or one decorated with precious stones symbolized Divinity.

What type of lamp is this? What does it illuminate? What fuels this lamp? Is it modern, or burning oil? Where is it sitting? What is it being used for? Who made it? For what purpose? What is it made of?

Who would own such a lamp? Who would turn their nose up at it? Is the lamp new or old? Why? What does this remind you of? See also CANDLE, FLAME, LIGHT.

THE FLAME OF A LAMP is an old symbol for love, desire, consuming passion, and a Divine Spark which willingly consumes itself in the service of the Light.

THE OIL OF A LAMP is an old symbol for the ocean, with all of its symbolism, and the personal devotion which sustains and gives birth to the flame.

THE WICK OF A LAMP symbolizes the Earth and the human mind.

LANDSCAPE

Landscapes or backgrounds most often represent the emotional environment or overall emotional undertone of your dream, meditation., or experience.

Landscapes are the settings for your personal dramas, and none of them ever are there by accident. Your subconscious has chosen its landscape for very specific reasons. Every piece of your landscape has a special meaning to you, each piece is an object and symbol.

Remember that *everything* in your dream is a symbol, including the stage setting. Interpret each object of the landscape itself as well as analyzing the landscape or background as a whole unit. What do the pieces tell you about the meaning of the whole?

Why is your dream or meditation (or life) taking place in this particular landscape, and not in some other? What kind of a person would be attracted by this landscape? What kind of a person

would avoid it? Why? How do you feel about it in your dream or meditation? How would your dream or life change if you changed the landscape or background? Why? See also all objects in the landscape.

LATE

Late almost always symbolizes that on some deep inner level you feel you are not using your time wisely, that you are running behind schedule.

Dreaming of being late can be telling you that you have too much to do in too little time, and need to relax and get back in touch with your natural rhythms. If you're late, you're late. What's the worst thing that will happen because of being late?

Being late also frequently symbolizes that you feel you have missed some opportunities, or are about to, at the time.

And late makes for some fun puns. Are you a day late and a dollar short? Is it too late to change now? Have you just missed the boat? Is your girlfriend late?

For what are you late? How do you feel about it? Why are you late? What caused you to be late, held your attention long enough to make you late? What will happen because you are late? Who will benefit, and who will lose?

Are you in the habit of being late when you are awake? Why, or why not? What does this tell you about your basic nature? How is this particular lateness different from the times you are late when you are awake? What kind of person is habitually late? What kind of person just doesn't care whether they are late or not?

LAUNDRY
Doing laundry or dealing with it in any form often symbolizes cleaning up or refreshing some of the roles you play in your life at the time, or that some part of you feels you should.

Is your laundry piling up? What type of clothing or laundry is it? What parts of your laundry are involved ? Do you use machines or are you scrubbing by hand?

What are you doing — washing, folding, hanging up, ironing? How do you feel about it? How do you feel about doing laundry when you are awake? What kind of person does laundry for a living? See also CLOTHES, HANG/Clothes, WATER.

LAW
Lawyers and dealing with the law in any way often symbolizes guidance, teaching, written legal authority, specialized knowledge, and protection or defense through legal authority. How you feel about the law and lawyers in general will determine how you are using this symbol.

Judges generally symbolize judgment of yourself by yourself. It can also be a reminder that you are in danger of judging the lesson other people have created for themselves. Has some part of you set yourself up as the judge, or is it in danger of doing so?

A jury would carry much of this same symbolism; there are just more parts of you doing the judging.

What is the purpose of the law? Who legislated the law in your dream of experience? Why? What is its impact on humanity? Does it solve anything, or create more problems?

What laws have been broken? What will be the penalty or sentence? What kind of a person would not conform to these laws?

Why is the lawyer or judge in your dream at all? What do they want to tell you? How would the dream change if the lawyer or judge was not there? See also GUARD, JAIL, and POLICE.

LEADER
Leaders are often messages to point you toward a very specific direction or course of action, usually in connection with your philosophy, belief, or action to be taken at the time.

Dreaming of a leader can also point to a feeling that you are, or would like to, follow a certain strategy or philosophy, that you would like to follow a leader or mentor, someone who knows the way.

But dreaming of a leader or of actually being the leader can also represent a strong inner hope or wish that someone else will take care of things for a while, that you literally are ready to follow the leader, not think for yourself right now.

Leaders of any kind, of course, may also be showing you leadership talents of your own that you are not utilizing, or even may not be aware that you have, and a desire to lead, not just keep on following. Is it time for you to step forward and take charge?

What kind of a leader is this leader? What are his or her strong and weak points? What and who gave this leader the right to lead? Who is being led? How do they feel about it?

To what or to whom are you being led? Is your leader a true leader, or a dictator in leadership clothes? What kind of a person would follow this leader? Why? Are you usually a good follower? Why, or why not?

How are leaders different from followers? What does this leader remind you of that is going on in your life at the time? See also FAMOUS, if the leader is a famous person.

LECTURE

Dreaming of attending or giving a lecture often symbolizes a strong desire to take in additional or deeper knowledge of the subject of the lecture.

A lecture can also be a message that you should begin listening more closely, maybe even take notes, about the subject of the lecture. And it can also be telling you that you sometimes lecture others or yourself too much, are just a little too pedantic about your facts.

And, of course, a lecture can also be a suggestion that some part of you would like to, or should, lecture or provide information for others. How you feel about the lecture will give you your best clue as to which interpretation is right for the occasion.

What is the lecture about? Who is doing the lecturing? Why did you and anyone else at the lecture choose to attend?

What kind of person would pay good money and time to listen to this lecture? Why? How would your dream change if the subject of the lecture changed? See also BODY/ Mouth, Throat, Tongue, SCHOOL, SPEECH, STAGE if lecture is delivered from a stage.

LEFT

There is no easy interpretation of either left or right, in or out of your dreams. But *in general*, the left symbolizes the Yin (female) qualities and characteristics — the receptive, nurturing, intuitive, psychic, creative sides of you, even if you are naturally left handed.

The left is an old symbol for the internal, passive, incoming energy of the Soul.

The left side of the brain is the intellectual, rational side, and controls the right side of the body. Some authorities also view the left as the past and the right as the future.

In Western cultures, the left side symbolizes the second seat of honor (right being the first), the place of the second-born son. For instance, in Hebrew tradition, Jesus originally sat on the left hand of God and Lucifer on the right — until Lucifer angered God by his wilful disobedience and pride. And it was always God's left hand that destroyed.

To the early Christians, the left was the sinister, dark, illegitimate, lunar aspect and represented the past and lustful desires. To be born on the left side of the blanket indicated someone who had been born out of wedlock.

But in ancient China, the left was the side of honor and represented the Yin side. The right, or Yang, side had a tendency toward violence ultimately leading to self-destruction through its own strength. It required the more passive Yin energy to temper this outgoing strength with gentleness and compassion. In times of war, however, these two positions of honor were reversed.

And in many cultures even today, the evil eye is believed to be the left eye. Most witches and sorcerers were said to use their left hand to cast spells, and to dance widdershins (moving left to right) rather than right to left in ceremonies, symbolizing the inversion of right action.

It is an interesting side note that any negative interpretation given to the left appears to have entered human symbolism shortly after many cultures (with the exception of the ancient Romans) shifted from matriarchal to patriarchal societies.

In the Western world, the seat on the right side of a power figure is the seat of honor. It was the left hand which was used by monarchs to bestow gifts and titles, while the right hand blessed.

In many ancient cultures, the right symbolized the mercy of God while the left represents God's justice or judgment. And it was the right hand which was also the choice of priests and priestesses for bestowing gifts and blessings.

The left can, of course, also be a great pun. What part of you feels left out or behind? What are you left of, or on? Are you left politically? Are you taking the left hand path?

What does left mean to you? Who or what is on the left? How do you feel about it? Why do you think you placed the person or object on the left rather than the right? How would the symbolism change if left became right? See also RIGHT.

LICENSE

A license of any kind usually represents your personal identity. It is a verification and proof of who you are, where you live, and often even what you are authorized or permitted to do in your society.

Licenses also symbolize that you have been granted special permission and the authority to go forward and to continue, or to perform the particular function that the license represents.

What type of license is it? Who grants it? What kind of person would hold this license? What would you have to do to get it? What would happen if you lost it? How does it define who or what you are or are allowed to do?

LOST

Being lost in a dream or meditation often symbolizes that you or some part of you is confused and is questioning your current direction in life.

Being lost can also be a symbol that your energy is getting low, a message to come out of the woods or maze of confusion, to get back on track, quit exploring and wandering around wasting time and energy.

Who is lost? How did they get that way? Where are they lost? Why? What is the best way for them to find their way back? What will happen when the lost person gets found? What is the overall feeling connected with the feeling of being lost? What changes once you or the object is no longer lost? See also MISSING and any object that got lost.

LOVER

Dream lovers most often symbolize the integration of your Yang (male) and Yin (female) qualities and characteristics. Dream lovers do not necessarily represent sex at all, even if your dream is blatantly sexual (sorry) — although of course it can also be exactly what it looks like. But even then, it will hold a lot of symbolism. There is a reason why you subconsciously chose the particular lover you did, for instance.

A lover also represents your natural desire and need for human physical love, a deep unfulfilled need to be touched, held, accepted, and appreciated by another for just who and what you are, just as you are.

Dream lovers can also symbolize qualities you may subconsciously feel are missing from your current relationship, or from your own capacities or willingness to "make love."

The Lover is also a very old symbol for the human Soul in its intense yearning and all-consuming desire to reunite with its Source, the Beloved. Many ancient erotic love poems and stories are really about this spiritual longing and desire, not about physical love.

How is your dream lover different from your current lover, or lovers you have had in the past? Why? Where would you meet such a lover? What would it take to please and hold such a lover? How would you like to meet this person in your waking life? Why, or why not? See also SEX.

M

MACHINE

Any kind of machine generally symbolizes an extension of the natural physical and mental powers of the person using it.

But machines can also be telling you that you have sacrificed your human attributes for a routine, machine-like existence. Does some part of you feel that you have become a machine, just another cog in the wheel?

What kind of a machine is it? What kind of energy does it run on? What is its function?

Who would own and use this machine? Who would maintain and repair it? Why would anyone need it? Does it make life easier, or more complicated and expensive?

How is this dream machine different from other machines just like it, or ones that can do the same job? What does the machine remind you of that is going on in your life at the time? See also TOOL, VEHICLE.

MAIL

Any kind of mail usually tells you that you are receiving information and messages from a distance.

But mail is also often a pun, substituting "mail" for "male."

If you are the one mailing something, what is it, to whom is it addressed, what type of postage does it require, what does it communicate? What will change when it is received? Why?

Where did the mail come from, who sent it, how did you receive it, was it sent by any special messenger? Who would send this kind of mail? Why? See also POSTMAN.

MAIL-RELATED SYMBOLS:

LETTER: Letters often symbolize receiving information or news from a distance, a communication of ideas and feelings, a message of some importance, and even a teaching of some kind. A letter represents a direct communication from a distant source through written symbols. See also ALPHABET.

What kind of a person would write this letter? To whom would such a letter normally be addressed? What type of paper is it on? Who delivered it? Why was it written? How will things change because of the letter?

NOTE: Receiving or writing a note is most often a simple but direct message to "take note" and pay special attention to the subject of your dream or meditation. As you have guessed, this one is a good pun.

PACKAGE, RECEIVING: Receiving a package often represents that you are being contacted by some unknown or unfamiliar part of yourself, that you are literally receiving a gift. What's in the package? From where did it originate? Who sent it? Why was it sent? How is it being sent: regular, third class, priority mail, specialized delivery? Why? What are you "packaging," and how? A potential pun, what are you packaging?

PACKAGE, SENDING: Sending a package often symbolizes that you are in the process of giving away a part of yourself, or even that you are projecting that part of yourself onto someone else. How do you feel about sending the package? To whom was it sent? Why? What will be the result once it's delivered? Why? How is it wrapped? How was it sent?

MALE

Male symbolizes the Yang (masculine) principle, the assertive, active, rational, practical, earthy, responsible, analytical, and intellectual side of yourself, whether you are male or female.

Traditionally, man or male represents the Cosmic Man (really the Cosmic Human), humanity as the Microcosm. The male's physical body represents Earth, the heat of his body represents Fire, the blood represents Water, and his breath, Air.

The Sufis define man as the "symbol of universal existence," but "man" within this and other ancient contexts actually translates to humankind, not just mankind.

The masculine principle is often symbolized by the sun and by anything phallic, upright, or capable of penetration (e.g., sword, needle, stinger), and is usually associated with heat and dryness (the Yin principle is considered to be "moist").

In some Native American cultures, the male principle is also represented by a white eagle feather, while the female is symbolized by a brown one.

In Taoism, Man is the central and mediating power of the Great Triad of Heaven-Man-Earth.

When all of the characters in your dream or meditation (other than the actual physical representation of you) are of the opposite sex, your dream is probably trying to tell you something about how you subconsciously feel about either that particular sex in general, a specific person of that gender, or a quality within you that is traditionally attributed to that gender.

However, it is important to note that men in general naturally tend to dream less about women that they do about other men, while women generally tend to balance the symbolism of men and women. And men are usually more concerned even in their dreams with their interactions with the other men in their dreams, while women tend to be more interested in social and emotional interactions with both sexes.

How do you feel about males in general? What is their function in your life? Other than anatomically, how are males different from females? Why do you think this is? How are males supposed to act?

What is the male in your dream doing? How is he acting differently from the males in your waking life? Why? How would you like to meet him? See also BOY, FAMILY/Husband, FEMALE, GIRL.

MARRIAGE

A marriage symbolizes a desire or strong need to integrate your heart with your mind, your intellect with your emotions.

Marriage also often represents spiritual union and the attainment of perfection through the process of the death of a former life (being single) into a new one, in which some give-and-take will be experienced.

And marriage represents union of the Soul with the Body and is symbolic of the union of Wisdom and Love, or Truth and Love, the union of the Higher Self with the now-purified Lower Self on the Higher Mental Plane of existence.

Marriage also symbolizes a uniting and merger of any one or more of the following: your ideas, your awareness, different parts of yourself, including your masculine (Yang) and feminine (Yin) qualities, and any dualities or opposites. And marriage symbolizes the mystic union of Heaven and Earth, priest and priestess, king and queen, sun and moon, the physical with the spiritual.

Dreaming of marriage often symbolizes that the Yin-Yang principles have or are about to merge, your intuitive abilities with your intellectual ones, your mind with your emotions. It represents the successful blending of any pair of opposites, not just man and woman.

Marriages can also symbolize a reconciliation of opposites, and coming to terms with, accepting, and appreciating the differences in any opposites. For instance, in alchemy, marriage represents the union of opposing, but equal, forces.

And, of course, a marriage can represent exactly what it looks like it does — that you want to marry the person in your dream or meditation. This is true even when the other person is a spiritual teacher or being, a common symbol when you are at the stage of yearning to be one with that person.

How are marriages different from weddings? How do you feel about marriage in general? How do you think the marriage couple will interact a year later? Why? See also CEREMONY/Wedding, FAMILY/Husband, Wife.

MAZE

Mazes or labyrinths are symbolic of the many detours and intellectual "what ifs" we use to occupy our minds so we can avoid seeing our part in creating a problem.Mazes are both entertaining and frustrating, but they can always give us an excuse for not finding our way of a situation or feeling.

Mazes also often represent your everyday life with its many twists and turns, detours, wrong turns or directions, unsuccessful efforts, and your tests and puzzles to be worked out.

And mazes don't have to look like traditional mazes to be mazes; city streets, forest paths, and office corridors make good mazes.

Mazes also symbolize your journey through confusion into clarity, making your way out of darkness into the light.

Mazes are an ancient symbol of an initiation of some kind, an invitation to use your ability to discover your own hidden spiritual centers, especially if your dream maze is underground and resembles a labyrinth Initiatory temples were often labyrinths for just this reason.

Your dream maze can also be telling you that you are refusing to make a decision of some kind, probably whatever is at the heart or center of the maze.

And mazes aren't easy to build, even in your sleep. Remember that the sleeping brain believes what it sees, so confusion is confusion. See also LOST.

Mazes can also be good puns. Are you feeling like a laboratory rat forced to run a maze or solve a puzzle for the enlightenment or at the whim of someone else? At what are you "a-mazed?"

How do you feel about the maze? Are you having fun, or are you frustrated and frightened? What is your maze made of? What will happen if you cannot find your way out?

Is anyone with you? Who would build this maze? For what purpose? Who would enjoy deciphering its puzzle?

MIRROR

Mirrors almost always symbolize the self coming face-to-face with itself, literally "self-reflection," looking directly into your true nature.

Mirrors reflect light, reversing the original image in the process. Things are not always as you see them in a mirror.

Mirrors also symbolize self-knowledge and your public self-image. And mirrors can represent your consciousness, unconscious memories of some kind, the clarity of intelligence, the mind itself, and the clear shining surface of Divine Truth. Mirrors also represent twins and echoes.

From the very earliest times, mirrors have been used as an ambivalent symbol. In many ancient cultures, mirrors symbolized the Creation reflecting Divine Intelligence. It was also a symbol of human consciousness or imagination in its capacity to reflect the form and reality of the visible world.

Mirrors are often connected symbolically to thought, especially thought as the instrument of self-contemplation. In some early cultures, mirrors were symbols of the multiple levels or facets of the Soul, and the Soul's ability to adapt itself to the many objects it encounters on its journey.

Mirrors are both a sun and a moon symbol, even though mirrors are usually viewed as passive rather than projective.

Mirrors are usually associated with the eye and face more than other parts of the body; see also BODY/Eye, Face. Mirrors are sometimes also used as a symbolic substitute for water; see WATER.

Since a mirror is a surface which reflects and reproduces an image, and even gives the appearance of absorbing it, they have almost always been a part of magic in legends and myths, and often credited with the power to retrieve images previously stored in them.

At other times, mirrors take on the symbolism of a door, especially a door into other dimensions of reality.

Even today, in many metaphysical systems it is believed that mirrors are tools for seeing your guides, especially guides who help with any psychic work. They are also used to aid in seeing the reflection of any past lives, to see your aura, and to deflect and send any negative or psychic attacks back to their sender.

A mirror is one of the Eight Precious Things in Buddhism, while in Japan, mirrors symbolize purity of the Soul and the Sun Goddess.

And seeing a mirror in your dream or meditation can be a wonderful pun, as in "it's all done with mirrors", "mirror, mirror on the wall..." How about "seeing eye-to-eye," "what you see is what you get?" Who or what is your mirror image?

What do you see in the mirror? What do you look like? Does your image change? How is it the same or different from how you feel you really look? How do you feel about your mirror image? What do you think he or she is like as a person? What objects are reflected in the mirror? Why?

HAND MIRRORS are ancient symbols of Truth, and in ancient China were a favorite as a gift to a bride, ensuring happiness in marriage and protection against evil influences. Many Chinese folktales are about the animal or spirit in the mirror. Mirrors also symbolize a wise, contemplative person who does not act, but who instead constantly reflects.

MISSING

Anything or anyone missing in your dream, meditation, or experience is often symbolic of parts of you that you miss, feel that you lack, or have somehow lost.

What or who is missing? How would your life be different if the missing object or person were never found? Why is it missing? How do you feel about it in your dream? What is actually missing from your life at the time? Have you missed the target? See also HUNT, LOST and the various missing objects, e.g., VEHICLE, WALLET, etc.

MISSED CONNECTIONS often symbolizes deep feelings of missing an opportunity or connection of some kind, that you might not be connecting to the right person or situation, even that you are not connecting to the subject of your dream or meditation, that you're missing the whole thing.

Missing a travel connection can also be a warning that your timing is off in the situation covered by your dream or meditation. Are you using the right time table? Is your timing off? What is the result of your having missed your connection?

This one is also a good pun. Have you just missed the boat? Been left standing at the station?

A MISSING OBJECT frequently represent specific parts of yourself as symbolized by the missing object. They can also represent a feeling of the loss of what the missing object symbolizes to you. Missing or lost objects can also be a warning of some kind about the object itself and what it symbolizes to you. Missing objects can also sometimes symbolize specific parts of your body, but don't get into a panic about this one. Missing your hands, for instance, doesn't imply that you're actually going to get them cut off. But you'll have to admit it would make a great symbol.

Missing objects are also any one of a number of good puns. Are you about to be found missing in action? What has gone missing? Are you missing an oar?

MONSTER

Monsters are most often attention-getting creations representing fear of your own personal power and energy, or fear of the ways you may be changing at the time.

Monsters are also symbols of any unreasonable fears you have consciously or unconsciously allowed to grow out of all proportion to their real strength or danger, and almost always because you have put off dealing directly with the fear — which is now relentlessly chasing you down.

To deal with your monsters, try to turn and face them in your dream or meditation, and ask it what part of you it represents, what it wants from you, what it wants to say to you. If it is a particularly terrifying monster, immediately upon waking imagine the monster stepping out of its monster suit and see what steps out. You will almost always be amazed at what's really inside that suit.

Talk with your monsters. Remember that it is really just a friend and ally who has come to bring you a strong message about yourself, and that the only way this particular message can get through is by frightening you enough to ensure you remember it. (Worked, didn't it?).

Throughout human history, monsters have symbolized cosmic or elemental forces at a stage of development just one step removed from chaos. Monsters are sub- or pre-human. Most of these elemental energies are in general not too fond of those of us who have earned the right to experience being human, so they tend to roar and gnash their incisors a lot, hoping we'll buy into their power.

Some authorities believe that monsters represent any imbalance of your psychic abilities, usually those which have been activated by too much emotion going to your desires or imagination. This imbalance of strong emotion is suppressed by the conscious mind, giving birth to "monsters." The form the monster takes gives you good clues to its meaning and which natural psychic ability you are in danger of suppressing or distorting.

But no matter what, the one thing you can say about monsters is that they always seem to get your attention, so you might as well face up to your inherent abilities and learn how to use them wisely. As your monster dreams usually show you, you can only run away for so long, and then...they pounce.

Monsters can, however, also represent latent and potentially dangerous energies and powers (always subconscious) in their more aggressive and destructive forms.

How free is this monster? Is it contained by anything at all? How do you feel about that? How much destruction or carnage can your monster cause? Why is it so angry? What is its nature and purpose? What actions is it carrying out? Who or what does it want to get at? Why? What does it remind you of?

What type of monster is this particular monster? What are its main strengths? Can it fly, swim, run fast, appear and disappear at will? What purpose does this monster serve? What has been the result of its appearance? What changed in your dream or meditation when you saw or felt its presence? Why? What does this tell you about what is going on emotionally in your life at the time?

How is this monster different from other monsters you have dreamed in the past? Why? How does this change what the monster represents to you? What actions are you taking to get away from your dream monster? See also CHASE, EMOTION/Danger, Fear, ENEMY, FOREIGN/Alien, NIGHTMARE, RUN, VICTIM.

COMMON MONSTER SYMBOLS:

BOGEYMAN: This term is believed to have Slavic origins. It was originally a nature spirit shaped like a goblin. The bogey usually acted maliciously toward human beings, and, oddly enough, was originally believed to be in charge of and hover over areas of decaying vegetation, not spend its time lurking in children's closets or under beds.

DEFEATING A MONSTER: Defeating a monster symbolizes the triumph of Light over Darkness and of conscious awareness over the area of the subconscious symbolized by your monster. You may also just have experienced a major victory over some "monstrous" part of yourself. Give yourself a treat as a reward — couldn't hurt.

A DESTROYING MONSTER: A monster wreaking havoc and devastation is symbolic of evil and tyrannical rulers, and your own tendency to destroy valuable parts of your territory and creativity just to satisfy the ego. Why is your monster angry? What does it gain by being so destructive? What would it take to pacify it? What changes because of the devastation?

FIGHTING A MONSTER: Fighting or struggling with a monster often symbolizes your struggle to free your consciousness from the terrible clutches of the dreaded subconscious.

It can also, of course, symbolize any fierce inner struggle going on at the time.

How do you feel fighting the monster? If your monster could talk, what would it tell you about itself, and about you?

GHOST: Ghosts or apparitions frequently symbolize a part of yourself you do not understand, and therefore fear and distrust.

If the ghost is in the form of someone you know, it can symbolize that you need to bring something in connection with that person into substantial reality, or what or who they represent to you, even if that person is actually dead. And it isn't just human beings who can end up a ghost.

Dream ghosts can also represent your own spiritual nature. Is the ghost earth-bound, or on its way home? Why? How does it feel? What does it want to say to you?

Some authorities believe that to dream of someone, even someone you do not know, who has died means that some part of the energy that was once that person (the "ghost") is actually with you at the time of your dream or meditation. This type of dream is called an apparition dream, and these apparitions almost always come to bring you a message — quite often a message that on some deep unconscious level some part of you is in danger of giving up, joining the ghost by becoming a ghost yourself.

Ghosts can also be a wonderful pun, as in "you don't have a ghost of a chance." Are you just a ghost of your former self? Are there ghosts in your machine?

How do you feel about the ghost? What does it look like? Does it remind you of anything going on in your life right now?

Are you interacting with the ghost? What does it have to say? How would you like to talk with or meet your dream ghost while you are awake? Do you believe in ghosts? What kinds of people become ghosts? Why? See also CEREMONY/Funeral, DEATH, EMOTION/Fear/Grief, GRAVE.

GOLEM: A golem is a figure carved from wood or sculpted from clay, wax, or metal (and sometimes by sewing dead body parts together) which is then given a personality by carving a sacred name into its forehead.

Golems are created to perform specific tasks for its creator, almost always for malicious or deadly reasons. Dr. Frankenstein's monster was a type of golem.

GROTESQUES: This is a very old name for the images we often see streaming by under our eyelids just before sleep, or during deep relaxation exercises. These images usually last only a few seconds or minutes, are vividly colored, and can be either beautiful or frightening.

It is generally believed that grotesques occur during the in-between stages of consciousness when the conscious mind relinquishes control to the subconscious. This particular state of consciousness is also sometimes called the hypnagogic state.

LAND MONSTER: In general, most land monsters represent your emotions closer to the surface of consciousness, while water monsters represent your deep, deep subconscious fears.

VAMPIRE: A vampire symbolize pseudo-immortality, the non-ordinary, the supernatural, great strength through use of the supernatural, beings who must take the energy of others in order to survive, and transfiguration and transmutation.

Vampires also represent a fear of your own "supernatural" powers, and a fear that you might somehow misuse it and damage others.

A vampire can also symbolize that you are losing energy to someone or something else, or that you yourself are draining someone of energy.

What does this vampire look like? What actions is it carrying out? Do you feel threatened by it? What is it wearing? How does it feel? How do you feel about vampires in general? What does it want to say to you? See also ATTACK, BLOOD, BODY/Fangs, EMOTION/Fear, DEATH, KILL, VICTIM.

WATER MONSTER: In general, water monsters symbolize fears and emotions at a much, much deeper level than land monsters.

WEREWOLF: No one is quite sure where the belief that people turned into raging animals of one kind or another began, but it is a belief common to many cultures around the world.

Lycanthropy was actually named for the ancient Greek deity Apollo Lycaeus, Wolfish Apollo, who was worshiped in the Lyceum, the Wolf Temple, the temple where Socrates taught.

Wolves are often associated with death and reincarnation legends. The wolf in this context symbolizes the positive and spiritual characteristics of humanity, as well as its diabolical and wild qualities.

The legends about the werewolf or any form of wereanimal always included the warning that "even a man who is pure of heart and says his prayers by night" was vulnerable to the attack of a werewolf, thereby himself transforming into this monster against his human will every full moon.

What is this werewolf or wereanimal doing? What does he or she want to say to you? How would it feel to become one every full moon? How would your life be different? What does this remind you of that is going on in your life at the time of your dream? See also ANIMAL, BLOOD, BODY/Fangs, DEATH, EMOTION/Anger, Fear, KILL, VICTIM.

MOUNTAIN

In all cultures where they exist, spiritually significant events take place on the mountain. Even today there are many sacred mountains.

Mountains have almost always represented the highest mental development of human beings and the closeness and protection of God, symbolizing the joining or connection of Heaven with Earth.

As an archetype, the Cosmic Mountain is a World Center, the Axis Mundi of the ancients. The highest point of the Earth is seen as central, the very summit of Paradise, providing passage from one Plane of Existence to another, and direct communication with the gods. It is probably for this reason that in many myths, mountains are often made almost entirely of gold and precious gems.

Mountains are imperturbable, almost indifferent to human beings, and often unapproachable and inhospitable. Does this remind you of anything going on in your life at the time?

Mountains symbolize constancy, Eternity, firmness, and stillness. Mountains also represent great effort, great beauty, obstacles to be overcome, and great or mountainous changes looming on your immediate horizon.

And dreaming of mountains often represents your spiritual awareness and your current progress within the situation your dream mountain represents.

A mountain also makes a good pun. Are you making a mountain out of a molehill? Since the mountain won't come to you, is it time for you to go to the mountain? What in your life has assumed mountainous proportions?

What kind of a mountain is this? How are you interacting with it? By what geologic process was it formed? What and who lives on, around, or in this mountain? Does it have any caves? How do you feel about it in your dream or meditation? See also HILL, VALLEY.

COMMON MOUNTAIN SYMBOLS:

CLIMBING DOWN or GOING AWAY FROM A MOUNTAIN: Climbing down or moving away from a mountain in a dream or meditation may symbolize you are heading in the wrong direction. But this action can just as easily symbolize that you have passed an initiation phase and are descending into the valley to share your lessons with others before climbing your next mountain. The total content of your dream or meditation will give you the best clue.

CLIMBING UP or GOING TO-WARDS A MOUNTAIN: Climbing up a mountain, especially a sacred mountain of some kind, symbolizes your rejection of material desires in favor of spiritual aspirations and your dedication to the sacred in your life at the time.

Going up or toward a mountain also symbolizes your step-by-step progress above your ordinary life and existence. Pilgrimages to

sacred mountains are still common today.

TOPS: Mountain peaks and tops symbolize the state of complete consciousness. Mountain tops are the "Abode of the Gods." What type of mountain is it? What is at the top? How do you get there? What or who lives there?

IN THE DISTANCE: Seeing mountains in the distance often symbolizes that you are moving toward your next stage of growth and development, or that you are getting close to some form of understanding or enlightenment.

Are you moving away from, or toward, these distant mountain? How do you feel about it? How far away is it? What kind of effort will you have to make to get there? What does this remind you of?

VOLCANO: An erupting volcano almost always symbolizes an explosive eruption of your severely suppressed life forces and energies. This includes your emotions, deeply buried anger and frustrations, repressed sexual feelings and energies, or all of the above together.

But volcanos also represent tremendous power available for your use during change and rebirth. After an eruption comes new life. How you feel about the volcano in your dream or meditation will tell you which is closer to your own truth.

Volcanos make good dream puns. Are you about to blow your top? What are you on fire or smoldering for?

What will be destroyed if the volcano suddenly blows? What is it getting rid of? What pressures have caused it to blow? What will spew out of its head? Is your volcano erupting, or just simmering? Why? Is there a lot of fire and magma, or just smoke and ash? Why? It is giving the chance for new life, or devouring everything in its path? How old is it? See also FIRE, EXPLOSION, HEAT, SMOKE.

A DORMANT VOLCANO symbolizes your deep inner power and your potential to nurture many forms of life. What kind of life forms are living on and around your sleeping volcano? Is it tropical or covered with snow? Why?

MOVIE
Dreaming of a movie is generally pinpointing a common theme in your life, or highlighting some plot or scene from of it at the time of your dream.

Your dream movie can also be a message that you are spending too much time observing life and not nearly enough participating in it.

And a movie can be symbolic of some part of you which feels you are only acting a part, not really experiencing the situation that is the plot of your dream movie.

But dreaming of movies can be pointing out your natural talents and creativity, that you ought to be

in pictures. Or are you just telling yourself a story about how you think things are?

Is your movie a soap opera, a tear-jerker? Is it helping you work out some inner suppressed anger or violence?

If your dream movie is being shown on television, it often symbolizes how you are handling your day-to-day roles, that you are probably trying to get a better look at them within the privacy of your own home.

What kind of TV set is it? Is it color or black and white, split screen? How big is the screen? What movie is on? Which channel? Are you flipping through the channels? Why, or why not? How do you feel about television in general? What kinds of people watch a lot of TV? What is the purpose of a television set?

What kind of movie is your dream movie? Who are its stars? What are the sets and costumes like? What's the plot? Who would pay to see your dream movie? Why? Are there any special effects? How do you feel watching your movie? What does it remind you of that is going on in your life at the time? See also FAMOUS, PLANET/Star.

MUD
Dreaming of mud often symbolizes that you feel stuck, or that you are in danger of getting stuck if you don't watch where you are going.

Mud can also symbolize confusion, muddy thinking, getting

mired down in your own intellect or emotions.

And if you are muddy and there is mud all around you, it is often a symbol that you need to clean up your life or thinking, or some part of it represented by the dream.

Mud can also be a great pun. Is someone slinging mud? What is clear as mud to you?

How is mud made; what are its components? What does this remind you of? How do you feel about mud? Did you like to play with it as a child? How is your dream mud being used? How do you feel about it in your dram? Where is it or what is it on? See also COLOR of mud, STORM/Rain, WATER.

MUSIC

This is an extremely complex symbol, but in general was used by the ancients as a symbol of the intermediary between the material world and the spiritual one. Music represents the order and harmony of the Higher Planes of Existence where there is perfect blending with the Whole, harmony with Divine Nature as It externally manifests.

Music symbolizes the flow of life by the creation of proper harmonies. Music is sound created to influence and change everything it touches; it effortlessly creates or destroys moods and feelings.

Music also symbolizes healing and pleasure through the ability to listen and enjoy what you hear.

What type of music is in your dream or meditation? What instruments are used to make the music? From where is it originating? Is it vocal or instrumental? Does the music please you, or do you find it jarring and intrusive? Are there words to the music? Why, or why not?

What kind of person would like this music? What kind of a person would like to play it? Who would pay money to hear or own it?

What is the title of the song? Does it remind you of anything going on in your life at the time? See also ORCHESTRA.

HEARING MUSIC in your dream or meditation is quite often reminding you of the divine influences surrounding you every second of your life. You have just forgotten to stay quiet enough to listen. And hearing music or singing can also be direct information concerning any higher energies. Pay close attention to the style of music it is and especially any lyrics that go with it.

A MUSICIAN is an ancient symbol for the mind able to access and manipulate the higher emotions, thereby coming into harmony for the brief time of the song with the Divine Nature of the Absolute.

In some early cultures, however, a musician was one of the symbols for death (transformation), especially when a harp was involved.

SACRED MUSIC is symbolic of Nature in its many ever-changing aspects. It symbolizes the Relative with its underlying reality, the

Absolute. Sacred music is specifically created to aid the listener in
reaching ever higher states of consciousness, and is a good example
of the phrase "The Relative is the
way to the Absolute."

N

NAIL

A nail symbolizes holding or putting something together by using strength, determination, and by taking a deliberate action through the sheer force of your will. Nail also shares much of the symbolism of the knot; see KNOT.

Nails are ancient symbols of the Axis Mundi around which the stars or heavens rotate. They were also a symbol of the North Star to ancient Northern European cultures.

In Central Africa, nails were part of various shamanic rituals, most often utilized in some ceremony to remind a Spirit of its true task here on Earth.

Nails were used as a message to the spirit inhabiting the object into which the nail was hammered that it was not to pay attention or obey anyone asking it for anything, except the shaman or master who hammered the nail, of course.

In Central Europe, pounding a nail into a tree or carved figure was symbolic of the presence of someone, and a notice of a visit from an outsider. In Christian symbolism, of course, nails are symbolic of the crucifixion of the Christ.

And nails show up in various magical ceremonies and spells. For instance, it was once believed that you could harm someone by nailing their footprint to the ground.

Nails also make great puns. Who is hard as nails? Did you just get nailed? By what or whom? Or have you just hit the nail on the head? What are you trying to nail down? Are you substituting one kind of nail for another, i.e., hand or toe nail, for the building kind?

What do the nails look like, what shape are they? What are they made of? Are they old, or new? What are they nailed into or allowing to be connected?

Who put them there? Why? How well are they doing their job? See also any object associated with the nail.

NAKED

Dreams of being naked in public are some of the most common, especially in early adulthood and anytime you are have prolonged periods of stress. At this age, nakedness is telling you how vulnerable and exposed you feel, especially in relation to the subject of your dream or meditation.

But to anyone past their early or mid-twenties, to dream that you are naked or nude most often symbolizes that you are feeling open, very comfortable with who you are, and that you have nothing to hide or be ashamed of at the time.

Nakedness represents your natural, innocent, original state of being, before you were taught you should be ashamed or feel guilty about something.

As an archetype, nakedness symbolizes Truth, Purity, Virtue, and, conversely, Lust.

Nakedness is an ancient symbol of creation, resurrection, and stripping the ego-based personality of its material earthy desires. It is also symbolic of freedom from the restrictions of matter and of your own human limitations, opinions and beliefs, the "clothes" of your physical personality nature.

Being naked in a dream can also be a symbol that you are ready to take off your current uniform or role you play, symbolized by the clothes you were wearing before you saw yourself naked. But it can also be telling you that some part of you is now feeling very uncomfortable and exposed, totally vulnerable to outside influences and opinions. How you feel about being naked in your dream will tell you how your subconscious is using this symbol at the time.

Who or what is naked in your dream or meditation? Why? What does this remind you of? Does anyone notice or respond to the nakedness? What would happen if you were naked in the same situation while you are awake?

How do you feel about the difference in meaning between the concepts of naked and nude? Why? See also BODY, CLOTHES.

UNDRESSING IN A DREAM or meditation frequently symbolizes a desire to expose your true self, your true feelings, or to change your role in life (by changing clothes). What part of your body are you unclothing? Why? What does this remind you of? Is anyone paying attention to your disrobing?

What type of clothing are you taking off? Are you putting on others? Why are you undressing at all? How do you feel about it in your dream? How would the dream change if you did not undress? Why?

NATIVE AMERICAN

Dreaming of Native Americans often symbolizes your own love of the Earth and a strong desire to live in harmony with all that is natural on this planet, even if you are a Native American.

Native Americans are also symbolic of strength, creativity, a strong sense of honor, and connection to Spirit.

And dreaming of a Native American can represent one of your teachers or guides.

What do these Native Americans look like? What tribe do you think they are from, and how is that tribe different from all others?

How are the Native Americans dressed? What actions are they taking? How do you feel about Native Americans in general? What do you think they are like as individuals? How are they the same as, or different from, you? What does this remind you of? See also RACE, HUMAN.

NET

Nets most often symbolize catching, or trying to catch, something you really, really, really want. A net can also symbolize unconscious feelings of being trapped, caught in a net, since nets can be used to snare and entangle as well as hold safely and securely.

And a net can symbolize an easy safe way to carry many things at one time, gathering things together, and a means of holding many pieces in one place until you can take care of them later.

Nets as an ancient symbol are related to seeking God and Illumination, representing the seeker whose only desire is to capture Enlightenment. And they were often used as symbols of the interconnectedness of all things. For example, The Great Mother is often depicted as a goddess with a net, or even the goddess of nets, goddess of the sea and fishing harvest.

Stars were also often symbolized by a net, the "net of heaven."

Nets are made by interweaving strands of some material together, their design often determined by what they will catch or carry. For example, in the Himalayas, "demon nets" are made from sticks and thread and used to capture and destroy evil spirits. And today of course we have our dream catcher nets. Of what is your net woven? Why? What will it hold?

Nets can also be a message that you are ready to come to terms with something deep within your subconscious, that you are ready to "go fishing." For what?

In ancient India, a spider web is also the Net of Cosmic Order and the radiance of the Divine Spirit. Conversely, the spider web also symbolizes the illusions of the physical senses; see also INSECT/Spider.

Nets are also great puns. In whose net are you in about to become entangled? Are you about to net a profit? What is net of what?

What is this net made of? What is its purpose or function? Who made it? Who would normally use this kind of net? Why? What condition is it in? What is captured in it? See also FISH, or any object held in the net, like hair.

NUMBER

Since volumes have been written on the symbolism of numbers and how to interpret and use them, we will list here only some of their common possible interpretations. If you are a student of numerology, numbers have a deeper significance to you than the rest of us, and will generally encompass a much wider field of interpretations than the ones below.

Symbolically, numbers are not just a way of pointing out the quantity of something but also represent ideas and forces. All numbers are derived from the number 1, which symbolizes Unity. The farther a number is from one (Unity), the deeper and more entangled within Matter the number and what it symbolizes has become.

In the Western world, the first ten numbers generally symbolize Spirit and its various characteristics and training levels, but in the Eastern part of the world the first twelve numbers carrying this symbolism.

But in both systems, the remaining numbers are considered combinations of these original ten (or twelve) basic primary numbers.

In addition, the sequence of the numbers symbolizes the belief that each being has an inherent tendency to push itself beyond its original limits and to confront itself with its opposites for the purpose of learning.

For example, the number two gives birth to the number three, symbolizing among other things production through union. The number three then gives birth to the number four, giving the symbolism of the three some of its own strength and stability, and so on.

To the Pythagoreans in the 6th Century B.C.E., numbers were the key to the harmonic laws of the Cosmos and symbolized Divine Order. It was their belief that every form could be expressed in numbers.

And many ancient cultures considered the numbers 6, 7, 10, and 1000 to be perfect numbers.

The discovery that vibrating strings cut to different lengths produced different cords led directly to our current concept of harmony, and was a first step toward mathematical analysis; see also MUSIC.

Each number you remember in your dream, meditation, or experience has its own direct message, so begin by interpreting them first individually. Then add multiple numbers together until you end up with a single digit.

For example, if you dream that four and twenty blackbirds have been baked in a pie, you first check the symbolism of the numbers 4 and 20; then add 4 + 20 for a total of 24.

Now keep adding to get your single digit number: 2 + 4 = 6. You will be amazed at how often each individual number is literally just breaking down the components of the final overall meaning of your single digit number. There is often little if any conflict in meaning between the parts and the whole.

If you find yourself dreaming or experiencing a lot of numbers, you might want to consider researching into the field of sacred numbers and geometry. See also ALPHABET.

ZERO: Zero symbolizes Spirit, the Source of all Being, the Cosmic Womb from which everything is born. And zero symbolizes Perfection, Spiritual Completion, Infinity encompassing the field of all possibilities, Unity, and Wholeness. In ancient symbolism, zero represented the "I am that I am."

Zero shares the symbolism of the circle and the egg, that of having no beginning and no ending. Zero symbolizes protection, non-being, non-existence, the Eternal, death as the state in which life is transformed, the Cosmic Egg, the Monad, the originator and container of all life.

Zero is a form and can contain forms within it, but it can also exist without form, without three-dimensional being.

As a pun, your zero can also be telling you that some part of you is feeling like a big zero. Or what are you trying to zero-in on?

ZERO NEXT TO ANOTHER NUMBER symbolizes the potential to recycle the symbolism of that number, to begin its lesson over again, and your ability to now move to the next level; e.g., 10 can symbolize all of the potential within the number 1, but at one turn higher on your growth spiral, while at the same time letting you know that you now have the knowledge to go one step higher.

A STRING OF ZEROS in a number can symbolize a strong desire or longing for grand or great things, or can be telling you directly that great things are about to happen. Multiple zeros greatly enhance the value and meaning of the number they follow.

ONE: The number one often shows up to remind you of your true spiritual essence, and that this essence exists in each one of us, that there is really only One. It could also be a message to return to the One. One is the starting place of all things, so 1 also symbolizes hidden intelligence, intelligence with all of the power of Creation available at the time.

The number one symbolizes the point of Being, new beginnings, the courage to stand alone, the Mystic Center, Infinity, the Supreme Power, the Universal Force, God, the Life Force, Light, and almost any kind of creative energy. And one is indivisible; it cannot be divided, even by means of itself.

One is also symbolic of Primordial or Original Unity, the First Mover, the Creator, All That Is, the sum of all possibilities, Prime Essence, isolation, the principle which through its very nature gives rise to duality and diversity, the number two.

The number one is also an ancient symbol for Adonai, the "I Am," and the Yang (male) principle.

And the dot or point shares much of the symbolism of the number one; see GEOMETRIC SHAPE/Dot.

One also makes a good pun. Is this the one? Which one are you? What is there one of in your dream or meditation? Are you "one of those?"

TWO: The number two symbolizes re-flection, counter balance of opposites, the balance of the Yang (male) and Yin (female) qualities and characteristics, the passage of time, Nature reflecting its Creator, the Moon and the Sun, the bi-sexuality of all things, twins, your shadow self, the Yin quality, the Life Force, wisdom and self-consciousness, a relationship to something, stability, the link between the Immortal and the mortal, any pair of opposites, any duality, desire, and anything terrestrial or partaking of the Earth.

The number two may be telling you that you are beginning to see and pay attention at the subconscious level to the connection or interrelationships of the subject of your dream, meditation, or experience.

But the number two can symbolize that you need to "get straight" or more balanced about the subject of your dream, become aware of the language of opposites, maybe even return to the symbolism of the number 1, or the One.

Two's are temporarily without and require no center of being. Two also symbolizes cooperation between two energies, forces, or beings, and often represent a peacemaker. Two reminds you of the relationship of things. In the number 2, things begin to grow and move, to happen, but from a temporarily stable position.

The geometric symbol for 2 is a straight line. A line takes you from here to there, among other things; see GEOMETRIC SHAPE/Line.

THREE: Three symbolizes mysticism, spirituality, love triangles, great strength achieved through minimum structure, one who gives or brings joy, optimism, and the process of obtaining perfection while in Matter.

Three can represent the end or solution of a conflict between opposites. Three also symbolizes your creative powers, growth, moving forward by overcoming or learning to work with and within duality.

The number three is also one of the numbers for the Soul, and has almost always been considered to be a "heavenly" number. For instance, the Law of Three is common to most mystical systems.

The number three symbolizes spiritual synthesis, and was believed by the ancients to be the formula for the creation of the world. Three is the harmonic result of the action of the Unity of the 1 upon the Duality of the number 2.

Three is the number concerned with basic principles, how Unity grows within a dual medium, within the Third Dimension of reality.

Three carries the authority and knowledge of accumulated effect, since the ancients believed that once or twice could be coincidence, but the third time gave the event certainty, a clear message from the gods. Even today we still say that the third time is the charm, and that events happen in three's.

Three also symbolizes any threesome, trinity, or triad: body-mind-spirit, physical-mental-emotional; mother-father-child, beginning-middle-end, etc.

Three carries with it most of the symbolism of a triangle and a three-sided pyramid. Within this context, three symbolizes a gathering together of spiritual forces, the three parts of the Self or the Soul. The triangle was the ancient Egyptian hieroglyph for woman and for the Moon goddess Men-Nefer. See also GEOMETRIC SHAPE/Triangle.

FOUR: The number four symbolizes growth within a structure of perfect balance and stability. Four represents balance in a partnership, foundation and building a foundation, security, achievement made tangible or real, and the orderly arrangement of what was once separate, the construction of something, and dependability.

Four symbolizes the Four Earth Elements of Earth, Air, Fire, and Water, and the four seasons of Nature.

Four also symbolizes the human physical body, especially the human male. It also symbolizes intellect and balanced spirituality, rational organization, the cross (with all of its multidimensional symbolism; see GEOMETRIC SHAPE/Cross), the Earth herself and all her terrestrial space, and

the human situation or condition in general.

From four was created the first solid three-dimensional shape, giving four the symbolism of completion of a thing, totality, the rational and stable, measurement, relativity, and justice.

And the number four represents the geometric square, the ancient symbolic formula for Divinity.

Four is also a good pun. What are you for? Who or what is square? Do you need a more solid foundation? See also GEOMETRIC SHAPE/Square.

FIVE: The number five is symbolic of the Center, love, health, progress and the natural progression of something, knowledge, meditation, religion, and the midpoint of something.

Five is the symbol of Essence acting upon Matter, and for this reason is often associated with the human Soul.

Five is the ancient number for change, since it is always in a state of fluctuation. The ancient Law of Five is the Law of Change. So, of course, five is also often a message that rapid changes are on the way, a symbol of great activity and movement.

Five also symbolizes the human body (the four limbs of the body with the head that governs them), and the five physical senses.
In many ancient cultures, five symbolized the emergence of humanity and the quickening of Consciousness, since it was

believed that the Soul did not enter the fetus until the fifth month. At one time, the fetus could be terminated before this time without committing a sin. It was not until 1869 that Pope Pius X announced that abortion was a mortal sin.

Five is abundant new growth and Spring, the 5-pointed star or pentagram, the four cardinal directions and their center, the harmonious union of Yin and Yang, the Five Manifold Planes of Nature in their gradations of Spiritual Matter, and the human microcosm.

Five was sacred to Isis, Aphrodite, and their successor goddesses. In ancient Qabalism, five symbolized fear, just one of the possible interpretations for the fruit eaten by Eve and Adam in Eden. See also FOOD/Apple.

SIX: Six is the number of the accomplishment of a specific purpose, one who is of service or wishes to be of service, and the completion of a process. Six often shows up at the end of a period of great change or activity (symbolized by the number 5). Within this context, six prepares the way for the seven of perfection.

Six is the number of the Philosopher's Stone, the Great Yantra, the Shield of David, Solomon's Seal, the six-pointed star, and the hexagram.

The number six symbolizes mystical dualism, the union of Fire and Water, which when properly combined gives rise to the human Soul. In ancient China, six was associated with the influences of Heaven.

Six is equilibrium and its opposite, ambivalence.

And six also symbolizes the six directions of Space, trial and effort, guidance, perfect balance, the meeting and merging of the Upper and Lower Worlds, and nonmovement or the cessation of movement.

Since it was the midpoint between 2 and 10, six was considered by the Pythagoreans to be a perfect number (the Pythagoreans did not consider 1 to be a number).

Six also represents sexuality and most sexual matters since the hexagram symbolizes the meeting of male and female; see GEOMETRIC SHAPE/Hexagram.

The ancient Greeks used six to symbolize the hermaphrodite or androgyne, harmony, the harmonious union of polarities, love, health, beauty, chance, luck, creation, and intelligence.

Six and the five preceding numbers together represent the process of the curving inward of all spiritual qualities into Matter, with all of the inherent lessons. (Seven represents the evolution from Matter back to Spirit).

To the early Christians, six was an ambivalent number, sacred when it represented the six days of Creation, but evil when associated with the Apocalypse; 666 is the number of the Apocalyptic animal or Beast (see 666 below).

SEVEN: Seven symbolizes a new beginning after completion of a cycle, understanding, The Alpha and Omega, consummation, completion of your former state of growth or being, and perfect order (3 + 4; see Three and Four above).

Seven follows the number six, which itself symbolizes completion of a process.

And since six and the five preceding numbers together represent the process of the curving inward of all spiritual qualities into Matter, the number seven represents evolution from Matter back to Spirit.

And seven symbolizes exceptionally good luck, intellect, spirituality, mystical relationships, a totality, the Macrocosm, the Universe, virginity, and The Great Mother.

Seven also symbolizes the three-dimensional cross, thus sometimes giving it the symbolism of pain caused by a particular cycle of growth.

Seven is the reconciliation of Earth (the 4) with the Sky (the 3). Seven also symbolizes the seven directions of Space, the 7-pointed star, the union of the Ternary (3) and the Quaternary (4).

Seven is the number forming the basic series of musical notes, of the basic colors, the Seven Heavens, Seven Hells, and of the seven planets as known to the ancients.

Seven also symbolizes the seven major Chakras or energy centers of the physical body; see CHAKRA.

To the ancient Buddhists, seven is the number of ascent and of ascending to the highest center. And seven was sacred to Osiris, Apollo, Athene, and Ares.

The number seven represents the process of the evolution of our spiritual qualities back to their original spiritual state, but now carrying with us the experiences gained through the preceding six numbers.

Seven has almost always been viewed as a particularly healing number. The number seven is generally agreed to be the "most mystical of numbers."

To the Moslems, 7 is the first perfect number and always involves "what is holy." Seven also symbolizes hidden or secret intelligence and knowledge.

And as if this weren't enough, there are seven cosmic stages of development, seven Ages of Man, and seven days in our week.

The geometric symbol for the number seven is a square with a triangle above it; see GEOMETRIC SHAPE/Square, Triangle.

EIGHT: Eight symbolizes the reality of the physical world, perfect balance and rhythm, Cosmic Consciousness, and Infinity. Eight is a strong symbol of regeneration, renewal, resurrection after an initiation, prosperity, and good judgment.

Eight represents the eternal spiraling movement of the Universe and Life.

And the number eight represents the goal of the Initiate and all possibilities available within manifestation.

Eight has the digit value of the ancient Hebrew IHVH. It was the magic number of the ancient Egyptian Thoth, later becoming the number of the Greek Hermes.

And the ancient Hindus held that the formula 8×8 equaled the order of the Celestial World as it is established here on Earth.

Eight contains the symbolism of two squares or cubes forming an octagon, giving eight the symbolism of each of these components, and, in fact the geometric symbol for eight is the cube; see GEOMETRIC SHAPE/Cube.

The two serpents of the Caduceus form the number eight, symbolizing the proper balancing of opposing forces and the balance of spiritual power with natural earthly power.

In the European Middle Ages, eight was the symbol of the waters of baptism and a symbol that planetary influences had been successfully overcome.

Eight was also an ancient symbol for entrance into a new state or condition of the Soul, and the duality of the aspects of the Four Lower Planes of Existence.

NINE: Nine symbolizes expanded awareness while still within a physical body, the recognition that separation is an illusion and that the true Self is connected to or is within the One at all times.

Nine also symbolizes the end of the old, a period of gestation, an initiation, magic, self-awareness, self-reliance, the attainment of a previous goal, Fate, luck, and integration of the previous eight levels of learning with the potential to now center yourself within them.

So if you are dreaming of nine or it is frequently showing up in your life, you may be getting the clear message that now is the time to focus on awakening to yourself as an individual within the One, or that you are near the completion of a cycle through the recognition of your individuality within the One.

The number nine also symbolizes Truth and Wisdom, since when it is multiplied by means of itself, it continually reproduces itself.

The number nine is the number of the Angels and of the Cosmic Spheres. It also represents the completion of the Three Lower (physical) Planes of Existence.

Nine is an emblem of the Muses, themselves representative of human accomplishment in science and the arts.

Nine is the triplication of three, a triple trinity or triad, the number of awareness which has been enormously expanded.

Nine symbolizes a complete picture of the Three Worlds (Heaven, Hell, Earth), and each Plane of human existence within Matter (physical, mental, spiritual).

The number nine also symbolizes completion of an entire cycle, the end of the numerical sequence before returning again to the 1 of unity. It is one of the most powerful numbers representing social things, the result of things coming together.

Nine is composed of the all-powerful 3 × 3, and in ancient China, nine was in fact the symbol for Heaven itself.

Geometrically, the number nine is the equivalent of the dot within the circle (see GEOMETRIC SHAPE). Within this context, the number nine symbolizes the knowledge of the Self as a distinct individual within the physical world of Matter, while at the same time retaining the knowledge that it is part of a greater whole, and will ultimately return to it.

TEN: Ten is the number of perfection through completion. Ten represents the all-inclusive and tells you that all things are possible, From the number ten, all numbers return to the One.

And ten is the symbol for the Cosmos, the All, the return to Unity, the totality of the Universe, both physical and meta-physical.

An important number in virtually all cultures on our planet, ten represents the geometric line and the circle, which produce a cross only when the lower Soul nature acts in direct opposition to the higher Soul nature.

Ten also symbolizes the completion of journeys, the successful completion of the Initiate, and his or her mystic return to Unity.

And since it represents the circle enclosing itself, ten often announces the recommencement of a series of events or lessons.

Ten is also a symbol of spiritual achievement, the number of Absolute Perfection, new beginnings but with the experience gained from completion of the previous nine levels of learning.

Ten is the completion of all previous nine numbers and what each symbolizes, and for this reason is often a symbol of marriage; see MARRIAGE.

To the ancient Qabalists, ten had the numerical value of Yod, the Eternal Word, the first letter of the Divine Name.

ELEVEN: The number eleven is symbolic of transition and the power to create the balance of Self.

In numerology, eleven is a Master Number 2. And in the Western world, eleven is often viewed as a good luck number.

The phrase "the eleventh hour" was used to represent the eleventh stage of the natural evolution of qualities manifested within material forms, qualities necessary before reaching the final stage, the twelfth.

But in many ancient systems, eleven symbolized sin or transgression, since the number ten was the number of the Law and by adding the number 1 to it, an excess had been created. So the number 11 often represented an excess of pride.

Sometimes called "the devil's dozen," eleven is a number in excess of the Perfection represented by the number ten, and was often used to symbolize a transgression of the Law and one in great spiritual peril.

So the number eleven has frequently symbolized conflicts and excesses carried to dangerous extremes. It is probably for this reason the number eleven is often associated with martyrs.

TWELVE: Twelve as a sacred number has been traced back as far as Babylonia and has almost always represented Divine Spirit in its male or Yang aspects (13 represents the Yin aspects).

The number twelve is considered by most systems to be a power unit, symbolizing Cosmic Order, salvation, and good fortune in earthly endeavors.

For instance, there are twelve gods in the ancient Greek pantheon, twelve Christian disciples, twelve months in the solar year, twelve planets, twelve signs of the zodiac.

The number twelve has always been linked to Time and Space and the wheel or circle, especially the Wheel of Life. And to the ancients, twelve was the number of good fortune.

This number can also symbolize a completed cycle of twelve, a full period of evolution completed, the Twelfth Hour or Stage of spiritual evolution.

THIRTEEN: The number 13 is symbolic of both birth and death, and represents renewal, beginning again — but beginning refreshed and renewed in strength and resolve.

Thirteen also symbolizes a spiritual gathering or council of some kind.

Thirteen is a lunar number, representing the 13 months of the lunar calendar. It was often an emblem of the feminine (Yin) aspects of the Soul and its reflection of God or All That Is, while it is the solar number 12 which represents the masculine (Yang) aspects.

Thirteen was a number widely used in ancient Aztec divination and in the Aztec calendar.

But, of course, the number 13 also represents bad luck, and could be a warning of some kind if it keeps showing up in your life. This number was believed to be unfavorable or unlucky by many ancient cultures, mostly because it followed the number of good fortune, the number 12.

During the Middle Ages in Europe, the number thirteen was symbolic of a witch's coven of 12, the attendance of the devil making it 13.

In spite of this, in many early Christian systems, thirteen was considered a holy number since it could not be divided, thereby symbolizing Infinity, completeness, and the complete and full union of humanity with God. Used within this context, the number 13 represented that which was responsible for the creation of the Christ.

FOURTEEN: The number 14 symbolizes justice, temperance, organization, goodness, mercy, and fusion with a thing. And 14 doubles the symbolism and power of the sacred number 7.

FIFTEEN: The number fifteen often symbolizes completing a condition or period of time. It is a multiple of 3 (a perfect number) and of 5, the number of change and the manifested Planes of Existence.

Conversely, in some systems, fifteen is the number of eroticism, and was therefore often linked with lust and the devil and demons.

TWENTY: The number twenty is symbolic of the Completed Human Being, the Whole Man and Whole Woman. Twenty also symbolizes a reckoning or totaling of the score.

TWENTY-ONE: Since it is the number 3 increased 7-fold, twenty-one is the number of Divine Wisdom.

TWENTY-TWO: The number twenty-two symbolizes the spiritual expression of balance and the integration of the Self. In numerology, it is a Master Number 4.

TWENTY-FOUR: The number twenty-four symbolizes the attainment of perfect balance within the physical world. It incorporates the symbolism of the 2 and 4, representing the accomplishment of

stability while still within the world of duality.

TWENTY-SIX: The number twenty-six was believed by the ancients to contain the fullest possible expression of Divinity while still within the material world.

For example, the body of the ancient Egyptian god Osiris was cut into 26 parts and scattered over the Earth, symbolizing the range of the power of Osiris within the physical world.

The Hall of Truth, an ascending passage inside the Great Pyramid, has a slope of 26 degrees, which some experts interpret as representing human evolution.

And the number 26 is symbolic of *Yod-Heh-Vau-Heh*, the sacred trapezoid in ancient Qabalism, and represents the four stages or elements of Creation and the four parts of Jehovah's name.

Twenty-six therefore often represents the ability and the extent to which you can manifest in the material world, and the limits under which you can physically operate at the time of the dream or experience.

Twenty-six is an aspect of the number eight and the Cube; see GEOMETRIC SHAPE/Cube and Eight above.

And today, there are still 26 letters in the English alphabet and 26 weeks between solstices and equinoxes.

THIRTY-THREE: The number 33 always symbolizes a Master Teacher.

THIRTY-SIX: The number 36 is a symbol of the cosmic relationships among Heaven, Earth, and humanity. It is a number of the Totality which has been finally achieved and earned by a human being.

FORTY: The number 40 has always had deep mystical significance for human beings. It is symbolic of a period of probation and testing, of fasting and seclusion, of initiation and sacrifice.

As an increase of the number four, forty represents wholeness and totality; see Zero above.

And while 40 is a number of change and death, it is also the number of reconciliation and a return to Divine Law.

Some authorities believe that the importance of the number 40 may have originated in Babylon, a culture responsible for one of the first written records of a great flood or deluge. Since the Pleidaes annually disappeared for a period of 40 days and 40 nights, bringing heavy storms, rains, floods, and their resulting dangers, 40 was associated with floods and destruction by water very early in human history.

In Babylonia, a bundle of 40 reeds was burned for the "40 days of evil power," and the return of the Pleiades was a time of great celebration for these ancient societies.

It takes 40 days to renew the human body and spirit, and for change to occur in order to make the transition to a higher perception.

The number 40 also represents the length of time it takes to recharge and renew the physical body after excesses of almost any kind. And, in fact, the word *quarantine* comes from the ancient Roman practice of isolating incoming ships for 40 days.

So dreaming or experiencing frequent 40's in any form can symbolize your strong need for rest and relaxation at virtually all levels of your existence, that you need time to integrate and digest your recently acquired experiences and information.

Forty is also the number of expectation and preparation. And 40 is symbolic of completion of a process on the Four Lower Planes of Existence.

FIFTY: Fifty symbolizes a spiritual quest aimed at conquering the myths of your mind.

The number 50 frequently shows up in ancient Sumerian, Assyrian, Egyptian, and Greek mythologies in connection with heroes and their quests, often representing the successful completion of the quest, the Great Year.

For example, Jason had 50 Argonauts, Anut (one of the aspects of Osiris) had 50 attending gods who sat on 50 golden thrones.

To the ancient Hebrews, 50 was symbolic of feasting and joy; every 50 years Hebrew slaves were freed by their captors, giving 50 its symbolism of starting fresh.

Even today there are 50 lunar months (4 years) between Olympic Games.

SIXTY: To the ancient Egyptians, 60 symbolized longevity, while to the ancient Chinese, it was just a life cycle number.

In some systems of thought even today, it is believed that a cycle becomes complete in all of its possible combinations in the 60th year.

SEVENTY: Seventy is the sacred seven multiplied ten-fold; see Seven, Ten, and Zero above.

The ancient Hebrews considered 70 to be the allotted human life span. And the 12 zodiacal divisions of the 7 planets were organized in groups of 10.

ONE HUNDRED: The number 100 symbolizes the essence of multiplicity completed within a greater totality. One Hundred symbolizes heavenly bliss and Paradise.

666: This number is and always has been an ambivalent number, in spite of all of its bad press in the Western world. While it is the "number of the Beast," it was also assigned to the Angel Hakathriel, the Angel of the Diadem, a symbol of supremacy over the physical human nature.

To the early Christians, of course, it was the mark of the Antichrist, and to the ancient Qabalists, it was the number of Sorath, the solar demon who opposed the Archangel Michael.

It has also been linked by scholars to Greek numerical values inscribed on the coin of the Roman Emperor Domitian, and some biblical scholars credit him today with being the Hebrew "beast."

This number is a solar number and one of the basic numbers in geometry.

888: In the ancient Hebrew alphabet, 888 is the sacred number of the Christ, the Messiah, the number opposed to the 666 of the Antichrist or Beast.

1001: This number is common in Eastern and Middle Eastern tales, and symbolizes the number of days it normally takes an Initiate to complete his or her spiritual training.

O

OPERATION

Operations often symbolize repair and healing on the emotional, mental, physical, or spiritual levels, or all and any combination of these.

A dream operation can also be telling you that some part of you is ready to be cut away, or feels like it is being cut away and is trying to get your attention before it is too late.

And an operation could also be a wonderful pun. Are you a smooth operator? Are you cutting yourself out, or in? Where and how do you operate best?

Where is the operation being performed? Who is performing it? Who is being operated on? Why is it necessary? How will things change after the operation?

What part of the body is being cut? Is there any fear or pain? Is there blood, and if so, which part of the body is bleeding? What does the operating room look like? On whose advise is the operation being performed? What does this remind you of?

How will you or the object operated on be changed after the operation? Why? See also BLOOD if any is present, BODY part affected, BUILDING where operation takes place, EMOTION if present, PAIN, if you feel pain, WEAPON/Knife, and any other instrument used in the operation.

ORGY

While a dream orgy often symbolizes the parts of you that are in the process of merging and integrating at the time of your dream, an orgy is almost always a strong message that this integration is being unnecessarily forced by wasting energy, and often through confused ideas about the things being merged, excesses of various kinds, a lack of control your emotions, or just a plain old lack of common sense.

Dreaming of an orgy can also be a signal that your sexual (or other) energy is going in too many directions at one time, or would like to. The busier you keep your emotions, including sexual ones, the less you have to deal with on the conscious level.

Orgies can also, of course, be telling you about unconscious excessive appetites and insatiability. What can't you get enough of (and not necessarily sex)?

But an orgy can be a clear, strong message to loosen up a little, to accept and enjoy the reality that you are in a physical body. Are you in danger of making too fine a line between the physical and the spiritual?

How do you feel in your dream or meditation about the orgy? How did you feel about participating in the orgy when you woke up? Why?

What is your personal definition of an orgy? What kind of person likes this kind of activity? How are you different from, or the same as, this kind of person? What does this tell you about yourself at the time? What part of you might this kind of person represent?

Who or what is participating in the orgy? How many members of each sex? Where is it taking place? How are the participants dressed?

What part(s) of you do your dream participants symbolize? See also ALCOHOL, PARTY, SEX.

P

PAIN

Pain most often symbolizes something from your past you are refusing to let go, or some part of you that you are causing pain through fear or plain old lack of attention.

Pain also represents a very strong suppression of feeling and emotion, a message that something is trying to get your attention by giving you pain.

To feel pain or to be hurt in your dream or meditation can also represent your normal everyday emotional disappointments and deep unconscious painful feelings.

Feeling pain can, of course, be an early health warning connected directly to what is hurting and what it symbolizes to you. Keep in mind that you get health information in plenty of time to correct the problem before it manifests on the physical body, so don't panic.

Dream pain also symbolizes a possible imbalance between your natural physical, emotional, intellectual, psychological, and spiritual natures, or any combination of these. And dream pain can be showing you that you sometimes tend to play the martyr. Do you feel this pain often? If so, when does it pop up? And what does this remind you of?

As an archetype, pain symbolizes the suffering of the Soul of bondage within Matter, and unnecessary limiting of spiritual energy, usually through the fear of acknowledging who you really are.

Pain also represents the Lower Self's illusion that it is in bondage to the physical world, and that it is needlessly living a life without the knowledge of the Higher Self. When you learn to look through your spiritual eyes as well as your human ones, pain becomes a little easier to handle.

Pain also symbolizes a transition from one stage or level to another, and especially one of passing from one stage of illusion to another. Is there more or less pain than before? Why? What does this tell you about where you are headed?

To find the true source of your pain, pretend you are the pain itself, and then, speaking as the pain, tell yourself why you are there and what your real purpose is. What does your pain want to tell you? What does it remind you of that is going on in your life at the time?

Pain can also be a good pun. Where is the location of your pain, in your neck, or your posterior? What gives you a tummy ache?

Who or what is hurt and feels pain? What causes the pain? What kind of a pain is it: dull or sharp? What will alleviate it?

How would your dream or life be changed if the pain were suddenly gone? What does it remind you of going on in your life? What kind of person normally suffers from this kind of pain? Why? What would alleviate it? Why is that action not be taken?

See also BLOOD if there is blood in your dream, BODY part feeling the pain, VICTIM, and any object causing the pain.

EMOTIONAL PAIN in a dream or meditation frequently symbolizes some truth that is being shown to you that you are unwilling or unable to accept in your waking life, that your once comforting illusions are being hurt by reality.

This type of pain can also be quite clearly showing you that your present illusions are what is actually causing you pain. Often, when you feel emotional pain it is a clear message that your expectations have been unrealistic. Anytime you feel deep emotional pain, look at your original expectations. Were they reasonable?

Where is the pain located? What does it remind you of? What would have to happen to take the pain away?

PHYSICAL PAIN in your dream or meditation usually symbolizes a self-imposed limitation of some kind. It clearly marks the place where this limitation is occurring.

What part of the body is hurt? How did it happen? What will make it feel better? See BODY part experiencing the pain.

PSYCHOLOGICAL PAIN in your dream or meditation almost always symbolizes ideas or beliefs which now don't fit the person you are becoming or want to become.

Like emotional pain, psychological pain is almost always caused by your stubbornly holding on to favorite illusions and psychological constructions or core beliefs which no longer fit who you are. You have just plain outgrown them, and you're trying to force yourself into the shoes of a ten year old when you are now an adult.

What is causing the psychological pain? How do you know the pain is psychological, rather than physical? What does this remind you of? What will it take to alleviate the pain?

PARTY
Parties, celebrations, and feasts are ancient symbols for the realization of Truth, Wisdom, and Love in a state of bliss or joy on the Higher Planes of Existence, or, in simpler words, that you finally mastered

the subject of your dream or meditation, you have reached the truth of the situation, and it's party time.

A celebration can also simply be telling you that you need to lighten up, have some fun, become freer in your emotions and behavior, and party once in awhile.

As an archetype, parties and celebrations are a symbol of the process of transmutation of the lower Soul qualities to a higher level of being.

Party is also a good pun. Are you a party of one? What are you party to? Or do you just need to party down?

What type of party is it? What event is being celebrated? What kinds of people would normally attend this party? Why? What kinds of food and beverages are being offered? Where is it being held? How do you feel in your dream or meditation? What are you doing? See also ALCOHOL, CEREMONY, FOOD, PEOPLE, and any objects involved in the party.

PEOPLE

Dream people almost always symbolize various facets of your own personality, your own beliefs, wishes, talents, abilities, and fears.

The people in your dream or meditation, however, can also represent your guides and teachers who have chosen the persona or image in your dream or meditation for specific symbolic reasons.

People can, of course, also represent people you know in your waking life and tell you a great deal about how you subconsciously see and interact with them.

But as we said, while on one level of your dream every dream object, including people, represents a part of you (even when you recognize the people in your dream), they will most often simply be a symbol for various personality characteristics of those people, and do not represent the actual people themselves. So always go for this interpretation first if you're serious about learning who you really are inside. What part of you is this person?

To understand how your subconscious is using this persona as a symbol, ask yourself what the dream person is like *as a person*, and be as honest in your description as you can. What qualities or characteristics do they have that makes them easy to recognize by anyone who doesn't know them?

Only an honest detailed description of the people in your dream or meditation can show you how your subconscious is using these people as symbols. This is not about judging or labeling; it's about getting to your unique use of symbols.

It is common to dream of people you don't know, even though they may feel familiar in the dream or meditation. Often they will show up in settings you have dreamed before, places you visit off and on in your dreams. And many authorities now believe that this type of dream experience represents real parallel existences, places you actually have visited or visit from time to time. What do these familiar people and their environment remind you of? How do you feel about them? Would you like to be with them when you are awake? Why, or why not?

How are these people dressed? To which race or culture do they belong? Why? How do you relate to them in your dream or meditation?

How are they different from, or the same as, people you generally associate with? What actions are they carrying out? Is this different from what you would expect from this kind of person? Why, or why not? What would they like to tell you if you were not the one writing their script? See also CROWD, RACE HUMAN, and STRANGER.

PHOTOGRAPH

Photographs generally symbolize how you saw things at the period of time in which the photograph was taken. Photographs freeze time, space, relationships, actions, and almost always conjure up specific memories and feelings when we see them.

Photographs can also be a reflection of the person or objects in the photo, a message to you to review the subject of the photograph.

And a photograph represents a self-examination of the person you were at the time, or a wish or need to freeze the action or preserve a certain time in your life. What does this photograph make you think of?

A photograph from your childhood, for example, may be a

message that you need to look at past memories from that same time period. You may not have learned the lessons associated with the experience, or you may be feeling the way now that you felt then, or somehow wish you were. How is your life different now from the way it was then?

Is the photograph in color or black and white? Why? How would its image change if it were one or the other? Why?

What does the photograph remind you of? What kind of person likes to take photographs? What kind of person values photographs? Do you normally save photographs yourself? Why, or why not? See also MIRROR, and any objects in your photograph.

PILOT

Pilots often symbolize a teacher or special guide of some kind, and frequently your Higher Self, or some other higher guiding part of you.

Pilots have the ultimate responsibility for all other objects on the vehicle they are piloting. What is the cargo?

This is another good pun. Are you about to begin a pilot project? Which Plane are you trying to pilot or master? Does your pilot have a manifest? What's your flight plan?

Who is the pilot? Male of female? Why? What does he or she look like? How are they dressed? How competent are they? How much training did it take to receive the license? Or do they have one?

What kind of vehicle is being piloted? What direction is it going? Where did it start from and what is its destination? Who would normally trust their life or cargo to this pilot? Why? See also LICENSE, and any object involved, like Water.

AN AIRPLANE PILOT often tells you that you are on your spiritual journey, and currently in control and "on your flight path". The pilot of a plane can also be showing you that you are ready to fly with the subject of your dream or meditation. See also VEHICLE/Airplane.

A SHIP'S PILOT often represents your emotional journey, life journey, or spiritual journey, or all three or any combination of the three; see also VEHICLE/Boat and WATER.

PLANT

Plants most often symbolize your growth — physical, emotional, psychological, and spiritual.

Plants are ancient symbols of simplicity, especially your simple uncomplicated instincts and feelings which just naturally reach up toward the light.

And plants are often used to represent a stage of spiritual growth that is slightly pre-human. Plants and any type of vegetation can also symbolize unconscious life, inactivity, and immobility. Are you in danger of vegetating?

What type of plant is it? Where does it normally grow? What type of an environment does it grow in best? How is this plant different from, or the same as, the same plant in waking life?

What color is the plant? What is its overall condition? Where is it located? Who would grow such a plant? For what purpose? Is it difficult, or easy, to cultivate? How do you feel about it in your dream? See also COLOR of plant, FLOWER, TREE/Leaves.

COMMON PLANT SYMBOLS:

EVERGREEN PLANT: All plants which can stay green year-round are symbols of hardiness, vitality, immortality and eternal life, youth, constancy, and enduring friendships. How healthy is your evergreen, and how green is it? See also COLOR/Green.

GREEN PLANT: Green plants most often symbolize healthy vibrant growth, new or continuing life, abundance, and being in tune with Nature; see COLOR/Green.

MISTLETOE: Mistletoe is an ancient symbol for the life essence, the divine substance, and thus immortality.

Mistletoe was believed by many ancient cultures to be all-healing. Interestingly, mistletoe is now being tested as a potential cure for some forms of leukemia.

Since it is neither a tree nor a shrub, it is also an old symbol for "that which is neither one nor the other," and therefore a symbol of freedom from limitations and labels.

Mistletoe was the Golden Bough of the Celtic Druids (see TREE/ Golden Bough), and represented the sacred female principle growing with and supported by the sacred male principle, the oak tree; see TREE/Oak.

And mistletoe symbolizes new life and rebirth, and was often used in ceremonies at the Winter Solstice. See also SEASONS/Winter Solstice.

WEED: A weed often symbolizes a bad habit, something a part of you feels should be weeded out of your life, beliefs, behavior, and thoughts.

But weeds also symbolize strength, tenacity, and great determination. Weeds continue to flourish even under the harshest of conditions, and wild flowers are "weeds." And many so-called weeds have great medicinal value.

What is growing like a weed in your life at the time? Where are these weeds growing? What type of an environment have they chosen? What kind are they? How healthy are they? How do you feel about weeds in general? How do you feel about the weeds in your dream?

PLANET

Planets often symbolize an idea or message of great importance and magnitude, literally something of "cosmic" significance.

A planet can also symbolize a particular teacher and his or her teaching. The type of planet will tell you they kind of teaching; see individual planets below.

To the ancients, the planets were strong symbols of the continual progression of human life through areas of light and dark, through periods of introspection and re-emergence in a same-but-new form, and the evolution of human life by experiencing all of its characteristics and qualities.

Planets appeared to follow a path of their own choosing, while the stars remained fixed in the heavens. Many ancient cultures even assigned specific Angels or beings to govern each of the planets.

What kind of life forms does this particular planet support? What type of atmosphere does it have? How did you get there? How do you like being there? What actions are you carrying out? Is anyone with you? Does any of this remind you of anything going on in your life right now?

COMMON PLANETARY AND CELESTIAL BODY SYMBOLS:

COMET: Comets and meteors most often symbolize that something of great, life-changing importance is taking place, or is about to. Comets were once believed to be precursors of both good and bad omens.

Comets are ancient symbols of elemental and highly disruptive forces, primarily on the Mental Plane of Existence, and therefore always good at producing feelings of unrest and anxiety.

To the ancient Alchemists, a meteor or comet was the Celestial Flower, and a flower was for them symbolic of the "work of the Sun". The deeper symbolism of the comet was then deciphered by the flower's color; see also FLOWER.

EARTH: The Earth symbolizes growth, grounding, learning and studying the lessons inherent within duality, compassion, and learning to live within physical time. Earth symbolizes Matter which when acted upon by Spirit is able to take form.

In ancient terms, the planet Earth was often a symbol for the lower Soul nature and the lower-mental, astral and physical Planes of Existence, the stage upon which the human ego acted out its dramas in order to learn.

In an Earth Mother context, the Earth represents the productive spiritual nature as the Divine expression on the astral and physical Planes of Existence, a place to guide the separated Self in order to discover its true nature.

INNER PLANETS: To the ancients, the inner planets of our solar system represented the new gods, while the outer planets represented the old and Ancient Ones. What does this remind you of going on in your life?

JUPITER: The planet Jupiter symbolizes wealth, expansion and expansiveness, an abundance of spiritual knowledge and expres-

sion, extraordinary good luck, and benevolence.

Jupiter also symbolizes the Creator, the Soul, the Law, limited space, the power of organization, decision, expansion, intellectual will, the Air, courage, and in many cultures the Eastern part of the world.

And Jupiter often symbolizes the direction East. Jupiter is usually linked to good judgment, direction, constructive order, and subjective good or right action.

The offspring of Jupiter was believed by the ancients to be Mars. Does this remind you of anything?

And to the ancient Chinese, Jupiter was the East, the Earth element Wood, and the color blue.

MARS: Mars symbolizes action, adventure, assertiveness, sexual energy, aggressiveness, war, hostility, passion, strength, masculinity, and warrior energy. Mars also represents the South and the Yang (masculine) qualities and characteristics; see MALE.

To the ancient Chinese, Mars was the South, associated with the Earth element Fire, and the color red.

Mars was believed to be the offspring of Jupiter and associated with the ancient Greek god Ares.

MERCURY: Mercury symbolizes the mind, intuition, telepathy, swift thought communication (especially communication from the gods), intuition, quick movement, illumination, and rapid changeability.

Mercury has almost always been called the Messenger of the Gods. And Mercury also often represented the Center.

To the ancient Chinese, Mercury was the North, the Earth element Water, and the color black.

Mercury was linked to Thoth by the ancient Egyptians and to Hermes by the Greeks. But the planet Mercury is used both as a masculine and androgynous symbol.

MOON: The moon is an exceptionally complex symbol but, in general, symbolizes any one or more of the following: your natural intuition and psychic awareness, creativity, the unconscious mind, love, peace, ice, death, emotions, responsiveness, magic, mysticism, and moisture and the Yin (feminine) receptive qualities, whether you are female or male.

Dreaming of the moon can also represent your spiritual ideals and spiritual progression, symbolized by the cycle or phase you are in at the time by the phase of the moon you see. In which phase was this moon? And what does that tell you about where you are at the time of your dream or meditation?

The moon also represents Time, all cycles, the powers of conception and regeneration, the Vital Spirit which holds body and Soul together, and involuntary and instinctual nature and behavior.

The moon has always been an emblem of The Great Mother, and of all Queens of Heaven.

The moon is able to give light only by reflecting the light of the sun, reflecting light from its source back onto the Earth. Symbolically, what does that say to you?

The moon is an object incapable of generating its own light by its own efforts, through no fault of its own. It can only shine by being willing to reflect the light of another source (see Sun below).

And the moon is constantly cycling through new faces, unable to hold or maintain its total identity for any length of time.

One of the oldest surviving names for moon translates to "Beloved of the Sun." It is also often called the "Eye of the Night."

The moon has represented the Goddess, especially the Crescent Moon (Hathor, Ishtar, Isis, Anaitis, Artemis, Diana, etc.) since patriarchal societies replaced the matriarchy, and for this reason even today is still strongly associated with fertility, receptivity, and sensual attunement with your body's chemistry.

There are, however, still several cultural exceptions to use of the moon as a symbol of the feminine. Some African and North American Indian, Japanese, Maori, Oceanic, and Teutonic cultures view the moon as a male fertility symbol, not a female one.

But all moon deities, female or male, are controllers of Destiny and Time, the weavers of Fate.

The moon also represents cycles and rhythms, the act of becoming naturally within a thing's own time or cycle.

The birth, death, and resurrection phases of the moon symbolize immortality and eternity. But it can also symbolize the dark side of Nature, the unseen aspects of something.

And the moon represents control of the seasons and tides, and thus the natural length and rhythm of life.

The moon also represents emotional confusion, even lunacy. And the moon, of course, represents romance and lovers. Are you telling yourself that you are moonstruck?

To the early Christians, the moon was the home of the Archangel Gabriel, while Michael's home was the sun.

A moon also makes a great pun. Have you just been mooned? Are you mooning about something instead of taking action?

Where is your moon? In which phase is it? What does this tell you? How much light is it giving? How do you feel about the moon in general?

A CRESCENT MOON symbolizes Light, growth, and renewal and regeneration.

To the ancient Egyptians, the crescent moon was a symbol of Isis, the Queen of Heaven, the "Maker of Eternity and the Creator of Everlastingness," "She Who Gives Birth to the Sun."

A crescent moon also symbolizes change within the world of form, the newly born, the Ship of Light which carries the Soul through the darkness into the light of a new dawn, the primordial waters, and magical powers with the force and energy necessary to transform other shapes.

The crescent moon is associated with intuition, ESP, dreams, and clairvoyant and other psychic abilities.

THE DARK PHASE OF THE MOON is an ancient symbol for death, and it was once believed that the dead actually stayed on the moon until their soul was reborn.

Within this belief system, only that which was beyond or above the moon had the ability to transcend the cyclic process of becoming form again, to break the karmic cycle.

The dark phase of the moon was also viewed as a particularly magical time, but usually pertaining only to a dark or negative magic. And the power of white or positive magic was believed to be greatly weakened during the dark of the moon.

A FULL MOON most often represents a harvest of some kind or that it is time to harvest, a completion, perfection, strength, and a fullness of spiritual power.

Full moons can also represent romance, dreams, and even very, very bizarre behavior. And the full moon is a perfect time to dump old outdated emotions and behavior.

A HALF MOON, depending upon whether the half moon is in the waning phase or the waxing, can symbolize either death and the dying of any form, passing away, and the waning power or energy, or its opposite, new growth, building, and renewing; see Waning Moon and Waxing Moon below.

A WANING MOON was believed by the ancients to be sinister, sometimes even demonic. This is the "dark of the moon" phase, and even today some of us won't plant anything in the dark of the moon. What does this remind you of?

A WAXING MOON, in general, represents new growth, new life, new or renewed love, and a time for making new plans and deciding what you want within the next cycle.

MORE THAN ONE PLANET SEEN TOGETHER symbolizes the Order of the Universe, and a very particular order, depending on which planets show up together. Which planets did you put together in your dream or meditation, and what does this remind you of? What do they symbolize individually and as a whole?

NEPTUNE: Neptune is an ancient symbol for all forms of mysticism, psychic awareness, the Unconscious, the Primordial Ocean from which all life arose, and the Source of All Things.

THE OUTER PLANETS were generally believed to be older dei-

ties or powers than the inner ones. These were the Ancient Ones. Which planets are your outer planets? What do they remind you of?

PLUTO: Pluto symbolizes deep hidden knowledge, transformation, and spiritual growth. During the European Middle Ages, Pluto was also often associated with the darker side of human nature.

SATURN: Saturn symbolizes deep and intense learning phases, self-discipline, refinement of a process of a particular state of being, a slowing down of physical time, and taking personal responsibility — with a large capital R.

Saturn is the principle of analytical thought, one of the things that sets us apart from other Earth life forms. It has almost always symbolized intense concentration and the rational mind.

Saturn often represents the North, and is linked with endurance, a reserved nature, peace, self-possession, subjective evil (believed in the European Middle Ages to be the abode of Satan), and Time.

To the ancients, Saturn represented the dark spirit within Matter lying captive and in wait for the unwary, and was often associated with dragons, vipers, foxes, cats, mice, and many night birds.

But to the ancient Chinese, Saturn was the Center, the element Earth, and the color yellow. And Saturn was the Ruler of the Golden Age and the Seventh Heaven, death and rebirth, the Destroyer, and no less than God of the Earth, Reason, and Intellect.

In ancient Alchemy, Saturn is lead which is able to attain a luminous state through its transformation into gold.

And in early Gnosticism, Saturn was both the Father and Son, young and old.

THE PLANETS SEEN AS A WHOLE symbolize the harmonious and natural interaction of all of the essential forces of the Universe.

A STAR most often symbolizes the direction you are to follow, your guidance, Light, clarity, and that you possess enormous self-generating energy at the time you experience the star.

Stars also symbolize higher, even excessively high, ideals. Are you reaching for the stars? And is that a reasonable reach at this time?

Star also often represents your mystical achievements and may be a message to go ahead, follow you star, now's the time, trust yourself and follow your star.

Stars can also symbolize an award or a pat on the back, your gold star.

In ancient times, stars were symbols of the spiritual light which pierces the darkness, and of spiritual constancy. Stars were often seen as dead heroines or heroes who had been transported to and set in the sky by the gods as stars

to watch over us. And the ancient Hebrews believed that every star was protected and governed by its own Angel.

Stars also announced the presence of a divinity or great teacher and represented the highest attainments, Angelic messengers, the Eternal, and Hope.

Stars have always been associated with the Queen of Heaven, who is often crowned with stars or surrounded by them. For example, the star was an emblem of Ishtar and Astarte in Babylon, of Aphrodite in Greece, and Venus in Rome, all goddesses of the morning and evening star. And stars were emblems of all sky deities who succeeded or replaced these goddesses.

In ancient Alchemy, stars symbolized the union of all opposites (Air, Earth, Fire, Water), often depicted as the six-pointed star.

A FALLING STAR frequently symbolizes a warning, and is often a warning that you are in danger of giving up hope, usually about the subject of your dream or meditation. See also Comet above. Why is the star falling? What will be the result? How do you feel about it at the time?

A FIVE-POINTED STAR is also known as the Shield of David or the pentacle and pentagram, and symbolizes the human microcosm; see GEOMETRIC SHAPE/Pentacle.

The five points of the five-pointed stare are generally labeled Spirit, Air, Fire, Water, and Earth. Like the circle, the five-pointed star has a long history of possessing the power to bind the Earth Elementals and all evil or destructive powers.

POINTING DOWNWARD, the five-pointed star symbolizes perversions and evil, humankind in reverse position and condition of its true spiritual nature, most likely why it is often associated with black magic ceremonies. See also NUMBER/5.

POINTING UPWARD, the five-pointed star symbolizes aspirations, Light, education, and all things spiritual.

A SIX-POINTED STAR is often called the Seal of Solomon. It is a double triangle symbolizing "as Above, so Below," the meeting and union of opposites, perfect balance between two complementary forces, the androgynous nature of the Divine, and humankind looking into its own nature.

The six-pointed star is also a symbol of The Preserver, and was believed by ancient cultures to give Spirit power over Matter, especially dominion over all magical beings like jinns and demons.

The six-pointed star also symbolizes Creation and the interpenetration of the invisible world with the visible world. See also GEOMETRIC SHAPE/Hexagram, NUMBER/6.

SOMEONE WHO IS A STAR making an appearance in your dream or meditation often represents some quality within that person, or his or her public image, that you admire and would like to incorporate into your own personality. What do you think this star is like as a person? How would you like to have them actively in your life? Why, or why not? See also FAMOUS.

THE SUN is an ancient symbol of Divine Light, life, fire, natural energy and power, the Yang (masculine) principle and qualities, healing, the Center, the heart of anything, instant intuitive knowledge or illumination, healthy growth, intense heat, wisdom, creativity, the incarnated personality and character of the individual human being, the power of feeling and believing, and imagination and inspiration of the intellect. It was one of the first symbols to be widely used by human beings.

All life on this planet depends on our sun. What does this remind you of?

The sun also symbolizes all solar deities, including the Archangel Michael. It symbolizes high spiritual ideals, the Light of Consciousness, and is a common 3rd or Solar Plexus Chakra symbol.

The sun has almost always been a symbol of the intellect (the moon symbolizing the intuition).

The sun also symbolizes the zenith, the highest point in the sky, and is linked symbolically to the

Will and to the active nature. And, of course, our sun is a star.

In ancient cultures, the sun was the Supreme Cosmic Power, the All-Seeing Divinity, the Heart of the Cosmos, the Center of Being, Enlightenment and Illumination, the Eye of the World, the unconquerable, and a symbol of supreme rulership and royalty.

The sun also symbolized Divine Will and guidance, the Light of the Buddha, the Logos, pure Spirit, and the World Door as the entrance to Knowledge and Immortality.

Some of the more common symbols which can themselves represent the sun are:

- revolving wheels or disks
- circles with a dot in the center
- swastikas
- rays, especially wavy or undulating rays
- chariots
- an eye. When the left eye represents the sun, it usually symbolizes the Yin (feminine) qualities. When it is the right eye, it reinforces the symbolism of the Yang qualities.
- a radiant face (in general, all forms of radiance symbolize new life received from divinity)
- a spider at the center of its web
- all solar birds and animals like eagle, hawk, lion, dragon, etc.

THE LIGHT OF THE SUN is an ancient symbol for direct knowledge and illumination, as opposed to indirect, intuitional, or lunar knowledge.

THE STRAIGHT LINES IN A SUN SYMBOL represent Light itself. In quantum physics terminology, straight lines would represent particles and wavy lines would be the waves.

THE WAVY LINES IN A SUN SYMBOL usually symbolize the heat and radiating power of the sun. In quantum physics terminology, wavy lines are the waves, straight lines are the particles.

URANUS: Uranus symbolizes out-of-the-ordinary abilities and talents, awakening, intellectual curiosity, extremes, transcendence, boundless space, the Unmanifest, the Will, and Celestial Space which must ultimately give birth to Time.

VENUS: Venus symbolizes Harmony, Beauty, Love, femininity, and emotion, and is often associated with the Crescent Moon.

As both morning and evening star, Venus is both a solar and lunar symbol, and represents the uniting and merging of the energies of these polar opposites.

Venus also symbolizes feminine passivity, passions and desires, the Creative Great Mother, imagination, synthesis, objective good, and defender of the innocent and helpless.

To the ancient Chinese, Venus was the West and associated with metal and the color white.

POCKET

Pockets most often symbolize a safe place to carry things. Pockets can also represent a wish or need for secrecy, a place to hide your feelings or something about yourself from public view.

Pockets also represent money, prosperity and wealth, as in you have "deep pockets."

A pocket can also be a good pun. Are you pocketing something? Does something have you in its pocket?

What is in the pocket? How did it get there? What type of clothing or other object is this pocket on or part of? Why? What would normally be carried in this kind of pocket? How is this the same or different from what you usually carry in your pocket? Why? See also CLOTHES, CONTAINER, and any object in the pocket.

POLICE

Police and security guards most often symbolize, safety, authority, and order through man-made laws and strictly enforced rules and regulations.

They can also be telling you that help is now on the way, or that you need or want to be rescued from something going on in your life at the time.

Conversely, police can symbolize restriction of your natural personal expression, your individuality and freedom, and limitations you feel are imposed upon you by society or from any outside source.

And police are good puns. Do you need to police your area? Is someone about to make your day?

What is the function of a police force? What is the function of this particular police or security guard? What actions are they taking? Why? How is this the same as or different from the actions they normally take?

How are these police dressed? What does this remind you of? How do you feel about them in your dream or meditation? How do you feel about the police in general? What do you think they are like as people? Why? See also GUARD.

POVERTY

Poverty or being poor often symbolizes that some part of you feels you are not using your potential to its maximum, or that you are not seeing your own worth and value.

Poverty can also symbolize your true feelings about money, or your fear of money and what it represents to you. Money and the lack thereof is a major lesson for most of us throughout our lives.

Dreaming of poverty can also symbolize that some valuable part or parts of you have been lost, and that you have become impoverished by this loss. Who feels the effects of this poverty? What part of you is that?

Who or what is in poverty? Why? What can be done about it? How do you feel about poverty in general? Why do human beings live in poverty — by choice or through circumstances beyond their control? Do you believe that people can be happy and wealthy at the same time? Why, or why not? Is it okay for spiritual seekers to be wealthy or comfortably well off? Why, or why not? See also EMOTION/Fear, LOST, WEALTH.

PREGNANT

Pregnancy often symbolizes that you are gestating a brand new beginning, or that a new part of yourself is being formed and will soon come into your waking consciousness.

But pregnancy can also represent the incubation or gestation period of an idea or belief, or that parts of yourself are still being formed, that you are literally pregnant with ideas and potential, but you aren't quite fully formed yet. To give birth to them now might be premature. Does this remind you of anything?

In ancient times, pregnancy symbolized the liberation from Time. It also represented wealth and security, since it exemplified continuity and immortality through the continuation of physical existence. The permanence of a family or genetic line is still of extreme importance in some cultures. So are you telling yourself to get back to the source of your beginnings?

But a dream pregnancy can be a message that you want to return to the womb, give up personal responsibility for your life as it is at the time, that you want to be nur-

tured and totally and completely taken care of by someone wiser and stronger than you.

And women often dream they are pregnant before any physical signs show up, and it is common for women to dream of pregnancy and babies (even dead babies) at the onset of, during, and shortly after menopause, the "change of life." Does this remind you of anything going on in your life at the time?

Pregnancy can also be a good pun, as in a pregnant pause, barefoot and pregnant, pregnant with possibilities. Or did you just get screwed?

Who is pregnant? Who is the child? Who are its parents? How long has the pregnancy been going on? What will happen after the baby is delivered? How does it feel to be pregnant in your dream or meditation? Is the pregnancy going well? How will life be different when this child is born? Why? How will your life change? See also BIG, FAMILY/Baby, SEX.

PURSE

Purses and wallets usually symbolize your personal identity and your feelings of security within that identity.

Purses and wallets also symbolize your connection to your culture and society, where you fit in, how you rank.

They can also represent a transition into new self images, that your old identity is no longer needed or appropriate for the new you, that you will have to replace your present identity with a newer version.

Why do human beings use purses and wallets? What kind of purse or wallet is it? What is carried in it? How do you feel about it in the dream? What is it made of? What color is it? What kind of a person would carry your dream purse or wallet? See also LICENSE, POCKET.

LOSING A PURSE or WALLET may be a symbol that you are not quite sure yet who you are or who you are becoming, that you aren't clear yet how to identify yourself, or on what you really want to spend your cash or credit; see also WEALTH.

Losing your wallet or purse can also be a symbol that you would like to lose your present identity, not be that personality any longer. This can also, of course, be a strong message from some part of you to be more careful with your identity and things of value.

Do you misplace your wallet or purse often when you are awake? If so, why do you think you do this? What does it tell you about some of your personality's characteristics?

A STOLEN PURSE OR WALLET may mean that you feel that you are losing your identity or power to other people or things, specifically to what the person or thing who took your purse or wallet means to you. What is being taken

from you? And what will be the ultimate result?

PYRAMID

Pyramids most often symbolize spiritual or mystical power, knowledge, and information. A pyramid also symbolizes a phase of initiation and that you are ready for it and doing well.

Pyramids are symbols of the Causal Body (the body that must conquer the three lower bodies) as it rests on the foundation of the Four Planes of Existence (symbolized by the four-sided base of the pyramid).

A pyramid can also be a message that you feel you are being, or are about to be, caught in a triangle; see GEOMETRIC SHAPE/ Triangle.

To many ancient cultures, a pyramid was the Center, an Axis Mundi symbolizing the Sacred or Cosmic Mountain, and it is probably for this reason that many pyramids are four-sided at their base.

And Plato used the pyramid to represent the element Earth (the cube was Air, the octahedron was Fire, isosahedron was Water, and the dodecahedron was the Ether or Air).

To the ancient Aztecs, the pyramid was symbolic of the fifth sun of Quetzalcoatl. And in ancient European cultures, the pyramid was symbolic of the Earth in her maternal roles.

In general, pyramids are a synthesis of other material forms. Its four-sided base represents the

Earth and its apex represents both a starting point and a point of completion. Joining the apex to the base gives the pyramid its triangular faces which symbolize Fire, divine revelations, and the threefold principle of Creation. Within this context, the pyramid symbolizes the whole of Creation within its three essential components or parts.

What is this pyramid made of? What would it be used for? Who would build it? Why? What do you believe about pyramids?

What kinds of people believe in pyramid power? Would you like to spend time in this one's inner chambers? Why, or why not? See also GEOMETRIC SHAPE/Square, Triangle, BUILDING, NUMBER/3, 4, and any objects in, on, or around the pyramid.

THE APEX and CAPSTONE of the pyramid are ancient symbols of the highest spiritual and initiatory attainments possible in this dimension of existence, the point from which you begin and to which you must return after completing the lessons symbolized by the base and sides of the pyramid.

The apex of a pyramid is also a symbol of the Higher Self. And the apex was a symbol of fire, a flame, solar and masculine energy and force, and a common phallic symbol.

A PYRAMID WITH CIRCLE AT THE TOP is an ancient Egyptian life force symbol and represents Eternal Life. Some authorities believe that the shape itself was created to give the wearer psychic abilities and "pyramid energy."

A PYRAMID WITH DECORATIONS AND LIGHTS is symbolic of the duality of life and death and associated with The Great Mother. It was often a substitute for the "hollow mountain," the place of ancestors; see also TREE/Christmas.

A PYRAMID ENTRANCE in ancient Egypt was always to the North, symbolizing the Lower Planes of Existence, and representing their belief that as the Soul rose from its lower physical nature, it entered the pyramid (its Causal Body) on the North side.

THE LOWER PASSAGES of the pyramid symbolized the narrow path from Earth to Heaven.

THE PASSAGE TO THE QUEEN AND KING'S CHAMBERS symbolized the Soul's progress to the highest spiritual levels, a state of consciousness of the love and wisdom of the Highest.

THE STEPS OF A PYRAMID symbolize the structure of the Universe and the various Planes of Consciousness, as well as the ascent of the sun.

THE STONES OF A PYRAMID were symbolic of the eternal nature and substance of Spirit; see also ROCK. And in the Near East, a stone pyramid symbolizes the element of Fire.

Q

QUARTZ CRYSTAL

Quartz crystal symbolizes the Spirit and the intellect associated with the Soul as the light of the Spirit.

Quartz crystals also symbolize your spiritual potential within the Third Dimension. They represent Truth received by the Mind as it operates through the medium of the personality.

Quartz is an ancient symbol for self-illumination, spiritual perfection and knowledge, perfect insight, and the passive aspect of the Will (the sword symbolizes the active aspect of the Will).

Quartz crystal also symbolizes purity, clarity, the union of opposites, the Immaculate Conception and the Virgin Mary, Truth conveying Knowledge to the human personality, Truth on the Higher Mental Plane (as does glass), and is also related to the symbolic meaning of diamond.

Quartz Crystal also represents the potential for human beings to attain "transparency," to be "in the world but not of it," to exist in Matter but not be trapped by nor enamored of Matter.

Quartz crystal belongs to the hexagonal crystal system and is a framework silicate; it builds its framework or structure first and then begins to fill it in.

Clear crystal offers little or no resistance to the Light. Quartz crystal won't burn, but it can be used to ignite a flame by allowing light to pass through it.

Quartz crystals can also represent a need or desire for clarity, a wish to be crystal clear about the subject of your dream or meditation.

Crystals boost and amplify all energy around them, are natural energy sources themselves, and can store information for long periods of time.

How do you feel about quartz crystals? Why? What do you believe about them? Do they remind you of anything in your life right now?

What kind of a person is a rock hound? What do these quartz crystals look like? Why are they there?

If they could talk to you, what would they want to say? See also STONE, WEALTH/Jewel.

A CRYSTAL BALL or SPHERE most often symbolizes the Light of God. Crystal spheres were sacred to the Roman goddess Selene and represented the celestial power of Light. See also GEOMETRIC SHAPE/Circle.

THE POINT OF A CRYSTAL symbolizes the 7th or Crown Chakra, and the potential we all have to know our spiritual nature through use of our inner knowledge and energy and through the proper use of the energy and knowledge contained within the other six Chakras; see also CHAKRA/7th.

THE SIX SIDES OF A CRYSTAL symbolize humanity and the six major energy points or Chakras of the human body; see also GEOMETRIC SHAPE/Hexagon.

R

RACE, Human

As a symbol, race is our mental-nature, the physical medium within which a consciousness experiences, learns, and ultimately progresses.

Each race represents a particular type of human learning, a particular range of possible experiences.

Which race is in this one? What are the people of that race like as human beings? (Be very specific and honest about answering this question so you will understand how your subconscious is using race as a symbol. This questions is not about prejudice or labels, it's about symbolism). How does this particular race differ from all other races?

Which race are you most often in your dreams and meditations? Why? How would they change if you were a different race?

How do you feel about this race when you are awake? How would you like to belong to this race? Why, or why not? What actions are these people taking in your dream or meditation? How do you feel about that?

RAPE

Dreaming of rape almost never represents a real-life rape or potential of it. It generally symbolizes that you are losing valuable personal energy to something or someone against your desire or will, that something intimate is being forcefully taken from you.

Rape usually tells you that you feel you are getting ripped off, taken unfair advantage of, are unable to fight back or defend yourself for some reason, that your feelings are being raped.

Dream rape can also be telling you that you feel unable to change or stop some situation going on in your life at the time of the dream.

Rape can, of course, also represent a deep fear of your natural sensual nature (and not just sexually), and that you have to be forced against your will to show the depth of your true feelings about the subject of the dream or meditation.

Some authorities take the view that the act of rape among ancient cultures was extremely rare, even though early Greek mythology uses rape as a favorite central theme. But the historical reality is that the ancient Romans and Saxons put a rapist to death, while the Normans merely put out his eyes and cut off his testicles.

Most Oriental cultures also imposed the death penalty on a rapist, even for a Hindu who raped a woman of a lower caste. These people were forever afterward declared untouchable and their soul never pardoned.

And the Byzantine culture mandated that a rapist must be put to death and all of his property confiscated and given to the victim, even if she were a slave.

In general, it was Medieval Europe that began, through their legal treatment of them, to change the status of rapists.

Would your dream rape be different if it had occurred in any of these time periods rather than the one it did? Why, or why not?

Who is being raped, and by whom or what? Are you or they fighting back? Why, or why not?

How do you feel in the dream? What kind of a person do you feel rapes another? What kind of a person do you feel generally gets raped?

How is the dream different after the rape? Does it remind you of anything going on in your life at the time? See also ATTACK, EMOTIONS, SEX, VICTIM.

RASH
Rashes symbolize deeply submerged anger, frustration, irritations, annoyances, or just plain old aggravations.

Rashes also make great puns. Are you about to do something rash?

On which part of the body does the rash appear. What color is it? Does it itch? How do you feel about it in your dream? What does it remind you of that is going on in your life?

ITCH: Itching frequently symbolizes a healing stage, new growth over an old injury, stretching your old perceptions, even that you have an inner itch for something.

An itch can also represent an annoying part of your life. What part of the body itches? What does this remind you of?

Another good pun, are you just itching to get at something or someone? Are you susceptible to the seven-year itch?

RIGHT
There are really no easy interpretations of right and left. But as an over-simplification, the right generally represents your assertive outgoing energies, and the left your passive incoming energies. The right projects and the left takes in; see also LEFT.

The right side *generally* symbolizes the Yang (male) principle, your outgoing creativity, your generosity, power, natural assertiveness or aggressiveness, your material responsibilities, the ability to understand symbols rather than words, non-linear thought, and your psychic capacities.

The right can also be a message that you are headed in the right direction at the time of your dream or experience. Right can literally be telling you that something is "right."

But since the right side of the body in general is controlled by the left side of the brain, right can also be symbolic of logic, the intellect, and language skills.

The right is also a symbol of the external, positive, outgoing, energy, the part of you that takes action and gets things done.

And the right represents your abilities to direct, delegate, and take command in and of the situation of your dream, meditation, or experience.

In the Western part of the world, the seat on the right side of a power figure is the seat of honor, while in the East it is the left (except in times of war when these positions are reversed).

In many ancient cultures, the right symbolized the mercy of God, while the left represented God's justice or judgment.

Today, the right hand is still used to give a blessing. It was the left hand which was used by monarchs to convey titles and other gifts; see also BODY/Hand.

As you can see, even more so than many other symbols, the interpretation of right and left will depend entirely upon the total content of your dream and the context within which you are using it at the time.

RING

A ring symbolizes a promise given, an oath taken for life, a sincere and binding commitment to something or someone, Eternity, fidelity, completion, perfection, wholeness, union, continuity, long relationships, and protection.

Rings also symbolize membership within a special or esoteric group or belief system.

All rings are believed to bind and hold energy, especially powerful energies. And rings, of course, are circles; see GEOMETRIC SHAPE/Circle.

A ring can also be a good pun. What has the ring of truth? Do you need to give someone a ring?

What kind of a ring is it? Where did you get it? How do you feel about it? Does it have jewels? What is it made from? Who would wear this ring? Which finger of your hand is it on? What happens if you lose this ring? See also BODY/Hand, Finger.

FINDING A RING often symbolizes your rediscovery or renewal of commitment to the subject of your dream or meditation.

LOSING A RING often symbolizes your current emotional feelings about a relationship or the condition of your relationship to what the ring symbolizes, but losing a ring is not necessarily confined to romantic relationships. You can be "married" to almost anything: habits, food, your work, a belief, an illness.

A RING AS A NECKLACE, especially if the necklace is jeweled, symbolizes the higher aspects of the mind and the higher emotions, the bridge between your higher and lower nature or characteristics.

The jewels themselves often symbolize wisdom and the capacity to connect and bring about union with the true Self; see also WEALTH/Jewel.

What type of necklace is it? What is it made of? Who would wear it? Why? How valuable is it? See also BODY/Neck.

ROAD

Roads generally symbolize your life, your current path, or your direction at the time of your dream, meditation, or experience.

A road can also symbolize the Way (the system) which will lead you to your goals or aspirations.

Is your road straight, steep, rocky, winding, paved, gravel, dirt? Are you moving up, or down? What vehicle have you chosen for your journey?

What shape is the road? Are there ditches by the side? Does it cross a river or ravine? How well maintained is the road? Who would be responsible for maintaining it?

Who would habitually use this road? Why was this particular road constructed? Whom does it benefit most? See also DIRECTION, TRIP, VEHICLE, and any objects on, around, or under your road, like DITCH or PLANT.

A BEND IN THE ROAD often symbolizes that you, or some part of you, is thinking about making a change in direction, taking a turn, and that there are new views and experiences ahead.

A CROSSROAD is an ancient symbol for a place of momentous meetings, and always a place possessing strong powers of spiritual transcendence. And crossroads sometimes share the symbolism of doorways; see BUILDING/Door.

In Europe, crossroads were magical and dangerous places, meeting places of witches and demons, ghosts, and other disembodied spirits.

Suicides, criminals, and vampires were buried at crossroads to make sure they would be confused if they tried to harass the living. And at one time, legal transactions were carried out at crossroads.

Crossroads were sacred to Hecate, one of the Greek goddesses of the Underworld, and dogs were ritually sacrificed at crossroads in her honor.

Crossroads also, of course, tell you that you have now choices, more than one direction you can go — even that you are literally at a crossroad in your life at the time.

A STRETCH or SEGMENT OF ROAD often represents a particular period of time. What does this stretch remind you of? Which stretch of your journey are you on?

ROAR

Hearing a roar in your dream or meditation usually symbolizes forceful emotions which have been up till now strongly suppressed but are now beginning to surface from the depths of your subconscious.

But a roar can also represent a need for recognition or attention from large numbers of people, an audience, a wish or need to hear the roar of the crowd. Or even to make a big noise yourself.

What generated this roar? What did it sound like specifically? Does it remind you of anything? What happens when the roaring stops? How does it make you feel in your dream or meditation? What would normally make a sound like your dream roar? See also ANIMAL if roar is from an animal, MONSTER, SOUND.

ROCK

Rock is an ancient symbol for permanence, durability, strength, solidity, the planet Earth, grounding or connection to the Earth, and your own personal power and beliefs as the rock upon which you stand.

Rocks also symbolize reliability, safety, steadfastness, and a place of refuge, especially when associated with water.

But rocks can also symbolize hardness, inflexibility, and coldness toward the subject of your dream, meditation, or experience.

To many cultures, rocks and stones are the bones of Mother Earth, while minerals are her body. And in ancient times, rocks were often used as symbols of human wishes. Rocks also symbolize the eternal substance of Spirit, especially if the rock or stone is glowing, pulsating, or luminous; see GLOW.

To the Chinese, rocks are Yang (masculine) and the opposite of the ever-changing Yin of water.

CLASHING ROCKS are a common symbol in myth and carry Yang symbolism, but with an added factor of danger for anyone careless or inexperienced in moving between the rocks.

DUAL ROCKS are symbolic of doorways and gateways, and almost always give access to other realms or dimensions, as do dual pillars.

THE LIVING ROCK is an ancient symbol of humanity's Primordial Self.

WATER GUSHING FROM A ROCK is an old symbol of the Source of all Life, the Life-giving Spirit.

ROPE

Ropes are another of the ambiguous symbols, but frequently represent your safety line, depending upon its use in your dream or meditation.

And rope is often associated with various spiritual rites of passage, as are ladders, bridges, trees, mountains etc.

Since ropes are often used to draw or pull things forward, the ancient Egyptians used rope as a symbol of the highest human qualities as they were evolved by physical skill and effort (the weaving of the rope) in the process of the refining or purifying the personality (the boat or object being drawn) for the purpose of aiding the Soul's progress (being pulling forward).

Ropes limit while at the same time allowing the possibility for escape to freedom. And ropes can make things secure by binding.

Ropes are sometimes used as substitute symbols for a snake or serpent and in mythology for the Golden Cord of Homer. For example, the cord that surrounds the Earth or the Cosmic Egg is a form of rope or golden cord.

In the pre-Buddhist beliefs of ancient Tibet, a rope was used to symbolize the connection between Heaven and Earth, and the gods were believed to come down this rope to mingle with human beings. But once the rope was cut, only the Soul was able to ascend by means of it, and the physical body had to be left behind.

"Cutting the rope" became a spiritual analogy for the mortality of human beings, and for the actual moment when we became mortal.

The famous East Indian rope trick symbolizes this almost magical ascent to Heaven, the ability to transcend all earthly conditions by extraordinary means.

And the Babylonian water god was often called the Rope or Bond of the Universe.

A rope can also be a great pun. Is some part of you feeling roped in, tied up, hamstrung? Are your hands tied in relation to the subject of your dream? Are you getting hung up somewhere, or about to? Who has roped what?

CLIMBING A ROPE can symbolize that you are moving by means of your own strength and effort, but that you may be using more energy and effort than you really need to. What is a simpler, easier way to ascend or descend than by this rope? Why is a rope being used instead of an elevator or ladder, for instance?

A ROPE NOOSE is an old symbol for Knowledge and the love of Truth and Right. Conversely, a noose can symbolize deep despair, even death. See also HANG and Hanged Man.

A ROPE PASSING THROUGH A WINGED DOOR is a Sumerian for the Mystic Link, the union between God and humanity.

BEING TIED WITH A ROPE may be a message that you are holding back or imprisoning some part of yourself, your life, your feelings, or your creative energy and power.

But being tied up can be a message that some part of you feels helpless, not able to function normally in some situation, that it literally feels all tied up; see also VICTIM.

RUN

Running in your dream or meditation most often symbolizes that you are running away from some part of who you are, from your feelings, or from life in general — or all of these, especially when you are being chased by something.

But running can also mean you are in a big hurry to reach a goal or destination. How you feel while you run and how effective the act of running is will tell you which symbol might apply.

How do you feel about running in your dream? What parts of your body are functioning the most efficiently during your run? Which are slowing you down? Does any of this remind you of anything going on in your life at the time See also CHASE.

RUNNING AWAY from anything almost always is a clear message that you are at some level actively avoiding what the object you are running from symbolizes to you.

But remember that even when you are running away from one thing, you are at the same time running toward another. What are you running away from? How will your dream or life be different when you manage to elude what you are running from? Why?

RUNNING A RACE often symbolizes that you are competing, and almost always with yourself at some level.

A race can also be a message that you need to slow down, you are pushing yourself too hard, depending on how you feel in the dream and the condition of your vehicle doing the racing.

And it could be a play on words, substituting racing for human race or any race within the human race.

RUNNING IN SLOW MOTION is a very common dream experience and often symbolizes that whatever it is you are running with, from, or toward is catching up with you. It is most likely also telling you that you don't feel you are making much headway concerning the subject of your dream and that you're beginning to run out of energy to either avoid it or keep up with it.

Running in slow motion can also be calling your attention to an unrecognized subconscious sense of feeling powerless, that you or some part of you feels you do not have the training or stamina to outrun, or even just keep pace with, the others in the situation represented by your dream.

And since your body is all but paralyzed during REM, slow motion running could just be a physical reaction to the brain trying to wake you up; see Glossary/Stage Three Sleep.

RUNNING TOWARD SOMETHING frequently symbolizes you are excited about a goal or part of your life, that you want to hurry up and get there.

S

SCAR

A scar frequently symbolizes an old emotional wound of some kind, and that while the wound itself may have healed, the deeper feelings associated with it have not yet been completely released, that you have grown some sort of extra protection over it.

But in some societies scars are medals of courage, and worn with great pride. Scars are even deliberately and ceremoniously created in some cultures. Have you earned your scars? How do you feel about them in your dream or meditation?

As an archetype, scars symbolize imperfections in your current perception of reality, misperceptions which have not been recognized for what they are and consequently have not had a chance to heal correctly or totally.

Where on your body is the scar? What color is it? What caused it? What kind of a person would be embarrassed by your scar? What kind of person would be proud of it?

In what stage of healing is it? Does this remind you of anything taking place emotionally in your life at the time? See also BODY part that is scarred, PAIN if present, and any object that might have caused the scar, such as WEAPON/Knife, etc.

SEASONS

The four seasons in general symbolize the natural orderly cycles of life and life's transitory nature.

Seasons are also symbolic of the four stages of growth of human life (infancy, childhood, adulthood, old age), and the four cycles of manifestation through which the Soul evolves.

What time of the year is it? Why? How would things change if the events took place in a different season? Why? Which season is your favorite? Which is your least favorite?

What does this remind you of?

SPRING symbolizes the beginning of a new life, new growth actively in process, freshness, renewal, rebirth, resurrection, planting for the future, the awakening of storms (see WEATHER), and the inexhaustible spiritual and emotional energy available to you at the time.

SUMMER symbolizes a time of great energy and activity, cultivation of things already planted, and rapid growth of things planted.

Summer is a time for relaxing and playing, using what you have learned before your next round of study or growth.

FALL symbolizes beginning to harvest your past experience and efforts, slowing down, that you should enjoy the fruits of your labor, and a reminder to prepare for the future.

WINTER symbolizes a time of deep rest, a time for preparing for the new beginnings of Spring, for living from the harvest you just brought in, and a time for inner and spiritual introspection and reflection.

THE SUMMER SOLSTICE takes place in Cancer and is known as "the Door of Man." It is symbolic of the descent and diminishing power and energy of the sun, with all that this symbolically implies; see PLANET/Sun.

And to the early Christians, the summer solstice was a symbol for John the Baptist.

THE WINTER SOLSTICE takes place in Capricorn, and symbolically is the day when the powers of Light conquer the powers of Darkness. For this reason, the winter solstice is often called "the Door of the Gods," and symbolizes the ascent and growing power and energy of the sun, and all that this implies.

In many ancient cultures, the winter solstice was the festival of the dying god. The Great Mother or the Queen of Heaven gave birth to the Son of Light during the Winter Solstice, somewhere around December 25th, and has always been a significant time in solar religions.

In ancient Egypt, Horus was reborn to Isis during the winter solstice, while in Alexandria it was Osiris who was reborn represented in the phrase "the virgin has given birth, the light grows."

In Mithraism, the winter solstice was the birthday of the Unconquered Sun. In Babylonian belief, it was the constellation of Virgo (the sign of the virgin mother goddess) who gave birth to the Sun. While in ancient Scandanavian tales, it was Baldur who appeared every December 25th.

In early Christian thought, the winter solstice represented the Christ and the birth of the Christ. And, of course, the Christian midnight mass ceremony today still incorporates the lighted candles of Mary as the Light-Bearer, the Virgin who brings forth the light.

SECRET

A secret in a dream or meditation most often represents your personal search or quest for the Truth, for the very secrets of life. Secrets also represent hidden knowledge, usually deep esoteric knowledge.

Secrets can also symbolize anything that parts of you do not want other parts to know. And they can symbolize something you not yet quite ready to share with others — maybe even yourself.

What is the secret? Whose is it? Who is telling it? To whom or what? Who wants to uncover it? What will happen if the secret becomes common knowledge? What does it remind you of that is going on in your life at the time? See also WHISPER.

SECRETARY

A secretary symbolizes the supportive, efficient, loyal and hard working side of yourself. A secretary can also represent any work overload and that you feel you need some help to get the job done right or faster.

Secretaries record minutes of meetings, keep files and records of events, keep their bosses on schedule, and have a good handle on what has been completed and what still needs to be done, and by whom. Does this remind you of anything?

Are you the secretary, or have you just hired one? Who is he or she? What are their primary duties? What salary level do you feel they are on? How good are they at what they do?

Who would normally hire your secretary? How is he or she dressed for the job? What do you think secretaries are like as people? Why? What social level do you feel they're on? What does all of this remind you of that is going on in your life?

SEX

Dreaming explicitly sexual scenes frequently simply symbolizes a merger or blending of energies, most often your Yin (female) and Yang (male) qualities, but it can just as easily represent a merger of any polar opposites.

Sexual intercourse is an ancient symbol of the union of the Mind with the Emotional Desires, which together produce ideas and feelings, which ultimately causes the creation and manifestation of a new life or form.

Erotic dreams can also symbolize an intense need or desire to merge with Spirit, the God Force, or life itself.

Dreams about sex are also often just your subconscious picking up on your body's natural chemical cycles while you are sleeping. Since the human body goes through sexual stages of arousal approximately every ninety minutes, your subconscious picks up on these cues and uses them symbolically. This is just one of the reasons why dreams involving sex aren't really always about sex at all. Many of your truly sexual dreams will be cloaked in symbolism, and it's very common to miss them altogether once you wake.

Dreaming of sex with a specific person can be telling you that you would like to merge with or blend the qualities of that person with your own, and not necessarily that you want to have a sexual relationship with her or him. But, of course, it can also be telling you just that.

Dreaming of sexual intercourse with a member of the same sex symbolizes how you feel about your own gender, and represents an intense merger of your energies and qualities with the energies associated with your own gender. Are you not giving enough recognition to the positive characteristics generally associated with your own sex?

Any form of dream eroticism or sex can also symbolize exactly what you think it does — that you need to pay attention to the physical, sensual part of yourself, that you need to remind yourself that you are a Spirit having a human experience, and that all human experiences are valuable. Keep in mind that growth is about integration, not denial or separation. Be more aware of your body's physical needs and requirements.

How well did the dream sex go? How is that the same as, or different from, your usual sexual experiences?

Are there a lot of interruptions? Are there other people around? If so, how do they react to your sexual activities? Where does the sex take place? Why? How would it be different in another setting; see also LANDSCAPE.

How do you feel about your dream sex partner? Does he or she remind you of anything emotionally going on in your life at the time of the dream — and not just sexually or romantically. Would you like to spend time with your dream lover when you are awake? Why, or why not? See FAMILY/Husband, Wife, KISS, LOVER, MAN, MARRIAGE. WOMAN.

SHADOW
Shadows often symbolize the Unknown, your favorite illusions, your hidden fears, your personal power, your subconscious mind, and your shadow self.

A dream shadow can also be a message that it is time to begin to integrate your shadow side. According to Carl Jung, the shadow self is the unconscious layers of the personality which are integrated into the complexities of the experienced world and can be transformed only through the process of individuation. In other words, it's time to grow up.

In many cultures, the shadow is considered to be an integral part of the Soul, and it is extremely important to see where the shadow of a person falls. For instance, strong taboos against crossing someone's shadow were very common. Some older languages even use the same word for soul, image, and shadow.

And an old superstition assures us that spirits appearing in human form and those who have sold their soul to the devil cast no shadow.

In Africa, the shadow is symbolic of the natural second nature of all things. In Buddhism, the shadow is a symbol for the illusion of the physical world.

Without shadows there can be no depth, and without light there can be no shadows. It is impossible for you to lose your shadow while you are standing in the light. Does any of this remind you of anything?

Dream shadows can also be a warning that some part of you feels it is in danger, being shadowed by something. Does some part of your personality feel overshadowed by other traits or habits?

Shadow is also a wonderful pun. Are you just a shadow of your former self? Who or what is shadowing you? In whose shadow are you standing? Are you afraid of your own shadow?

What or who is casting a shadow? What is the light source causing the shadow? What does this remind you of?

How large is the shadow? Why? What shade is it? How would your dream be different without the shadow? How do you feel about it? What would cause the shadow to disappear? What does all of this remind you of that is going on in you life at the time? See also COLOR of shadow, and any object casting and causing the shadow.

SHELL

A shell symbolizes direct communication with the Earth element Water and the many life forms contained within it. Shells also symbolize serenity, protection, natural beauty, and peace.

And shells are sometimes used in ceremonies, including baptism.

A shell can be telling you that you are living in a shell, or would like to. Are your exterior surfaces too rigid and unyielding, even if they are attractive and cozy?

In ancient times, shells symbolized the Yin (feminine) principle and quality, the Universal Matrix, birth, regeneration, life, love, marriage, fertility, the moon and all lunar deities, and virginity.

To the ancient Chinese, shells represented a good life in the next world and good fortune in this one, especially when used in conjunction with Jade's Yang (masculine) principle.

To the early Greeks and Romans, shells symbolized resurrection, a journey across the seas, sexual passion and union (since the two halves of a shell are tightly held together), and were symbols of Aphrodite, Venus, and Boreas in his guise as the North Wind.

To the Buddhists, a shell is the Voice of Buddha preaching the Law, learning, sound, victory over Samsara, and one of the Eight Symbols of Good Augury.

Shells can also be a good pun. Are you just a hollow shell? Is someone trying to pull the old shell game on you? What are you shelling out? Are you trying to live in a shell?

How do you feel about shells in general? Why? What type of shell is this? What color is it?

What kind of life form once lived in it? Where did you find it? Why? How would its meaning change if you found it in some other environment? What does it remind you of?

THE CONCH SHELL symbolizes the rising and setting sun, the lunar spiral, and the waters of the world — with all of their own symbolism.

To the ancient Chinese, the conch shell symbolized royalty and a prosperous voyage. To the Greeks and Romans, it was a symbol of Poseidon, Neptune, Triton, Aphrodite, Venus, and Boreas as the North Wind.

The conch shell is sacred to the Hindu, symbolizing Vishnu as Lord of the Waters. It is believed that the primordial creative word *OM* came from the conch shell. And to the Moslems, the conch is "the ear which hears the Divine Word."

THE SCALLOP SHELL was dedicated to Aphrodite and Venus, "she who is born of the sea," and so incorporates all of the symbolism of The Great Mother, love, compassion, and life.

To the Medieval Christian, the scallop shell symbolized pilgrimage, originally to the Shrine of Saint James, the Great and Rich.

THE MOLLUSK SHELL symbolizes the moon, purity, and virginity.

SHOT

Being shot or shooting in your dream often symbolizes that you are damaging and may actually be in danger of killing off or seriously wounding parts of yourself, or feel that you would like to.

But shooting or being shot can also symbolize that you are aiming at the target, hitting the mark, drawing a bead on the subject of your dream or meditation. How you feel about the shooting will lead you to your interpretation.

Who or what is getting shot? Why? Who is doing the shooting? What kind of a weapon is being used? Why that one and not some other type?

How do you feel about the whole thing in your dream? Is there any sound involved? Is there blood? Any pain? How would your dream be different when the dream object being shot at is killed off? Does any of this remind you of something going on in your life at the time of your dream? See also BLOOD if blood is present, HURT, PAIN if present, VICTIM, WAR, WEAPON.

SICK

To dream of being ill is usually telling you that your energy is dangerously low. It can also, however, be a symbol that you are in the process of getting rid of unwanted toxins of almost any kind, depending on the illness and your dream reaction to it.

In ancient times, dreaming of being sick was a symbol of a sickness of the Soul, believed to be caused by a one-sided development of the lower more physical Soul qualities, and caused by a failure of the mind to control or correct this error in development.

Sick of course can also be an early health warning. Are you getting enough rest? How is your nutrition? Need more natural vitamins and herbs?

This is also be a good pun. What or who in your life is making you sick? What are you sick and tired of? What would you like to sic on what?

What kind of illness is it? What parts of the physical body are affected by it? What are the normal symptoms? Do you actually feel ill in your dream? How does it feel?

Are you doing anything about the illness in your dream? How would your waking life be different if you managed to get sick? See also BODY parts affected by illness, COLD if there is a chill, HOT if there is a fever, etc.

SKI

Snow skiing often symbolizes that you will be able to slide right over the next the subject of your dream or the next life lesson — assuming you are skiing well, of course.

Snow skiing can also tell you that there is new ground to cover, especially if the trail is fresh untouched snow.

Skiing also symbolizes freedom of movement, and personal balance gained by honing the skills

you take the time and effort to learn well. After all, no one is born knowing how to ski.

SKI TRACKS AHEAD OF YOU is most likely trying to show you the path or road right in front of you at the time, how smoothly you can breeze right through it, and that others have been this way before. Maybe it's time to look for a role model, mentor, or teacher?

SKI TRACKS BEHIND YOU often tells you that you have already moved through something, and probably fairly rapidly and smoothly.

The key to your personal use of this symbol is how you feel about skiing in your dream, and how you feel about it when you are awake.

What color is the snow? How well are you skiing? How's your balance? Are you alone? How are you dressed? Do you feel cold?

Are there any obstacles in your way? How do you feel when you are skiing? What does it remind you of? How do you feel about skiing in general?

See also COLOR of snow, ROAD, WEATHER/Cold, Snow, and any objects around you, like MOUNTAIN, TREES, etc.

SKY

The sky symbolizes Infinity, the Heavens as the blanket covering all of us, the order of the Universe, sovereignty, the realms of bliss, and transcendence over the mundane worldly things in your life.

Throughout human history, sky deities have been mostly creators, not destroyers. They are often guardians of The Law, or of specific laws. Under matriarchies, sky deities were usually female, but it was not uncommon for sky deities to be asexual.

Sky can also symbolize your future, the things about to happen in your life.

And sky makes a good pun. Is the sky the limit? Do you have some pie in the sky idea? How high are you?

What color is the sky? What time of day or night is it? Why? Are there birds or other flying objects in your sky? How do you feel about it? How's the weather? Why? See, also, COLOR of sky, WEATHER, and any objects in the sky.

A BLACK SKY in the daytime often symbolizes a coming storm, problems or emotional turmoil building up — but often for someone else in your life, not you. Black skies can also be showing you that you need more light on the subject of your dream, that you're not quite clear about it yet.

But a black sky at night makes a perfect background for stars. How do you feel about your black sky? Why is it black? What would it take to change its color? What is in the black sky?

A BLUE SKY usually symbolizes great happiness, contentment, peace, and that there is fair weather ahead and good things coming your way.

A GRAY SKY often symbolizes depression, that you feel you have a problem, or that you are in danger of creating too gloomy a view of the subject of your dream or meditation. A gray sky can be a very direct message to lighten up a little, turn up the light.

SLEEP

Dreaming that you are sleeping may be telling you that you are not paying attention when you are awake, that you need to wake up, become aware of what's really going on around you, especially as related to the subject of your dream or meditation.

Sleeping in a dream can also symbolize an unwillingness to make a conscious (awake) change in your thinking, behavior, beliefs, and life. And sleeping or napping in your dream can represent the parts of you that would like to stay asleep. What does this remind you of? What parts of your character like to sleep a lot? Why?

And dreaming that you are asleep can also be a message to you that you are about to or are already in a lucid dream; see Glossary/Lucid Dreams.

And it can, of course, simply be telling you that you are not getting nearly enough rest and sleep, and that to feel rested, you even have to sleep when you sleep.

Sleep can also be a good pun. Whom or what are you sleeping with? Should you let sleeping dogs lie?

Who or what is sleeping? Why? Where are they sleeping? At what point in your dream did they decide to go to sleep? What does this tell you about your emotions at this point in the dream?

What is the sleeping environment? How do you feel about sleeping in your dream? Are you getting enough sleep in your waking life? What will happen if you do not get to sleep in your dream? What kind of people normally sleep a lot? How do you feel about them? See also FURNITURE/Bed, Pillow.

SMOKE

Smoke is a combination of air and fire, and therefore symbolizes a connection and merging of these two elements.

Smoke also symbolizes the Soul ascending after purification by the fire of Spirit. It is an ancient symbol for the union of Spirit with Matter, and of Heaven with Earth.

And smoke symbolizes prayer ascending to the heavens, a direct invitation and request for a deity to come in or to be present.

In some Native American traditions, smoke can also symbolize purification and cleansing. For instance, smudging is an important part of many ceremonies and rituals. And at one time, important messages were sent over long distances by smoke.

Smoke rising from the center of a tepee or temple symbolizes the Axis Mundi, the Center, the path of escape from Time and Space into the Eternal non-confinement of Infinity.

But to the early Christians, smoke symbolized anger, vanity, and the shortness of fame and life.

Smoke also may be telling you that something is hidden from view, that you may be dealing with an issue which you are not willing or ready to look at directly yet; see also WEATHER/Fog.

Smoke is also used to preserve and to flavor, and smoke protects by keeping wild animals and insects away. Is something prowling around or bugging you?

Smoke is also a great pun. Is smoke getting in your eyes? Is it a smokin' deal? How about "Where there's smoke, there's fire?" Who's blowing smoke? Who just got smoked?

What color is the smoke? Why? Where is it coming from? Is its source smoldering, or a roaring blaze? How do you feel about the smoke in your dream or meditation? What is the smoke hiding or obscuring from view? What does this remind you of? See also COLOR of smoke, FIRE, WEATHER/Fog.

SOUL

The human soul is often symbolized in dreams, meditations, and in works of art as a bird in flight.

In ancient Egypt, the human soul was frequently depicted as a bird with a human head and hands. In ancient Greece, it was symbolized leaving the body as a serpent. And the human soul was symbolized as a young child emerging naked from the mouth in early Christian art, representing new birth and resurrection.

Some of the more common symbols which can themselves represent the human soul are:

- Birds, especially white birds
- Stones and jewels or gems, especially pulsating or glowing
- Flowers of almost any variety and color
- Magical or "cosmic" infants
- Cocoons, caterpillars, and butterflies
- Spheres of any kind
- Balls of light
- Seeds
- Fruit, especially delicious fruit
- The colors blue, gold, silver, violet, white
- Glowing objects of almost any kind

SPORTS

Sports frequently symbolize your ability to temporarily cooperate with others to achieve a special goal, how you are learning the rules of the game (symbolized by the sport being played), and how you feel about those rules and how you may or may not be following them at the time.

And, of course, each sport has its own rules and regulation. How is basketball different from football? What are athletes like as people? Do you like sports? Why, or why not?

Sports are also good puns. Are you being a good sport? Do you have a sporting chance? Have you just dropped the ball? Is someone or something trying to end-run you? Are you being sent to the showers? Did you just hit a home run? Are you a player? How about a hole in one?

Which sport are you playing? *Are* you playing, are you a spectator? Why? What is the difference between a player and a spectator?

Who is on the team? How is this sport usually played? What time of year is it played? How are the players dressed? What are the normal rules of the sport? How is this particular sport different from other sports?

What is the object of the sport? What kind of people like this sport? Why? How involved do they get with it? What kind of person likes sports in general? How are they different from people who are not interested in sports? What does this remind you of going on in your life at the time?

STAGE

Dreaming of a stage often symbolizes the roles you are playing at the time, how you present yourself to your public, or how you would like to.

A stage can also be a message that you need or want to be center stage or up front about the subject of your dream or meditation. And it can be telling you that your ego needs a little stroking, a little boost, or conversely, a little toning down. Are you over acting?

Stages are also good puns. Are you about to stage an event or production of some kind? What stage of your growth are you in? Is the curtain about to go up, or down? Who or which part of you is hogging the spotlight in your life?

Are you actually on stage or in the audience? Why?

What is taking place on your dream stage? How are the players interacting? How is your dream audience responding? Are costumes involved? What type of lighting does your dream stage have? What is your dream stage made of? Where would it normally be found? See also BUILDING/ Curtain, Theater; CLOTHES; LECTURE.

AN AUDIENCE very often symbolizes your strong need to be heard, seen, appreciated, and even applauded. Audience is also a good candidate for a play on words. With whom would you like an audience?

Who is in this audience? For what occasion? How are they dressed? How large is the audience? What kind of a person would perform for this audience? See also CROWD, PEOPLE.

AN APPLAUDING AUDIENCE usually means just what you think it does, that you are getting a pat on the back, a gold star.

A BORED OR RESTLESS AUDIENCE usually symbolizes that some parts of you are not listening to other parts, and that they've probably heard this song and dance routine too many times

before, that you should deepen the plot, speed up the action, get on with the subject of your dream or meditation.

STONE

Even though most of us see rocks and stones as the same thing, they are not only geologically different but symbolically different as well. And being lovers of stones, we just naturally had to separate the two.

A stone symbolizes some type of spiritual truth, and is almost always a symbol for Spirit, especially Spirit's manifestation into Matter, into the material world. Stones are also often symbols for the human Soul, and inner growth and knowledge.

And stones represent solidity, strength, durability, reliability, the planet Earth, all or any of the planets, the physical Universe, and the entire Cosmos.

Conversely, stones can symbolize something that is static, at a standstill, and that there is little change going on, or going on much too slowly.

Stones can also be good puns. What is hard and cold as stone? Who got stoned? Is your dream or meditation a cornerstone? What might be in danger of becoming stone cold dead?

THE KA'ABA STONE was ancient and revered centuries before Mecca became the center of Islam. No one is sure where this stone originated, or even what it is since no one is allowed to touch it.

But in general, the Ka'aba Stone symbolizes the potential of the hidden Spirit within the Soul.

STONES BEING THROWN, believe it or not, is an old symbol for the positive power of the mind or the intellect.

More often, of course, throwing stones takes its opposite symbolism, that of the unproductive, prejudiced, outdated parts of the mind and intellect.

Who threw the stones, what kind they are, what or at whom they are being thrown, and why, will lead you to which of these two interpretations applies.

BUILDING STONES symbolize the parts of the Self that have been shaped and purified and are now part of the immortal body.

They are often a message that some part of the old you has been sacrificed in order to become usable for constructing the new.

Building stones also symbolize the beliefs upon which you build your life, stone by stone.

CARVED OR POLISHED STONES symbolize your personality or character traits which have been consciously worked upon, shaped, polished, even tumbled around a lot.

A CORNER STONE is a very old representation of the spiritual perfection of the Inner Self. Who placed this corner stone? Why? What would happen if someone removed it?

A STONE COVERING ENTRANCE OR WELL symbolizes the conditions imposed and the natural obstacles you must understand and master before the treasures of hidden knowledge can be reached and used. You must metaphorically "roll away the stone." How heavy is this stone? What does it cover or protect? Who placed it there? Why? See also WATER/Well.

A CUBIC STONE symbolizes stability, passive perfection, the foundation of something, the stone on which the Universe is built, and the Number 8.

A ROUND STONE symbolizes the moon, the Yin (feminine) principle, all lunar deities, and the Soul.

A TALL UPRIGHT STONE, including mountains, pillars, columns, and obelisks, symbolizes the Axis Mundi, the Cosmic Axis, the central point of Space and Time.

AN UNCARVED STONE often symbolizes the raw material of your personality, the parts of your character which have not yet been worked on. But an uncarved stone can also symbolize something in its pure, raw, natural state, something that requires no work or artificial adornment.

STRANGER
It is common to not recognize the people in your dreams and for them to be vague faceless strang-

ers, even though you often feel you do know them while you are dreaming.

In general, strangers simply tell you that these are some of the more unfamiliar parts of yourself, the actors you have placed on your dream stage to represent different qualities of your personality.

Strangers, however, can also represent teachers or guides who have taken on a certain persona to strengthen their message to you.

In older cultures, the stranger represented the one who was destined to replace the one in power, symbolizing the possibility for unseen change, the future made present, or a transformation or mutation in general.

How do you feel about the strangers? What are they doing? Are they mostly male or female?

Why? How are they dressed? Which race or culture do they belong to? What are they saying? How would you like to meet any of them when you are awake? Why, or why not? See also CROWD, FOREIGN, PEOPLE.

STRUGGLE

Struggle of any kind in your dream, meditation, or experience is most often a message that you are making the subject much, much harder than was meant to be.

Struggles also frequently represent part of you struggling with some other part, usually some trait or habit which is trying to gain dominance over the current dominant personality trait. Does this remind you of anything going on in your thinking right now?

Struggle can also be a clear message to slow down, relax, go with the flow, let things happen in their own time, quit fighting to have everything your way, don't force it; let the rose unfold naturally on its own in its own time.

What are you struggling against or for? Why? How do you feel about it at the time? How much energy is involved? What happens if you or your opponent loses the struggle? See also ATTACK, and any weapons or objects used in the struggle.

A FIGHT most often represents battles or struggles you are having with some part or parts of yourself.

But a fight also symbolizes the struggle between the physical and the spiritual, as in the biblical Jacob wrestling with an Angel.

A fight can also be showing you blocked 1st, 2nd, and/or 3rd Chakra energy movement trying to release itself, movement which has built up to a potentially violent result if something isn't done to help release this energy log jam.

[NOTE: It is important to know that, in general, all men tend to dream more violent actions than do women, and the older a man is, the more violent his dreams *may* become. Remember that dreams are a safe place to work out and release stress and potentially destructive feelings, and that all of your dreams exaggerate to some degree.]

SUITCASE

A suitcase most often represents your normal everyday baggage, the things you believe are necessary to get through your trip.

Suitcases are also often a symbol that you are turning something which is really very simple into something very heavy and cumbersome.

But suitcases also symbolize that you are ready to move on, travel, go exploring, get a change of scene. And a suitcase can, of course, simply be telling you that it's time for a vacation, go pack your bags.

This is one of your subconscious' least subtle puns. Are you still worried about dragging around your stuff when you could be traveling light? Are you about to pack it all in? Who or what is excess baggage? Is it time to just pack your bags and leave?

Are you packing things away that you should just throw out? Are you packing your bags in an attempt to run away from your problems?

What is the suitcase made of? What color is it? What size is it? What is in it? Who put the stuff in it? Is it light, or heavy? Awkward or easy to handle? Is your suitcase old or new? Is it yours, or does it belong to someone else?

Are you packing, or unpacking? Is anyone helping you with your baggage? What kind of travel tags are attached? Have you lost your luggage? Who would own this suitcase? Why? How often do you dream this symbol? Can you connect it to specific emotional events in your life at the time?

See also CLOTHES, GARBAGE, JUNK, and any dream object in the suitcase.

SWIM

Swimming frequently symbolizes your lessons and tasks in life at the time, and how good you are at staying afloat while learning and handling them.

Swimming can also be a message to you about a different way to handle the situation that is the subject of your dream or meditation.

The symbol of the swimmer has been used in several cultures to represent the spiritual seeker, and swimming can represent your present spiritual activities, and again, how well you are doing with them.

A person who is walking or driving also contains the potential to be a swimmer with the proper training, enabling him or her to move safely through a potentially hazardous element, water, even though this might not be his or her normal mode of moving around. Does this remind you of anything?

Who is swimming? In what are they swimming? What is the swimmer wearing? How well are they swimming? What is the color of the liquid in which they are swimming? How do you feel about swimming in general? Does this remind you of anything going on in your life at the time? See also FISH, WATER.

T

TEACHER

Dreaming of a teacher is almost always an especially important message from You to you.

And teachers frequently represent things you would like to really dig into and study, lessons you are in the process of learning at the time, that you have just completed a particular course of study, even that you are looking for a good teacher at the time.

Teachers can also be telling you that you would like to teach and that now is the time, you're ready.

What subject is this teacher qualified to teach? What type of school or organization would hire this teacher?

How do you feel about teachers in general? What is being taught? Who else is learning it? Who would choose to take classes from this teacher? Why?

How is the teacher dressed? Why? How effective is this teacher at helping students learn? Is the teacher male or female? Why? How would their presentation change if they were the opposite gender? See also SCHOOL, SPEECH, STAGE.

TELEPHONE

Telephones often symbolize communication from a distance by the use of voice and sound. Dreaming of a telephone is frequently letting you know that a significant message is coming in, a message that can't wait for slower styles of communication. Receiving or sending a Fax, E-Mail, or using the Internet would imply even greater speed.

And if you are the one making the call and dialing the numbers, don't forget to look up the specific numbers.

Telephones can also be good puns. Are you about to make the call? Is this a situation of "Don't call us, we'll call you?" Would you like to hang up on someone, or do you have a hang-up? Who has just "dropped dime" on you? Would you like to reach out and touch someone?

What type of phone is being used? What does it remind you of?

Where is the phone located? Who owns it? What kind of a person or business would purchase this type of phone? What color is it?

How are telephones different from other forms of communication? Why do human beings use telephones rather than letters or meeting in person? What words or sounds are coming from the telephone? What language is being spoken? See also BELL, MAIL, NUMBERS if you dialed a number.

TEST

Dreaming that you are back in school and taking a test is an extremely common dream and is almost always telling you that the way you felt when you took tests at that time in your life is the way you are feeling now about something at the subconscious level. What does this remind you of?

What emotional things were going on in your life at that age? How does that connect to what you are experiencing at this time? Are you being tested on or by something or someone when you're awake?

Tests often symbolize your past, your old belief patterns which now need to be tested for their present validity.

Dream tests are frequently about deep inner self-esteem feelings and how comfortable you are about something going on in your life at the time.

And taking a test often symbolizes a strong desire to study more

or to get more out of what you are already studying.

Tests can also be good puns. Is this a test, or the real thing? What would you like to test?

Are you taking, or giving, the test? How do you feel about it in your dream or experience? What is the subject matter covered by this test?

What will happen if you do not pass the test? Is anyone else being tested with you? When was the last time you remember feeling this way? Does it remind you of anything going on in your life at the time?

What kind of a person usually takes this test? Who usually requires it and actually gives it? What is the usual result? How is this test different from, or the same as, tests you have already taken? See also BUILDING\School, TEACHER.

TOOL

Tools of any kind are generally symbols of your ability to extend and enhance your physical body through your strength and skill.

So tools symbolize the different options and choices you have to get the job done at the time, and your present power and ability to build, restore, repair, create, renew, and tear down or disassemble the subject of your dream or meditation (e.g., a wall or structure).

Tools also symbolize the skills, tools, and knowledge available to you at the time to help complete any task at hand.

Tools can, of course, also be great puns. Do you have to be hit in the head with a hammer before you get it? Are you sawing the floor out from under you? Have you painted yourself into a corner? Do you need to pound sense into someone? Did you just get screwed? Does something have you in a vise? What's the drill? Is it the nail that stands up that gets hammered, or have you just hit the nail on the head?

What type of tool is being used? Why that one and not another? What does it look like? How is it different from all other tools like it?

What kind of a craftsman would normally choose this tool? How effective is it in your dream? Would it be better to use a different one? What does that remind you of that is going on in your life at the time?

TOY

A toy frequently symbolizes a strong desire or need to play, to take some time out for the child-like parts of yourself, to loosen up and be more creative with the things around you.

But dream toys can be telling you that you are not taking the subject of your dream, meditation, or life quite seriously enough, that you should stop playing around and get on with this game called your life.

A toy can, of course, also be telling you that you feel you are not being taken seriously enough by the people around you in your life,

that you are just a toy, or that they are toying with your feelings.

And toys are often harmless copies of the real thing. Does this remind you of anything going on in your life at the time?

Toys obviously make great puns. What or who are you playing around with? What kind of games are you playing? Are you just toying with something when you should be more sincere about it?

What kind of toy is your dream toy? Why kind of child would play with it? How is it different from other toys? What is it made of? What color is it?

Is it new, or old and broken? How do you feel about toys in general? What were your favorite toys as a child? How closely does your dream toy resemble these?

Did you ever have a toy like this one? When? What does it remind you of that is going on in your life at the time? See also FAMILY/Child.

TRAP

A trap of any kind often symbolizes a trap you have set for yourself somewhere along the way, at some level of your life.

Traps can also tell you that you are now seriously about finding and trapping something, often a natural more instinctual part of yourself, some element of your nature that you would like to capture, or, conversely, keep safely tied up or caged.

Traps also represent deep feelings of being caught or trapped in the situation represented by your dream or meditation.

And a trap makes for a good pun. Should you keep your trap shut? Are you setting a tender trap for someone?

What kind of trap is it? What is it made of? Who or what will it catch? What kind of a person would normally set this trap? For what purpose? What will this trap catch? How do you feel about the whole thing?

See also ANIMAL, HUNT, VICTIM/Captive, and any other object associated with the trap.

TREE

Trees are very ancient and complex symbols, but in modern times often symbolize great and enduring strength and your present rate of growth and development, spiritual and otherwise.

Trees provide protection and nourishment for a wide variety of life forms, and shade for living things. Trees can also be places of safety from things at or below ground level.

As an archetype, trees symbolize the Cosmic Tree or Axis Mundi, the World Axis or Center; the whole of manifestation unfolding from a single seed; the synthesis of Heaven, Earth, and Water; access to and the correct use of solar powers and energies; the Great Awakening; and The Great Mother, the matrix and power of inexhaustible nourishment and shelter.

Trees have almost from human beginning represented oracles as the "mouthpiece of divinity," especially the oak, sycamore, ash, beech, hazel, yew, peach, plum, and mulberry tree.

COMMON TREE SYMBOLS:

ALMOND TREE: The almond tree is a symbol of alertness, early awakening, and rebirth, while the nut of the almond is itself symbolic of the Essential Self, and that which is concealed behind and within a deceptive shell.

ASH TREE: The ash tree symbolizes modesty, adaptability, discretion, prudence, solidity, and stability. It is often associated in various legends with the blood of castration, and was the ancient Scandanavian Cosmic Tree, the tree holding together heaven, earth, and hell.

The ash was also sometimes attributed with the ability to drive away serpents, probably just one of the reasons a wooden stake made from the ash was believed to be especially effective against vampires; see ANIMAL/Snake.

And the Asherah was an early Semitic symbolic tree representing the feminine aspects of divinity, especially Ashtoreth or Astarte.

BEECH TREE: The beech tree symbolizes prosperity and divination, and was sacred to Zeus. Today, it is still the emblem of Denmark.

To the Freemasons, the beech symbolized endurance and steadfastness. However, in ancient Greece the beech tree was sacred to Hades and Cybele, and is still considered to be a tree of the dead in that part of the world.

BIRCH TREE: The birch symbolizes Spring, the young girl, fertility, light, protection against evil spirits and witches (just one of the reasons it was used on the backsides of disobedient children). And birch trees symbolize understanding, and relationships that heal.

The birth tree was sacred to Thor, Donar, and Frigga, and the ancient Scandinavian culture held that the last battle of the world would be fought around a birch tree.

The birch is also often the Cosmic Tree of shamanism, and the shaman ascends either seven or nine branches or notches of the trunk of the birch or a birch pole, symbolizing ascent through the planetary spheres to reach the Supreme Source of All.

BRANCH: A tree branch symbolizes fertility, one of the reasons why branches or boughs were and still are common at weddings.

Branches are also symbolic of the renewal of youth, fame, honor, and immortality. And a branch can take on the symbolism of an oar, a wand, or a pole.

Even the Tree of Life can itself be symbolized by just a single branch.

CLIMBING A TREE: Climbing a tree in your dream or meditation is often a symbol that you are moving from one level to another by your own strength, skill, efforts, power, and energy.

Climbing a tree is also a symbol of the attainment of knowledge gained through your ability to keep your balance, level by level as you climb. If you are afraid while climbing, it probably only shows you how deeply some part of you is afraid of changing, or afraid of its own power and knowledge.

CEDAR TREE: Cedars symbolize strength, incorruptibility, stateliness, beauty, and nobility. Cedar is believed to have been the sacred wood used in Solomon's Temple.

To the Sumerians, the cedar tree was the Cosmic Tree and the Tree of Life, and believed to possess supreme magical powers.

CHERRY TREE: Since cherry trees create their fruit before their leaves, a cherry tree often symbolizes humankind born naked and without possessions or adornment.

To the Japanese, the cherry tree symbolizes riches and prosperity, and is still a flower emblem of Japan.

Cherries and cherry trees are also often shown in Christian art as symbols of the Christ Child, good works, sweetness, and the blessed.

THE CHERRY BLOSSOM is an old symbol of Spring, youth, hope, feminine beauty, virility, and the Yin (female) principle.

CHRISTMAS TREE: A Christmas tree symbolizes the Winter Solstice and a new year with fresh beginnings and brand new possibilities.

The Christmas is the tree of rebirth and immortality, the Tree of Paradise shining by night.

Each light on the Christmas Tree represents a Soul, but can also be representative of the sun, moon, and all of the stars or lights of Heaven.

The sacred pine tree of Attis was hung with gold and silver bells, ornaments, and gifts or offerings to the gods, and the tree was burned after the ceremonies. See also Evergreen Tree, Pine Tree, and Pine Cone below.

THE COSMIC or WORLD TREE: The Cosmic or World Tree is one of the most ancient of symbols. It has its roots around the Earth and its branches in Heaven, symbolizing the potential inherent within humanity to ascend from the dense dimension of Matter into the pure dimension of Spirit.

In the ancient Scandinavian cultures, the World Tree was known as *Yggdrasil*, the Cosmic Tree, the Mighty Ash, the Ever Green, the Fountain of Life. As you can imagine, it was a strong symbol for eternal life and immortality, and the gods themselves held their councils beneath the World Tree.

The roots of the Cosmic Tree grow from the Underworld; its trunk moves through the Earth, the waters, and humankind, uniting all, with its branches reaching into the heavens.

It was through the root of the World Tree that the River or Fountain of Time ascended. And the root of the World Tree was constantly under attack by the more malevolent forces of the Universe, usually symbolized by *Nidhogg*, the Dread Biter.

Odin's horse nibbled at the leaves of the World Tree and an eagle and serpent were often shown in its branches, symbolizing light and darkness in their endless conflict.

It was from this tree that Odin sacrificed himself by hanging for nine nights and discovered the meaning of the sacred Runes, symbolizing rejuvenation through sacrifice, the smaller sacrificed to the greater Self; see HANG/Hanged Man.

The variety of tree representing the Cosmic Tree is usually culturally very different, but in almost all human cultures any dying or sacrificed god is killed on a tree of some kind, and a sacred bird sits in its branches.

COTTONWOOD TREE: The cottonwood tree is symbolic of the power of inner adaptability and resiliency. It also represents patience and acceptance of the very real physical needs of your physical body.

CYPRESS TREE: The cypress is an ancient symbol for grief and strife, strife almost always caused by negative emotions, just one of the reasons why you see so many of them in cemeteries. And it was once believed that cypress had the power to preserve the body from corruption.

Cypress trees are strong phallic symbols, and an emblem of Apollo, Zeus, Hermes, and Venus, and in this context represent life and continuing life. In ancient Phoenicia, the cypress tree was a sacred emblem of Astarte and Melcarth and was the Tree of Life.

But the cypress was also sacred to the Greek Hades, and in this context symbolized death and the funereal.

To the early Christians, the cypress symbolized perseverance in virtue, the just human being, and endurance, but also represented mourning and death.

And the ancient Chinese chose cypress as the symbol of happiness, grace, and — you guessed it — death.

DECIDUOUS TREES, trees that loose their leaves at the end of their season, symbolize the world in its state of constant renewal and regeneration, the power to die-to-live-again, resurrection, reproduction, and the Life Principle itself.

THE ELM TREE often symbolizes dignity, and to the early Christians, the spreading branches of the elm tree represented the strength of the Holy Bible.

However, in some cultures it is believed that the elm tree doesn't like human beings very much, which might account for so many nightmares on streets lined with them.

AN EVERGREEN TREE of any variety symbolizes everlasting life, immortality, and the undying Spirit; see also Christmas Tree above.

THE FIG TREE symbolizes life, prosperity, peace, knowledge, enlightenment, and fertility.

In some cultures, it is the fig tree that is the Tree of Knowledge. Within this context, the fig tree combines symbols of both the masculine and feminine principles, the fig leaf being male and the fruit female. And, of course, the fig leaf itself is often used even today to symbolize lust, sexual passions, and shame caused by those feelings.

Some authorities believe that it was this tree under which the Buddha sat when he attained enlightenment, the bodhi tree.

The fig tree was also sacred to Dionysos, Bacchus, Priapus, Jupiter, and Silvanus.

In Islam, the fig tree is a Tree of Heaven and sacred, since Mohammed swore by it.

A FOREST is a highly complex symbol and used in many legends, myths, and folktales world wide.

Forests are almost always connected at all of symbolic levels with The Great Mother and the female Yin principle.

Dreaming of a forest can symbolize one or any combination of the following: protection, healing, a restorative nurturing environment, peace, connection to the Earth, the Earth herself, and all natural things and behaviors — anything being its own nature.

A forest is a peaceful, healing place where the human spirit can recharge and regain its direction.

And forests can be places of seclusion from the civilized, demanding, fast-paced world, and good places to remind ourselves what this is really all about.

In many ancient traditions, a forest symbolized the subjective state of mind where consciousness withdraws from all external attractions into the higher intellectual levels. Within this context, forests are strong symbols of spiritual concentration to the point of total self-involvement. Forests are places of testing and initiation, a secret which must be penetrated by spiritual insights in order to find your way safely out again.

But since the plant growth in the forest often hides the light, it can sometimes be symbolic of something that is opposed to the power and light of the sun.

It is hard for us in our modern concrete and electric world to completely relate to the original deep symbolism of the forest — impenetrable, completely engulfing, both life-giving and life-threatening. Magical and other-worldly experiences overtake any naive or reckless human who wanders into the deepest parts of the forest, and worst of all is unwise enough to fall asleep there. Children who wander into its depths are rarely seen again. Does any of this remind you of anything?

Forests play important roles in many cultures as sacred groves and mystical places, mysterious realms where good and evil gods and spirits live, not to mention fairies, sprites, wildmen, and various demons, jinn, and afrits.

All forests hide and camouflage their secrets, their many life forms. For this reason as much as any other, forests sometimes represent the subconscious mind, and Carl Jung believed it was for this reason that forests turned up in so many children's stories.

Within this context, a forest symbolizes our deep natural fear of the Unconscious, and its very real power to hide or even devour our rational, reasonable mind.

In Celtic Druid symbolism, the forest was given in marriage to the sun. To the Hindu, the forest dweller symbolizes someone who has left the mundane material world for a contemplative life. And to all shamans everywhere, the forest is the dwelling place of spirits.

The Australian aborigine sees the forest as the place of initiation, the Beyond, and the place of the spirit of those who have died.

Forests can also represent irrational or hidden things, often symbolized by being lost in a forest.

So if you find yourself lost in a forest, it may be telling you that you are off your path, that can't see the forest for the trees. Being lost in a forest or woods can be a clear message from You to you to take control of your life again, find your way back home, get back in the light — or the big bad wolf will get you.

What life forms inhabit this forest? What types of plants grow there? How would you like to be in this forest in waking life?

How do you feel while you are there? Would you like to really walk there? Why, or why not? How is it the same as, or different from, forests you have been before? Have you ever been in this particular forest? What does it make you think of?

THE GOLDEN BOUGH to the ancients was a link between this world and the next, a passport or bridge to the heavenly realms, and represented initiation and even sometimes a "magic" wand.

The Celtic Druids believed that mistletoe was the Golden Bough; see also PLANT/Mistletoe, and Silver Bough below.

AN INVERTED TREE is a important and common universal symbol and is always a magical or mystical tree.

The roots are in the air and symbolize the Life Principle; its inverted branches symbolize unfolding manifestation in inverse action, or that which is on high descending to that which is below.

The inverted tree also symbolizes bringing knowledge back to its roots, to its source.

In many initiation ceremonies, the inverted tree symbolizes reversal and the symbolic death of the initiate. Many inverted trees are of Cabalistic origin.

TREE LEAVES are old symbols of fertility, growth, renewal, health, and great abundance. In ancient China, the leaves of the Cosmic Tree symbolized all being in the universe, the "Ten Thousand Things"; see also Cosmic Tree above.

The leaves of a tree can be symbolizing the lessons you have already learned, the stages of growth you have already accomplished. Leaves are the visible result of your growth up to the point of your dream, meditation, or experience.

Leaves can also be showing you your next phase or cycle of growth. On what type of plant are these leaves? Why?

And leaves make good puns. What are you leaving? Do you feel as helpless as a leaf in the wind? Are you about to turn over a new leaf?

AUTUMN LEAVES represent the winding down of a cycle of growth, especially one where you have experienced great activity. Autumn is the time of preparing for the winter, completing a harvest.

And autumn leaves can symbolize a strong life change of some kind that is either on the way or already beginning. The type of change and how you may be feeling about it is symbolized by the color of the leaves and the context within which your subconscious is using this symbol; see also SEASONS/Autumn.

How do you feel about autumn leaves in general? How are these the same or different as ones you have experienced before?

A CROWN OF LEAVES symbolizes a divinity, a victory, and personal dedication to what the leaves themselves symbolize.

DEAD LEAVES represent rest between the stages of renewal and new growth, but can also symbolize a sadness for a time just ended, or even be an early warning about your health. See also DEATH. What caused the leaves to die? How do you feel about them at the time? What do they remind you of going on in your life?

GREEN LEAVES most often symbolize renewal of hope, a change for the better in your energy, vibrant health, productive and natural growth, and great abundance and life. What type of plant are these leaves on? Why?

A LEAFLESS TREE usually symbolizes a time of hibernation, a temporary rest period, your natural renewal process, and the end of a the particular cycle which symbolized by the type of tree this is.

Again, how you feel about the tree will help you find your own best interpretation. Is your tree leaf leafless by nature, has the wind blown them all away, has something destroyed the tree's ability to grow leaves, or is it merely time for the tree to rest?

LEAVES ON THE GROUND generally represent lessons you have already learned dropped, or ones you are about to let go of because they have outlived their purpose. What color are the leaves? How do you feel about them being on ground? What happens to them next? And what does this remind you of?

In what stage of growth were the leaves before they fell? What type of tree or plant were they on? What color are they? Are they healthy, dormant, plastic, silk? See also COLOR of leaves, PLANT, and Autumn Leaves above.

LIMBS: Limbs of a tree most often symbolize your talents, gifts, and abilities, either ones you already have and are using or ones you might want to develop or grow.

Limbs are also the way you reach out from your trunk, your source and support system.

As an archetype, limbs often symbolize the manifestation of individuality growing from and nurtured by the Unity, the Source.

A limb can also be a good pun. Are you out on a limb? What or whom would you like to tear limb from limb? Are you using limb as a substitute for arms or legs?

How strong and healthy are the limbs? What is on them? What type of tree or plant are they growing on? What time of year is it? What would their wood normally be used for? How many are there? Why?

MAPLE TREE: Maples are symbols of giving and receiving unconditional love. In fact, in Japan the maple leaf is the symbol for lovers.

MULBERRY TREE: Since the mulberry cycles through three distinct stages of growth (its berries changing from white to red to black), it became a symbol early-on for the three stages of initiation and the three stages of life.

To the ancient Chinese, the mulberry tree was a Tree of Life, believed to have magical powers against all dark forces. But to the ancient Greeks, mulberry symbolized tragic love affairs.

OAK TREE: Since oak is one of the hardwood trees, it is an ancient and common symbol for immortality, long life, endurance, steadfastness of purpose, unshakable power, durability, unyielding strength, growing by means of your own inner strength, the Yang (masculine) principle, and heroism.

The oak was sacred to many ancient deities, both male and female, and was believed to have been especially chosen and favored by the gods.

It was once a common belief that the oak tree actually attracted lightning, and that anyone who drew energy from the tree was therefore assured of ascending to heaven; see also WEATHER/Lightning.

And the oak tree symbolizes the human body, humanity in general, masculine strength, and the weakness inherent in strength which causes it to resist rather than bend to the wind.

The oak was sacred to the ancient Celtic Druids, to Zeus and Jupiter, Thor, and many other deities of the sacred grove, as well as sky, thunder, lightning and various fertility deities.

The ancient Greeks believed that oak groves were the home of a form of nymph known as a dryad. And the ashes of a burned oak were believed to protect crops from diseases, while an arrow of oak wood would keep away snakes and serpents.

The oak tree has a long, long history for use as a psychic and divinatory tool in almost always cultures where it could be found.

ACORNS were eaten by the Celtic Druids before making prophecies. But in most every other culture, the acorn was a phallic symbol and was often worn by men as a talisman.

OAK LEAVES were once believed to have the power to transfix lions, and possess the ability to speak to human beings.

Even today, the US Army gold oak leaf is reserved for the rank of major, and a silver one for the rank of lieutenant colonel.

A WREATH OF OAK LEAVES symbolizes a powerful ruler, and was often worn by those who saved lives.

OLIVE TREE: The olive tree was sacred to Athene and symbolized mental strength, purification, vital energy, fertility, victory, peace, reconciliation, and knowledge.

Since its oil provided fuel for lamps, it also symbolized bringing forth light from your own essence.

ORANGE TREE: The orange tree and its blossoms symbolize fruitfulness, fertility, good fortune, immortality, and pure love, and was one of badges of Diana.

The fruit of the orange tree is believed by some authorities to have been the Golden Apple of the Hesperides.

THE TREE OF PARADISE: All trees of Paradise are frequently heavy with precious stones rather than flowers or fruit.

PEACH TREE: The peach tree is both a Tree of Life and Tree of Immortality in some cultures. In any case, it always symbolizes immortality, Spring, youth, marriage, wealth, femininity and feminine charm, good wishes, longevity, and magical fairy fruit. PEACH STONES are often carved and worn as amulets for any or all of these reasons.

PEAR TREE: The pear tree is a symbol of transience, delicacy, the fragility of life, and mourning.

During the Middle Ages in Europe, it was one of the emblems of the Virgin Mary.

PINE TREE: The pine is the second highest conductor of tree energy on this planet, redwood being the highest.

So dreaming of a pine tree often is telling you that it is time to get back in touch with the energy of Nature, recharge yourself, or just to relax, take a deep breath and take in some clean air.

Pine is soothing, cleansing, and naturally healing. Anytime you need a serious energy recharge, stand or sit with your back against the trunk of a pine tree. And then remember to say "thank you."

Pine trees also symbolize straightness in your growth pattern, uprightness in action and stature, and strength of character.

Pines are ancient symbols of courage, faithfulness, longevity, and are emblems of many deities and teachers, including the Buddha.

In ancient Egypt, the pine tree was sacred to Serapis, while I ancient Greece, it was one of the trees sacred to Zeus. And to the ancient Romans, the pine was sacred to Diana, Venus, and Jupiter. And in the Middle East, the pine tree was associated with Mithra.

PINE CONE: The pine cone is a phallic fertility symbol and a symbol of good fortune and abundance. The pine cone also represents Spirit with its many layers or leaves in most cultures where it is found.

The pine cone was an emblem of Serapis, Cybele, Sabaszios, Astarte, Artemis, and the represented the heart of Bacchus/ Dionysos. Pine cones also share the symbolism of vortexes and whirling spirals.

A WHITE PINE CONE was an emblem of Aphrodite.

QUAKING ASPEN: The quaking aspen tree symbolizes moving from anxiety to excitement about the possibilities of your new awesome opportunities and challenges. It is a symbol of the ability to turn in the wind as needed.

In some Native American cultures, quaking aspen is called "noisy leaf" because of the way its leaves chatter in the wind.

It is the quaking aspen which is one of the first trees to regenerate on any land that has been burned, in the process providing shade for tender new plants and trees. How's *that* for a symbol?

SHADE: Shade symbolizes relaxation, rest, protection, and shelter from the heat of the sun or day; see DAY and PLANET/Sun

Dreaming of shade can also symbolize that you want to hide something, not let the light shine too brightly on the subject of your dream or meditation.

In older cultures, shade was often a symbol of The Great Mother who always provides shelter for those in her care.

Shade can also be a great pun. What feels shady to you? Do you want to pull down your shades and rest? Are you wearing shades? Would you like to just stay in the shadows?

What is providing the shade? What is the source of light that allows this shade to exist and manifest? How do you feel about it in your dream? What does it remind you of going on in your life at the time? See also HOT, SHADOW, SUN.

THE SILVER BOUGH: The Silver Bough, usually from an apple tree, symbolizes the link between this world and the world of fairies. At one time, breaking the Silver Bough symbolized the death of the fairy king.

SNOW-COVERED TREE: Snow-covered trees symbolize peace, purity, silence, truth, and soft protection by gently covering. But a snow-covered tree can be showing you that a part of you feels shut down, cold, ignored, alone, that your true nature is hidden. How do you feel about the tree? Why? How is it the same as, or different from, snow-covered trees you have seen before? See also COLD, WEATHER/Snow.

STUMP: A stump symbolizes something which has been cut off, growth which has been forcefully and deliberately stopped; see also DECAPITATION. How you feel about the stump in your dream will tell you whether your subconscious feels this cutting off has been a good thing or not.

A stump can also be a wonderful pun. What has you stumped? Did you make the cut? Do you feel cut off? Has someone just cut you down?

What was growing above the stump before it was cut? Why was it cut down? What was used to make the cut? Has the cut healed? Did it heal well, or is it still raw? Is the stump in the way of something else that now wants the room to grow, was it an obstacle of some kind, or did it serve an important purpose?

A STUMP BEING PULLED OUT is often symbolizing one of your old no longer useful beliefs, thoughts, or behavior patterns, which are now in the process of being pulled out by the roots. Removal of the stump will allow a more productive use of the area being cleared.

By what process is the stump being removed? What will happen when it is gone? What will change? What does this remind you of going on in your life at the time?

THE TREE OF LIFE: The Tree of Life and the Tree of Knowledge grow in Paradise in virtually all cultures.

The Tree of Life is at the Center, and symbolizes regeneration and return to the primordial or perfect original state of being, and the beginning and ending of a long cycle of evolution.

Immortality is gained in many legends by either eating the fruit of the Tree of Knowledge, or by drinking the liquid extracted from the fruit of the Tree of Life.

And the Tree of Life is also a symbol for the human body. The spinal cord represents its trunk and the nerves its many branches. Within this context, the nerves are responsible for many different fruits as they experience touch, taste, smell, sound, and sight.

THE TREE OF KNOWLEDGE: The Tree of Knowledge symbolizes the inherent duality of true knowledge, the knowledge of the reality behind good and evil — in short, the knowledge of the gods. So it is no surprise that the Tree of Knowledge is connected in many cultures with the first man and first woman and their fall from a state of paradise or divine grace.

Immortality is attained in many myths by either eating the fruit of the Tree of Knowledge, or by drinking the liquid extracted from the fruit of the Tree of Life.

The Tree of Knowledge is also sometimes characterized as a vine rather than a tree; see also ALCO-HOL/Wine.

And the Tree of Knowledge symbolizes the cerebro-spinal nervous system of the physical body, the system that was developed to allow and facilitate human choices.

A TREE WITH THREE BRANCHES or BIRDS: This is a very ancient symbol for the lunar cycle; see PLANET/Moon.

A TREE WITH 10 or 12 BRANCHES or BIRDS: This is a very ancient symbol for the solar cycle; see PLANET/Sun.

A TWISTED TREE: A twisted tree symbolizes magic and all things sacred, either good or evil.

For example a bonsai tree symbolizes Nature in its deep wisdom and simplicity.

THE TREE OF LIGHT: The Tree of Light is an ancient symbol for the rebirth of the Soul. Each Soul created was originally symbolized by a candle on the Tree of Light, but in more modern times electric lights have replaced the candle.

Our Christmas trees are trees of light, as are the tree used at Buddhist feasts of the dead. This custom has been traced back to the legends of Attis, Dionysos, Atargatis, and Cybele, indicating that its origin is probably much, much older. See also CHRISTMAS TREE above.

The tree of Attis and Dionysos were always hung with offerings to the gods, but the fir tree of Woden was believed to give gifts back to those who honored his sacred tree.

WOOD: Wood itself often symbolizes support, a framework, practical functioning, safety, calm and comfort, protection from the elements, and Nature which has been worked and shaped to a specific form and function by a craftsman.

As one of the oldest and most important raw materials available on this planet, wood symbolizes Matter in general and the Prima Materia and Vital Energy in particular.

As an archetype, wood also symbolizes the wholeness of Paradise, that which gives shelter at birth and at death, and forms the lunar boat, and the marriage bed.

To the ancient Buddhists, wood was Brahman, the "tree from which they shaped heaven and earth." In China, wood represents Spring, the East, and the colors blue and green. See, also, any object made from the wood.

And this one, of course, in prime for a play on words — "wood" for "would."

THE YEW TREE: To both the ancient Celts and early Christians, the yew tree was a strong symbol of immortality. The Celts believed it was a magic tree, and the Celtic White Wand was traditionally fashioned from yew.

Conversely, to many other early cultures, the yew tree was a symbol of mourning and sadness and was commonly used at funerals.

THE YULE LOG: Burning a yule log is a very old custom and most often symbolizes the death of Winter and the rebirth of the power of the sun. Burning the yule log is an old symbol representing the sacrifice of the dying god, with his continuing renewal and rebirth.

Yule logs were usually of oak, the Cosmic Tree of the ancient Druids, or of pine, the sacred tree of Attis, Dionysos, and Woden.

Ivy was traditionally wound around the yule log to symbolize Dionysos or Osiris, depending upon which culture you were in.

Lights and luminous balls on the yule log or tree symbolized the light of the sun, the moon, and the stars in the branches of the Cosmic Tree. Sometimes these lights were also symbols of souls.

A WILLOW TREE: The willow of antiquity was believed to be sterile, and therefore often symbolized chastity, purity, and virginity.

Since an endless number of cuttings can be taken from the willow without harming the original, it was also a symbol of a source and supply of limitless wisdom and life.

Willow is also an old symbol for deep heartache, especially pain caused by an unhappy love affair, and of mourning for the dead.

All willows were believed to be enchanted and were sacred to various moon goddesses in many cultures. Willow wands were used to invoke the Muses, later turned into the wizard's and witch's wand. But to the ancient Greeks, willow wands provided protection during travels through the Underworld. Willow was sacred to Helice, the goddess Hecate in her virgin aspect.

The willow was believed to be magical, possessing enormous healing powers, and was a dwelling place for spirits, witches, wizards, and mystical beings.

To the Chinese, willow symbolized meekness, Spring, feminine grace and charm, artistic ability,

and sorrowful partings. Willow is often associated with Kwan-yin, who sprinkles the waters of life with a willow branch.

To the Taoists, willow symbolizes strength in weakness, the strength-weakness of one wise enough to bend to outside forces when necessary rather than break or be torn out by the roots.

TRIP

A trip or journey most often symbolizes your life path, your quest for spiritual goals and the meaning of your life.

But trips and journeys also symbolize the focused and determined exploration of yourself. During any dream or meditation journey, you will often be moving along a path or road toward a specific goal or destination, almost always with delays and obstacles to be overcome — your hero or heroine's journey.

The difficulties or obstacles encountered along your trip are highly significant, and tell you what you are working with at the time of your dream, meditation, or experience. Watch these obstacles and delays change as you change. They aren't there just to annoy you. What do they symbolize that is going on in your life at the time?

What type of vehicle are you using for this trip? Who is with you? Where you are headed? Which direction?

What time of day or night is it? What are your surroundings? How much preparation did you make for your trip? Or did you have time to make any?

How long is your trip? How much baggage are you taking? What is the purpose of this trip? What will happen when you reach your destination? Are you coming back?

Another good potential pun, what have you just tripped over? Have you just taken your first step along the journey of a thousand miles? What has tripped you up? See also ROAD, SUITCASE, and VEHICLE if one is being used.

TUNNEL

A tunnel often symbolizes a safe way travel through levels of consciousness. In this context, the walls of the tunnel help protect you from absorbing too much energy or information too fast and suffering from sensory overloads. You can't see what's the tunnel is allowing you to move through, you can only see the beginning and ending points.

But a tunnel showing up in a dream or meditation can also symbolize a deep feeling of being trapped, undermined, forced to move through something that makes you (or parts of you) very uncomfortable. Do you like tunnels? Why, or why not?

Tunnels are also good symbols of the subconscious. What is this tunnel going through? Is it being used as a shortcut through something that would otherwise take much more time and effort?

How you feel about the tunnel will tell you which interpretation may be right at the time.

Tunnels also make good puns. Are you being told you have tunnel vision? Are you in the process of tunneling your way to freedom? Is there light at the end of your tunnel? Are you being told to hang in there, that you are almost out of the tunnel?

Why was this tunnel constructed? By whom? How much effort and energy did it take? Where is it? Where does it lead?

Who uses it on a regular basis? Why? Does it make their life easier, or harder? Why? Is it free, or do you have to pay to use it? Why?

How do you feel about tunnels in general? How did you get into this particular tunnel? Are you alone?

Where does the tunnel begin, and where does it end? What will happen once you are out of the tunnel? And what does all of this remind you of going on in your life at the time?

U

UMBRELLA

An umbrella symbolizes protection, usually from emotions raining down on you. Umbrellas also protect you from strong heat and sunlight, your strong heated emotions; see DAY, PLANET/Sun.

An umbrella also frequently symbolizes your basic belief systems, beliefs which are at the time now "under one umbrella."

As an archetype, the umbrella symbolizes the Solar Wheel, the canopy of Heaven, protection of the Soul from Above, shelter of the branches of the Cosmic Tree, and both worldly and spiritual power.

To the Chinese, an umbrella or parasol represented dignity and one of high rank, protection, and good luck. And to the Hindu, it was a symbol of the Universal Spiritual Truth which covers all.

How is this umbrella being used? How is it the same as, or different from, a real umbrella? Who would pay good money for this umbrella? What color is it? Why? See also COLOR of umbrella, and any object your

umbrella is being used to protect you from.

UNDERGROUND

Anything underground in your dream or meditation usually symbolizes your subconscious mind with its deeply hidden beliefs and feelings at the time.

And the underground also represents the Collective Unconscious, the Underworld of the ancients.

Being underground is almost always a clear message that something or some feeling is deeply buried, and that now is a good time to bring it up. The deeper underground you are, the less you are consciously aware of the issue represented by your dream or meditation.

Being deep under water often shares this same symbolism; see WATER.

Being underground can also be telling you about a deep desire or need to hide or rest, to get away from the bright lights and noise for awhile.

Why are you underground? What does it feel like? Is it damp, musty, dirty? Or is it peaceful, a good place to hide from storms and the confusion of everyday life?

Are you looking for something while underground? Where are you underground? How much light is there? How do you feel about it in your dream or meditation? How is this feeling the same as, or different from, the way you would feel in your everyday world?

Are you normally comfortable being underground? What does this underground place remind you of that is going on emotionally in your life at the time? See also HOUSE/Basement and TUNNEL.

UNEMPLOYED

To dream of being unemployed generally symbolizes that a part of you feels that you are not using (employing) your talents or creative abilities to their fullest potential, that the best parts of you are not being used to their true capacity.

Which of your talents and skills are not employed at the time? Why? How would your life be different if you employed these skills and talents, put them to work for you? What parts of you do these things represent? How do they feel about being unemployed? Why?

Unemployment can also represent a very real fear of loss of support of some kind, and a loss not necessarily related to the business world or your job.

However, if you are consciously aware of the fear of actually being unemployed, losing your job is probably not what your dream is about, so keep digging.

Being unemployed in your dream can, of course, also be representing a strong subconscious desire to actually be unemployed in the field you are now in. What would you decide to do if your present career or job vanished overnight? What keeps you from doing that now?

Why are you unemployed? What work or activity are you unemployed from? How do you feel about it in the dream or meditation?

How did you become unemployed? Did you quit, get laid off, fired? How would your life change if you became unemployed? What does this remind you of going on in your life at the time?

V

VALLEY

As an archetype, a valley is Yin and symbolic of the womb. A valley is the counterpart of the male Yang of the mountains.

And a valley frequently symbolizes the "path of spiritual enlightenment" a deepening of your knowledge and experience before climbing up to the next stage or level.

And dreaming of a valley can be telling you that you are now ready to rest and recuperate before the next segment of your goal or journey begins.

Conversely, a valley can symbolize an emotional or spiritual loss of some kind, that you have descended from the heights into the valley of despair. How you feel about the valley will give you your clue as to which might apply to your valley.

Valleys are also symbols of prosperity and plenty in contrast to the austerity of the mountains.

Valleys symbolize an opportunity to strike out in a new direction, climb a different mountain from the one you are on or thinking about tackling, or the one you just climbed.

Valleys are places of growth and great productivity as well as beauty. They are strong symbols of descending, depth, contrast, and protection (see also DIRECTION/ Down).

What does the valley look like? Where is it located? What kind of mountains are near it? What geological forces caused it to form originally? Does this remind you of anything going on in your life at the time?

What grows in this valley? In which season of the year? What kind of animals live there? What kind of person would choose to live in this valley? Would you? Why, or why not? What does the valley remind you of? See also HILLS, MOUNTAINS, and any objects in the valley, e.g. FARM.

VEHICLE

As an archetype, any vehicle used for moving from one place to another symbolizes the Self and the current method of movement chosen to get where you want to go spiritually at the time. And a vehicle can also be telling you something about your emotional subtle energy body.

On a more worldly level, any type of vehicle is you (your physical body and personality), whether it's a bicycle, car, train, plane, ox cart, or chariot. Vehicles are the way you get around in your life, the method you prefer to get out and about, to get from one place to another and take an active part in life.

Your subconscious quite often prefers one vehicular symbol over another, so your dream vehicle can also be one of your key dream symbols over the years. Watch how it changes as you change — because it will. For instance, even if you always dream of a car, that car changes over time.

And while cars, trucks, trains, and buses are able to move over the earth and therefore symbolically more "physical," planes fly and ships float, and so are often symbolizing something less physically focused.

What type of vehicle is this? How is it different from the vehicle you use in your everyday life? How does it move around? What type of fuel does it run on? How is it different from all vehicles in its class?

Who is in control of the vehicle? Are there passengers? Why, or why not? What is the overall condition of the vehicle? What color is it? Why? Is it an automatic or manual shift? Why? Which do you normally prefer? Why?

Where is it going, where has it been? What is the vehicle made of? What is its path? What kind of surface is it moving over? How fast or slow is it moving? How does it feel to be in it?

How does the vehicle feel about being in your dream, meditation, or experience? If it could talk to you, what would it say? See also DIRECTION, ROAD.

AIRPLANE: The general definition of any flying vehicle is that you are beginning the process of awakening, literally flying to and in new levels of experience, and into space you have yet to master.

Airplanes are at home and at their best in the air. They are able to achieve flight against many odds, not the least of which is their own weight.

Airplanes are vehicles of both land and air. They travel at very high speeds, can carry many different cargos, and must have a very specific flight plan and schedule to maintain. Does this remind you of anything? This would also make a good pun. Which "Plane" are you on at the time? Or do you feel plain?

What type of an airplane is it? Is it on the ground, taking off, landing? Is the flight going well? Why, or why not?

What kind of weather is it flying into, and out of? Where are you in the airplane? Who is the pilot? What kind of passengers or cargo does it carry? Where is it headed? How would you like to fly in this airplane when you are awake? Why are you in a plane, and not a car or on foot? Do you like to fly? Why, or why not? See also FLY and Pilot below.

BOAT: Boats or ships symbolize safe passage across whatever the water symbolizes to you, assuming your boat is in no danger, of course; see WATER.

As an archetype, a boat or ship is an ancient symbol of the seat of the Higher Self, the causal body. In this context, the Soul floats upon the Sea of Life.

Boats are also frequently symbols of teachers, places of safety while you are learning, especially while you are learning spiritual lessons.

Boats were the vehicles of the sun and moon, responsible for transporting them across the sky. To the ancient Egyptians, the two boats of Ra (Sektet, the evening boat, symbolizing accumulating strength through the ascent toward Spirit, and Atet, the morning boat, symbolic of losing strength through the descent into Matter).

Boats also symbolize a place of safety while you are in deep water; see WATER. And boats and ships represent transitions, crossings from one environment to another.

Boats make for great puns. Have you just found your dream boat? Is your ship about to come in? Or have you missed your boat? Who is in the same boat with you? Are you one oar short?

What kind of a boat or ship is it? What shape is it? Who owns it? Where is it headed? What condition is it in?

Are you the captain, engineer, sailor, passenger? Why? How would the dream or experience change if your role changed? What is the main purpose of this boat? Who would use it? Why?

BRAKES: Using the brakes symbolizes your sense of control of the situation that is the subject of your dream, meditation, or experience.

Braking in your dream can be a fairly straightforward message to slow down in some part of your life or in some aspect of your growth. Or is some part of you afraid of your present forward movement?

Dreaming of brakes can also be a very strong health message. Are your brakes worn? Are they not working at all? What part of your body is symbolized by the brakes? What will happen if the brakes fail? What does this remind you of going on at the time?

Your dream may also, of course, be reminding you of information your subconscious has picked up about the brakes on your real vehicle. Had yours checked lately?

Brakes are also a good play on words, sometimes substituting brake for "break." If you can't or don't brake, will something break? Do you need to give someone a break?

How did you feel in your dream? What does it remind you of? Did you take control? Why, or why not?

CAR: A car often represents you and your feelings of personal freedom, how you are able to freely move around in your life.

Cars also represent your physical body, your personality, and your emotional subtle body.

Car also carries some of the ancient symbolism of chariot (see Chariot below), substituting the car's modern methods of movement for those of the horse. How many horse power does this car have? How many is it using?

How in control is the driver? Are you driving, a passenger, or taking a back seat to the driver and passenger? And how does this feel?

What kind of a car is it? How is it different from other cars? What color is it? Is it parked, moving, broken down, having problems?

Is anyone in the car with you? Who is driving? How do you feel about cars in general, what do they symbolize to you?

How easy is this car to handle? How fast or slow is it moving? Why are you traveling by car rather than by plane, horse, boat, train, bus, or walking?

CHARIOT: Chariots symbolize the human body as a vehicle. The driver of a chariot represents the mind, the intelligence, or the Spirit directing and driving the vehicle; the power of the horse symbolizes the spiritual energy and Will available or used at the time.

The qualities and real intentions of the driver are symbolized by the animals pulling the chariot; e.g., a chariot pulled by griffins symbolizes the solar, the spiritual, or purity, while Freya's cat-drawn chariot is lunar and magical. Doves draw the chariot of Venus, Cybele's chariot is powered by lions, Poseidon's by white horses or Tritons, Juno's chariot is drawn by peacocks, Zeus prefers eagles, Dionysos chooses goats or leopards, Vulcan likes dogs, and Pluto uses black horses.

The reins in the driver's hands symbolize the ability of the intelligence or mind to control the power drawing the chariot. So how you hold the reins will tell you how in control of the subject of your dream or meditation you are at the time.

Chariots drawn by white or golden horses are symbolic of attributes of sky deities who drive the sun-chariot across the sky.

And chariots were often battle emblems, especially of heros, victors in battle, and solar deities.

The two wheels of the chariot symbolize Heaven and Earth in perfect harmony, balance, and cooperating to accomplish a specific task.

PASSENGER: When you are the passenger in any type of vehicle, it generally symbolizes you are assuming a passive rather than an active role in the situation, that you are letting some other part of you or someone or something else take control and responsibility for getting you where you want to do. How you feel about being a passenger will give you your clue about whether this is a productive or unproductive thing at the time.

Passenger can also symbolize that you are not taking responsibility for your actions on a day-to-day basis, or that you would like not to have to do so.

But dreaming of being a passenger, or preferring to be one when you are awake, can also symbolize that you are very comfortable with the situation, and are that you are literally willing to go along for the ride, to see where the driver takes you, maybe even take a back seat concerning this particular situation. How's the view from where you are? Are you comfortable with the driver taking control?

Passenger can also be a great pun. Do you feel that you are being driven? Are you about to get taken for a ride? Are you taking a back seat? Do you deserve to be chauffeured about? Is it time to turn over the reins to someone else or some other part of yourself?

How does the passenger feel? Why has the passenger given over control of the vehicle? How do you feel about driving in general? What does this remind you of?

STEER: Steering is most often a symbol of authority, skill, and control. So if you are steering something in your dream or meditation, it often symbolizes that you are taking charge, or are ready to do so.

Steering can also be a dream pun, substituting one kind of steer (the action) for another (the animal). Or is someone steering you wrong, giving you a lot of bull?

What are you steering? Which direction are you headed? Is it difficult, or easy? What are you using to steer? What will happen if you lose control? How does it feel in the dream?

TIRES: Tires symbolize how safely and smoothly you are moving yourself (your vehicle and all it symbolizes) through life. How is the ride on or because of these particular tires?

A FLAT TIRE may be a message that you need to add more Spirit (air) to your support systems, or just that you need to slow down and get some rest, that you are in danger of having a blow-out from too much wear and heat.

IF MISSING A TIRE, it is often a symbol that you need to start looking for replacements, and that this time you might want to make sure they are steel belted and better suited to your vehicle and the environment. Or maybe you have outgrown the vehicle your tires are on altogether. Is it time to trade in your vehicle for one that better reflects who and what you are at the time?

But missing tires could also be telling you that some part of you feels that it does not have enough or adequate supplies or energy to move smoothly and effortlessly ahead. What may you have forgotten to check before you headed out?

Tires can also be a clear early health warning of some kind. What part of your physical body do your tires represent to you? What condition are these tires in?

And tires are also, of course, wheels and circles, with all the symbolism they both carry.

See also type of vehicle the tires are on, and NUMBER of tires.

TRUCK: Trucks are work vehicles, giving you many more options than cars for both the terrain they can cover and the load they can carry from one place to another.

What tasks was this truck designed to perform? How well is it performing this task? What color is the truck? Why? How would the truck be different if it were a different color?

What is its overall condition? Who maintains it? What kind of tires does it take? Who would want to own this truck? Why? How is a truck different from a car? What does this remind you of?

WHEELS: Wheels are extremely ancient symbols, showing up even in cultures that did not use the wheel. For instance, The four-spoked wheel has been dated back to early Neolithic times, and wheels are a common Maya and Aztec symbol even though there is no evidence they ever used wheels as labor-saving devices.

Wheels symbolize the various cycles of life, your support system for moving around in your life, and how smoothly or efficiently you are moving at the time of your dream, meditation, or experience.

Since wheels combine the symbolism of the circle with that of movement, wheels also symbolize the coming into being and passing away of something, in this case the subject of your dream or meditation.

As an archetype, wheels are one of the strongest sun symbols and are almost always associated with all solar deities, both male and female. Within this context, wheels represent the Wheel of Law or Wheel of Karma, the Wheel of Fortune, the Wheel of Life, and the Wheels of Chance, Time, and Fate.

As sun symbols, wheels also represent the movement of light through the darkness and through the entire Cosmos or Universe.

The wheel is also often associated with the lotus (in the East) and the rose (in the West) as the solar matrix, especially when used as a symbol of the Chakras. And the zodiac is also often compared to a wheel.

To the early Christians, the wheel symbolized God and Eternity. To the Buddhists, it symbolizes the many forms of existence and the teachings of the Buddha. And the golden wheel symbolizes spiritual power.

Another great pun, do you feel like you're just spinning your wheels? Are you a big wheel, or a small one? Who is wheeling and dealing? Did you just pop a wheely?

See also GEOMETRIC SHAPE/ Circle, and Tires above.

VICTIM

A victim most often symbolizes that some part of you feels that you are unwilling at the time of your dream, meditation, or experience to take personal responsibility for your own life and experiences.

Victims can also represent unrecognized strong feelings of being a victim, or of wanting to place someone else in the position of being *your* victim. Victims always find other victims; they always know instinctively who wants to play the victim-martyr game.

In any form of sacrifice, the sacrificer and the victim become one with each other and with the Universe, symbolizing the meeting of the Microcosm and Macrocosm and attainment of unity. Does this remind you of anything?

What kind of a victim is this? What part of you may be feeling victimized by which part? How is it being victimized? How can it break free?

Who is the victim and who is the villain? In what environment is the victimization being carried out? What kind of person would allow themselves to be this kind of victim? Why?

What kind of person would want to take advantage of this victim? Why? See also any object used to carry out the victimization.

COMMON VICTIM SYMBOLS:

CAPTIVE: A captive of any kind most often symbolizes that some part of you feels it is giving up its power and freedom to act to someone or something else, or to some other part of you, that it's hands are tied, it is helpless in the situation represented by your dream or meditation.

A captive or captives can be a strong clear message that you are feeling so much restriction in your emotions or your life that you are literally thinking or behaving like a slave.

Dream captives can also, of course, be a clear and direct message that you feel trapped in the situation represented by your dream.

And to be a captive can be telling you that you have given up personal responsibility for yourself, even at the level of the basic survival levels of food and shelter.

Dreaming of being a captive can also be a message that you are subconsciously resenting the fact that others expect you to be in control when you actually feel "all tied up," hampered, and just generally unable, unwilling, or inadequate at helping.

And a captive can represent a need or desire to capture the essence of the object or person being held captive. What would you like to trap and have at your disposal?

And a captive man or woman is often a symbol for your higher emotional nature that is latent (held captive) by your concentration on your lower more everyday feelings and desires. Is your captive male or female? Why? What part of you is that?

Who is being held captive? Why? What can they do about it? How does the captive feel? What kind of a person would hold this person or thing captive? Why?

How can the captive escape? How dangerous will the attempt be? What kind of a person would allow herself or himself to become a captive in these circumstances? What does the captive gain? What does he or she lose? How do you feel about that?

See also any object responsible for securing the captive; e.g., GUARD, ROPE.

MARTYR: Martyrs generally symbolize the parts of you which feel an exceptionally strong lack of self-love and respect. This feeling often is the driving force behind a strong need to sacrifice a part of yourself to some belief, person, organization, or situation, and just to be accepted or to relieve some deep inner feeling.

Most often, however, dreaming of a martyr is a message that you are spending too much time on others and not nearly enough on yourself. Remember that taking responsibility for others is one of the ways to avoid focusing on your own growth and fixing your own problems. The old Chinese curse of "May you live in interesting times" carries just this meaning.

But no matter what, dreaming of martyrs almost always is a strong message to accept responsibility for your own life, and to honor those you love by having enough

faith in them to let them to do the same.

Dreaming of a martyr can also be telling you that the ego part of you has a strong need to feel important, that you subconsciously feel that no one else can fix the subject of your dream, meditation, or experience but you, and that only you can save the situation.

Who is being martyred? Why? What part of you feels it is being sacrificed by or to other parts?

How is the martyrdom being carried out? Is any kind of ceremony involved? How would your dream be different if the martyr chose not to be the willing sacrifice?

Who will ultimately benefit from the martyrdom? How?

See also BLOOD if blood is present, CEREMONY/Sacrificial, DEATH, KILL, and PAIN if pain is present.

WAR

War almost always symbolizes some violent battle going on within yourself at the time.

But as an archetype, war and battle symbolize the natural cycles of disintegration and reintegration, the annihilation of disorder and the establishment of a new order out of the chaos of war.

And war is an ancient symbol for the ongoing battles between good and evil, the spiritual battle of humanity with its own nature as the Holy War. The spiritual warrior's battle is always with the nature of his or her own personality traits and desires.

Wars or battles are also strong symbols of the conflict between your mind and your emotions, your thoughts with your actions, your spiritually energized mental qualities against your physical passions, instincts, and the desires of your lower spiritual nature, as in the Biblical Jacob wrestling with the Angel.

It is also fairly common for men to dream of war, sometimes so graphically they even feel the bullet hit. Just remember that's it's all symbolic and trying to tell you something about how you feel at the time.

Who is fighting this war? What is the war about or over? What weapons are being used? How effective are they? What are the uniforms like? What does this remind you of going on in your life at the time?

Which side is going to win? Why and how? Where is the war taking place? Who started the war? Why? What will happen when one side triumphs over the other?

What role are you playing in this war? How do you feel in your dream? What does this remind you of that is going on in your life at the time? How are wars different from battles?

See also BLOOD if blood is present, CLOTHES/Uniform, DEATH if someone dies, DESTRUCTION, EMOTION, EXPLOSION, KILL, and any WEAPON used.

WATER

Water is an extremely complex symbol with one of the widest ranges of interpretations, depending even more than other symbols on how it is being used. Water can symbolize many things all at one time at different levels, and in fact rarely has just one interpretation.

Dreaming of water, however, often symbolizes, first, your emotional state at the time of the dream. But it can also be symbolic of your Spirit, your Consciousness, your life force and energy, your subconscious, the Creative Mother from which all life sprang — or any combination of these, depending upon the context of its use.

Water is traditionally the Mother of Creation, especially large bodies of water like oceans and seas. Water is the source of all potentials within physical existence. It can symbolize the Unmanifest, the very first form taken by Matter.

All waters are associated in some way with The Great Mother, with birth, the Yin (feminine) principle and qualities, the Universal Womb (the Cosmic Egg often floats on water), fertility, refreshment, cleansing and purifying, and the Fountain of Life.

Water is also associated with the continuity and yet constant change inherent within all physical life.

Water, like the grove, mountain and stone, can also symbolize the Cosmos in its entirety.

Water is ultimately uncontainable and ever-changing, and always only temporarily conforming to the container which holds it.

The color of the water, what type of water it is, how it is behaving, and who or what is on or in it will help you with your interpretation of this complex symbol. But take heart in that there is really no slick easy way to get to the heart of how you're using it, and that we all have the same problem with this particular symbol.

COMMON WATER SYMBOLS:

AGITATED: Agitated water often symbolizes some part of you which feels that decisions need to be made or something handled before you can calm your emotions.

Agitated water also symbolize the illusions in your everyday life. What is causing the disturbance in the water? What does it remind you of? How would things change if the water suddenly calmed?

This one makes a good pun. Are you in troubled waters? Are you about to get caught in a riptide? Who's making big waves or a big splash?

BATH: As a universal symbol, showers and baths represent mystical union, rebirth, renewal, and refreshment of your spiritual qualities, a call to remember who you are and why you are here.

Taking a bath or shower in your dream frequently symbolizes a cleansing and purification of some kind. But either one can also symbolize a need for relaxation, even a small sensual but allowable self-indulgence.

A bath or shower can also symbolize the renewal of a relationship, especially the relationship with emotional or spiritual forces (represented by the water).

When do you usually take a bath or shower? Under what emotional conditions? Why? How do you feel both before and after the bath or shower? What does this remind you of going on at the time?

Baths also make wonderful puns. Are you about to take a bath in a relationship or business deal? Who is all wet? With what are you being showered?

What is in this bath with you? What does the water look like? Why are you taking a bath at all? Where is the room or location where the bath is taking place located? Why?

Are there other people there? Are they paying attention to you, or oblivious of the whole thing? What does this remind you of?

How do you feel in your dream? Why? How is it different from, or the same as, you would feel if the same scene took place when you are awake? Why?

CALM: Calm water most often symbolizes that a decision has been made on the subconscious level, and that you are now literally calm and untroubled, that right now there is no more inner agitation.

Calm water can also be telling you that now it's okay to just relax and float, let what water symbolizes to you carry you gently on its surface, that things are going well and you should trust the natural flow.

But calm water can be telling you that some part of you is becoming bored, things are much too calm, so let's go shoot the rapids. And calm water can be telling you that you are too neutral right now about the subject of your dream or meditation and in danger of stagnating if you don't stir things up a little.

How do you feel about the calm water? What color is it? What is it a part of? What does it remind you of that is going on in your life at the time?

CLEAR: Clear water often symbolizes that you are in control of your life and emotions at the time of the dream or meditation, that you have nothing to hide and are clear about the subject or situation.

Conversely, clear water can also be telling you that you might want to begin to stir things up a little, that you have been too passive lately and are in danger of becoming too remote and self-contained unless you get moving again. How do you feel about the clear water? What color is it? Why?

CROSSING OVER WATER: Especially if the water is a river, lake, or sea, crossing over water is a strong symbol for the end of one form of life and moving on to another, the transformation inherent within life and death.

What is on the side you are leaving, and what are you moving toward? Why? What changes when you get across the water?

What kind of water is it? Calm, or rough? What color? What body of water is it part of? Why? How would your symbol change if you changed the water you are crossing over? What kind of vehicle or medium are you using to get across? Why? See also, BRIDGE, and VEHICLE/Airplane, Boat above if either is being used.

DEEP WATER: All deep water is and almost always has been connected with supernatural beings, beings especially close to the Mother of Creation.

Deep water is also often a strong symbol for the subconscious mind and the Collective Unconscious, and often associated with the dead.

This can also, of course, be a good pun. Are you getting into deep water? Are you in over your head? How do you feel about deep water in general? What color is it? Where is it? Why? What does this remind you of at the time?

DIRTY: Dirty water frequently symbolizes that your feelings, emotions, or thinking are unclear, slightly muddy.

Dirty water can also be an early health warning of some kind. What part of your body might the dirty water represent? Where is it flowing? Or is it backing up? What does this remind you of?

Where is the dirty water? How do you feel about it in your dream or meditation? What makes it dirty? What will it take to clean it

up? What does this remind you of? How will things change once the water is clean again?

DIVING INTO WATER: Diving into water usually tells you that you are searching for the ultimate mystery, the true meaning of life, or maybe just a deeper meaning of the subject of your dream or meditation.

It can also be telling you that you are now ready to get more than just your feet wet, that you're ready to dive into the subject or situation.

How deep did you dive? How did you feel? Is this an action you would take when you are awake? Why, or why not?

Into what are you diving? Head first, feet first, belly flop? What does this dive remind you of?

DROWN: Drowning in a dream is often a clear symbol that you are emotionally overloaded at the time and literally drowning in your own feelings, that you are going under. Take immediate action to relieve this stress, the first step of which is of course to own up to it.

Drowning can also symbolize physical, even spiritual, overloads (and, yes, you can get spiritual indigestion when you try to take in too much, too fast; give your physical body and mind time to catch up. Greed, after all, is greed — even in a good cause).

But drowning can also be a message to relax and just tread water for awhile, but to do it NOW. Stop struggling, don't be so intense or your muscles are apt to cramp and you'll go down needlessly.

But as a universal symbol, drowning represents the loss of the ego or Lower Self in the ocean of Unity or Cosmic Consciousness.

What are you drowning in? What has caused you to be drowning? Are there other people around? How are you dressed? Why are you drowning and not swimming or safely on board a ship?

How do you feel in your dream? How could you have saved yourself? What actions could you have taken that you did not, and how would that have changed this dream? What does this remind you of that is going on in your life at the time?

FLOOD: Floods almost always symbolize excesses of emotion, that you are feeling completely overwhelmed by them at the time of your dream, and that as a result some part of you feels strongly threatened and in danger for its very life; see Drown above.

As an archetype, a flood symbolizes the Waters of Truth pouring forth from human logic rather than from Spirit, and represents the first cause of erroneous thinking and opinions, one of our first steps away from Truth.

In the same vein, a deluge is an ancient symbol for the awakening of the human mind, but an awakening in ignorance and error, a mind out of control.

The symbolism of a deluge is found in literally all parts of the earth. But as a catastrophe, a deluge is never seen as final since it takes place under the sign of the lunar cycle and within the regenerating properties of water.

A deluge can destroy forms, but never forces or energies, always leaving open the potential for reemergence into a new form of life. Consequently, a deluge often symbolizes the final stage of any cycle, often coinciding with the astrological sign of Pisces.

Torrential rains always have some of the same symbolism of a deluge. Every kind of rainfall, in fact, symbolizes purification and regeneration of some kind; see also Rain below.

While floods symbolize the more violent, destructive qualities of water, throwing yourself into flooding water is an old symbol that you are ready to throw yourself into the Unknown, to caste your fate upon the waters.

Floods also represent the lunar aspects of water and the end of a particular cycle. Floods can cause death, but are also sources of fertilization and a chance to build new structures from the ground up, to begin all over again.

And a flood may be telling you that you feel out of control emotionally, and in danger of being swamped or swept away. Or maybe even that some part of you feels that you have too many dangerous passionate feelings. How long have you been treading water?

But floods not only destroy the old or the status quo, the prepare the way for the new, and in fact make rebuilding from scratch inescapable.

Floods also symbolize the aspect of water which devours without regard for anything but its own force and movement and buries everything in its path, moving first and quickest through the areas of least resistance. What part of your personality do you think this is?

And floods can represent a flood of ideas as they literally pour out from the source of Truth or from your own creative source.

What is the source of this flood? How do you feel it in your dream or meditation? What actions is it causing you to take that you might not otherwise have attempted?

What color is the flood water? What actions are you taking, or not taking, to avoid the flood? Are you in it, watching it, running from it?

What stage is your flood in? What is its flood level? When will it crest? What will things look like when the flood waters have receded?

Have you ever been in a real flood; if so, how is this flood the same as, or different from, that one? What does this flood remind you of that is going on in your life at the time?

See also DESTRUCTION, EMOTION/Danger, Fear if fear is present, and any object in, on, or around the flood water.

FOUNTAIN: A fountain most often symbolizes the flow of your life energy, your spiritual energy, your Kundalini energy (see SNAKE/ Kundalini), how well the *chi, ki, prana* is flowing and moving through and out.

Fountains also symbolize happiness or joy literally pouring out in a free-flowing display for all to see and enjoy.

As an archetype, fountains are common symbols as the Fountain of Life and the Fountain of Youth, both symbolizing fertility, renewal, the mother-source, and eternal life.

And fountains represent the sudden flow of knowledge or the opening of the "eye of the heart." The Fountain of Life is often found in Paradise flowing from the Tree of Life and is the source of the Four Rivers of Paradise.

FOUNTAINS IN THE CENTER of courtyards, squares, walled gardens, etc. symbolize the Cosmic Center, a source of living waters and eternal youth or immortality.

FOUNTAINS or JETS OF WATER COMING FROM A MOUTH symbolize the power of speech, the Word or Logos, instruction, and refreshment through these things.

FOUNTAINS OF LIGHT are symbolic of light and water which originate from the same source.

A SEALED FOUNTAIN is an ancient symbol of virginity.

THE HIGHER WATERS: The Higher Waters is an ancient term

symbolizing the world of unifying waters. The Higher and Lower Waters are usually associated with the Lesser and Greater Mysteries, which it is necessary to combine to create the One.

LAKE: Lakes are symbols of collected wisdom and are almost always considered Yin (female). Many magical feminine powers inhabited lakes.

And lakes were often called the "open eye of the Earth." Lakes within this context are symbols for the subconscious and intuitive aspects of the human mind.

But lakes were also inhabited by monsters who were able to lure human beings to their destruction through their hypnotic magical powers of illusion.

In ancient Egypt, a lake symbolized the Lower Waters; see Higher Waters above and Lower Waters below (no pun intended this time).

Lakes are also an old symbol for the limiting of Truth, since they are too small to hold large fish (the Self); see FISH.

Dreaming of ponds or lakes might also be a dream pun, as in "a big frog in a little pond."

Where is your lake or pond? What kind of a person would like to visit it? What kind of life lives in and around it? What colors are in and the lake?

How do you feel about it in your dream? Why is it a lake or pond and not a sea or ocean? See also COLOR of lake or pond, and any objects in or around the lake.

LIQUID: Liquids of any kind usually represent your fluidity, how easily you are "in the flow," and the flexibility of your emotions and beliefs at the time.

What kind of liquid is it? How is it different from other liquids? For instance, how is honey different from milk?

How sluggish or free-flowing is it? Why? How do you feel about it? What color is it? Is it drinkable? Why, or why not? Can you swim in it, float on it, take a bath in it? Why, or why not? See also specific liquid, such as BLOOD, FOOD, etc.

THE LOWER WATERS: The Lower Waters is an ancient symbol for the constantly changing material physical world.

The Higher and Lower Waters are usually associated with the Lesser and Greater Mysteries, which are necessary to create the One.

MUDDY WATER: Muddy water frequently symbolizes that you are feeling extremely unclear about the subject of your dream or meditation, and that if things don't clear up soon you might get stuck where you are.

Muddy water also represents, of course, a blending of earth with water, Matter with Spirit. What's the ratio of soil to water in the muddy water? What caused it to be muddy? How would things change if it were clean or clear? Why? What does this remind you of?

OCEAN: Oceans have always symbolized Universal Life, Cosmic Consciousness, the beginning of all life itself, the Mother of All, the subconscious mind, and the Collective Unconscious out of which the sun is continually reborn.

Oceans also symbolize inexhaustible vital, creative energy, Matter as Primordial Truth which brings forth all qualities and form out of the Absolute.

An ocean can also represent the range of moods and mystical powers of the human psyche.

And the ocean symbolizes perpetual movement and change, and the formlessness of water. It is symbolic of tremendous dynamic forces of energy, and all transitional states between the solid of earth and the formlessness of water.

To some authorities, the ocean also symbolizes unlimited illogic, and Consciousness dreaming its own dreams and being still asleep within its own reality, but still carrying the seeds of its possibilities. The ocean within this context represents the sum total of all possibilities of a particular Plane of Existence.

Oceans are also strong symbols of Woman with both her nurturing life-giving and destructive natures.

The ocean is also, of course, the home and mother of monsters of the deep. In general, water monsters symbolize emotions and fears at a much deeper level than any of your land-based monsters; see also MONSTER.

Oceans are deep rather than shallow, profound rather than superficial. They are dangerous but support and create life.

Conversely, an ocean can also represent strong, deep emotions and fear of the unknown or of any deep compelling emotions you have not yet experienced. Are you feeling "lost at sea," "out of your depth?"

What kind of life does this ocean support? How would you like to sail on this ocean when you are awake? Why, or why not? Is it calm, or stormy?

Where are you in relation to the ocean in your dream or meditation? What does this remind you of that is going on in your life at the time?

See also COLOR of ocean, and any object in or around the ocean.

OVERFLOWING WATER: A very common dream symbol, overflowing water frequently symbolizes an abundance of life, depending upon the kind of water overflowing.

Overflowing water can also symbolize overflowing emotions, or emotions that are not able to flow correctly because something is blocked, backed up, or stopped. Is the overflowing water clean, or dirty? How would changing its condition change your dream or meditation? What does it remind you of going on in your life at the time?

See also HOUSE/Bathroom, Toilet, and Flood above.

RIVER: Rivers generally symbolize the way you feel about how your life is moving at the time. But rivers also symbolize your personal spiritual journey and your "true destiny."

And rivers symbolize the twists and turns, the pools and eddies in your life at the time.

Rivers are ancient symbols for the journey between this life and the afterlife. They are also strong symbols of the flow of the world in its many manifestation, the passage and natural flow of life and time, and a return to the Source.

A river can also be a good pun. Are you about to cross over the river of no return? Are you paddling upstream, or going with the flow? Do you want to cry a river?

Is the river moving, or standing still? Which direction is it flowing? What color is the water? What lives or grows in this river? How do you feel about that?

Are you swimming, wading, floating, or in a boat? Is there a bridge across this river? Why, or why not? How easy is it to cross the river?

Is the river flooding? Does it have rapids, dams, or other obstructions or features? What kind of environment does it flow through? Why? See also COLOR of river.

COMMON RIVER-RELATED SYMBOLS:

FLOWING RIVER: A flowing river is the universal symbol for Time, transitoriness, and perpetual renewal. And a flowing river is your life, your energy, your thoughts, your stream of consciousness floating by. How well is the river flowing? What is it carrying with it? And, of course, what color is the water? Is it at flood stage?

THE FOUR RIVERS OF PARADISE FLOWING FROM ONE SOURCE: This is a symbol common to many cultures. The four rivers usually flow outward from the Tree of Life, from a single mountain or rock, or from the four cardinal points of the Earth, representing the four ages or four phases of development of humanity: birth, childhood, maturity, and old age.

GOING FROM ONE BANK OR SHORE TO ANOTHER: This is a strong symbol for an initiation or rite of passage.

It is also an ancient symbol for death and the beginning of a new life in a new form. But keep in mind that it is extremely rare to have a precognitive dream about your own physical death. Death, in the dream world, is almost 99.999% symbolic.

What is on the shore you are leaving, and what awaits you on the other shore? How do you feel in your dream or meditation? How is that different from, or the same as, the way you feel when you are awake?

MOUTH OF A RIVER: The mouth of a river has the same

symbolism as that of a door or gateway — it is the entrance to the Higher Mind through which your consciousness is able to perceive other dimensions of reality.

The mouth of the river is its source, its place of creation and perpetual birth.

In what environment is the river's mouth? Is it wide, narrow, large, small? Why? What flows from it? Who discovered it?

RIVER OF LIFE: The River of Life is in and symbolizes the Land of Divinity, the Macrocosm. It is the life force, the life energy sustaining all.

RIVER OF DEATH: The River of Death symbolizes the world of change, the Microcosm, and is in fact the only place where the River of Death can be found.

RUNNING WATER: All running water (e.g., fountains, springs, even faucets, etc.) are symbols of the Water of Life, the Living Waters, and the Fountain of Youth.

It is a common superstition that ghosts, demons, werewolves, and vampires cannot cross running water, and so running water can symbolize your protection from the unknown, supernatural, and things that go bump in the night.

Conversely, running water could be telling you that your emotions turned on high, especially if the running water will eventually cause flooding; see Flood and Fountain above.

SHOWER: Showers symbolize cleansing and purification by means of fast-moving water (and all that water symbolizes) which is capable of forcefully washing off the surface or outer layer. Showers are capable of refreshing both the body and Spirit with rapidly-moving energy instead of the slower method represented by a bath.

Showers are also good puns. What are you being showered with? How is a shower different from a bath? What kind of person usually prefers a bath to a shower? Why? What kind of water is coming out of the shower?

What kind of a room is it in? Are there other people around? How do you feel about it? Are they noticing you at all? How do you feel about showers in general? Is someone you know giving you a shower? Of what?

SURROUNDING WATER: Water surrounding anything (e.g., castle, island, etc.) Is an ancient symbol of the enclosing of a special or sacred space by the action and protection of Spirit.

Surrounding or enclosing water is almost always both protective and purifying, and rarely threatening.

What is the water surrounding? Does it make you feel safe or threatened? Why? What lives in the water? What would happen if the water were suddenly gone? How is it possible to get across the water? What does it remind you of?

WATER IN ITS ORIGINAL UNFORMED STATE: In many cultures, both ancient and modern, water is seen as the creator, the primal origin of all life. So any kind of water in its original and unformed state is symbolic of the immense potential and limitless possibilities at your disposal at the time, literally representing your primal source of energy and power.

Water in its original unformed state of being is also symbolic of all that is, was, and ever will be.

How will things change when the water takes a form or is contained? What do you feel its next form will be? What does this remind you of?

WATERFALL: The illusion of a consistent, solid form given by a flowing waterfall is a symbol for the true transitoriness and many illusions of life.

Waterfalls are symbolic of Yin (female) energy passing and energizing and in turn being energized by the Yang (male) energy of the cliff or mountain it is falling from. Many waterfalls throughout human history were sacred sites.

Waterfalls can also represent the free, unhindered flow of life, energy, Spirit, and anything else that water represents to you.

Waterfalls also represent a forceful generation of positive energy, or a need for it.

Pay particular attention to where and when the water changes as it gets closer to the drop off.

Where will it land? What will be the result? Who or what will benefit, and who or what might not like it?

What is the source of the waterfall? How high is it? How large? To what kind of an environment does the waterfall contribute? What happens if the water stops flowing? What does any and all of this remind you of?

WAVES: Waves symbolize the force and power of your emotions, consciousness, life force, and/or spiritual growth at the time of your dream or meditation — or all or any combination of all four.

Waves are water in precise measurable rhythm and motion, and therefore often symbolize freedom, change (either gentle or tumultuous, depending on the wave), illusions, and even uncontrollable and potentially destructive power and energy. Waves eventually wear away even the hardest stone.

Waves could also be telling you that some part of you feels out of control and tossed around by your emotions or some part of your life.

And waves make good puns. Who or what is causing waves? Or do you need to think about "waiving" something? Have you substituted a water wave for the wave of a hand, or the military Wave?

How large are the waves? What color are they? What is causing them? How do you feel about them in your dream or meditation? What will happen if they get larger, or smaller?

WELL: A well was often believed to be a passage to and contact with the Underworld. Many wells were healing wells and dedicated to The Great Mother in her many forms.

As an archetype, a well is a symbol of the Wisdom of God brought up from the depths of Eternal Truth. It is also a strong symbol for the Psyche and the Soul.

A well also symbolizes a natural reserve of power, spiritual and emotional energy, and a deep source of strength, wisdom, and the renewal of life.

And wells symbolize a need or deep desire to bring more magic into your life. Is your well a wishing well?

A CLOSED WELL symbolizes virginity, especially virginity to the point of self-imposed sterility.

DRAWING WATER FROM A WELL is symbolic of drawing information up from spiritual or psychic depths.

FALLING DOWN A WELL may be telling you that you are afraid of your own power or emotions. But falling down a well can also be telling you of a strong desire to make contact with your subconscious or the deeply hidden portions of your Soul or Spirit.

Conversely, falling down a well be telling you that some part of you feels so trapped or hemmed in that it is in danger of falling into a deep depression, a hole it will have trouble getting out of. See also TUNNEL, UNDERGROUND.

A WELL FED BY A STREAM symbolizes the union of male and female, the merger of your consciousness with your subconscious.

SACRED WELLS are doorways to other worlds or dimensions and are believed to possess magical and exceptional healing powers. For example, people still travel to Lourdes today.

WATER AND CLAY: Water and clay together symbolize Creation, the raw stuff of the Universe, with its unlimited potential to create form. Clay represents Matter, and when blended with the water of Spirit takes on a life of its own.

WATER AND FIRE: When depicted together, water and fire symbolize the two conflicting elements or dualities within the material world. While they remain in a state of conflict, they create heat and moisture, both of which are necessary for the continuation of life. If they merge completely, one will always extinguish the other.

Burning water symbolizes the union of these opposites in the process of consuming themselves.

WATER AND WINE: Water and wine together are ancient symbols of the blending of human nature with Divine nature, divinity immersed in and blended with humanity. See also ALCOHOL.

WALKING ON WATER: Walking on water is an ancient symbol for the transcendence of the conditions and limitations of the physical world. Many great sages and teachers throughout human history are attributed with this power.

WEALTH

Wealth of any kind most often symbolizes your accumulated wisdom and knowledge, your creative or spiritual powers, your feelings about wealth and money in general, and anything else you personally associate with wealth.

COMMON WEALTH SYMBOLS:

JEWEL: Jewels always symbolize something of supreme value, something very precious and rare, that you have achieved a special status or level of some kind.

Jewels can also represent a beloved person, idea, philosophy or teaching, even the Soul itself, especially if the jewels are glowing or radiating color or energy.

And no less an authority than Carl Jung believed that dreaming of jewels symbolized the various aspects of your Higher Self.

DIAMOND: Diamonds represent the Center of Consciousness shifted from focus on the personal ego to its original source of being.

And diamonds symbolize integrity of the highest order, faith, and fidelity and constancy in relationships. It is often referred to as the Gem of Reconciliation and was once believed to enhance the love between a husband and wife.

Diamonds also symbolize invincibility and fearlessness in action. In fact, the Greeks called diamond *adamas*, meaning invincible, while the East Indian cultures referred to it as "fragments of Eternity."

Diamonds are formed under enormous pressure over an unimaginable period of time, and have always represented the indestructible and invulnerability, and so, of course, symbolize the Eternal Soul.

EMERALD: Emeralds symbolize great wealth; physical, mental, and emotional stability; a raised consciousness; and protection. One of the oldest legends about emeralds is that they were brought to Earth from the planet Venus by "the Lord of the Flame." And like the ruby and diamond, emeralds were believed to change color when their owner was in danger.

GLOWING: Glowing jewels and stones symbolize the emerging True Self, the true essence of your Soul. What kind of a jewel is it? What does that tell you about yourself?

JADE: Jade symbolizes the balance of your emotions with your intellect. Jade also symbolizes peace, purity, and great good fortune.

And Jade sometimes symbolizes a karmic lesson of some kind, represented by the subject of our dream or meditation.

The ancient Chinese believed that Jade increased health and

longevity, and that it contained all five of the qualities necessary to create a civilized human being: Charity, Courtesy, Modesty, Justice, and Wisdom.

Jade also represents vital energy and cosmic forces. This precious stone was considered to be food and nutrition for immaterial and spiritual beings.

And to the ancients, Jade represented immortality and protection from decay, just one of the reasons it is found in so many ancient tombs all around the planet.

In Central America, Jade is the symbol of the Soul, the Spirit, and the Heart. Jade received its name from the Spanish conquerors who called it *hijade*, meaning "hip stone," since it was believed to relieve kidney problems and was worn on that area of the body.

PEARL: The pearl symbolizes the Soul, the Whole Self. Pearls also symbolize perfect peace, perfection, purity, the Yin qualities and energies, compassion, justice, gentleness, love, natural beauty, and great wisdom. And, of course, pearls are created in water.

One of the most interesting beliefs about natural pearls is that they can both generate and hold psychic energies, but will "die" if used or worn by an unhappy person. And in fact the normal "lifespan" of a pearl is approximately 100 tp 150 years, although some today are over 400 years old.

RUBY: Rubies symbolize the highest form of true love. The ruby always symbolizes enormous accumulated power and tremendous passion.

Ruby is also a symbol for a symbol, the Mystic Rose; see FLOWER/Rose.

Rubies have been symbols of mystical and magical powers for several millennia, and it was commonly believed that rubies could be used to pool and hold energy for use later. They have almost always been credited with heightening telepathic abilities.

It was also believed that rubies changed color when their owner was in danger, a belief common to many other precious stones, including diamond and emerald.

TURQUOISE: Turquoise symbolizes the ability to speak Truth, power, protection, the throat and 5th Chakra, and the spiritual path or Warrior's Way.

Turquoise also symbolizes a strong personal connection to the planet Earth. This semi-precious stone symbolizes your ability and willingness to speak your own personal truth from a position of integrity, even when you don't have all the pieces to the puzzle yet.

MONEY: Dream money generally symbolizes your security, safety, independence, freedom, social status, and personal power as it is generated from external sources.

Money is man-made and can only be obtained from other people.

Only human beings put any value in money or how much they can accumulate.

Money also represents anything at all of value, and especially the value human beings place on objects that can be traded for money.

But money can represent the equal and fair exchange of personal values and energies.

Traditionally, to dream of coins meant that small changes were on the way, or was a warning to "watch the pennies." To dream of bills or paper money meant that large changes were on the way. Notice the numbers on the bills or coins and look up the definitions of the numbers themselves.

If money is popping up a lot as a symbol for you, now is the time to begin working on this lesson. And take heart; there's no one on this planet who doesn't have the same lessons.

How do you feel about money in general? How do you feel about the money in your dream or meditation? Is there ever enough money? Why, or why not? How much is enough for you?

What type of currency it being used? What is it made of? Who has it? For what can it be exchanged? What does this remind you of?

TREASURE: Treasure often symbolizes your buried, undiscovered, unused creative talents, your underground power, your own personal slice of the Divine spark, the "treasure buried in a ruin" of legend and myth.

Dreaming of treasure can also be a symbol for your search for earthly treasure, wealth, and power, and/or your search or quest for spiritual knowledge and wisdom.

It is common for treasures to be guarded by menacing animals or mythical monsters like serpents, dragons, the Gorgon, the Hydra, etc.

What are the components of this treasure? Did you manage to find it in your dream or meditation? Who buried it? How did you hear about it? Who or what guards it? How can this treasure be used when you bring it into the light? See also any object guarding the treasure.

WEAPON

Weapons, like tools, are extensions of the physical body and personal power.

A weapon of any kind almost always tells you that you are ready to or already are using your energy and power with great deadly force and determination, especially if hunting is involved.

A weapon can also represent a hidden desire or need to control or defend the subject of your dream or meditation.

Weapons, however, also represent protection in the face of great danger and against enormous odds. What part of you may be feeling that it needs defending by extraordinary means? From what other part of you?

What is your the weapon? How is it being used? Who owns it? What kind of a person would pay money to own this weapon? Why?

How do you feel about the weapon in your dream? How do you feel about it when you wake up? What does it remind you of?

How would the dream change if you changed weapons? See also ATTACK, EMOTION, WAR

COMMON WEAPON SYMBOLS:

ARROWS: Arrows are ancient symbols of lightning, rain, virility, and fertility. An arrow also represents the Higher Self as a ray of the Soul.

And arrows represent war and the qualities of personality usually attributed to a warrior.

Arrows are strong phallic symbols, representing the piercing, forceful, outgoing energy of the Yang qualities. They are strong solar symbols, representing the rays of the sun.

ARROWS SHOT FROM A BOW symbolize the consequences of your actions which cannot be taken back once released.

THE FLIGHT OF AN ARROW is symbolic of the ascent to the heavens, or the path your actions are taking at the time.

A HEART PIERCED BY AN ARROW symbolizes the union of they symbolism of the arrow with that of the heart, the union of Yang and Yin, Mind with Emotions, and of course the sweet piercing pleasure-pain of love.

A FEATHERED ARROW symbolizes a flight to heaven by transcendence of the material state of being.

BOW AND ARROW: Symbolically, the bow is Yin (feminine) and the arrow Yang. The bow and arrow together symbolize spiritual Truth which can bring down even the high, can raise the low, and supply physical and spiritual needs.

They also represent fertility and offspring, and personal strength, skill and ability.

To the Buddhists, the bow is mind which sets loose the arrows of the five physical senses. And to the Hindu, the human mouth is the bow, the arrow shot from it is the sound of the eternal *OM* as it penetrates the ignorance of sleep.

And the *OM* can also represent the bow from which the arrow of ego speeds back to the One, the true target.

The Japanese and Islamic technique of shooting an arrow at a target while blindfolded symbolizes the ability to let go of the ego's need to direct and control.

And arrows shot from a bow can symbolize the consequences of your words and actions which cannot be taken back once released.

The bow itself also symbolizes the crescent moon, personal will power, your worldly power, and the power of God. It is also symbolic of the vital life energy and power, capable of precisely aiming and hitting its target.

GUN: A gun most often symbolizes immensely powerful, explosive, masculine (Yang) energy, and for this reason is often a symbol for sexual energy.

But guns can also be a warning about any unacknowledged lethal anger or energy building up to potentially explosive levels. Guns shoot other objects out of them at extremely high speeds through the process of internal explosion.

Guns are an impersonal form of violence since is it not necessary to touch or even be close to someone to use a gun effectively.

Guns give warnings of danger or potential threat, and can be effective deterrents when used wisely. Is the gun keeping something at bay? Is it protecting, or threatening? How effective is it?

Guns are also good puns. Are you loaded and ready for action? Are you being asked a loaded question? Who or what is holding a gun to your head? Is someone about to make your day?

If you or someone in your dream has been shot, which part of the body has been injured? And what does this remind you of? See also SHOT.

What type of gun is this gun? What kind of bullets does it use? Who it holding it? Where is it aimed? Who will pull the trigger? What does this remind you of? How do you feel about the gun in your dream? How do you feel about guns in general? Why? What kind of person likes guns? What kind of person hates them? And what does all of this remind you of?

KNIFE: Knives are tools for cutting away, trimming, transforming, creating or destroying, sacrificing, and for preparing food for nutrition. But knives also wound, disfigure, and kill.

Traditionally, a knife is a symbol for the personal will which can either cut away desires or to facilitate progressive new growth by pruning back or cutting out the old or out of control growth.

Knives are also used to facilitate healing in the physical body. And a knife is sometimes used symbolically as a substitute for the tongue.

In ancient Egypt, the pharaoh's dagger within its sheath was symbolic of the Soul or Spirit sheathed by its physical body.

How the knife is being used and who is using it will help you find your personal interpretation. How is this knife different from other knives? Who owns it? What is it made of? What kind of a person would normally like this knife? Why? How do you feel about knives in general? How do you feel about the one in your dream? Why? How are knives different from guns? How are knives different from swords? What does this remind you of going on in your life at the time?

SWORD: Swords almost always symbolize power (both personal and spiritual), Truth, honor, justice, protection, and the strong cutting power of the mind and intellect. Swords also symbolize powerful extensions of your physical arm.

Swords are power tools for shamans, priests, heros, heroines, and warriors, belonging to the same archetype as the wand and the staff.

A sword is created by human beings, symbolizing your ability to be developed from raw materials through conscious training, effort, and skill.

Often, the sword symbolizes the Mind which knows how and when to make the cut. And swords are related to a mastery of an active imagination and intellect.

Swords can also be a purely sexual symbol, making them good puns. Who's the swordsman?

And there are many magical swords in myth and legend.

What type of sword is it? What is it made of? Who crafted it? Who uses it? Why? What was it originally designed to be used for? How well is it carrying out that function?

Who would like to own this sword? Why? How heavy is it? How easy is it to use? Where is it when not in use?

WEATHER

Weather in a dream or meditation represents the state of your emotions and the way your life and energy is moving at the time, and how you feel about it.

The weather is a strong factor in creating your dream environment and the environment and tone of your dream will change as the weather changes. And remember that the environment and landscape set the emotional tone for the dream and meditation. You never choose an environment just because it fits or looks good — it's all symbolic.

Weather can also be a great pun. It something or someone as unreliable and changeable as the weather? Will you be able to weather your storm? How about "whether" for "weather?"

COMMON WEATHER SYMBOLS:

CLOUDS: Clouds are ancient symbols of fertility, blessings from the Life Force of gods, good works, compassion which can cover and protect all things, and the unseen aspects of Divinity.

Clouds were held by the ancients to be the dwelling places of the gods, especially clouds surrounding high places.

And clouds represent concealment, and since they both protect and obscure the view, they symbolize the penetrating light of the gods shielding you from this all-consuming light until you can withstand its intensity.

Clouds also symbolize the mist, itself representing the intermediate world between Form and Non-Form, the place and time just prior to taking physical shape.

In ancient China, clouds that dissolved in the sky were a symbol of the necessary transformation to which all who desired to be wise must submit in order to dissolve (or control) their earthly personalities and enter Eternity.

The Five Clouds of Fortune (clouds colored by five colors) were considered peace symbols, since they were believed to be created by the union of Yin and Yang.

To the early Christians, clouds were the throne of God, especially in connection with the Last Judgment. And in Islam, a cloud symbolizes the inscrutability of Allah.

And in many pantheistic belief systems, clouds are fertility symbols which only give up their life-giving waters when struck by thunderbolts.

On a more earthly level, clouds and rain were often used in erotic literature to refer to sexual intercourse, again representing the union of male and female energies.

Clouds are also good puns. What is chasing away the clouds? What is clouded over? Is your cloud cover good, or obstructing your view? Are you feeling partly cloudy at the time?

How do you feel about clouds in general? What kind of clouds are in your dream? Are they calm, or stormy? Are they stationery, or moving? Why?

Are the clouds shielding you from a too-intense sun (light), or keeping you from it? How does it feel to be a cloud in your dream? If it could write its own dialogue, what would it say to you?

AN ANGEL OR PERSON IS STANDING ON A CLOUD, symbolizes the celestial, heavenly qualities of the person or being.

A HAND EMERGING FROM A CLOUD symbolizes Divine omnipotence, a being who is all-powerful.

COLD: Feeling cold sometimes symbolizes an unwillingness by some part of you to change and get moving, that your energy is just moving too slow.

Dreaming of cold can be a message that you are cutting yourself off from your emotions and feelings, especially when ice is involved. Dream cold can also symbolize that some part of you feels isolated from you or from other people, literally left out in the cold.

And this can be a direct early warning health message that you are in danger of catching a cold, especially if some type of attack or invasion is a part of the dream. Do you need to beef-up on your vitamin C, rest, and general nutrition?

Human beings also keep things cold to preserve them, to keep them from spoiling, and sometimes just to enhance their taste. It your cold really a frozen delight of some kind?

In the metaphysical world, cold often announces the approach of inferior slower moving energies, the theory being that these energies have to siphon off existing heat just to penetrate the physical world at all. It is this type of energy-stealing which results in the famous cold spots in haunted houses, for instance.

Cold is also a metaphysical term used to describe interior messages from psychic sources given to the public without any preparation or previous notice to your guides or helpers. To give a "cold" message or reading is believed by some sources to attract only energies that remain close to the Earth, rather than those from "higher" dimensions.

What is causing the cold? How do you feel about it? What kinds of life forms would flourish in this cold? What would happen if the cold suddenly turned warm? See also FOOD/Ice Cream, and Snow and Hot below.

FOG: As an archetype, fog represents the Primal Substance of the physical world of Matter.

Fog frequently symbolizes something that has not yet taken shape or something still partially hidden from view, the indefinite, and a transition from one condition or state to another.

And fog can also symbolize your unwillingness to look directly at subject of your dream or meditation.

But fog can be a symbol of protection, since it can both keep dangerous and frightening things from seeing you, and you from seeing them. For instance, an old proverb tells us, "Do not curse the fog if it is hiding you from a man-eating tiger."

Fog also symbolizes the fantastic, the unreal, and all manner of hidden, ephemeral things.

Fog is composed largely of water, and fog muffles and makes it difficult to tell with accuracy where a sound is coming from.

And dreaming of fog could be a message that you now need rest, especially mental rest.

Fog can be a direct message that you "really don't have the foggiest idea," or that you are not clearly focused on the direction in which you want to be going or the lesson on which you should be working at the time that you are literally "walking around in a fog."

How do you feel about this particular fog? How do you feel about fog in general? See also SMOKE, WATER.

HURRICANE: A hurricane, tornado, or cyclone most often symbolizes that you feel caught up by an emotional storm which literally has the power to blow you away.

These types of storms are bigger and stronger than you are, are caused by events outside of your control, and can generally be survived only if you take appropriate action and wait for it self out or move on.

And these intense storms can be telling you that sudden, drastic, life-changing things are coming straight at you. How do you propose to handle them? Will it blow you off course, or just create new beginnings for you by the destruction of your former way of living? Or are you in the eye of a storm?

But strong wind storms of any kind are also symbols of strong, uplifting sources of energy (quite often spiritual) which can carry you to new places and in almost any direction, even into totally new ways of living and being. The cyclone that lifted Dorothy and Toto from Kansas to the Land of Oz is a good example of this kind of symbolism.

What actions are you taking in your dream or meditation to survive this storm? How do you feel about the storm? Do you have personal experience of a hurricane, tornado, or cyclone?

Are there any colors involved? What do you think about them? Do they remind you of anything going on in your life at the time?

See also Lightning if any it present, Rain, Rainbow, WATER if present, and any objects you use to protect you from the hurricane or severe wind storm.

LIGHTNING: Lightning has a long tradition for symbolizing the active Spirit, the Will of God, and the sudden, searing Awakening of the Soul.

Lightning is symbolic of fertilizing and cleansing, as well as destruction. It can both wound and heal, but it always makes changes in that which it passes through.

Lightning has the ability to transform through instantaneous, searing, shattering energy and power. Lightning also represents

flashes of insight or intuition obtained and experienced through special states of contemplation or meditation.

And it represents sudden, unexpected, often overpowering inner changes.

To the ancients, to be struck by lightning was to be instantaneously transported to the heavens. To shamans, it symbolized instant and total illumination. And lightning was a Manichean an emblem of the Virgin of Light.

And lightning symbolizes spiritual illumination, sudden revelation, instantaneous realization of Truth, the destruction of ignorance, fertility, and masculine Yang power.

Lightning also symbolizes enormous supernatural and psychic powers and energies. And lightning was often used as an omen, predicting both good and bad things to come.

Lightning is connected to all storm deities, and often depicted by a zig-zag, a trident, an axe, a hammer, a dorje, an arrow, and even a bird of prey.

Lightning is also one of the 3rd or Solar Plexus Chakra symbols; see CHAKRA/3rd.

In some Native American traditions, lightning is one of the Thunder Beings, representing the fire sticks as they create a bridge between Father Sky and Mother Earth.

And lightning symbolizes the awesome, uncontrollable power of Nature.

Dream lightning may also be a message that you are being "too cool," that there is a need for a sudden, jolting change in your attitudes, thinking, behavior, and way of being. The Tower card in the ancient tarot carries much of this kind of symbolism.

And lightning can be one of several wonderful puns. Are you causing a lot of static about something? Have you been struck by lightening? Is lightening about to strike twice in the same place? Do you need to be hit by a bolt from the blue before you get it? Have you just been struck by the white flash?

How do you feel about lightning in general? Are you afraid of it? What color is this particular lightning? What form does it take: vertical, horizontal, ball?

What has it struck, or what or who is it about to strike? How will your dream or meditation object be changed after lightning strikes it?

Is there thunder or a storm accompanying the lightning, or has it literally come out of the blue? What does all of this remind you of that it going on in your life at the time?

See also DESTRUCTION, FIRE, LIGHT, and Thunder below.

RAIN: Rain most often symbolizes a renewal and rejuvenation through cleansing, new or continued growth, refreshment, and Spirit supplying life to all it touches. Rain creates the environment required for the continuation of growth and life.

Rain is an ancient symbol for Truth, especially Truth pouring down and influencing the human emotions and spirit. And rain symbolizes the effects of Heaven upon the Earth, and is always one of the Divine blessings.

Rain symbolizes revelations coming from above (both intellectual and spiritual), and the fertilizing effects of Father Sky upon Mother Earth.

To ancient cultures, rain causing a flood symbolized the flood of Truth inundating the errors of the lower mind, errors in thinking which cannot stand against the power of Truth. See also Flood above.

RAINBOW: Rainbows are very ancient symbols indeed, and used by virtually every culture on this planet.

In general, rainbows symbolize harmony, restored balance, happiness and good health, and Divine promises and covenants, especially the promise of a new beginning or way of being.

Rainbows are always strong symbols of transformation, the communication between Heaven and Earth, and the harmony between all states of Consciousness.

In most cultures, rainbows are the bridge between this world and some form of celestial paradise, and the throne of the celestial gods.

The colors of the rainbow symbolize not only the color itself but the movement of Consciousness through the various levels of growth each color represents. For example, we can see the color red because its vibratory movement is the slowest on the human color spectrum, and the color violet because it vibrates the fastest.; see COLOR.

Rainbows symbolize a time of peace and calm after a devastating storm, and can be a message that you have weathered your personal storm after all, or a promise that you soon will, that all is or soon will be well.

As an archetype, rainbows symbolize the Higher Mental Planes forming the bridge between our higher (spiritual) and lower (physical) natures.

Rainbows are caused by reflections of light (Spirit) within drops of water (the Self and Truth). Rainbows are also associated with the Rainbows are the Celestial Serpent in many cultures, the serpent who is the guardian of great and magnificent treasures; see WEALTH/Treasure.

To the Buddhists, rainbows represent the highest state attainable in the realm of Samsara before attaining the clear light of Nervana.

To the ancient Chinese, rainbows were sky dragons, while to the Greeks, they were a manifestation of the goddess Iris, the winged messenger of the gods (especially the gods Hera and Zeus).

To the Hindu, the rainbow body was the highest yogic state attainable in the realm of Samsara, and the rainbow itself is the Bow of Indra.

And to the early Christians, the rainbow symbolized pardon and the reconciliation between God and humanity.

What did your dream or meditation rainbow look like? How big was it, how much sky did it cover? What caused it to appear? What colors were in it?

In which landscape or setting did you place it? Why? What does it represent to you within the context of your dream, meditation or experience? Is there a pot of gold at its end? Why, or why not?

SNOW: Snow symbolizes purity, peace, innocence, truth, and a fresh start and clean beginning.

Snow also symbolizes spiritual purification, especially when the snow is pristine, untouched and uncontaminated.

Snow is an ancient symbol of Truth solidified and therefore still latent and as yet unexpressed. Ice and frost share much of this same symbolism.

But dreaming of snow can symbolize that you are in danger of letting your emotions get frozen and cold, especially if objects are frozen in your dream, like water for instance. How is water as snow different from water as rain?

Dreaming of being trapped in or by snow may be telling you that some part of you feels trapped, snowed in, buried under heavy thoughts or emotions, even though on the surface everything may appear sparkling and full of the potential for fun. But if you happen to like being snowed in, the meaning would be just the opposite. And it could be telling you that you need a rest, it's time to hibernate, chill out.

Snow also represents any current problems you feel are insurmountable or a will be a real mess or chore to clean up. But again, only if you dislike dealing with snow.

Snow, of course, makes a great pun. Who is trying to snow you? Is some part of you feeling snowed under? And, of course, there are different types of snow — legal and otherwise.

In general, how do you feel about snow? What color is this particular snow? Where are you in relation to it? Why?

Is it freshly fallen, or turning to slush? Are there any tracks in the snow? What kind? Is it a heavy snow, or light? Wet, or dry? What actions are taking place on or in the snow? See also Cold above, COLOR of snow, SEASONS/Winter, and any objects in or around the snow, like TREE/Snow-Covered.

STORM: Dreaming of a storm or a storm warning often tells you that deep and potentially life-altering inner changes are about to take place, and how the various parts of you feel about these changes at the time. These dynamic changes are approaching from outside your normal range of control, or some part of you feels they are.

Storms also represent the enormous energy and power of your unexpressed anxieties, fears, and other emotions, both productive and unproductive, depending upon how you feel about storms in general and this storm in particular.

Storms also represent sudden, even violent, outbursts of emotion and desire, your passions, and your very strongest feelings and reactions

And storms can symbolize extreme mental and psychological emotional agitation and turmoil.

Storms are forceful, basic and elemental, and therefore also represent your innate instinctual nature, your primal energies, and your natural creative and psychic powers.

Storms also make wonderful puns. Is it the quiet before the storm? Who or what would you like to storm? Would you like to go storming out of something? Are you creating a tempest in a teapot?

THUNDER: Since thunder always follows lightning, to the ancients thunder was the Voice of God, and one of the Divine attributes. Thunder also represented the Divine Will of God, especially expressing God's displeasure on the Lower (physical) Planes of Existence.

As an archetype, thunder represents thoughts, beliefs and opinions, often erroneous and out of control, and passions disrupted by the Voice of God to remind you to develop better states of being as an individual.

Many thunder deities have assistant smiths who do the actual forging of lightning and thunder with clubs, hammers, etc. For instance, Thor is often called "the Hammer of Odin."

In some Native American cultures, Thunder is one of the Thunder Beings who announces the union between Father Sky and Mother Earth, and tells of the beauty and power of their love for one another.

And thunder often symbolizes any forcibly contained or suppressed anger and any other deep passionate emotions.

How do you feel about thunder? What is causing it in your dream? Is it also raining or storming? What does the sound of thunder remind you of that is going on in your life at the time? See also BELL, ROAR.

WHIRLWIND: The whirlwind is an ancient symbol and represents the vibrant evolution of the Universe. Whirlwinds also symbolize vortices, energy points, and rapid change charged by these energy forces.

And it is often a whirlwind which announces the imminent approach of a divinity.

As a Universal Symbol, a whirlwind represents resonating vortices within the atoms of both the Higher and Lower Planes of Existence as they are generated and set in motion by spiritual energy.

Whirlwinds within this context are symbolic of the chaos which gives birth to the evolution of the True Self. And since all things are interdependent, this evolution greatly affects everything around it.

And the feeling of being caught in a whirlwind is often reported by people who experience out-of-body dreams; see Glossary/OBE.

And whirlwinds make wonderful puns. Do you feel caught up in a whirlwind, swept off your feet, about to get blown away by an uncontrollable energy?

WIND: As an archetype, wind symbolizes Spirit energizing all it touches at the material level; is it *chi, prana,* Divine energy, the vital breath of the Universe. It is the wind as Divine power which energizes the mental aspects of the Soul in order for the lower (physical) vehicle to be prepared for the Soul's re-energization.

Wind also symbolizes the power of Spirit to sustain life and hold it together.

And wind itself is sometimes symbolized by a fan or wings.

Throughout human myth and legend, winds are messengers of the gods and often the heralds of an approaching divinity, especially a whirlwind; see Whirlwind above.

The wind is invisible and intangible, elusive, transient, changes direction quickly and without warning, is always moving, and can be both energizing and destructive, depending upon its speed and content.

Wind makes strange and inexplicable noises, wears away the strongest mountains and structures, moves and even sometimes picks up parts of large bodies of water, tears down and then builds up again in totally new forms.

WHISPER

The word we translate as whisper, could just as easily be translated as "small, still voice," and within this context, a whisper represents a message from the greater you, your Higher Self.

The ancients believed that ghosts and spirits spoke to human beings in whispers, and almost all supernatural beings of any kind were identifiable by their whisper-soft voices.

And a whisper in your dream may be telling you that you have difficulty in or fear of a more open, direct communication, that you aren't comfortable with speaking up, raising your voice. Or, conversely, that you are much too vocal in your opinions and ought to soften and tone it down a little so that it's easier for others to hear.

A whisper can also represent your fear of what others say about you, or of what some part of you thinks about other parts or of other people. Within this context, your dream whisper could be your own conscience trying to get through to you. Are you listening when you are awake? Why, or why not?

Whispers also make great puns. What is being whispered in the wind? Do you have an angel or little devil whispering in your ear? What should be whisper soft?

Who is doing the whispering? What is being whispered, and why? Why is there a need or desire to whisper rather than speak in a normal voice?

What will happen if the whisper changes to normal levels of speech or to a shout or scream? See also BODY/Mouth Throat, Tongue, SECRET, YELL.

WHISTLE

Whistling is an old symbol for attracting the attention of totem and sacred animals. There is a taboo against whistling in many primitive cultures.

It was a common archaic belief that women who whistled practiced witchcraft and could cause storms, could literally whistle up the wind, not to mention the devil.

Whistling, of course, today almost always means someone who is so happy they just have to let it out. And whistling represents appreciation. Whistling is sometimes used as a code and signal to those who can understand the coded message.

Who or what is doing the whistling? For what reason? How do you feel about whistling in general? Do you ever whistle? When? What does this remind you of?

WILL, Last

Dreaming of a last will and testament almost never symbolizes an actual physical death. Wills generally symbolize getting your material affairs in order, taking inventory of your talents and accumulated knowledge and wealth, and even a desire to now share your assets with others.

A will can be a message from some part of yourself to review your life up to the time of the dream or meditation, re-evaluate your priorities and get them in order, review what you would like to accomplish in this lifetime while you still have the time.

Wills are also a way for some part of you to tell the rest that you are paying far too much attention to the acquisition of material values and things, and not enough to real assets. And, of course, once you have your material affairs in order, you are freer to concentrate on non-material things.

And will can be a good play on words. Are you giving your will away? Is someone trying to manipulate or influence your will? Or are you trying to control others through your will?

Whose will is it? Why was it prepared? What kind of paper is it on? Who were the witnesses to it? Who drafted it? Who will benefit from it? How do you feel about wills in general? How do you feel about this will? Why? Why do human beings have wills? See also CEREMONY, DEATH, LAW.

WILL, Human

Human will, often referred to by the ancients as the Will of Mankind, represents the spiritual center of relative reality as it exists in the lower mind of illusions. It is from this center of Will that higher choices can arise and then manifest.

The Lower Mind itself is symbolic of human passions and desires which are not yet properly directed, while the Higher Mind represents these same desires and passions after they have been transformed by the awakened Soul.

WORM

Worms very often symbolize the parts of yourself you are not willing to look at, things you literally do not want to handle or touch, depending upon how you feel about worms in general, of course.

As an archetype, the worm symbolized decay, death, dissolution, and the element of earth.

And the snake and serpent were often referred to as the Great Worm; see ANIMAL/Snake.

Worms are also, however, used to tempt fish to grab the hook, and worms are superb at aerating the soil. Birds love them and spend a lot of time listening for them. Does any of this remind you of anything?

Worms also make good puns. Who is opening a can of worms? Is someone or something trying to worm its way into your life? Is some part of you using another part as bait? To hook what? Is there a worm in your life?

How do you feel about worms in general? How do you feel about these particular worms? Why are they there at all? What actions are they taking?

If they could talk, what would they like to say to you? What color are they? How it this the same as, or different from, the natural color of worms?

X

X is a symbol for the inversion of a thing. It is also one of the many cross symbols, representing perfect balance and completion through perfect balance; see GEOMETRIC SHAPE/Cross. X was the Cross of St. Andrew, for example.

X also represents an unknown ingredient or quantity. And, of course, buried treasures are marked by an X on a map.

X is the Roman numeral 10; see NUMBER/10. And people who could not read or write signed their name with an X, they "made their mark."

And X's make great puns. X marks the spot. Have you just made your mark? Are you dealing with an unknown? What is your X factor? Should your dream be X-Rated? Are you sending kisses to someone? Crossing something or someone off your list?

X-RAY

X-rays often symbolizes a strong desire to examine the subject of your dream or meditation from the inside out, to be literally see into or through someone or something, to get the full story.

It could also, of course, be an early health warning of some kind. What is being x-rayed? Does it remind you of any part of your physical body?

X-ray can also be a good pun. Who has x-ray vision? Or are you being zapped by an X ray from outer space?

Z

ZODIAC

The zodiac is an ancient symbol for the cycles of life through which the Soul is able to complete its development, the spiritual journey and quest.

The Soul, the in-dwelling Self (symbolized in the zodiac by the sun), advances along its way on a spiral course. Its cyclic progression is symbolized by the twelve signs of the zodiac, each successive stage of its learning represented by each of the twelve signs.

The zodiac relates to human life through the Archetypal Man, and each part of the zodiac is a stage of development which relates to the whole. Each sign symbolizes a particular kind of human experience for our progression and growth, and ultimate return to the center, the sun.

The zodiac is approximately 18 degrees wide, the sun traveling completely through it once each year. It is divided into 12 constellations of stars, and appears the same to virtually all locations on Earth, although the 12 images in the constellations have been seen and named differently by various cultures. For example, what we see as Cancer, the Chinese see as the Cat.

Many authorities believe that the zodiac is responsible for the symbolism of the Wheel of Life and other cosmic wheels.

In astrology, the various constellations correspond to various life forms. The astrological signs form a connection between many systems using symbols; e.g., alchemy and medieval medicine.

The 12 animals of the zodiac even show up in early Christian art, and symbolized, among other things, the passing of Time and the Divine which is beyond all change.

The 12 signs of the zodiac also make for some great puns, so watch carefully.

What part of the zodiac have you dreamed or experienced? What does it symbolize to you? What kind of people are interested in astrology? How do you personally feel about it? Why?

ZOO

A zoo generally symbolizes the variety of personality changes you have available to you at the time of your dream or meditation, especially any parts that feel naturally wild and caged.

A zoo can also be telling you that some part of you, or many parts, feels that it has been put on public display for the sole purpose of entertainment, even that you are trapped by the curiosity and superficial scrutiny of others.

And a zoo is a good pun, as in "This place it really a zoo!"

What is in this zoo? Are the animals caged? If not, how are they contained, and why do they need to be contained, kept from the everyday life of the general public? Is it to protect the animals or the people?

Which zoo animals are your personal favorites in waking life? Why? Which ones do you rarely take time to see? How do you feel about zoos in general? How do you feel about this zoo? How is it the same as, or different from, any zoo you normally visit?

What kind of person would like to work in this zoo? Why? Who would pay money to see it? How do you feel about that?

See also ANIMAL in the zoo, CONTAINER, VICTIM/Captive.

Glossary

DREAM SYMBOLS: *Everything* in your dream is a symbol. Nothing appears there by accident or to fill in the scenery and make a logical picture. Action, for instance, is a symbol, as is non-action. Symbols are always very personal to the dreamer, even when they are "universal." Symbols are able to carry and convey much, much more information than words, so keep unraveling each symbol until it bores you stiff. You will be amazed at how much is stored in your subconscious that you had no idea was there. Get acquainted with it — you won't be sorry, and we promise it won't hurt.

INCUBATING: Incubating a dream just means to tell your subconscious mind to answer a question for you in your dream. Dream incubation is also sometimes referred to as having a "dream intent" — it's all the same thing. Dream incubation is an ancient technique and can give you information on just about anything you want.

Incubating is an excellent way to get additional information about a dream you have already had and can't quite figure out. And you can find out how your subconscious feels about your job, relationship, money — anything at all stored in your memory banks.

You should only incubate one question per night, and even then you will probably need to analyze your dream symbols to get to your answer. Remember that you have your own built-in consulting team, right inside your own head. Nobody knows what's better for you than you do.

So, to incubate a dream, several times during your day, think about a particular problem or question you'd like more information on. Think the question through to ensure you are clear and precise about what it is you really want to know. Get to the essence of the question or problem, then end each of these waking sessions with the command that tonight you get the answer in your dream. Keep everything present tense. Your subconscious simply does not compute the future.

Keep all statements to your subconscious, awake or asleep, in present tense terms only. No wishy-washy "I want's" or "I will's." This puts everything across the future boundary, and your subconscious simply doesn't comprehend the future. It only thinks in terms of NOW.

Before you go to sleep, condense your question to one simple statement. You can even write the question down on a piece of paper to help reinforce your dream intent. But only one question at a time; asking more than one gets you no answer, or a very confused one.

When you wake up, write down any dream, dream fragments, and feelings you remember. Don't try to analyze anything at this point, just record it. And even if you don't instantly understand it, you did get your answer. Believe it, and keep at it. And never ask a question you don't really want an honest answer to. This stuff works.

LUCID DREAM: Realizing *in your dream* that you are dreaming is a lucid dream. Lucid dreams will usually feel more "real" and you may have a hard time convincing yourself that the situation didn't actually happen, that you just dreamed it. Lucid dreams can and do occur naturally, but controlled lucid dreaming for use as a tool for self- examination, exploration and growth can be learned as a skill. See Additional Reading for some of the best books on lucid dreaming.

OUT-OF-BODY DREAM: Out-of-body experiences, waking or sleeping, are often called OBEs (O-Bees). There is a continuing disagreement by experts on whether anything at all actually leaves the physical body at night during dreaming, and if something does leave whether that "something" is part of your consciousness, purely some form of energy, or your soul or spirit.

Out-of-body dreams are known for their exceptionally vivid colors and feelings, although the same is true of a lucid dream. However, in out-of-body dreams, your sense of taste and smell will probably be slightly diminished, while in a lucid dream these two physical sensations will be heightened. See Additional Reading for some of the best books about OBE's.

PSYCHIC DREAM: True psychic dreams are generally hard to prove to anyone but the dreamer, another good reason to record your dreams. The term "psychic" itself simply means "beyond the five senses." Psychic dreams will almost always contain some information you would not normally know or have access to in any other way.

We all have psychic dreams at some point in our lives, but usually miss them because they are very ordinary and don't seem "important" at the time. One of the main functions of any psychic dream is to show you that there are things, or dimensions, beyond your five physical senses, and to help you with the process of trusting yourself about information that usually has nothing to do with your intellect (and, boy, does your intellect hate that part).

NON-REM SLEEP: Non-REM sleep is dream sleep that occurs without the telltale rapid eye movement of REM. It most often happens in Stage Two or Stage Four sleep and is the subject of ongoing research. Non-REM dreams appear to be distinguished by their lack of emotion and are often in black and white, leading some researchers to speculate that Non-REM may occur in the theta brain wave state (REM occurs in alpha and is always in color).

REM SLEEP: REM stands for Rapid Eye Movement, named for the side-to-side eye movement made during Stage 3 sleep. And by the way, this eye movement appears to have no correlation to what you are seeing in your dream, yet another puzzle for researchers. It is REM which generally signals the beginning of a dream, although current research seems to indicate that some dreaming does occur in stages of sleep other than REM, which, oddly enough, is called Non-REM. And when you know that newborn babies spend approximately 80% of their sleep time in REM, it sort of makes you wonder, doesn't it? What do babies dream about?

UNIVERSAL SYMBOLS: It is estimated that we each dream from 3 to 4 Universal Symbols each night of our lives. "Universal" in this context simply means that the symbol is a very primary and basic one, common to almost everyone on this planet. For example, dreaming of a snake could have a purely universal meaning — symbolizing, among other things, wisdom and spiritual energy — in addition to any personal meaning the dreamer has for the concept of snake.

THE FOUR STAGES OF SLEEP

The "average" sleep cycle is approximately 90 minutes, but varies from person to person. To be on either side of this 90-minute cycle does not mean there is something wrong.

STAGE ONE: Stage One sleep is the lightest level of sleep. This is where most of your hypnogogic images will occur (see MONSTER/ Grotesques). Your brain is beginning to check the body's systems and shut down unnecessary power functions while you are sleeping to get your body ready for the rest and recharging periods it must have for optimum performance. At this point, you are neither quite awake nor quite asleep, and are literally between stages of consciousness, shifting gears, so to speak. It's common to experience sudden muscular twitches or jerks during this stage, especially if you've been doing very active things, like moving furniture.

STAGE TWO: Stage Two sleep usually begins five to ten minutes after you go to sleep. Your heart beat will slow and your breathing becomes more regular. Body temperature begins to lower.

STAGE THREE: Stage Three is where most of us experience our dreams. This is the REM stage of sleep and can last anywhere from 10 minutes in the first 90-minute sleep cycle to 60 minutes by the end of your sleep period. Your body will be unable to move during Stage Three, the only exceptions being your eyes moving rapidly back and forth and a part of your inner ear still picking up sound. You will spend more and more time in Stage Three as your sleep cycles progress, and less and less in Stages One, Two and Four. And in some elderly people, Stage Four all but disappears. Your brain is in the alpha brain wave state during REM and alpha experiences are in color. Yes, folks, we do dream in color. In fact, it appears that all mammals do.

STAGE FOUR: Stage Four is where your physical body rests and recharges. This is the stage of sleep where growth hormones are released and where your nervous system gets revitalized. Stage Four will last approximately 20 minutes during your first 90-minute cycle of sleep, but may last as little as 1 to 2 minutes by the end of the night, depending upon how physically tired your body and brain are. You will spend less and less time in Stage Four as your night progresses. Following Stage Four, you will return to Stage One and on through your sleep cycle throughout the night in your cycles of approximately 90 minutes. Stage Four sleep can disappear altogether as the body ages, just one of the reasons elderly people are sometimes irritable.

QUESTIONS TO QUESTION YOUR QUESTIONS

When analyzing your dreams, it is often as important to know which questions to ask and when to ask them as it is to ask the questions at all.

Each of your dream symbols can be questioned directly, just as if it were a person. It is also useful to "gestalt" the symbol — become the person or object in your dream and then ask the "new" you the questions. Gestalting can also be a lot of fun, especially in a group and if you have ever wanted to be an actor.

Another highly effective method was developed by Dr. Gayle Delaney, who pretends she is an alien from another planet when questioning her clients. This method forces the dreamer to explain the symbol in detailed simple terms, how the particular object functions on earth, and why humans carry out certain actions. Again, a lot of fun to play with, and it works.

Keep hammering away at your symbols until you "know" you have finally extracted the truth. Remember that you will often consciously still be resisting deciphering your symbols, and that it is the norm to not be able to easily get to the bottom of your dream messages. There is no need to ever be embarrassed for not understanding your own dreams. Even the experts go to other experts. Above all, don't get discouraged with the process.

Become a dedicated investigative reporter. You want to know who, when, why, where, and how. And you won't give up until you have your news story.

You cannot over-analyze any of your dreams. And remember that you cannot take any symbol out of the context of the whole dream. A car in one dream may be representing something very different in another. The overall "universal" meaning of "car" will remain the same, but your subconscious's creative use of this basic symbol can vary from dream to dream.

Here, as in waking life, assume nothing. Question, question, question — and then question your questions. Dreams are almost never what they appear to be on their surface.

Questions are also fun to use to help others work on their dreams and learn more about themselves and the process of dream work. And please do question them. You don't do them any favors when you give them the answers. It's much more fun to get to the Aha! by yourself, isn't it? So, here we go.

ACTION

Every single part of your dream is a symbol, even action or non-action. And remember that dreams always exaggerate slightly, very much like the old silent movie melodramas. Don't be overly concerned about any dream violence. Research shows that we all tend to be slightly more violent in our dreams than we are when awake.

Men seem to naturally dream more violence than women, and this dream violence increases as a man gets older. Analyze dream actions, including violence, symbolically. Dreams are a safe arena to release all of your bottled up and unacknowledged emotions and stress, with no one getting hurt, not even you.

1. What is the main action in this dream?

2. What does this remind you of that is going on in your life at the time?

3. What is the central plot of your dream, what's the main storyline? Is it a comedy, melodrama, suspense story? Why? And how would it change if the plot changed?

4. Does this plot remind you of anything going on in your life at the time?

5. Why are your dream characters (including you) performing the action(s) they are? How do they each feel about that?

6. How does it, or would it, feel to actually live your dream actions when you are awake? Is this something you would ever really do? Why, or why not?

7. What kind of a person or thing would normally carry out these action(s)? Why? What are they getting out of it?

8. Have you ever done the same things while you are awake? If so, how did you feel about it at the time, and what does that remind you of now? If not, why not?

9. What part of you is performing your dream action(s) for you, or to you? Why?

ANIMALS

Animals are generally more common in children's dreams than in adult's. Children will dream some type of animal approximately 25% of their dream time until adolescence, while adults seem to dream about animals only about 5% of the time. In general, women tend to dream about small, soft animals like cats, and men tend to dream more about large animals, like horses. So if you are way outside these "averages," you are probably telling yourself something very important.

1. How is this dream animal different from the same animal in the waking world?

2. Describe your dream animal in detail. What color is it, what shape is it, what type of fur or hide does it have, how does it move, what does it eat, how healthy is it, etc.

3. Do you like this animal? How would you like to spend time with one?

4. How do you feel about the animal *in* your dream? Why?

5. What part of you or your personality could your dream animal represent?

6. If your dream animal could talk, what would it say to you?

7. How does the animal feel in your dream?

8. How would your dream be different without the animal in it?

9. What actions is your dream animal taking? How are they different from the way the same animal would behave in the waking world? What does this remind you of going on in your life at the time?

FEELINGS

Since your dreams are all about your feelings, your honest answers to these questions become doubly revealing. Remember that your dream feelings are subconscious ones. If you were aware of these feelings while you are awake, or how deep they go, you would not need to dream them.

1. What is the main overall feeling you experienced in your dream? When was the last time you felt this way while you were awake?

2. Does this feeling remind you of anything going on in your life right now?

3. If your dream emotion (fear, happiness, love, etc.) could talk, what would it want to tell you?

4. What are your strongest feelings in this dream? How many different feelings were experienced by you or others in this dream?

5. How do you feel about your dream setting? (Remember that your dream setting or landscape often tells you the overall emotional background).

6. What feelings are you most aware of while you are in the dream, not after waking? Look especially for the duality of your feelings. For example, if you are happily playing with an animal you would normally be afraid of when awake, what makes the difference in your dream?

7. When was the last time you remember feeling this way while you were awake?

8. Did your feelings change while you were in your dream? If so, where, when and why?

9. How do you feel about this dream overall? For instance, how did you feel the minute your eyes opened?

10. How did you feel at the very end of your dream? Did this feeling change from the feeling you had at the beginning? How? Why?

11. Have you ever felt this way before? When was the last time? Why?

12. How did you feel *immediately* upon waking up? If that feeling was different from the feeling in the dream, how was it different? Why?

13. Did your feelings about the dream change after you had been awake awhile? If so, why?

14. What was the central underlying feeling tone of your whole dream?

15. Can you give your dream a title by describing this central feeling?

16. If your dream feelings were colors, what colors would each of them be? Why?

17. Ask yourself how you feel now and how you felt in your dream about every single object in your dream.

18. Dream anger is almost always directed at yourself, not your dream object or person. What part of you is angry at which part? Why? Is that anger valid, or can it be discarded? How are you expressing the dream anger? How is the way you handle dream anger different from, or the same as, the way you handle your anger while awake? How is your dream anger resolved in your dream? What will happen in your dream if you act on your anger? What will happen if you choose to transmute the anger into love?

OBJECTS

Dream objects are not necessarily confined to physical objects. In fact, in dream terms, everything in your dream is an "object."

1. Describe each dream object in detail. Describe absolutely everything you remember about it.

2. What is a [your dream object]?

3. What is it normally used for in waking life?

4. How is your dream object different from the same object in waking life? How is it the same?

5. How does [your dream object] work or function?

6. Do you own one? Do you, or would you, use one? Why, or why not?

7. Do you like [your dream object]? Why, or why not? [Get into your feelings about your dream object].

8. What kind of a person would own or use your dream object? Why?

9. Does the dream object as you describe it remind you of anything? Pay close attention to the words and phrases you use to describe any dream object; they often give you the key to the overall meaning of the dream.

10. Is there anything different or unique about your dream object? How is it different from all other objects just like it?

11. In what condition is your dream object? Is it antique, new, not finished, shiny, ready to be discarded, etc.?

12. How could your dream object be incorrectly used? What would be the consequences of any mishandling of the object?

13. What color is your dream object? How is the color the same or different from the usual color of the object?

PEOPLE

The people in your dream are seldom who they seem to be on the surface and are usually extensions or projections of some quality of yourself, or qualities you admire and wish you had. In the dream world, three or more people other than yourself constitute a "dream crowd," which can often signal that a decision of some kind needs to, or is being, made. Your choice of dream people, then, can often show you the different choices you have and how you feel about it. Be exceptionally detailed in describing all of your dream people. Dreaming "faceless" unknown strangers, by the way, is very common, and these strangers also represent unfamiliar parts of you; see PEOPLE and STRANGER.

1. What is your dream person like *as a person*? Describe the person in detail. Saying that someone is "nice" or "funny" isn't enough of a description to show you how your subconscious is using the person as a symbol, or why. Describe the person so that someone else would recognize their unique energy pattern without being told who that person is.

2. What part in your dream movie is your dream actor playing? Why? How is that the same as, or different from, their usual role in the waking world?

3. What is this person doing in your dream at all? What action(s) is he/she carrying out? Why?

4. What is your dream person saying? Why? (Remember that actions can count as words).

5. Does this dream person remind you of anything or anyone in your life now or in the past?

6. What would you, or the rest of the world, lose if your dream person disappeared or died or disappeared? How would your life be different?

7. How do you feel about the person in your dream? Why?

8. How do you feel about your dream person while awake? Why?

9. Does this dream person remind you of anyone you know?

10. How would you like to meet or spend some time with this dream person? Why, or why not?

11. How is your dream person dressed? Why? (Clothes often show us how we see the different roles we play in life; see CLOTHES).

12. What kind of a person would be attracted to your dream person? What kind of a person would avoid them? Why?

13. What kind of a career choice would your dream person be most likely to make? What does that tell you about their personality?

14. Of what race or nationality is your dream person? Why?

15. What do all of these descriptions remind you of that is going on in your life at the time?

SETTINGS
Your dream settings are very often strong clues to the underlying emotional tone of the dream. Technically, every time you change scenes or settings in a dream you are considered to be in a "new" dream. Pay particular attention to any scene changes. They very often signal changes in your feelings. Nothing shows up or happens in your dream just to fill in the picture. We can't say this too many times — *everything in your dream is a symbol*. Your dreams take place in a particular setting or landscape for a very specific reason, never by accident.

1. Describe your dream stage setting in detail. What colors are in it? What type of decor or landscape? What is the atmosphere like? Are there animals, plants, people, machinery, buildings? What time of day or night is it? What direction are you going or facing? What is the weather like? What time of year is it?

2. What sort of person would live, work, play, get lost, in your dream setting? Why?

3. Who owns your dream stage setting? How did they get it?

4. What kind of person would like this dream stage setting? What kind of a person would intensely dislike it? Why?

5. How does it feel for you to be there? Would you like to go there while you are awake? Why, or why not?

6. If the setting is familiar or reminds you of something, between what years did you live there, or in a place similar to it? What does this remind you of that is going on in your life at the time?

7. How would most people usually feel in this setting?

8. How is your dream setting different from the same setting in waking life? How is it the same?

9. Would you like to make changes in your dream setting? If so, how would you change it, and why?

SEX
Keep in mind that dream sex can, and often does, have meanings far beyond purely sexual ones, and that truly sexual dreams are more often symbolic in nature than explicit. The good news is that most of us will continue to have sexual and erotic dreams throughout our lives.

1. Why do human beings have sex? What do they get out of it? (Get very clear on your feelings about this one).

2. How did your sexual rendezvous feel in your dream?

3. Did the sex go well? Or did you get to that point in your dream? If you did, were there interruptions or problems? How is that the same as, or different from, your waking sex life?

4. Does this remind you of any feelings or circumstances in your waking life? And not just sexual ones, by any means.

5. Give a good detailed physical and emotional description of your dream lover.

6. Does this person remind you of anyone or anything in your life at the time?

7. What does this dream say about how you might be feeling about your current sexual relationship?

8. Where does your dream sexual experiencer take place? How is that place the same as, or different from, a place where you might normally have such an experience?

9. Does this sexual encounter involve any type of infidelity or "cheating?" If so, what does this remind you of that is going on in your life at the time, and not just sexually or romantically?

10. Would you like to be with your dream lover in waking life? Why, or why not?

11. How is your dream lover different from any other dream lovers you have ever had?

12. Are other people present during this experience? If so, describe them. Are they paying any attention to what you are doing? What does that tell you about your current sexual relationship? How do you feel about other people being there? How does your dream lover feel about it? Why?

13. How are your feelings in your dream different from, or the same as, your feelings during your waking sexual experiences? Why?

Bibliography

Each book listed in this Bibliography is highly recommended to anyone who wants to increase their understanding of dreams and symbols. Without the previous hard work of each of these authors, this book would not have been possible. Thanks to each and every one of you.

The Dream Book: Symbols for Self-Understanding, Betty Bethards, Inner Light Foundation, 1983.

A Dictionary of All Scriptures and Myths, G.A. Guskell, Avenel Books, 1981.

Dream Symbols and Psychic Power, Alex Tanous and Timothy gray, Bantam Books, 1990.

The Herder Symbol Dictionary, translated by Boris Matthews, Chiron Publications, 1986.

A Dictionary of Symbols, Second Edition, J.E. Cirlot, translated by Jack Sage, Dorset Press, 1971.

An Illustrated Encyclopeadia of Traditional Symbols, J.C. Cooper, Thames and Hudson, 1978.

Medicine Cards, Jamie Sams & David Carson, Bear & Company, 1988.

Dictionary of Symbols: Cultural Icons and the Meanings Behind Them, Hans Bierdermann, Facts On File Books, 1992.

The Woman's Encyclopedia of Myths and Secrets, Barbara G. Walker, Harper Collins, 1983.

Signs of Life: The Five Universal Shapes and How to Use Them, Angeles Arrien, Arcus Publishing Company, 1992.

Lucid Dreaming, Stephen LeBerge, Ph.D., Ballentine Books, 1985.

The Donning International Encyclopedic Psychic Dictionary, June G. Bletzer, Ph.D., Whitford Press, 1986.

Crystal Personalities: A Quick Reference To Special Forms of Quartz, Patricia Troyer, Stone People Publishing Company, 1995.

Other Council Fires Were Here Before Ours, Jamie Sams & Twylah Nitsch, Harper Collins, 1991.

The Secret Language of Symbols: A Visual Key to Symbols and Their Meanings, David Fontana, Chronicle Books, 1994.

Numerology, Astrology & Dreams, Dusty Bunker, Whitford Press, 1987.

Animal-Speak: The Spiritual & Magical Powers of Creatures Great & Small, Ted Andrews, Llewllyn Publications, 1994.

Animal Energies, Gary Buffalo Horn Man and Sherry Firedancer, Dancing Otter Publishing, 1994.

Trees For Healing: Harmonizing with Nature for Personal Growth and Planetary Balance, Pamela Louise Chase & Jonathan Pawlik, Newcastle Publishing Company, 1991.
Earth Changes Report, Jordan Michael Scallion, Matrix Institute.

ADDITIONAL READING

The inclusion or exclusion of any book on our suggested reading list in no way implies that these are the only books on dreams and the exploration of consciousness worth reading. There are many, many excellent books, addressing all facets of dreams, dream work, and the use of symbols, and more appear every day.

Exploring Lucid Dreaming, Stephen LeBerge, Ph.D. and Howard Rheingold, Ballentine Books, 1990.

A Little Course in Dreams: A Handbook of Jungian Dreamwork, Dr. Robert Bosnak, Shambala, 1988.

The Dream Workbook, Jill Morris, Ph.D., Fawcett Crest, 1980.

Dream Power, Dr. Ann Faraday, Berkely Books, 1980.

Breakthrough Dreaming: How To Tap the 24-Hour Power of Your Mind, Dr. Gayle Delaney, Bantam, 1991.

Lucid Dreams in 30 Days, Keith Harary, Ph.D. and Patricia Weintraub, St. Martin's Press, 1989.

Psychic Dreaming: A Parapsychologist's Handbook, Loyd Auerback, Warner Books, 1991.

Realities Of The Dreaming Mind, Swami Sivananda Radha, Timeless Books, 1994.

The Art of Dreaming, Carlos Castenadas, Harper Collins, 1993.

Control Your Dreams, Jayne Gackenbach and Jane Bosveld, Harper Perennial, 1989.

Dream Telepathy: Scientific Experiments in the Supernatural, Montague Ullman, M.D. and Stanley Krippner, Ph.D. with Alan Vaughan, MacMillan Publishing Co., Inc., 1973.

Dreams and Healing, Joan Ruth Windsor, Berkley Books, 1987.

Night and Day, Jack Maguire, Fireside Books, 1989.

Women's Bodies, Women's Dreams, Dr. Patricia Garfield, Ballentine Books, 1988.

ORDER FORM

To order copies of *Letters From Home* send requests along with check to:

>Stone People Publishing Company
>P.O. Box 4650
>Apache Junction, AZ 85278-4650 USA

For Phone Orders: 602/671-7913
For FAX Orders: 602/671-7914
800 Orders: 800-205-8254

Book Price: $19.95 US Dollars, Soft Cover.

Sales Tax: Please add 7.05% sales tax for books shipped in Arizona.

Shipping Costs:Book Rate $3.00 for the first book and $.75 for each additional book, domestic. Surface shipping may take 2 to 3 weeks. For UPS or air mail add $4.00 to total shipping.

SHIP TO: _____

                     _____

                     _____

                     _____

NUMBER OF BOOKS ORDERED: _____

TOTAL AMOUNT DUE (including sales tax & shipping): $_____

WOULD YOU LIKE YOUR BOOK AUTOGRAPHED? Yes ____ No ____

Please make checks payable to:
Stone People Publishing Company
(Do Not Send Cash).

Don't forget to ask about other Stone People products. Write for details or to receive our free catalog.

Thank you for your order.
Stone People Publishing

Notes

Notes

Notes

Notes

Notes

Notes

Notes